THE
APOCRYPHA
AN AMERICAN TRANSLATION

THE
APOCRYPHA
AN AMERICAN TRANSLATION

BY
EDGAR J. GOODSPEED

With an introduction by
Moses Hadas

Vintage Books
A Division of Random House, Inc.
New York

Vintage Books Edition, September 1989

Copyright © 1959 by Random House, Inc.
Copyright © 1938 by Edgar J. Goodspeed

All rights reserved under International and
Pan-American Copyright Conventions.
Published in the United States by Vintage Books,
a division of Random House, Inc., New York,
and simultaneously in Canada by
Random House of Canada Limited, Toronto.
Originally published, in hardcover, by
the University of Chicago Press.

Library of Congress Cataloging-in-Publication Data
Bible. O.T. Apocrypha. English. Goodspeed. 1989
The Apocrypha : an American translation /
Edgar J. Goodspeed ;
with an introduction by Moses Hadas.
p. cm.
Reprint. Originally published: Chicago, Ill. :
University of Chicago Press, c1938.
ISBN 0-679-72452-4
I. Goodspeed, Edgar Johnson, 1871-1962. II. Title.
BS1692 1989
229'.05209–dc20   89-40158
                                          CIP

Manufactured in the United States of America
9B8

PREFACE

THE APOCRYPHA FORMED AN INTEGRAL part of the King James Version of 1611, as they had of all the preceding English versions from their beginning in 1382. But they are seldom printed as part of it any longer, still more seldom as part of the English Revised Version, and were not included in the American Revision.

This is partly because the Puritans disapproved of them; they had already begun to drop them from printings of their Geneva Bible by 1600, and began to demand copies of the King James Version omitting them, as early as 1629. And it is partly because we moderns discredit them because they did not form part of the Hebrew Bible and most of them have never been found in any Hebrew forms at all.

But they were part of the Bible of the early church, for it used the Greek version of the Jewish Bible, which we call the Septuagint, and these books were all in that version. They passed from it into Latin and the great Latin Bible edited by St. Jerome about A.D. 400, the Vulgate, which became the Authorized Bible of western Europe and England and remained so for a thousand years. But Jerome found that they were not in the Hebrew Bible, and so he called them the Apocrypha, the hidden or secret books.

It must not be supposed, however, that Jerome gathered them into a group and put them at the end of his Old Testament version. On the contrary, they are scattered here and there through the Vulgate, just as they are through the Greek Bible. They are also scattered through the versions made from the Vulgate—the Wyclif-Purvey English translations and the old German Bible, both products of the fourteenth century. It remained for Luther to take the hint Jerome had dropped eleven hundred years before, and to separate them in his German Bible of 1534 from the rest

of the Old Testament, and put them after it. This course
was followed the next year by Coverdale, in the first printed
English Bible, of 1535; and the English Authorized Bibles,
the Great Bible, the Bishops' and the King James, all followed the same course. The Catholic English Old Testament of 1610, however, followed the Vulgate arrangement
and left them scattered among the books which we include
in our Old Testament. It still contains them, but on the
Protestant side both British and American Bible Societies
more than a hundred years ago (1827) took a definite
stand against their publication, and they have since almost
disappeared.

Great values reside in the Apocrypha: the Prayer of
Manasseh is a notable piece of liturgy; I Maccabees is of
great historical value for its story of Judaism in the second
century before Christ, the heroic days of Judas Maccabeus
and his brothers, when Pharisaism had its rise. The additions to Esther impart a religious color to that romantic
story; Judith, Susanna, and Tobit while fascinating pieces
of fiction, were meant by their writers to teach important
lessons to their contemporaries. Wisdom and Ecclesiasticus
are among the masterpieces of the Jewish sages.

But to us this appendix of the Old Testament is important as forming a very necessary link between the Old
Testament and the New; and if we had no Old Testament
at all, the Apocrypha would still be indispensable to the
student of the New Testament, of which it forms the prelude
and background. This is why I have prepared an American
translation of the Apocrypha, to complete our American
translation of the Bible, and to make its various books more
intelligibly accessible to college and university students and
to the general reader. The strong contrast they present in
sheer moral values to the New Testament is most instruc-

tive. And they form an indispensable part of the historic
Christian Bible, as it was known in the ancient Greek and
Latin churches, in the Reformation and the Renaissance,
and in all Authorized English Bibles, Catholic and Protestant.

The excellent critical Greek text of the Septuagint recently published at Stuttgart by Alfred Rahlfs has in general
been followed in this translation, supplemented, of course,
by other studies on the Apocrypha, especially the volumes
edited by R. H. Charles at Oxford in 1913. For II Esdras,
for which only a Latin text buttressed by oriental versions
survives, I have made use of the critical labors of Bensly,
James, Box, and Violet. The Revised Version and the
translations of individual books by some of the contributors
to Charles's volumes (*Apocrypha and Pseudepigrapha*) and
others have greatly helped the translator. In the vexed
matter of the numbering of the verses the King James Bible
of 1611 has been followed. The bracketed verse-numbers
in II Esdras 7:[36–105] mark the missing portion discovered
by Bensly at Amiens and published in 1875. My brother,
Charles T. B. Goodspeed, has very kindly read the translation through in proof.

On the whole, the translation of the Apocrypha has been
surprisingly neglected. The translators of the Septuagint,
Thomson in 1808 and Brenton in 1844, studiously omitted
the apocryphal books they encountered in it, and not all of
Charles's associates in his impressive volumes made new
translations. Single books have here and there been translated from the Greek by individual scholars, but, while
Bissell ably revised the King James Apocrypha in 1880, I
cannot find that the Apocrypha as a whole have been translated into English since Coverdale in 1535 and Gregory
Martin in 1582 translated them from the Latin Vulgate
(Martin's version remained unpublished until 1610); or

that the Greek Apocrypha as a whole, that is, all the books
except II Esdras, have ever before been directly translated
from Greek into English.

Coverdale's translation of the Apocrypha in his Bible of
1535 was made from the Latin Vulgate, with the aid of
Pagninus' Latin and of recent German translations, especially Luther's. Coverdale's Bible became the basis of
successive revisions—Matthew, the Great Bible, the Bishops',
and the King James. The Geneva revisers of 1560, however, knew Greek, and contributed retranslations from the
Greek of two of the books, along with revisions of the others.
Revision of the translation in the light of the Greek continued to some degree in the Bishops' and the King James
Bibles; in the English Revised Version of 1895 six more
books appear virtually retranslated from the Greek, and the
rest revised. But even in it, five books remain revisions, however faithful, of Coverdale's translation of the Vulgate, so
that our standard versions of the Apocrypha (and aside from
Bissell's revision there are no others), though three or four
times revised, still to a substantial degree rest ultimately
upon the Latin Vulgate.

In contrast with them, the translation here presented is,
except for the Latin II Esdras, based directly upon the
Greek text.

EDGAR J. GOODSPEED

CONTENTS

INTRODUCTION

1. An Age of Fusion

The period of which the books in this volume are a significant monument, roughly the last two centuries B.C., is of
central importance for the cultural history of Europe, for it
was then that elements from disparate sources combined to
determine the directions and the contours our civilization
would take. Separately the major elements are known to us
with reasonable fullness for a millennium before the period,
and they and others which have entered the composition
after its character was determined may still be identified and
are still operative severally; but whereas an effort of the
imagination is required to enter into the spiritual and intellectual climate of classical Greece or of the Old Testament,
there is no such strangeness in the Hellenistic and Roman
world. The premises of conduct, of relations between man
and man and man and external authority, the canons of
taste, the goals of aspiration, are all familiar.

The catalyst for the new compound was Alexander the
Great. His conquests had broken down the insulation which
separated peoples and had enormously enlarged intellectual
as well as geographical horizons. Deprived of the political
entities which had absorbed their loyalties and had sheltered
them from the outer world, men were forced to turn in upon
themselves and to devise new attitudes for asserting themselves in a world grown overwhelmingly large. On the Greek
side, where the evidence is more plentiful, the changes are
palpable, in literature, in philosophy, in art. In all, the
movement is from the heroic, the ideal, the general to the
bourgeois, the actual, the individual. Literature deals not
with huge personages who die gloriously but with ordinary
men who wish to live happy ever after. Philosophy seeks to

redress the imbalance between tiny man and the colossal world either by making man part of the divine (as the Stoics did) or by depriving the world of divinity (as the Epicureans did). Sculptors no longer gloze over individual idiosyncrasies, as their classical precursors had done, but emphasize crooked features and wrinkles and anguished expressions.

The people on the eastern periphery of the Greek world were similarly stripped of insulation and constrained to find new attitudes to confront a changed world. Hellenism's penetration of the east was rapid and pervasive. The influence of the east upon the west came somewhat later in time and initially affected the lower classes, from which it gradually forced its way upward. Greek influence in the east affected the upper classes at once. Greek was the language of government, of business, and of fashion, and Greek ways offered a fuller and more stimulating life. Upper-class natives so far identified themselves with the Greek outlook that they spoke of themselves as barbarians, and even when they emphasized the worth of their native traditions they did so to show that they were respectable by Greek standards. Individuals or groups who refused to participate in the new ways would have proven themselves barbarians indeed and have been left stagnant in a backwater of civilization.

Because the Jews represent the major non-Greek element in the eventual fusion it is important to observe that their reaction to Hellenism was initially no different from that of other non-Greek peoples. Even in Jerusalem, as we see from the opening chapters of I Maccabees, the high-priesthood was contested by rivals each of whom bore a Greek name and was apparently very ready to adopt Greek ways. The Maccabean uprising, at least in its initial stages, was not against Hellenism but for national independence. And when independence, real or nominal, was secured, the object of the Maccabean principality was to hold its head up among other principalities that had arisen out of the ruins of the Seleucid Empire; there was nothing like an anti-Greek program.

It was only after the rise of Christianity and the fall of Jerusalem (A.D. 70), when exclusive loyalty to religion was the only means of preserving the identity of the group, that the barrier against alien influence was erected. But the way of life which the barrier was designed to protect had already assimilated significant quantities of Hellenistic influence, and so thoroughly that they were no longer felt to be alien. This influence is obvious in archaeological remains and in Jewish books written in Greek, but it is present also in books written in Hebrew, and in some included in the Old Testament. It is likely to be most significant where it is least obvious. It is very likely, for example, that the organization and discipline of the Essene-like community of Qumran near the Dead Sea were influenced by Pythagorean patterns; and the path from the Essenes to Christianity is straight and smooth.

New forms, whether in political organization, artifacts, or literature must inevitably influence content. If Canticles, Chronicles, Ecclesiastes, Job, and Jonah do indeed follow the forms of Hellenistic love poetry, historiography, diatribe, tragedy, and aretalogy, as it is quite likely they do, then consciously or otherwise their outlook must also have been affected. But when a new language is adopted, even a literal translation from the old must import new connotations. It is natural for a Greek translator to render the Hebrew word for soul by *psyche,* but by so doing he adds whole layers of meaning which had been attached to *psyche* by the Greek philosophers. The interesting thing is that these new meanings now inhere in the notion of "soul" even for Hebrew writers. There are numerous similar cases, where the innovation may have been inadvertent. Sometimes it appears to be intentional. At

Exodus 3.14 the puzzling phrase *ehyeh asher ehyeh,* commonly translated "I am that I am," is rendered in the Greek Bible by *ho ōn,* "I am being," which must be an intentional Platonism.

By collecting and arranging instances of fusion in forms and words and ideas it is possible to trace the process from its tentative beginnings to its consummation. The best field for studying the union of Greek and Hebrew strands into a single skein is the religious literature of the intertestamentary period, of which the Apocrypha constitutes a clearly defined group. We must now see how it is defined, first by external criteria and then by character.

2. Apocryphal and Apocrypha

In current usage the adjectives *Apocryphal* and *apocryphal* have separate meanings. Written with *a* the word means "of dubious authority," "spurious," often with a hint of "esoteric"; written with *A* it refers to the collection of books printed in this volume, with no pejorative connotation. The process by which the distinction arose will clarify the nature and standing of the books in question.

Apocryphon (of which *apocrypha* is the plural) is a Greek adjective meaning "hidden," and, as applied to writings, originally designated such as contained "secret" doctrine, Phoenician, Zoroastrian, or other. In early ecclesiastical usage the term came to be applied to writings regarded as inspired by various heretical sects, whether or not they were "secret." Presently *apocrypha* was used to designate not heretical books but books of religious interest which lacked the inspiration and hence the authority of books actually included in the Bible. The criterion is the canon of the Bible; books not contained in an authoritative Bible are apocrypha.

But the contents of the Hebrew and the Greek Bibles are not identical. The men who made the Greek translation of the Old Testament called the Septuagint included in their work a number of books (specifically, those in our present collection) which bear a general resemblance to analogous works in the Hebrew Old Testament and which for the most part were written in Hebrew (or Aramaic) but which are not in fact present in the Hebrew Old Testament. If the Hebrew Old Testament is the criterion, these books are apocrypha. But the Bible of the early Church was not the Hebrew but the Greek, and its contents are reproduced in Jerome's Latin version called the Vulgate, which is the Bible of the Roman Catholic Church. In the usage of the Catholic Church, therefore, the books here called Apocrypha are canonical, and the word Apocrypha is applied to a group of books which are in neither the Greek nor the Hebrew Old Testament.

But Jerome himself (though he is the only early writer to do so) speaks of the books found in the Greek but not in the Hebrew Old Testament as apocrypha. It was on Jerome's authority that the Wycliffe Bible (1382) included only such Old Testament books as were found in the Hebrew. Coverdale's "Great Bible" (1539) did include the extra works, but introduced an innovation in arrangement. Previously they had been placed where they seemed to belong, logically, or chronplogically, among the Hebrew books; now they were put together by themselves. At the Reformation the decisive step of denying inspiration to these books was taken. Protestants accept as canonical only those books found in the Hebrew Old Testament; those found only in the Greek Bible are *the* Apocrypha. The Council of Trent (1546) reaffirmed the Catholic position that these books are canonical. To the books which the Catholic Church called apocrypha, Protestants applied the term pseudepigrapha.

The distinctions suggested by this terminology are, however, inexact and hinder rather than help appreciation of the books concerned. The term pseudepigrapha, which

means "writings of falsely ascribed authorship," is appropriate enough as a designation for Enoch, The Testaments of
the Twelve Patriarchs, The Letter of Aristeas, and the like,
but it is equally appropriate for a number of writings in the
Apocrypha: Jeremiah, Baruch, Manasseh, and Solomon
cannot have written the works ascribed to them. In the books
labeled pseudepigrapha we recognize that the false ascrip-
tions are not a deception but a literary device to enhance
the dignity of an imaginative work. But the books of the
Apocrypha (with the exception of Maccabees) are similarly
imaginative works, artistically superior, indeed, and therefore following accepted literary forms more faithfully. Hellenistic literature gave a respected place, for example, to
historical romance calculated to foster political or religious
loyalty; audiences were not deceived because they knew
what kinds of truth the romance was intended to communi-
cate. If, by reason of its association with Old Testament
history, we read Judith or Tobit as a chronicle of actual
events, we must either resort to most implausible interpretation or dismiss the chronicler as an ignorant bungler; but if
we realize that such books were intended as edifying roman-
ces for the purpose of inculcating and strengthening loyalties
under trying conditions, we can appreciate them as honest
and effective pieces of literary art.

3. Between Canon and Pseudepigrapha

In the total body of Jewish religious writing surviving from
the last centuries B.C., then, the Apocrypha occupies a place
below the later books of the Old Testament and above the
pseudepigrapha. There is enough common ground between
them to give the three groups a certain unity, not only in
date and place but even in religious outlook and literary
merit, but there are perceptible gradations. Enoch, the most
influential of the group, and similar apocalypses, may have

been too vivid in their eschatology and too chaotic in form to be acceptable. Jubilees and The Testaments of the Twelve Patriarchs may have dealt with the patriarchs too imaginatively. IV Maccabees, which is the most elegant book of the group and most attractive to the modern reader, may have been excluded by reason of its late date or possibly Antiochene provenience. These books would all be anomalous if they were included in the Bible.

But this is not true of the books of the Apocrypha, and it is difficult to see why some of them were not in fact included. Those who argued for their retention in the canon could maintain that the Wisdom of Solomon and Baruch are at least as useful for religious instruction as Ecclesiastes and the Song of Songs, that if Esther is worthy of inclusion so is Judith also, that the Books of Maccabees are as deserving as Chronicles and Ecclesiasticus as Proverbs. If Wisdom was not actually written by Solomon, neither were Ecclesiastes or the Song, which make the same claim. The Maccabees and Ecclesiasticus, it is true, admit to dates in the second century B.C., and this may have been sufficient reason for excluding them; but modern scholars are quite certain that Ecclesiastes and the Song of Solomon and Daniel and Esther are as late or later. The history of the establishment of the Old Testament canon, which is to say, the decision on whether or not a given book was inspired, is full of uncertainties. About the inclusion of the first two divisions, the Law of the Prophets, there could be no question. The third category, called Writings, is not so firmly defined, for the Jews attributed a lower authority to it; the rationale for accepting or rejecting books for this category is not always clear. All that can be said is that a modern panel of religious teachers might well question the inclusion of certain books now found in the Hebrew Bible and advocate the inclusion of others found only in the Greek Bible.

4. Theme and Variety

Like the Old Testament itself the Apocrypha is rather a library than a single book. As in the older library so in the later the unifying theme is the relations between God and Israel. The actual working out of the theme in politics and war is described in the historical books, in our case Esdras and Maccabees. Instruction and encouragement in the proper attitude to the relationship is provided in the Wisdom of Solomon and in the additions and annexes to Esther, Daniel, and Jeremiah. Edifying examples of the proper relationship are offered in Judith and Tobit, and Ecclesiasticus shows how awareness of the relationship can ensure a reasonable practical life.

Except for Maccabees and Ecclesiasticus, where the actual historical situation is plainly indicated, the materials are retrojected to a fictive date in the remote past—as are some books in the Old Testament also. Wisdom is ascribed to Solomon, but its author has plainly learned from, and polemicizes against, current philosophic doctrine. The annexes to Jeremiah are naturally placed in Jeremiah's own time. Tobit, Judith, and the additions to Esther and Daniel are referred to the period of the Babylonian exile or earlier; actually the books of Daniel and Esther were themselves written not earlier than about 164 B.C. There is evidently purposeful conformity to the literary forms and doctrines of the Old Testament, but the characteristics of a later age are apparent nevertheless. Judith shows the influence of Hellenistic romance as plainly as Maccabees shows the influence of Hellenistic historiography. Wisdom is influenced by the form of the Cynic-Stoic diatribe, which may itself have been an eastern invention. Moreover Wisdom is the first Jewish (not Greek) writing to promise not merely national survival but a personal immortality. The phraseology of Wisdom, incidentally, shows striking parallels with that of the New Testament. This need not imply direct influence, but it does indicate a common climate of theologic discourse.

5. *The Essential Link*

But interesting as the connections of the Apocrypha with its Old Testament antecedents may be, its connections with the New Testament are more instructive. Between the Old Testament conceived of as a totality and the New Testament, there is as wide a gap as that which separates Homer and tragedy from the literature of Rome. Both later literatures presuppose the earlier to the degree that they are completely intelligible only in the light of the earlier; but just as the literature of Alexandria supplies the essential link between the classical literatures, so the Apocrypha does for the Testaments. Scholarly commentaries on individual books of the New Testament as of the Apocrypha point to specific echoes of phrases and images and ideas from books of the Apocrypha in books of the New Testament; what is more illuminating is that the Apocrypha reflects the social and intellectual climate, the religious premises and the literary forms, of the area and the culture out of which the New Testament grew.

6. *The Individual Books*

In the sense that they derive from a single culture and a single conjuncture of history the books of the Apocrypha have a certain homogeneity, greater, it may be, than the homogeneity of the Old Testament, and for the reader of a translation this homogeneity is enhanced, as in the case of canonical books, by the circumstance that all are translated by a single hand or in a uniform style. But the character of the group can better be apprehended by considering the books severally, and an inventory may incidentally be serviceable to readers who may not wish to start at the beginning and read through to the end. The order, which is that in which the books are regularly printed, has no relation to genre and but little to date, except that the books associated with Ezra are put first and those on the Maccabees last. Fuller treatments will be found in the Prefaces to the individual books.

A. I Esdras is an uninspired chronicle of the exile to Babylonia and the return to Jerusalem, largely identical with the narrative in Ezra and Nehemiah. The most attractive section is the story of the three young guardsmen (3.1–5.6) for which there is no extant analogue. The date may be late third century B.C.

B. II Esdras is an apocalypse. Its mature reflections on the continuing problems of human life and God's justice make it an important document in the history of religious thought. It was written after the death of Nero (A.D. 68); chapters 1, 2, 15, and 16 are Christian additions, and it may be that other parts are influenced by Christian teaching.

C. Tobit combines pre-existing novella motifs into an edifying romance. Characterization and plot construction are effective, and the piety genuine and moving. The emergence of individuality and of personal religion and the fusion of elements from disparate sources are characteristic phenomena of the Hellenistic age. The date of Tobit is probably early second century B.C.

D. Judith, of similar date, is another romance based on identifiable Hellenistic patterns. The story of the virtuous heroine who saved her people by decapitating the enemy general whose lust she had aroused is probably the most familiar in the Apocrypha.

E. The Additions to the Book of Esther comprise six separate fragments inserted at appropriate junctures in the canonical book of Esther. The passages may have been added to correct the secular tone of that book, or, less probably, they may represent a fuller early recension of the story. A likely date is the early first century B.C.

F. The Wisdom of Solomon, perhaps of the same date, is important for the development of theology. It is the first Jewish book specifically to promise individual retribution after death. It is also a good example of the fusion of Greek and Hebrew ideas. The book is a composite, with the break at chapter 11. The first part is probably a translation from Hebrew, and the second a Greek continuation by the translator of the first.

G. Ecclesiasticus, otherwise called The Wisdom of Jeshua the Son of Sirach, is the longest and most attractive book in the Apocrypha. The author is concerned for religious truth but his emphasis is on worldly wisdom that comes from experience. Ecclesiasticus was written about 180 B.C.

H. The Book of Baruch is the closest approach in the Apocrypha to the style and spirit of Old Testament prophecy. The themes are confession of sin, encouragement to pursue Wisdom, and comfort for affliction. Echoes of Daniel indicate a date later than 164 B.C. The appended Letter of Jeremiah, which can hardly be earlier than the first century B.C., is mainly an admonition against idolatry.

I. The Additions to Daniel comprise three separate pieces whose date must be later than 164 B.C.:
1. The story of Susanna, who rejected the solicitations of two lustful elders who surprised her at her bath, was accused by them of adultery, and vindicated by the youthful Daniel, as she was being led to execution.

2. The Song of the Three Children, which comprises a long prayer of Azariah (the Hebrew name of Abednego), and a formal hymn purportedly recited by the three prospective martyrs in the fiery furnace.

3. The story of Bel and the Dragon, which ridicules the worship first of Bel and then of a sacred serpent.

J. The Prayer of Manasseh purports to be the prayer which Manasseh is reported (in II Chronicles 33.18) to have recited while he was captive in Babylonia.

K. I Maccabees is a concise and competent account probably by an eyewitness and a devoted partisan of the Maccabees, of the course of events during the years 167–134 B.C. The book was written in Hebrew but exhibits the characteristics of Hellenistic historiography.

L. II Maccabees is not a continuation but a parallel account, covering the years 175–160. Its author describes it as an abridgment of a five-book work by Jason of Cyrene. It too rests ultimately on eyewitness accounts, but it is more emotional, more rhetorical, and more avowedly propagandistic than I Maccabees.

7. *Apocrypha in Literature and Art**

Tobit, Judith, Susanna, Maccabees evoke memories even for readers who have never encountered the books in which their stories are told. The limbo into which these have been relegated has estranged ordinary readers, but poets and painters and composers of earlier centuries could assume that their audiences were familiar with the Apocrypha. For artists Judith has understandably been the great favorite.

---

* For "The Pervasive Influence of the Apocrypha" see the admirable chapter so entitled in Bruce M. Metzger, *An Introduction to the Apocrypha* (New York, 1957), 205–238.

Her story has been painted by Baldassare, Botticelli, Cranach, Giorgione, Michelangelo, Tintoretto, Van Dyck, Veronese, and a dozen other masters. Pictures suggested by the story of Susanna are almost as numerous, and there are a good number drawn from Tobit. Of the numerous echoes of the Apocrypha in literature perhaps the most interesting is the tenth-century English (West Saxon) epic on Judith. The Monke's Tale in Chaucer tells the story in brief. And Shakespeare could count on his audience catching the allusion to the Susanna story when he has Shylock speak of Portia as "A Daniel come to judgment." In music, aside from frequent allusions in hymnody, mention ought be made of Handel's stately oratorios on Susanna and on Judas Maccabaeus.

8. *Translations and Introductions*

Even after the Reformation excluded the Apocrypha from the canon, it continued to be recommended as "useful for instruction" and selections were read in public worship. But as early as the time of Elizabeth, Puritans objected to the public reading of these "inferior" writings, and complaints became more vocal during the eighteenth century. But the ordinary editions of the English Bible included the Apocrypha. The British and Foreign Bible Society, founded in 1804, included the Apocrypha in the English and foreign-language Bibles it subventioned, but the practice was vigorously protested, especially by the Edinburgh branch of the Society. The protesters had their way, and in 1826 a rule was formally adopted: "The Principles of the Society exclude the circulation of those Books, or parts of Books, which are usually termed Apocryphal." The action of the London society confirmed the American Bible Society (founded at New York in 1816) in its own practice, and commercial publishers naturally followed the same practice. In consequence general familiarity with the books of the Apocrypha declined, though they were included in small editions of the Authorized Version issued by the Oxford and Cambridge presses and also in separate printings. But in their work on the Apocrypha the King James translators were careless and perfunctory, so that it is inferior to the rest of their work in both accuracy and style. To remedy these defects and to make the Apocrypha more generally accessible Professor Edgar J. Goodspeed published his "American translation" in 1938. More recently (1957) a Revised Standard Version Apocrypha has been prepared by a committee of American scholars. But the freshness and directness of Professor Goodspeed's version and its closer approach to a dignified vernacular make it more desirable for the general reader, and it has therefore been chosen for presentation in the present volume.

A welcome by-product of the nineteenth-century debate on the worth of the Apocrypha was a spurt of scholarly activity on text and interpretation. A precipitate of this activity, still highly useful, is available in R. H. Charles, *Apocrypha and Pseudepigrapha of the Old Testament,* in two quarto volumes (Oxford, 1913). The handiest modern Greek text is Alfred Rahlf's *Septuaginta* (Stuttgart, 1935, and reprints). Series of translations of individual books with commentaries are published by Catholic, Protestant, and Jewish organizations. The three most useful introductions to Apocryphal literature are by American scholars. The most technical is C. C. Torrey, *The Apocryphal Literature* (Yale University Press, 1945); the most devout is Bruce M. Metzger, *An Introduction to the Apocrypha* (Oxford University Press, 1957). Far the fullest, with due account taken of other scholarly opinion, is R. H. Pfeiffer, *History of New Testament Times with an Introduction to the Apocrypha* (Harper's, 1949).

THE FIRST BOOK OF ESDRAS

This book reproduces the substance of the end of II Chronicles, the whole of Ezra and a part of Nehemiah. In the Septuagint, where Ezra and Nehemiah are called I and II Esdras, this book is called III Esdras (or, by modern scholars, The Greek Ezra), but it is placed before *the other two, and Josephus' account of the period* (Antiquities *11.1–5) uses it and ignores the others. What the precise literary relationship between the parallel accounts may be, whether one is a revision of the other or both derive independently from a common source, is a much debated question; both versions are more concerned with inculcating special views regarding the Temple and the observance of the Law than with the historical course of events.*

What is new in I Esdras and most attractive is the story of the three guardsmen (3.1–5.6). The story probably originated in Persia, was translated into Aramaic, and then adapted to the purposes of this book. Our author has named the victorious guardsman Zerubabel to cement the connection with his history and to magnify his favorite personage; for his prize Zerubabel craves and obtains the privilege of rebuilding the walls of Jerusalem and the Temple. Zerubabel's eloquent defense of his thesis that truth is strongest (familiar in world literature as magna est veritas et praevalebit) *has been acclaimed a precious bit of Achaemenid literature, perhaps of importance for the development of the doctrine of the* logos. *The vicissitudes of the story offer an instructive example of the Hellenistic melting pot at work. The date of I Esdras is somewhere near the beginning of the common era.*

THE FIRST BOOK OF ESDRAS

1] **W**HEN JOSIAH CELEBRATED THE PASS-
over festival in Jerusalem to his Lord, he sacrificed the Passover on the fourteenth day of the
2 first month, placing the priests in their divisions, clad in
3 their vestments, in the temple of the Lord. And he ordered
the Levites, the temple slaves of Israel, to consecrate themselves to the Lord, when they put the holy chest of the
Lord in the house of the Lord, which Solomon the king, the
4 son of David, had built; and he said,

"You will not have to carry it on your shoulders any
more; so now worship the Lord your God, and serve his
people, Israel, and prepare yourselves by your families and
5 kindreds, as David, king of Israel, wrote, and with all the
magnificence of Solomon his son; and take your places in
the temple, according to your ancestral groups as Levites
6 before your brothers, the Israelites, in proper order, and
sacrifice the Passover, and get the sacrifices ready for your
brothers, and observe the Passover, in accordance with the
7 Lord's command which was given to Moses."

And Josiah gave the people that were present thirty thousand lambs and kids, and three thousand calves; these were
given out of the king's revenues, as he promised, to the
8 people and the priests and Levites. And Hilkiah and
Zechariah and Jehiel, the rulers of the temple, gave the
priests for the Passover two thousand, six hundred sheep
9 and three hundred calves. And Jeconiah and Shemaiah
and Nathanael, his brother, and Asabiah and Ochiel and
Joram, colonels of regiments, gave the Levites for the Pass-
10 over five thousand sheep and seven hundred calves. And
it was done; the priests and Levites, with the unleavened
bread, stood in proper order, according to their kindreds
11 and their family divisions, before the people, to make the

3   1:1–11

offering to the Lord, as it is prescribed in the book of Moses; this they did in the morning. They roasted the Passover 12 with fire in the proper way, and boiled the sacrifices in caldrons and basins, with savory odors, and set them before all 13 the people. Afterward they prepared some for themselves and their brothers the priests, the sons of Aaron; for the 14 priests were offering the fat until late, so the Levites prepared meat for themselves and for their brothers the priests, the sons of Aaron. The sacred musicians, too, the sons of 15 Asaph, were in their places, according to the regulations of David, with Asaph and Zechariah and Eddinus, who were of the king's circle, and the doorkeepers stood at each door. 16 No one needed to interrupt his duties for the day, for their brothers, the Levites, prepared meat for them. So the things 17 that had to do with the Lord's sacrifices were carried out that day, in celebrating the Passover and offering the sacri- 18 fices on the altar of the Lord, as King Josiah commanded. So the Israelites who were present at that time observed the 19 Passover and the festival of Unleavened Bread for seven days. No such Passover had been celebrated in Israel since 20 the times of the prophet Samuel, and none of the kings of 21 Israel had celebrated such a Passover as Josiah and the priests and the Levites and the Jews celebrated with all the Israelites that were present in their dwellings in Jerusalem. It was in the eighteenth year of the reign of Josiah that this 22 Passover was observed. And the doings of Josiah were up- 23 right in the Lord's sight, for his heart was full of piety. And 24 the events of his times have been recorded in the past about those who sinned and acted wickedly toward the Lord, beyond any other nation or kingdom, and how they grieved him keenly, so that the words of the Lord rose up to condemn Israel.

After all these doings of Josiah, it happened that Pharaoh, 25

1:12-25

king of Egypt, came to make war at Carchemish on the
26 Euphrates, and Josiah went out to encounter him. And
the king of Egypt sent word to him, saying,

27 "What do you want of me, King of Judah? I was not sent
against you by the Lord God, for my war is on the Euphrates. And now the Lord is with me! The Lord is with
28 me, urging me on; depart and do not oppose the Lord."

But Josiah would not turn back to his chariot, but tried
to fight with him, disregarding the words of Jeremiah the
29 prophet, spoken by the mouth of the Lord, and joined battle
with him in the plain of Megiddo, and the leaders fought
30 against King Josiah. And the king said to his servants,
"Take me away from the battle, for I am very sick."
And his servants immediately took him out of the fray.
31 And he got into his second chariot, and was taken back to
Jerusalem, and departed this life, and was buried in the
32 tomb of his forefathers. And they grieved for Josiah all over
Judah, and Jeremiah the prophet lamented for Josiah, and
the principal men, with the women, have mourned him to
this day; and it was ordained that this should always be
33 done, throughout all the nation of Israel. This is recorded
in the scroll of the histories of the kings of Judah; and every
one of the deeds of Josiah, and his splendor, and his understanding of the Law of the Lord, and what he had done before, and these present deeds, are told in the scroll of the
kings of Israel and Judah.

34 And the men of the nation took Jeconiah, the son of
Josiah, and made him king, to succeed Josiah his father,
35 when he was twenty-three years old. And he reigned three
months in Judah and Jerusalem. Then the king of Egypt
36 deposed him from reigning in Jerusalem, and he assessed
the nation a hundred talents of silver and one talent of gold.
37 And the king of Egypt appointed Jehoiakim, his brother,

king of Judah and Jerusalem. And Jehoiakim put the 38
nobles in prison and seized his brother Zarius and brought
him back from Egypt.

Jehoiakim was twenty-five years old when he became king 39
of Judah and Jerusalem, and he did what was wrong in the
sight of the Lord. And Nebuchadnezzar, the king of Baby- 40
lon, came against him, and put him in chains of brass and
took him to Babylon. And Nebuchadnezzar took some of 41
the sacred dishes of the Lord and carried them off and set
them up in his temple in Babylon. But the stories about him 42
and his uncleanness and his impious behavior are written
in the chronicles of the kings.

And Jehoiachin, his son, became king in his stead; for 43
when he was made king, he was eighteen years old, and he 44
reigned three months and ten days in Jerusalem, and did
what was wrong in the sight of the Lord. And a year later, 45
Nebuchadnezzar sent and removed him to Babylon, with
the sacred dishes of the Lord, and appointed Zedekiah king 46
of Judah and Jerusalem, when Zedekiah was twenty-one
years old. And he reigned eleven years. And he did what 47
was wrong in the sight of the Lord, and disregarded the
words that were spoken by Jeremiah the prophet, from the
mouth of the Lord. And although King Nebuchadnezzar 48
had made him swear by the name of the lord, he broke his
oath and rebelled, and he hardened his neck and his
heart and transgressed the laws of the Lord, the God of
Israel. And the leaders of the people and of the priests did 49
many impious acts and surpassed in lawlessness all the unclean acts of all the heathen, and polluted the temple of the
Lord that had been consecrated in Jerusalem. And the God 50
of their forefathers sent by his messenger to call them back,
for he would have spared them and his dwelling; but they 51
mocked his messengers, and whenever the Lord spoke to

1:38-51

52 them, they made sport of his prophets, until he grew angry with his people because of their ungodliness and ordered the
53 kings of the Chaldeans to be brought against them. These killed their young men with the sword around their holy temple, and did not spare youth or maiden, old man or
54 child, for he delivered them all into their hands. And all the sacred dishes of the Lord, great and small, and the chests of the Lord, and the royal treasures they took, and
55 carried them off to Babylon. And they burned the house of the Lord, and tore down the walls of Jerusalem, and
56 burned down their towers, and completely ruined all her glories. And those who survived the sword he removed to
57 Babylon. And they were his servants and those of his children, until the Persians began to reign; to fulfil what the Lord said by the mouth of Jeremiah,
58 "Until the land enjoys its sabbaths, all the time of her desolation she shall keep the sabbath, until the lapse of seventy years."
2] In the first year that Cyrus reigned over Persia, to fulfil
2 what the Lord said by the mouth of Jeremiah, the Lord stirred the heart of Cyrus, king of Persia, and he made a proclamation throughout all his kingdom, and put it in
3 writing, saying,
"Thus speaks Cyrus, king of Persia: The Lord of Israel,
4 the Lord Most High, has made me king of the world, and directed me to build him a house in Jerusalem, in Judah.
5 So if anyone of you is of his people, his Lord be with him, and let him go up to Jerusalem, in Judah, and build the house of the Lord of Israel; he is the Lord who lives in
6 Jerusalem. So let a man's neighbors, who live in each
7 place, help him with gold and silver, with presents, with horses and cattle, beside the other things added as vows for the temple of the Lord in Jerusalem."

Then the heads of families of the tribe of Judah and the 8
tribe of Benjamin arose, and the priests and the Levites, and
all whose hearts the Lord had stirred to go up to build the
house in Jerusalem for the Lord. And their neighbors 9
helped them with everything, with silver and gold, with
horses and cattle, and a great many vows from many
whose hearts were stirred.

And King Cyrus brought out the sacred dishes of the 10
Lord, which Nebuchadnezzar had carried off from Jerusalem, and deposited in the temple of his idols; but Cyrus, king 11
of Persia, brought them out, and delivered them to his
treasurer Mithridates, and they were turned over by him to 12
Sheshbazzar, the governor of Judah. And this was the num- 13
ber of them: a thousand gold cups, a thousand silver cups,
twenty-nine silver censers, thirty gold bowls, two thousand,
four hundred and ten silver bowls, and a thousand other
dishes. So all the dishes, gold and silver, five thousand, four 14
hundred and sixty-nine, were taken and carried back by 15
Sheshbazzar, along with those who had been in captivity,
from Babylon to Jerusalem.

But in the times of Artaxerxes, king of Persia, Bishlam, 16
Mithridates, Tabeel, Rehum, the recorder, and Shimshai,
the scribe, and the others associated with them, living in
Samaria and other places, wrote him the following letter,
against those who lived in Judah and Jerusalem:

"To King Artaxerxes our Lord, your servants Rehum, the 17
recorder, and Shimshai, the scribe, and the other judges of
their court in Coelesyria and Phoenicia; now be it known to 18
our lord the king, that the Jews who have come up to us
from you have reached Jerusalem and are rebuilding that
rebellious and wicked city and repairing its bazaars and
walls and laying the foundations of a temple. Now if this 19
city is rebuilt and its walls completed, they will not submit

2:8-19

20 to paying tribute, but will even resist the kings. And since
the matter of the temple is now under way, we think it
21 right not to neglect such a matter, but to address our lord
the king, so that, if you approve, a search may be made in
22 the records of your forefathers; for you will find in their
chronicles what is written about them, and you will learn
that this city was rebellious, troublesome to kings and
23 towns, and that the Jews were rebels and organizers of warfare in it from ancient times; that was why the city was laid
24 waste. We now therefore inform you, lord king, that if this
city is rebuilt, and its walls restored, you will no longer have
a way of access to Coelesyria and Phoenicia."

25   Then the king wrote in reply to Rehum, the recorder, and
Shimshai, the scribe, and their associates, who lived in
Samaria, Syria, and Phoenicia, as follows:

26   "I have read the letter which you sent me. I accordingly
ordered search to be made, and it was found that this city
27 from ancient times used to rebel against the kings, and the
people created revolts and wars in it, and that stern and
powerful kings ruled in Jerusalem, and took tribute from
28 Coelesyria and Phoenicia. Therefore I have now given
orders to prevent these men from rebuilding the city, and
29 to take measures that nothing further be done and that
these wicked undertakings go no farther, to the annoyance
of the kings."

30   When the message of King Artaxerxes was read, Rehum
and Shimshai, the scribe, and their associates proceeded in
haste to Jerusalem, with horsemen and a crowd of troops
and began to hinder the builders. So the rebuilding of the
temple in Jerusalem was suspended until the second year of
the reign of Darius, king of Persia.

3]   Now King Darius made a great banquet for all his subjects, and all his domestics, and all the nobles of Media and

Persia, and all the viceroys and provincial and district 2
governors under his sway, in the hundred and twenty-seven
provinces from India to Ethiopia. And they ate and 3
drank, and when they were satisfied, they went home, but
Darius the king went to his bedroom, and fell asleep, and
then awoke. Then the three young men of his bodyguard, 4
who kept guard over the person of the king, said to one
another,

"Let us each say what one thing is strongest, and Darius 5
the king will give rich presents and great honors to the one
whose words seem the wisest, and have him dressed in 6
purple, and drink from gold plate, and sleep on a gold bed,
and give him a chariot with gold bridles, and a linen headdress, and a necklace around his neck, and because of his 7
wisdom he shall sit next to Darius, and be called Darius'
kinsman."

Then they each wrote his own answer and put his seal on 8
it, and put them under the pillow of King Darius, and said, 9

"When the king wakes up, they will give him the writing,
and the one whose choice the king and the three princes of
Persia judge the wisest, shall be considered the victor in
what he has written."

The first wrote, 10
"Wine is strongest."
The second wrote, 11
"The king is strongest."
The third wrote, 12
"Women are strongest, but truth prevails over every-
thing."

So when the king awoke, they took the writing and gave it 13
to him and he read it. Then he sent and summoned all the 14
nobles of Persia and Media, and the governors and officers
and magistrates and officials, and he took his seat in the 15

3:2–15

council chamber, and what was written was read before
16 them. And he said,

"Summon the young men, and let them show their reasons."

17 And they were summoned, and came in. And they said
to them,

"Explain to us about what you have written."

18 So the first one, who had told of the strength of wine, began and said,

"Gentlemen, how supremely strong wine is! It leads the
19 minds of all who drink it astray. It makes the mind of the
king and the mind of the fatherless child alike; the mind of
20 the menial and the freeman, of the poor and the rich. It
turns every thought to mirth and merrymaking, and forgets
21 all grief and debt. It makes all hearts rich, and forgets kings
and governors, and makes everybody talk in thousands.
22 And when they drink, they forget to be friendly to friends
23 and brothers, and very soon they draw their swords. And
when they recover from their wine, they cannot remember
24 what they have done. Gentlemen, is not wine supremely
strong, since it forces them to act so?"

When he had said this, he stopped.

4] Then the second, who had told of the king's might, began
to speak:

2 "Gentlemen, are not men strongest, because they control
3 land and sea, and all that is in them? But the king is supremely strong, and is lord and master of them, and every
4 command he gives them they obey. If he orders them to
make war on one another, they do so; and if he sends them
out against the enemy, they go, and surmount mountains,
5 walls, and towers. They kill and are killed, but they do not
disobey the king's command. And if they are victorious,
they bring everything to the king, the spoils they take and

3:16–4:5

all the rest. And those who do not go to war or fight, but till 6
the soil, again, when they sow and reap, bring it to the king,
and they compel one another to pay taxes to the king. He 7
is only one man; but if he orders them to kill, they kill; if he
orders them to release, they release; if he orders them to 8
strike down, they strike; if he orders them to lay waste, they
lay waste; if he orders them to build, they build; if he orders 9
them to cut down, they cut down; if he orders them to plant,
they plant. So all his people and his troops obey him. Be- 10
sides, he reclines at table, he eats and drinks and sleeps, and 11
they keep watch about him, and they cannot any of them
go away and look after his own affairs, or disobey him at all.
Gentlemen, how can the king not be strongest, when he is 12
so obeyed?"

And he stopped.

Then the third, who had spoken of women and of truth— 13
his name was Zerubbabel—began to speak:

"Gentlemen, is not the king great, and are not men many, 14
and is not wine strong? Who is it then that rules over them
and masters them? Is it not women? Women have borne 15
the king and all the people, who are lords of sea and land;
from them they are sprung, and they brought them up, to 16
plant the vineyards, from which the wine comes. They 17
make men's clothes, they make men's splendor, and men
cannot exist without women. Why, if men amass gold and 18
silver, and everything of beauty, and then see one woman
remarkable for looks and beauty, they let all these things go, 19
and gape at her, and stare at her with open mouths, and
would all rather have her than gold or silver or any thing
of beauty. A man will leave his own father, who brought 20
him up, and his own country, and be united to his wife.
With his wife he ends his days, and remembers neither his 21
father nor his mother nor his country. Hence you must 22

4:6–22

recognize that women rule over men. Do you not toil and
23 labor, and bring it all and give it to your wives? A man
takes his sword and goes out on expeditions to rob and steal,
24 and to sail the sea and the rivers; he faces the lion and walks
in the darkness, and when he steals and robs and plunders, he
25 brings it back to the woman he loves. So a man loves his
26 wife better than his father or mother. Many have lost their
heads completely for the sake of women, and become slaves
27 for their sakes. Many have perished, or failed, or sinned for
28 the sake of women. Now do you not believe me? Is not
the king great in his power? Do not all lands fear even to
29 touch him? Yet I have seen him with Apame, the king's
concubine, the daughter of the noble Bartacus, sitting at the
30 king's right hand, and taking the crown from the king's
head, and putting it on her own, and she slapped the king
31 with her left hand. At this the king stared at her open-
mouthed. If she smiled at him, he laughed; if she grew
angry at him, he flattered her, so that she might be recon-
32 ciled to him again. Gentlemen, how can women not be
mighty, when they act like that?"

33   Then the king and the nobles looked at one another, and
he began to speak about truth:

34   "Gentlemen, are not women mighty? The earth is vast,
and heaven is high, and the sun is swift in his course, for he
circles about the heavens and hastens back to his own
35 starting-point in a single day. Is he not great who does
these things? So truth is great, and mightier than all other
36 things. The whole earth calls upon truth, and heaven
blesses her; all his works quake and tremble, there is no
37 wrongdoing with him. Wine is not upright, the king is not
upright, women are not upright, all the sons of men are not
upright, and all their doings, all such things, are not upright; there is no truth in them, and through their un-

righteousness they will perish. But truth endures and is 38
strong forever, and lives and reigns forever and ever. There 39
is no partiality or preference with her, but she does what is
right, rather than all that is wrong and wicked. All men
approve her doings, and there is no injustice in her judgment. 40
To her belongs power and the royal dignity and authority
and majesty in all the ages; blessed be the God of truth!"

When he stopped speaking, all the people shouted and 41
said,

"Truth is great and supremely strong."

Then the king said to him, 42

"Ask whatever you please, beyond what is written here,
and we will give it to you, since you have been found the
wisest. You shall sit next to me, and be called my kinsman,"

Then he said to the king, 43

"Remember the vow that you made, the day you succeeded to your throne, to rebuild Jerusalem and send back 44
all the dishes taken from Jerusalem, which Cyrus set aside,
when he vowed to destroy Babylon, and to send them back
there. And you vowed to rebuild the house, which the 45
Edomites burned, when Jerusalem had been laid waste by
the Chaldeans. So now, my lord the king, this is what I ask 46
and request of you, and this is the princely liberality to come
from you: I beg you to carry out the vow that you vowed
with your own lips to the King of Heaven that you would
carry out."

Then Darius, the king, got up and kissed him, and he 47
wrote letters for him to all his managers and magistrates and
officers and governors, to escort him in safety with all who
were going up with him to rebuild Jerusalem. And he wrote 48
letters to all the magistrates in Coelesyria and Phoenicia and
to those in the Lebanon, to bring cedar timbers from the
Lebanon to Jerusalem and that they should help him to

49 rebuild the city. And he wrote in the interest of all the
Jews who were going up from his kingdom to Judah, to
secure their freedom, that no noble or governor or magis-
50 trate or manager should forcibly enter their doors, and that
all the country which they were to occupy they should
possess free from tribute; and that the Edomites should give
51 up the Jewish villages which they controlled, and that
twenty talents a year should be given for the rebuilding of
52 the temple, until it was completed, and ten talents a year
besides, to provide burnt offerings to be offered daily upon
the altar, in accordance with the command they had to offer
53 seventeen, and that all who came up from Babylonia to rebuild the city should have their freedom, they and their
54 children and all the priests who came up. He wrote providing their expenses also, and the priestly vestments in which
55 they officiate. And he wrote that the Levites' expenses
should be provided until the day when the house should be
56 finished and Jerusalem rebuilt. And he wrote that lots of
land and wages should be given to all who guarded the city.
57 And he sent back all the dishes from Babylon, which Cyrus
had set aside; and all that Cyrus had ordered done he commanded them to do and to send back to Jerusalem.

58 When the young man went out, he lifted his face to
heaven toward Jerusalem, and praised the King of Heaven,
59 saying,
"From you comes victory, from you comes wisdom; to
60 you belongs glory, and I am your servant. Blessed are you,
who have given me wisdom; I praise you, Lord of my forefathers."

61 And he took the letters and went to Babylon, and re-
62 ported it to all his brothers. And they blessed the God of
their forefathers, because he had given them relief and
63 liberty to go up and rebuild Jerusalem and the temple

which was called by his name; and they banqueted with music and gladness for seven days.

After this the heads of families were chosen to go up, according to their clans, with their wives and sons and daughters, and their male and female slaves, and their cattle. And Darius sent with them a thousand horsemen, to escort them back to Jerusalem in peace, with music of drums and flutes (for all their brothers made merry); he made them go up with them.

These are the names of the men who went up, by their families within their tribes, for their priestly office: of the priests, the sons of Phineas, the son of Aaron; Jeshua, the son of Jozadak, the son of Seraiah, and Joakim, the son of Zerubbabel, the son of Salathiel, of the house of David, of the line of Phares, of the tribe of Judah, who uttered wise sayings before Darius, the king of Persia, in the second year of his reign, in the month of Nisan, the first month.

These are those from Judah who went up after their sojourn in captivity, whom Nebuchadnezzar, king of Babylon, had removed to Babylon, and who returned to Jerusalem and the rest of Judah, each one to his own town, going with Zerubbabel and Jeshua, Nehemiah, Seraiah, Resaiah, Bigvai, Mordecai, Bilshan, Mispar, Reeliah, Rehum, and Baanah, their leaders; the numbers of those of the nation, and their leaders: the descendants of Parosh, two thousand, one hundred and seventy-two; of the descendants of Shephatiah, four hundred and seventy-two; the descendants of Arah, seven hundred and fifty-six; the descendants of Pahath-moab, of the descendants of Jeshua and Joab, two thousand, eight hundred and twelve; the descendants of Elam, one thousand, two hundred and fifty-four; the descendants of Zattu, nine hundred and forty-five; the descendants of Chorbe, seven hundred and five; the descend-

13 ants of Binnui, six hundred and forty-eight; the descendants
of Bebai, six hundred and twenty-three; the descendants of
Azgad, one thousand, three hundred and twenty-two;

14 the descendants of Adonikam, six hundred and sixty-
seven; the descendants of Bigvai, two thousand and sixty-
six; the descendants of Adin, four hundred and fifty-four;

15 the descendants of Ater, the son of Hezekiah, ninety-
two; the descendants of Kilan and Azetas, sixty-seven;
the descendants of Azuru, four hundred and thirty-two;

16 the descendants of Annias, one hundred and one; the
descendants of Arom: the descendants of Bezai, three hundred and twenty-three; the descendants of Jorah, one

17 hundred and twelve; the descendants of Baiterus, three
thousand and five; the descendants of Bethlehem, one hun-

18 dred and twenty-three; the men of Netophah, fifty-five; the
men of Anathoth, one hundred and fifty-eight; the men of

19 Bethasmoth, forty-two; the men of Kirjath-jearim, twenty-
five; the men of Chephirah and Beeroth, seven hundred and

20 forty-three; the Chadiasans and Ammidians, four hundred
and twenty-two; the men of Ramah and Geba, six hundred

21 and twenty-one; the men of Michmash, one hundred and
twenty-two; the men of Bethel-Ai, fifty-two; the descend-

22 ants of Magbish, one hundred and fifty-six; the descendants
of the other Elam and Ono, seven hundred and twenty-five;
the descendants of Jericho, three hundred and forty-five;

23 the descendants of Senaah, three thousand, three hundred
and thirty.

24 Of the priests: the descendants of Jedaiah, of the house
of Jeshua, among the descendants of Anasib, nine hundred
and seventy-two; the descendants of Immer, one thousand

25 and fifty-two; the descendants of Pashhur, one thousand,
two hundred and forty-seven; the descendants of Harim, one
thousand and seventeen.

5:13–25

Of the Levites: the descendants of Jeshua and Kadmiel 26
and Bannas and Sudias, seventy-four; of the sacred singers: 27
the descendants of Asaph, one hundred and twenty-eight;
of the doorkeepers: the descendants of Shallum, the de- 28
scendants of Ater, the descendants of Tolman, the descendants of Akkub, the descendants of Hatita, the descendants
of Shobai—in all, one hundred and thirty-nine.

Of the temple slaves: the descendants of Ziha, the de- 29
scendants of Hasupha, the descendants of Tabbaoth, the
descendants of Keros, the descendants of Siaha, the descendants of Padon, the descendants of Lebanah, the descendants of Hagabah, the descendants of Akkub, the 30
descendants of Uthai, the descendants of Ketab, the descendants of Hagab, the descendants of Shamlai, the
descendants of Hanan, the descendants of Cathua, the
descendants of Gahar, the descendants of Reaiah, the de- 31
scendants of Rezin, the descendants of Nekoda, the descendants of Chezib, the descendants of Gazzan, the descendants
of Uzza, the descendants of Paseah, the descendants of
Hasrah, the descendants of Besai, the descendants of
Asnah, the descendants of the Meunites, the descendants
of Nephisim, the descendants of Bakbuk, the descendants
of Hakupha, the descendants of Asur, the descendants of
Pharakim, the descendants of Bazluth, the descendants 32
of Mehida, the descendants of Cutha, the descendants of
Charea, the descendants of Barkos, the descendants of
Sisera, the descendants of Temah, the descendants of
Neziah, the descendants of Hatipha.

Of the descendants of Solomon's servants: the descend- 33
ants of Hassophereth, the descendants of Peruda, the descendants of Jaalah, the descendants of Lozon, the descendants of Giddel, the descendants of Shephatiah, the de- 34
scendants of Hattil, the descendants of Pochereth-hazza-

5:26-34

baim, the descendants of Sarothie, the descendants of
Masiah, the descendants of Gas, the descendants of Addus,
the descendants of Subas, the descendants of Apherra, the
descendants of Barodis, the descendants of Shaphat, the
35 descendants of Ami. In all, the temple slaves and the
descendants of the servants of Solomon were three hundred
and seventy-two.

36   These are those who went up from Telmelah and Tel-
harsha, under the leadership of Cherub, Adan, and Immer,
37 but were not able to show by their families or lineage that
they belonged to Israel: the descendants of Delaiah the
descendant of Tobiah, the descendants of Nekoda, six
38 hundred and fifty-two. And of those of the priests who had
assumed the priesthood but were not found registered: the
descendants of Habaiah, the descendants of Hakkoz, the
descendants of Jaddus who married Agia, one of the
39 daughters of Barzillai and was called by his name. And
when the ancestry of these men was looked for in the
register, and could not be found, they were excluded from
40 officiating as priests. And Nehemiah and the governor told
them not to share in the consecrated things until a high
priest should appear clothed in the Manifestation and the
Truth.

41   In all, there were: of Israel, over twelve years of age, besides male and female slaves, forty-two thousand, three
42 hundred and sixty; of their male and female slaves, seven
thousand, three hundred and thirty-seven; of musicians and
43 singers, two hundred and forty-five. There were four hundred and thirty-five camels, and seven thousand and
thirty-six horses, two hundred and forty-five mules, and
five thousand, five hundred and twenty-five asses.

44   And some of the principal heads of families, when they
reached the temple of God in Jerusalem, vowed that they

would erect the house in its old place, to the best of their
ability, and that they would give to the sacred building 45
fund a thousand minas in gold and five thousand minas
in silver, and a hundred priest's garments.

So the priests and the Levites and some of the people 46
settled in Jerusalem and the country, and the sacred singers
and the doorkeepers and all Israel settled in their villages.

When the seventh month came, and the Israelites were 47
all at home, they gathered as one man in the square in front
of the first gate toward the east. And Jeshua, the son of 48
Jozadak, and his brothers the priests, and Zerubbabel, the
son of Salathiel, and his brothers took their places and prepared the altar of the God of Israel, in order to offer on it 49
burnt offerings, as is directed in the book of Moses, the man
of God. And they were joined by some of the other peoples 50
of the land, and they erected the altar in its place; for
though they had been hostile to them, all the people in the
land supported them, and brought sacrifices at the proper
times, and the morning and evening burnt offerings for the
Lord, and they kept the Camping Out festival, as it is pre- 51
scribed in the Law, and they brought sacrifices every day,
when it was proper, and besides these the regular offerings 52
and sacrifices on sabbaths and new moons and all the sacred
festival days. And all who had made voluntary gifts to 53
God began to offer sacrifices to God, beginning with the
new moon of the seventh month, though the temple of God 54
was not yet rebuilt. And they paid money to the masons
and carpenters, and gave food and drink and carts to the 55
Sidonians and Tyrians, to bring cedar timbers from the
Lebanon and convey them in rafts to the harbor of Joppa,
as Cyrus, the king of Persia, had commanded them in
writing.

In the second year Zerubbabel, the son of Salathiel, came 56

to the temple of God in Jerusalem, and in the second month
he began with Jeshua, the son of Jozadak, and their
brothers, and the Levitical priests and all who had come
57 back from the exile to Jerusalem, and they laid the foundation of the temple of God on the new moon of the second
month, in the second year, after they came to Judah and
58 Jerusalem. And they appointed the Levites who were over
twenty years old to have charge of the work of the Lord.
And Jeshua rose up and his sons and his brothers and Kadmiel his brother and the sons of Jeshua Emadabun and the
sons of Joda, the son of Iliadun, with their sons and brothers,
all the Levites, as one man pressing forward the work on the
house of God.

59 And the builders built the sanctuary of the Lord, and the
priests stood in their robes, with musical instruments and
trumpets, and the Levites, the sons of Asaph, with their
60 cymbals, praising the Lord and blessing him, according to
61 the directions of David, king of Israel, and they sang loudly,
giving thanks to the Lord, with hymns, because all Israel
62 enjoys his goodness and his glory forever. And all the people sounded trumpets and gave a great shout, praising the
63 Lord for the erection of the house of the Lord. And some of
the Levitical priests and the older men among the heads of
their families, who had seen the house that preceded this
one, came to the building of this house with outcries and
64 loud lamentation, while many came with trumpets and a
65 great shout of joy, so that the people could not hear the
trumpets on account of the lamentation, for the multitude
sounded the trumpets loudly, so that it was heard a long way
off.

66 And when the enemies of the tribe of Judah and Benjamin heard it, they came to find out what the sound of the
67 trumpets meant. And they learned that those who had re-

turned from captivity were building the sanctuary for the Lord, the God of Israel, and they went to Zerubbabel and 68 Jeshua and the heads of families, and said to them,

"We will help you build, for we, like you, obey your 69 Lord, and have sacrificed to him from the days of Esarhaddon, king of Assyria, who brought us here."

Then Zerubbabel and Jeshua and the heads of families of 70 Israel said to them,

"It is not for you and us to build the house for the Lord our God, for we will build it by ourselves for the Lord of 71 Israel, as Cyrus, the king of Persia, has commanded us."

But the heathen of the land pressed upon those who were 72 in Judea, and, blockading them, hindered them from building, and by making plots and stirring up the people and up- 73 risings they prevented the completion of the building all the lifetime of King Cyrus. So they were kept from building for two years, until the reign of Darius.

But in the second year of the reign of Darius, the prophets [6 Haggai and Zechariah, the son of Iddo, prophesied to the Jews who were in Judea and Jerusalem, prophesying to them in the name of the Lord, the God of Israel. Then 2 Zerubbabel, the son of Salathiel, and Jeshua, the son of Jozadak, got up and began to build the house of the Lord that was in Jerusalem, while the prophets of the Lord joined them and helped them.

At that very time there came to them Sisinnes, the gover- 3 nor of Syria and Phoenicia, and Sathrabuzanes and their companions, and said to them,

"By whose orders are you building this house, and com- 4 pleting this roof and all these other things? And who are the builders who are carrying this out?"

Still the elders of the Jews were shown favor, for the Lord 5 had regard for the captives, and they were not prevented 6 from building until Darius was informed about them and orders were issued.

7   This is the copy of a letter which Sisinnes, the governor of Syria and Phoenicia, and Sathrabuzanes and their companions wrote and sent to Darius:

8   "Greetings to King Darius. Let it all be known to our lord the king that when we went to the country of Judea and entered the city of Jerusalem, we found the elders of the

9   Jews, who had been in captivity, building in the city of Jerusalem a great, new house for the Lord, of costly hewn

10 stone, with timbers set in the walls, and we found this work proceeding with haste, and the undertaking prospering in their hands, and being completed with all glory and dili-

11 gence. Then we inquired of these elders and said,

   " 'At whose command are you building this house, and laying the foundations of these works?'

12 "Then in order to inform you and write to you, we inquired of them what men were the leaders, and asked them for a list of the names of those who were taking the lead.

13 And they answered and said,

   " 'We are servants of the Lord who created the heaven

14 and the earth. And the house was built many years ago by a king of Israel who was great and strong, and was finished.

15 And when our forefathers sinned against the heavenly Lord of Israel and provoked him, he delivered them into the hands of Nebuchadnezzar, the king of Babylon, the king of

16 the Chaldeans; and they tore the house down and burned

17 it, and carried the people away as captives to Babylon. But in the first year of the reign of Cyrus over Babylonia, Cyrus

18 the king wrote an order that this house be rebuilt. And the sacred dishes of gold and silver that Nebuchadnezzar had carried away from the house at Jerusalem, and set up in his own sanctuary, Cyrus the king brought forth again from the

6:7–18

sanctuary in Babylon, and they were given to Zerubbabel
and Sheshbazzar, the governor, and he was instructed to 19
carry all these dishes back and put them back in the sanctuary in Jerusalem, and that this sanctuary of the Lord should
be rebuilt on the same spot. Then this Sheshbazzar, after 20
coming here, laid the foundations of the house of the Lord
that is in Jerusalem, and although it has been under construction from then until now it has not reached completion. Now therefore, if it meets your approval, O king, let 21
search be made in the royal archives of our lord the king
in Babylon, and if it is found that the building of the house 22
of the Lord in Jerusalem was done with the consent of
Cyrus the king, and it meets the approval of our lord the
king, let him give us orders about this."

Then King Darius ordered a search to be made in the 23
royal archives that were deposited in Babylon. And in the
castle of Ecbatana, in the land of Media, was found a roll
in which this was recorded:

"In the first year of the reign of Cyrus, King Cyrus 24
ordered the rebuilding of the house of the Lord in Jerusalem, where they sacrifice with perpetual fire; the height of 25
it to be ninety feet, the width ninety feet, with three courses
of hewn stone and a course of new native timber, and the
cost to be provided from the house of Cyrus the king; and 26
that the sacred dishes of the house of the Lord, of gold and
silver, which Nebuchadnezzar carried away from the house
in Jerusalem and removed to Babylon, be restored to the
house in Jerusalem to be placed where they were." And he 27
further ordered that Sisinnes, the governor of Syria and
Phoenicia, and Sathrabuzanes and their companions and
the local governors appointed in Syria and Phoenicia
should take care to let the place alone, and to permit
Zerubbabel, the servant of the Lord and governor of Judea,

6:19–27

and the elders of the Jews, to build the house of the Lord in
28 its old place. "And I command that it be completely built
and that they seek earnestly to help the returned captives
29 of Judea, until the house of the Lord is finished; and that
a grant from the tribute of Coelesyria and Phoenicia be particularly given these men for sacrifices to the Lord, that is,
to Zerubbabel, the governor, for bulls and rams and lambs,
30 and likewise wheat and salt and wine and oil, regularly
every year, without objection, as the priests in Jerusalem
31 indicate they are daily used, so that libations may be
offered to the Most High God for the king and his children,
and that they may pray for their lives."

32   And he commanded further that, if any transgressed or
disregarded any of the things said above or added below, a
beam should be taken from his house and he should be hung
33 on it, and his property be taken for the king. "Therefore
may the Lord, whose name is called upon there, destroy any
king and nation that shall stretch out their hands to hinder
34 or damage that house of the Lord in Jerusalem. I, King
Darius, have decreed that it be done in exactly this way."

7]   Then Sisinnes, the governor of Coelesyria and Phoenicia,
and Sathrabuzanes and their companions, obeying the
2 orders of Darius the king, looked after the holy work very
attentively, assisting the elders of the Jews and the governors
3 of the temple. And the holy work progressed, while the
prophets Haggai and Zechariah prophesied; and they com-
4 pleted it at the command of the Lord, the God of Israel;
and with the consent of Cyrus and Darius and Artaxerxes,
5 the kings of Persia, the holy house was finished by the
twenty-third day of the month of Adar, in the sixth year of
6 King Darius. And the Israelites and the priests and the rest
of the returned exiles who had joined them did according to
7 what was in the book of Moses. And they offered at the

dedication of the temple of the Lord a hundred bulls, two
hundred rams, four hundred lambs, and twelve he-goats 8
for the sin of all Israel, to correspond to the number of the
twelve princes of the tribes of Israel; and the priests and 9
the Levites stood robed, by tribes, in charge of the service
of the Lord God of Israel in accordance with the book of
Moses, and the doorkeepers stood at each gate.

And the Israelites who had returned from exile held the 10
Passover on the fourteenth day of the first month, for the
priests and the Levites had been purified together, but all 11
the returned exiles had not been purified, for the Levites had
all been purified together, so they sacrificed the Passover for 12
all the returned exiles and their brothers the priests and
themselves. And the Israelites who had returned from exile, 13
all who had separated themselves from the accursed doings
of the heathen of the land and sought the Lord, ate it. And 14
they observed the festival of Unleavened Bread for seven
days, rejoicing before the Lord, because he had changed the 15
attitude of the king of Assyria toward them, so as to
strengthen their hands for the service of the Lord, the God
of Israel.

Afterward, in the reign of Artaxerxes, the king of Persia, [8
there came Ezra, the son of Seraiah, the son of Azariah, the
son of Hilkiah, the son of Shallum, the son of Zadok, the son 2
of Ahitub, the son of Amariah, the son of Uzzi, the son of
Bukki, the son of Abishua, the son of Phineas, the son of
Eleazar, the son of Aaron, the chief priest. This Ezra came 3
up from Babylon as a scribe, skilled in the law of Moses,
which was given by the God of Israel, and the king showed 4
him honor, for he found favor before him in all that he
asked. And there came with him to Jerusalem some of the 5
Israelites and the priests and Levites and holy singers and
doorkeepers and temple slaves, in the seventh year of the 6

7:8-8:6

reign of Artaxerxes, in the fifth month (that was the king's seventh year); for they left Babylon on the new moon of the first month, and they reached Jerusalem on the new moon of the fifth month, so prosperous a journey had the

7 Lord given them for his sake. For Ezra possessed great knowledge, so that he neglected nothing that was in the Law of the Lord or the commandments, but taught all Israel all the statutes and ordinances.

8 Now the written commission came from Artaxerxes, the king, to Ezra, the priest and reader of the Law of the Lord, and the following is a copy of it:

9 "King Artaxerxes sends greeting to Ezra, the priest and
10 reader of the Law of the Lord. As I have taken a friendly attitude, I have given orders that those of the Jewish nation who wish to do so, and of the priests and Levites and of the others in our realm shall, if they choose to, go to Jerusalem
11 with you. So let all who think of doing so, set out with you,
12 as I and the seven friends and councilors have decided, to look into matters in Judea and Jerusalem, in accordance
13 with what is in the Law of the Lord, and to carry to the Lord of Israel in Jerusalem the gifts that I and the friends have promised; and that all the gold and silver that can be found in the country of Babylonia for the Lord in Jerusalem,
14 with what has been given by the nation for the temple of their Lord at Jerusalem be collected, both gold and silver for bulls and rams and lambs and the things incident to them,
15 so as to offer offerings upon the altar of their Lord that is
16 in Jerusalem. And all that you with your brothers wish to do with gold and silver carry out, according to the will of
17 your God, and deliver the sacred dishes of the Lord that have been given you for the use of the temple of your God
18 that is in Jerusalem. And anything else that occurs to you as necessary for the temple of your God, you are to give

8:7-18

from the royal treasury; and I, Artaxerxes the king, have 19
commanded the treasurers of Syria and Phoenicia that
whatever Ezra, the priest and reader of the Law of the Most
High God, sends for, they shall take care to give him, up to 20
a hundred talents of silver, and likewise up to a hundred
measures (fifteen hundred bushels) of wheat and a hundred
measures (a thousand gallons) of wine and salt in abundance; and let everything prescribed in the Law of God be 21
scrupulously performed to the Most High God, so that
wrath may not come upon the realm of the king and his
sons. You are also instructed to lay no tribute or any other 22
tax upon any priests or Levites or sacred singers or porters
or temple slaves or persons employed in this temple, and
that no one has authority to lay any such tax upon them.
And you, Ezra, must appoint justices and judges to judge all 23
through Syria and Phoenicia all who know the Law of your
God; and those who do not know it you must teach. And 24
all who transgress the Law of your God and of the king will
be suitably punished, either with death, or by some other
punishment, a fine or imprisonment."

Blessed be the only Lord, who put this into the king's 25
heart, to glorify his house in Jerusalem, and gave me honor 26
in the sight of the king and his councilors and all his friends
and grandees. So I was encouraged by the help of the Lord, 27
my God, and I gathered men from Israel to go up with me.

These are the principal men, by their families and their 28
groups, who came up with me from Babylon, in the reign of
Artaxerxes the king: of the descendants of Phineas, Ger- 29
shom; of the descendants of Ithamar, Gamael; of the descendants of David, Hattush, the son of Shecaniah; of the 31
descendants of Parosh, Zechariah, and with him a hundred
and fifty men enrolled; of the descendants of Pahath-moab, 32
Eliohenai, the son of Zerahiah, and with him two hundred

8:19–32

men; of the descendants of Zattu, Shecaniah, the son of
Jahaziel, and with him three hundred men; of the descendants of Adin, Obed, the son of Jonathan, and with him
33 two hundred and fifty men; of the descendants of Elam,
Jeshaiah, the son of Gotholiah, and with him seventy men;
34 of the descendants of Shephatiah, Zeraiah, the son of
35 Michael, and with him seventy men; of the descendants
of Joab, Obadiah, the son of Jehiel, and with him two hun-
36 dred and twelve men; of the descendants of Bani, Shelo-
mith, the son of Josiphiah, and with him a hundred and
37 sixty men; of the descendants of Bebai, Zechariah, the son
38 of Bebai, and with him twenty-eight men; of the descendants
of Azgad, Johanan, the son of Hakkatan, and with him a
39 hundred and ten men; of the descendants of Adonikam,
those who came last, and these were their names: Eliphelet,
40 Jeuel, and Shemaiah, and with them seventy men; and of
the descendants of Bigvai, Uthai, the son of Istalcurus, and
with him seventy men.

41 So I assembled them at the river called Theras, and we
42 camped there for three days, and I observed them. And
when I found none of the descendants of the priests or of the
43 Levites there, I sent to Eleazar and Iduel and Maasmas
44 and Elnathan and Shemaiah and Jarib, Nathan, Elnathan,
Zechariah, and Meshullam, who were leaders and intelli-
45 gent men, and I told them to go to Iddo, who was in com-
46 mand at the place of the treasury, and ordered them to tell
Iddo and his kinsmen and the treasurers at that place to
47 send us men to serve as priests in the house of our Lord. And
by the mighty hand of our Lord they brought us competent
men of the descendants of Mahli, the son of Levi, the son
of Israel, Sherebiah and his sons and his kinsmen, eighteen
48 in all; and Hashabiah and with him Jeshaiah, his brother,
of the descendants of Hananiah, and his sons, making

twenty men; and of the temple slaves, whom David and the 49
princes had given to work for the Levites, two hundred and
twenty temple slaves; their names were all listed.

Then I proclaimed a fast there for the young men before 50
our Lord, to seek from him a safe journey for us and our
children and our cattle that were with us. For I was 51
ashamed to ask the king for foot soldiers and cavalry and an
escort to make us safe from those who opposed us; for we had 52
told the king,

"The power of our Lord will be with those who seek him,
and will give them every support."

And we prayed to our Lord again about these things, and 53
we found him merciful. Then I set apart twelve men of the 54
chiefs of the priests, Sherebiah and Hashabiah, and ten of
their kinsmen with them, and I weighed out to them the 55
silver and the gold and the sacred dishes, of the house of our
Lord, which the king himself and his councilors and the
grandees of all Israel had given. And I weighed and turned 56
over to them six hundred and fifty talents of silver, and silver
dishes to the value of a hundred talents, and a hundred
talents of gold, and twenty gold bowls, and twelve bronze 57
dishes of fine bronze that glittered like gold. And I said to 58
them,

"You are holy to the Lord and the dishes are holy, and
the silver and gold are a gift to the Lord, the Lord of our
forefathers. Be watchful and guard them until you deliver 59
them to the chiefs of the priests and the Levites and to the
heads of the families of Israel in Jerusalem, in the chambers
of the house of our Lord."

And the priests and the Levites took the silver and the 60
gold and the dishes which had been in Jerusalem, and
carried them into the temple of the Lord.

And we set out from the river Theras on the twelfth day 61

of the first month, and entered Jerusalem, because the mighty hand of our Lord was upon us, and he saved us from

62 every enemy on the way, and we reached Jerusalem. And when our third day there came, the silver and gold were weighed and turned over in the house of our Lord to Mere-

63 moth, the son of Uriah, the priest, who had with him Eleazar, the son of Phineas, and they had with them Joza-bad, the son of Jeshua, and Moeth, the son of Binnui, the

64 Levites; it was all counted and weighed, and the total

65 weight of it was immediately recorded. And those who had come back from captivity offered as sacrifices to the Lord, the God of Israel, twelve bulls for all Israel, ninety-six

66 rams, seventy-two lambs, twelve he-goats for a thank-

67 offering—all as a sacrifice to the Lord. And they delivered the king's orders to the royal treasurers and to the governors of Coelesyria and Phoenicia, and they showed honor to the people and the temple of the Lord.

68 When this was accomplished, the principal men came to me and said,

69 "The people of Israel and the leaders and the priests and the Levites have not separated from the alien heathen of the land and the impurities of them, the Canaanites and Hittites and Perizzites and Jebusites and Moabites and Egyptians

70 and Idumaeans, for they and their sons have married their daughters, and the holy race has been mixed with the alien heathen of the land, and from the beginning of this matter, the princes and nobles have shared in this iniquity."

71 As soon as I heard this, I tore open my clothes and my sacred mantle, and pulled out some of my hair and beard,

72 and sat down gloomy and grieved. And all who were moved at the word of the Lord of Israel gathered about me, as I grieved over this iniquity, and I sat grief-stricken until the

73 evening sacrifice. Then I got up from my fast with my

clothes and my sacred mantle torn, and I knelt down and
stretched out my hands to the Lord, and said,   74

"Lord, I am ashamed, I am abashed before you. For   75
from the times of our forefathers, our sins have risen higher
than our heads, and our mistakes have mounted up to
heaven, and we have been involved in grievous sin, even to   76
this day. And because of our sins and those of our fore-   77
fathers, we have been delivered with our brothers and our
kings and our priests to the kings of the earth, to be slain and
taken captive and plundered, in shame, unto this day. And   78
yet how great has been your mercy to us, Lord, that a
root and a name should be left to us in the place of
your sanctuary, and that a light has been disclosed to us in   79
the house of our Lord, and that food is given us in the time
of our bondage. Even in our bondage we have not been for-   80
saken by our Lord, but he has brought us into favor with
the kings of Persia, so that they have given us food and   81
glorified the temple of our Lord, and raised Zion up from its
desolation, to give us a stronghold in Judea and Jerusalem.
And now, Lord, what can we say, when we have these   82
things? For we have disobeyed your commands, which you
gave through your servants the prophets, when you said,
'The land which you enter to possess is a land that has been   83
polluted with the pollution of the aliens of the land, and they
have filled it with their impurity. So now you must not   84
marry your daughters to their sons, and you must not take
their daughters for your sons; and you must not seek ever   85
to have peace with them, so that you may grow strong and
eat the good things of the land, and bequeath it to your
descendants forever.' And all that has happened to us has   86
happened because of our wicked deeds and our great sins.
For you, Lord, have lightened our sins, and have given us   87
such a root as this, but we have turned back again, to trans-

8:74-87

gress your law, to mingle with the impurity of the heathen
88 of the land. Are you not angry enough with us to destroy
89 us, until there is left no root or stock or name of ours? Lord
90 of Israel, you are true; for we are left, a root, today. Now
here we are before you, in all our iniquity, for in view of it
we cannot any longer stand before you."

91   Now while Ezra was praying and making his confession,
lying on the ground before the temple weeping, there
gathered about him an immense throng from Jerusalem,
men, women, and children, for there was great lamentation
92 among the multitude. And Shecaniah, the son of Jehiel, one
of the Israelites, called out and said to Ezra,

"We have sinned against the Lord, and have married
foreign women from the heathen of the land, yet there is
93 still hope for Israel. Let us make oath to the Lord about
this, that we will expel all our wives who are of foreign
94 origin, with their children, as you and all who obey the Law
95 of the Lord decide. Get up and take action, for it is your
business, and we will support you in taking vigorous action."

96   Then Ezra got up, and made the chiefs of the priests and
Levites of all Israel swear to do this, and they swore to it.

9]   Then Ezra got up from the court of the temple, and went to
 2 the priestly chamber of Jehohanan, the son of Eliashib, and
spent the night, and he would not eat bread or drink water,
 3 but mourned over the great iniquity of the multitude. And
a proclamation was made all over Judea and Jerusalem to
all who had returned from the captivity that they should
 4 gather in Jerusalem; and if anyone failed to meet there
within two or three days in accordance with the decision of
the ruling elders, his cattle should be confiscated, and he
should be excluded from the multitude of those who had
returned from exile.

 5   And the men of the tribe of Judah and Benjamin gathered

in three days at Jerusalem (it was the ninth month, on the
twentieth day of the month), and all the multitude sat in 6
the square before the temple, trembling because of the
winter weather. And Ezra got up and said to them,   7

"You have broken the Law, and have married foreign
women, to increase Israel's sins. Now make your confession 8
and give glory to the Lord God of our forefathers, and do 9
his will, and separate from the heathen of the land and
from the foreign women."

Then all the multitude shouted and said in a loud voice, 10
"We will do as you say. But the crowd is great and it is 11
wintertime, and we are not able to stand out-of-doors, and
cannot do so, and this is not a thing we can do in a day or
two, for we have sinned too much in this matter. So let the 12
princes of the people remain, and let all those in our settle-
ments that have foreign wives come at the times appointed,
with the elders and judges of each place, until we free our- 13
selves from the Lord's wrath over this matter."

Jonathan, the son of Asahel, and Jahzeiah, the son of 14
Tikvah, undertook the matter on these terms, and Meshullam and Levi and Shabbethai sat with them as judges. And 15
the returned exiles acted in accordance with all this.

And Ezra the priest picked out for himself the leading men 16
of their families, all of them by name, and on the new moon
of the tenth month they held a sitting to inquire into the
matter. And the case of the men who had foreign wives was 17
brought to an end by the new moon of the first month.

And among the priests the ones who presented themselves 18
who were found to have foreign wives were: of the de- 19
scendants of Jeshua, the son of Jozadak, and his brothers:
Maaseiah and Eleazar and Jarib and Jodan; they pledged 20
themselves to cast off their wives, and gave rams in atonement for their mistake. And of the descendants of Immer: 21

Hanani and Zebadiah and Maaseiah and Shemaiah and
22 Jehiel and Azariah. And of the descendants of Pashur·
Elioenai, Maaseiah, Ishmael, and Nathanael, Gedaliah.
and Elasah.
23 And of the Levites: Jozabad and Shimei and Kelaiah,
24 who was Kelita, and Pethahiah and Judah and Jonah. And
25 of the sacred singers: Eliashib and Zaccur. Of the porters·
Shallum and Telem.
26 Of Israel: of the descendants of Parosh, Ramiah,
Izziah, Malchijah, Mijamin, and Eleazar, and Asibias, and
27 Benaiah; of the descendants of Elam, Mattaniah and Zecha-
28 riah, Jehiel and Abdi, and Jeremoth and Elijah. And of
the descendants of Zattu, Elioenai, Eliashib, Othoniah,
29 Jeremoth, and Zabad and Zerdaiah. And of the descendants of Bebai, Jehohanan and Hananiah and Zabbai
30 and Emathis; and of the descendants of Bani: Meshullam,
31 Malluch, Adaiah, Jashub, and Sheal and Jeremoth. And of
the descendants of Addi: Naathus and Moossias, Laccunus
and Naidus, and Bescaspasmys and Sesthel, and Balnuus
32 and Manasseas. And of the descendants of Annan: Elionas
and Asaias and Melchias and Sabbaias and Simon Chosa-
33 maeus. And of the descendants of Hashum: Mattenai and
Mattattah and Zabad and Eliphelet and Manasseh and
34 Shimei. And of the descendants of Bani: Jeremai, Maadai,
Amram, Joel, Mamdai and Bedeiah and Vaniah, Cara-
basion and Eliashib and Machnadebai, Eliasis, Binnui,
Elialis, Shimei, Shelemiah, Nethaniah. And of the descendants of Ezora: Shashai, Azarel, Azael, Shemaiah,
35 Amariah, Joseph. And of the descendants of Nebo: Mat-
36 tithiah, Zabad, Iddo, Joel, Benaiah. These had all married
foreign women, and they cast them off with their children.
37 So the priests and the Levites and the men of Israel settled
in Jerusalem and in the country. On the new moon of the

9:22-37

seventh month, when the Israelites were in their communities, the whole multitude gathered under a common impulse 38 in the square before the east gate of the temple and told 39 Ezra, the high priest and reader, to bring the Law of Moses, which had been given him by the Lord, the God of Israel. And Ezra, the high priest, brought the Law for all the multi- 40 tude, men and women, and all the priests to hear, on the new moon of the seventh month. And he read aloud in the 41 square before the gate of the temple from morning till noon, in the presence of both men and women, and the whole multitude gave attention to the Law. And Ezra, the 42 priest and reader of the Law, stood in the wooden pulpit which had been prepared, and beside him stood Matti- 43 thiah, Shema, Anaiah, Azariah, Uriah, Hezekiah, and Baalsamus, at his right, and at his left, Pedaiah, Mishael, 44 Malchijah, Lothasubus, Nabariah, and Zechariah. Then 45 Ezra took up the book of the Law before the multitude, for he was seated in a conspicuous place before them all, and 46 when he opened the Law, they all stood up. And Ezra blessed the Lord, the Most High God, the God of Hosts, the Almighty, and all the multitude shouted "Amen." 47 And they lifted up their hands and fell on the ground, and worshipped the Lord. Jeshua and Anniuth and Sherebiah, 48 Jamin, Akkub, Shabbethai, Hodiah, Masseiah and Kelita, Azariah and Jozabad, Hanan, Pelaiah, the Levites, taught the Law of the Lord, and read the Law of the Lord to the multitude, putting life into the reading.

Then the governor said to Ezra, the high priest and 49 reader, and to the Levites who were teaching the multitude, to all,

"This day is sacred to the Lord" (and they were all 50 weeping as they heard the Law) "so go and eat the fat and 51 drink the sweet, and send portions to those who have none,

9:38–51

52 for the day is sacred to the Lord. Do not mourn, for the Lord will honor you."

53   And the Levites commanded all the people, saying, "This day is sacred; do not mourn."

54   And they all went off to eat and drink and enjoy themselves, and to give portions to those who had none, and to

55 hold a great celebration, for they had been inspired by the words which they had been taught, and for which they had come together.

THE SECOND BOOK OF ESDRAS

*Where the book preceding is called III Esdras this book is
numbered IV Esdras; frequently it is given the more descriptive
title of The Ezra Apocalypse. Like Revelation, it is rather a
series of apocalypses. After the two initial chapters which (like
the two concluding chapters) are Christian additions, the scene
is set in Babylon in the year 556 B.C. "I Salathiel who am
Ezra" suggests that the prophecy of the unknown Salathiel
was attributed to Ezra to enhance its credit and to unite it with
the Ezra apocalypse which begins at chapter 14. The problem
for which the seer who speaks seeks an answer is the enigma of
God's dealings with the children of Abraham. Why are they enslaved while the heathen prosper? The reply, delivered by an
angel and in a series of dream visions, is a lofty justification
of the ways of God to man. In chapters 7 through 9 the seer
receives answers to his questions on the resurrection of the dead,
the last judgment, the messianic age, and why so few are to be
saved. A mourning woman who disappears and gives place to a
magnificent city symbolizes the past and future of Jerusalem.
The vision of the eagle in chapters 11 and 12 prophesies the destruction of Rome, which was expected (as in Revelations) with
the death of Nero; the confusion in the picture is due to altera-
tions which became necessary to account for the imperial suc-
cession after Nero. The final chapter of the original tells how
Ezra, after drinking from a cup divinely provided, was enabled
to recall and dictate to amanuenses not only the Law and the
Prophets and the Writings but also seventy "outside books."
Even the portions of II Esdras that were not obviously Chris-*

tian may well have been affected by Christian doctrine; suspicion must attach to passages like that at 3.21 f. which envisages the doctrine of original sin. In any case, II Esdras is not only a mature and devout attempt to deal with a central problem which is a continual stumbling block to men who grope after religion, but a valuable index to the climate and quality of religious thought in the first century.

THE SECOND BOOK OF ESDRAS

1] **T**HE SECOND BOOK OF EZRA THE PROPHET, the son of Seraiah, the son of Azariah, the son of Hilkiah, the son of Shallum, the son of Zadok, the son of

2 Ahitub, the son of Achiah, the son of Phineas, the son of Heli, the son of Amariah, the son of Azariah, the son of Meraioth, the son of Arna, the son of Uzzi, the son of Borith, the son of Abishua, the son of Phineas, the son

3 of Eleazar, the son of Aaron, of the tribe of Levi, who was a captive in the country of the Medes in the reign of Artaxerxes, king of Persia.

4 And the word of the Lord came to me, saying,

5 "Go and declare to my people their crimes and to their sons their iniquities which they have committed against me,

6 so that they may tell them to their children's children. For the sins of their parents have increased in them, for they have forgotten me and have offered sacrifice to strange gods.

7 Was it not I who brought them out of the land of Egypt, out of the house of bondage? But they have angered me,

8 and scorned my counsels. Shake out the hair of your head and hurl all evils upon them, because they have not obeyed

9 my law, but they are a rebellious people. How long shall I bear with them, when I have conferred such benefits upon

10 them? I have overthrown many kings for them; I struck

11 down Pharaoh with his servants, and all his army. I destroyed all nations before them, and I scattered the people of two provinces in the east, Tyre and Sidon, and I slew all

12 their enemies. But you must speak to them and say,

13 " 'Thus says the Lord: Surely it was I who brought you across the sea and produced broad highways for you where there was no road; I gave you Moses for a leader and

14 Aaron for a priest; I gave you light from a pillar of fire, and

did great wonders among you; but you forgot me, says the
Lord.

" 'Thus says the Lord Almighty: The quail were a sign 15
to you; I gave you camps to protect you, yet you grumbled
in them; and you have not triumphed for my sake over the 16
destruction of your enemies, but even now you still grumble. Where are the kindnesses I have shown you? When 17
you were hungry and thirsty in the desert did you not cry
out to me, saying, "Why have you brought us into this 18
wilderness to kill us? It would have been better for us to
serve the Egyptians than to die in this desert." I pitied your 19
groaning and gave you manna for food; you ate the bread of
angels. When you were thirsty, did I not split open the 20
rock, and waters flowed out in abundance? On account of
the heat I covered you with the leaves of trees. I divided 21
fertile lands among you; the Canaanites, the Perizzites,
and the Philistines I drove out before you. What more can
I do for you? says the Lord. Thus says the Lord Almighty: 22
When you were in the desert, at the bitter river, thirsty and
blaspheming my name, I did not give you fire for your 23
blasphemy, but I put wood into the water and made the
river sweet.

" 'What shall I do to you, Jacob? You would not obey 24
me, Judah. I will turn to other nations, and give them my
name, so that they may observe my precepts. Since you 25
have forsaken me, I will forsake you. When you seek mercy
from me, I will not have pity on you. When you call upon 26
me, I will not hear you; for you have stained your hands
with blood, and your feet are quick to commit murder. It 27
is not as though you had forsaken me, but yourselves, says
the Lord. Thus says the Lord Almighty: Have I not 28
begged you as a father begs his sons, or a mother her
daughters, or a nurse her little ones, to be my people, and 29

1: 15–29

that I should be your God, and you should be my sons and
30 I should be your father? I gathered you as a hen gathers
her brood under her wings. But now what shall I do to you?
31 I will cast you out from before my face. When you make
offerings to me, I will turn my face away from you, for I
have repudiated your feast days, and new moons, and cir-
32 cumcisions of the flesh. I sent my servants the prophets to
you, and you took them and killed them, and tore their
bodies in pieces; and their blood I will require of you, says
the Lord.

33   " 'Thus says the Lord Almighty: Your house is desolate;
34 I will drive you forth as the wind drives stubble; and your
children shall have no children, because they with you have
neglected my command, and have done what is evil in my
35 sight. I will give your houses to a people that is to come,
who without having heard me believe. Those to whom I
have showed no signs will do what I have commanded.
36 They have not seen the prophets, yet they will call to mind
37 their uprightness. I call to witness the gratitude of the
people that is to come, whose little ones rejoice with gladness, though they do not see me with physical eyes, but in
spirit they will believe the things I have said.' "

38   And now, Father, look upon me with glory, and see the
39 people coming from the east, to whom I will give to lead
them Abraham and Isaac and Jacob, and Hosea and Amos
40 and Micah, and Joel and Obadiah and Jonah, and Nahum
and Habakkuk, Zephaniah, Haggai, Zechariah, and Mal-
achi, who is also called the Messenger of the Lord.

2}   " 'Thus says the Lord: I brought that people out of
bondage, and gave them commandments through my
servants the prophets; but they would not listen to them, but
2 made my counsels void. The mother that bore them said to
them, "Go, my children, for I am a widow and deserted;

I brought you up in gladness, but in grief and sorrow I have 3
lost you, for you have sinned before the Lord God and done
what is evil in my sight. But now what can I do for you? 4
For I am a widow and deserted. Go, my children, and ask
for mercy from the Lord." I call you, father, as a witness, 5
in addition to the mother of the children, because they
would not keep my agreement, to bring confusion upon 6
them, and to give their mother up to pillage, so that they
may have no descendants. Let them be scattered among 7
the heathen, let their names be blotted out from the earth,
because they have scorned my agreement.

" 'Alas for you, Assyria, who conceal the unrighteous with 8
you. O wicked nation, remember what I did to Sodom and
Gomorrah, whose land lies in lumps of pitch and heaps of 9
ashes. So I will make those who would not listen to me,
says the Lord Almighty.'

"Thus speaks the Lord to Ezra: Tell my people that I 10
will give them the kingdom of Jerusalem, which I was going
to give to Israel. And I will take back to myself their glory, 11
and I will give to these the everlasting dwellings which I
had prepared for those others. The tree of life will give them 12
fragrant perfume, and they will not toil or be weary. Ask, 13
and you will receive; pray for few days for yourselves, that
they may be shortened; the kingdom is already prepared
for you; be on the watch. Call heaven and earth to witness; 14
call them to witness, for I have left out evil and created good,
because I live, says the Lord.

"Mother, embrace your sons, bring them up in gladness 15
like a dove, strengthen their feet, for I have chosen you, says
the Lord. And I will raise up the dead from their places, 16
and bring them out of their tombs, because I recognize my
name in them. Do not fear, mother of sons, for I have 17
chosen you, says the Lord. I will send to help you my 18

2:3–18

servants Isaiah and Jeremiah, for whose counsel I have consecrated and prepared for you twelve trees loaded with dif-
19 ferent fruits, and an equal number of springs flowing with
milk and honey, and seven huge mountains on which roses
20 and lilies grow, with which I will fill your sons with joy. Do
justice to the widow, judge the fatherless, give to the needy,
21 protect the orphan, clothe the naked, cure the injured and
the weak, do not laugh at a lame man, defend the maimed,
22 and let the blind man behold my glory. Preserve the old
23 man and the youth within your walls. When you find any
who are dead, give them burial and mark the place, and I
24 will give you the first place in my resurrection. Pause and
25 be quiet, my people, for your rest will come. Good nurse,
26 nourish your sons, for you must strengthen their feet. As
for the slaves whom I have given you, not one of them shall
27 perish, for I will require them from your number. Do not
worry, for when the day of affliction and anguish comes,
others will lament and be sad, but you will be joyful and
28 rich. The heathen will be jealous, but they will be not able
29 to do anything against you, says the Lord. My hands will
30 cover you, so that your sons will not see the Pit. Be joyful,
mother, with your sons, for I will rescue you, says the Lord.
31 Remember your sons who are asleep, for I will bring them
forth from the hiding-places of the earth and show mercy to
32 them, for I am merciful, says the Lord Almighty. Embrace
your children until I come, and proclaim mercy to them,
for my springs run over, and my favor will not fail."

33   I, Ezra, received a command from the Lord on Mount
Horeb, to go to Israel; but when I went to them, they re-
34 fused me and rejected the Lord's command. Therefore I
say to you, heathen, who hear and understand, expect your
shepherd; he will give you everlasting rest, for he is close at
35 hand, who will come at the end of the world. Be ready for

the rewards of the kingdom, for everlasting light will shine upon you forever. Flee from the shadow of this world, receive the enjoyment of your glory. I call my Savior to witness publicly. Receive the approval of the Lord, and rejoice, with thanksgiving to him who has called you to heavenly realms. Get up and stand and see the number of those who are marked with his seal at the feast of the Lord. Those who have removed from the shadow of the world have received splendid garments from the Lord. Receive your number, Zion, and close the list of your people who are clothed in white, who have fulfilled the Law of the Lord. The number of your sons whom you desired is full; intreat the Lord's power that your people which was called from the beginning may be made holy.

I, Ezra, saw on Mount Zion a great throng which I could not count, and they all praised the Lord with songs. And in the midst of them was a youth of lofty stature, taller than all the rest, and he put crowns upon the heads of each of them, and he was still more exalted. But I was possessed with wonder. Then I asked the angel, and said,

"Who are these, sir?"

And he answered and said to me,

"These are those who have laid aside their mortal clothing, and have put on immortal, and have confessed the name of God; now they are crowned and receive palms."

And I said to the angel,

"Who is that young man, who puts the crowns on them and the palms in their hands?"

He answered and said to me,

"He is the Son of God, whom they confessed in the world."

Then I began to glorify those who had stood firmly for the name of the Lord. Then the angel said to me,

2:36–48

"Go, tell my people what kind of wonders of the Lord you have seen, and how great they are."

3] In the thirtieth year after the destruction of the city, I, Salathiel, who am Ezra, was in Babylon, and I was troubled
2 as I lay on my bed, and my thoughts filled my mind, because I saw the desolation of Zion, and the wealth of those who
3 lived in Babylon. And my spirit was agitated, and I began to utter devout words to the Most High, and I said,

4 "O Sovereign Lord, was it not you who in the beginning when you formed the earth, and all alone too, spoke and
5 commanded the dust, and it gave you Adam, a dead body? But he was both himself a formation of your hands, and you breathed into him the breath of life, and he was made alive
6 before you. And you led him into Paradise which your right
7 hand planted before the earth appeared; and you enjoined upon him your one concern, and he transgressed it, and you immediately ordained death for him and his peoples; and there sprang from him nations and tribes, peoples and clans
8 without number. And every nation followed its own will and behaved wickedly in your sight, and you did not hinder
9 them. But again, in time, you brought the flood upon the
10 inhabitants of the world, and destroyed them. And the same fate befell them; as Adam experienced death, they ex-
11 perienced the flood. But you left one of them, Noah, with his household, all the upright people that were descended from him.

12 "And it came to pass that when the inhabitants of the earth began to multiply, and sons and peoples and nations grew very numerous, that they began again to be more un-
13 godly than their predecessors. And it came to pass that when they did what was wrong in your sight, you chose for
14 yourself one of them, whose name was Abraham, and you loved him, and to him alone you revealed the end of the

3:1–14

times, secretly at night. And you made an everlasting 15
agreement with him, and told him that you would never
forsake his descendants; and you gave him Isaac, and to 16
Isaac you gave Jacob and Esau. And you set Jacob
apart for yourself, but you cut off Esau, and Jacob became
a great multitude. And it came to pass, when you led his 17
descendants out of Egypt, that you brought them to Mount
Sinai. And you bent the heavens, and shook the earth, and 18
moved the universe, and made the deeps tremble, and disturbed the world. And your glory passed through the four 19
gates of fire and earthquake and wind and cold, so that you
might give the Law to Jacob's descendants, and your command to the posterity of Israel.

"Yet you did not take from them their wicked heart, so 20
that your Law might bear fruit among them. For the first 21
Adam, burdened with a wicked heart, transgressed and was
overcome, as were also all who were descended from him.
So weakness became permanent, and the Law was in the 22
heart of the people with the evil root; and what was good
departed, and what was evil remained. So the times passed 23
and the years came to an end, and you raised up for yourself a slave named David. And you told him to build a city 24
to bear your name, and to offer to you offerings of your own
in it. This was done for many years; then those who lived 25
in the city sinned, acting in all respects just as Adam and 26
his posterity had done, for they too had the wicked heart.
And you delivered your city into the hands of your enemies. 27
Then I said to myself, 'Do those who live in Babylon do any 28
better? and is it on this account that she has conquered
Zion?'

"For it came to pass, when I had come here, that I saw 29
acts of ungodliness without number, and in this thirtieth
year my soul saw many sinning, and my heart sank, for I 30

3:15–30

have seen how you bear with them when they sin, and have spared those who act wickedly, and have destroyed your

31 people, and preserved your enemies, and you have not shown anyone at all how this way should be given up.

32 Does Babylon do better deeds than Zion? Or has any other nation known you except Israel? Or what tribes have be-

33 lieved your agreements like that of Jacob? Yet their reward has not appeared, and their labor has not borne fruit. For I have gone all about the nations, and I have seen them abounding in wealth, yet unmindful of your command-

34 ments. Now therefore weigh our iniquities and those of the inhabitants of the world on the scales; and which way the

35 movement of the pointer turns will be found out. Or when did the inhabitants of the earth not sin in your sight? Or

36 what nation has kept your commandments so well? You will find names of men who have kept your command-ments, but you will not find nations."

4] And the angel who had been sent to me, whose name was

2 Uriel, answered and said to me,

"Your mind has utterly failed in this world and do you expect to understand the way of the Most High?"

3 And I said,

"Yes, my lord."

And he answered me and said,

"I was sent to show you three ways, and to set three

4 figures before you. If you can solve one of these for me, I will show you the way you want to see and teach you why the heart is wicked."

5 And I said,

"Go on, my lord."

And he said to me,

"Come, weigh me the weight of fire, or measure me a measure of wind, or call back for me the day that is past."

And I answered and said,   6
"Who that is born can do that, that you should ask such
things of me?"
And he said to me,   7
"If I had asked you, 'How many dwellings are there in
the heart of the sea, or how many streams at the source of
the deep, or how many ways above the firmament, or what
are the ways of leaving Paradise?' perhaps you would have 8
said to me, 'I have never gone down into the deep, nor into
Hades, nor have I ever climbed up into the heavens.' But 9
now I have only asked you about fire and wind and the day,
through all of which you have passed, and without which
you cannot live, and you have given me no answer about
them!" And he said to me, "Your own things that grow 10
up with you, you cannot understand; and how can your 11
frame grasp the way of the Most High, or one already worn
out by the corrupt world understand incorruption?"
And when I heard this, I fell on my face and said to him, 12
"It would have been better that we should not be here
than to come here and live in ungodliness, and suffer, without understanding why."
And he answered me and said,   13
"I went to a forest of trees of the field, and they took
counsel and said, 'Come, let us go and make war on the sea, 14
so that it may retire before us, and we may make more forests for us.' In like manner the waves of the sea themselves 15
also took counsel and said, 'Come, let us go up and conquer
the forest of the field, so that there also we may win ourselves more territory.' And the thought of the forest was in 16
vain, for the fire came and consumed it; so was the thought 17
of the sea waves, for the sand stood firm and stopped them.
Now if you were their judge, which of them would you have 18
undertaken to justify, and which to condemn?"

4:6-18

19 And I answered and said,

"It was a foolish plan that both formed, for the land is given to the forest, and the place of the sea is given it to bear its waves."

20 And he answered me and said,

"You have judged rightly; and why have you not judged
21 so in your own case? For just as the land is given to the forest, and the sea to its waves, so those who live on the earth can understand only the things that are on the earth, and those who are above the heavens, the things that are above the height of the heavens."

22 Then I answered and said,

"I beseech you, sir, to what end has the capacity for
23 understanding been given me? For I did not mean to ask about ways above, but about those things which pass by us every day: why Israel is given up to the heathen in disgrace; the people whom you loved are given up to godless tribes; and the law of our forefathers is made of no effect,
24 and the written agreements are no more. And we pass from the world like locusts, and do not deserve to obtain mercy.
25 But what will he do for his name, by which we are called? It is about these things that I have asked."

26 And he answered me and said,

"If you live, you will see, and if you survive, you will
27 often marvel; for the age is hurrying fast to its end; for it will not be able to bear the things that are promised to the upright in the appointed times; for this age is full of sorrow and
28 weakness. For the evil about which you ask me is sown, but
29 the harvest of it has not yet come. So unless what has been sown is reaped, and unless the place where the evil was sown passes away, the field where the good is sown cannot come.
30 For a grain of evil seed was sown from the beginning in the heart of Adam, and how much ungodliness it has produced

4:19–30

up to this time and will produce before the judgment comes. Estimate for yourself how great a crop of ungodliness a grain 31 of evil seed has produced. And when ears without number 32 are sown, how great a threshing-floor they will inevitably fill!"

And I answered and said,   33

"How long and when shall this be? Why are our years few and evil?"

And he answered me and said,   34

"You cannot hurry faster than the Most High, for you hurry for your own self, but he who is above hurries for many. Did not the souls of the upright ask about these 35 things in their rooms, saying, 'How long must I hope thus? And when will the harvest of our reward come?' And 36 Jeremiel, the archangel, answered them and said, 'When the number of those who are like you is complete, for he has weighed the world in the balance, and has measured the 37 times with a measure, and carefully counted the hours, and he will not move or disturb them, until the prescribed measure is reached.' "

And I answered and said,   38

"O Sovereign Lord, but all even of us are full of ungodliness. And let not the harvest of the upright be perchance 39 kept back, on account of the sins of those who live on the earth."

And he answered me and said,   40

"Go and ask a woman who is with child if when she has completed her nine months her womb can keep the child within her any longer."

And I said,   41

"No, sir, it cannot "

And he said to me,

"In Hades the storehouses of souls are like the womb, for 42 just as a woman who is bearing a child makes haste to escape the inevitable birth, so these places also make haste

43 to give up those things that were intrusted to them from the beginning. Then those things which you desire to see will be disclosed to you."

44 And I answered and said,

"If I have found favor in your sight, and if it is possible,

45 and if I am fit for it, show me this also, whether there is more to come than is past, or the greater part has gone by us.

46 For what is past I know, but I do not know what is to come."

47 And he said to me,

"Stand at my right and I will show you the meaning of a figure."

48 And I stood there and looked, and behold, a burning furnace passed before me, and it came to pass, when the flame had gone by, that I looked and, behold, the smoke re-

49 mained. After that, a cloud full of water passed before me, and stormily sent down a heavy rain, and when the rain-

50 storm had passed, the drops remained in it. And he said to me,

"Consider for yourself; for as the rain is more than the drops, and the fire is more than the smoke, so the quantity that has past has far exceeded, but the drops and the smoke remained."

51 Then I prayed and said,

"Do you think I shall live until that time?"

52 He answered me and said,

"About the signs of which you ask me, I can tell you of them in part, but as to your life I was not sent to tell you, but I do not know.

5] "But about the signs: Behold, the days will come, when when those who live on the earth will be seized with great dismay, and the way of truth will be hidden, and the land will be barren of faith. And iniquity will be increased be- 2 yond what you yourself see, and beyond what you ever heard of. And the country which you now see ruling will 3 be waste and untrodden, and men shall see it deserted. But 4 if the Most High grants you life, you will see it after the third day thrown into confusion, and the sun will shine suddenly in the night and the moon in the daytime. Blood shall 5 trickle out of wood, and a stone will utter its voice, and peoples will be troubled, and the courses will be changed. And 6 one will reign for whom those who live on the earth do not hope, and the birds will fly away together, and the Sea of 7 Sodom will cast forth fish, and one whom the many do not know will utter his voice in the night, but all will hear his voice. And there will be darkness in many places, and fire 8 will often break out, and wild animals will go outside their haunts, and women in their uncleanness will bear monsters. And salt waters will be found in sweet, and all friends will 9 conquer one another, and intelligence will hide itself, and understanding retire to its room; and it will be sought by 10 many and will not be found, and unrighteousness and lack of self-control will increase on the earth. And one country 11 will ask its neighbor, and say, 'Has uprightness, or a man who does right, passed through you?' and it will answer, 'No.' At that time, it will happen that men will hope and 12 not obtain; they will work, but their ways will not prosper. These signs I am permitted to tell you, but if you pray 13 again and weep as you do now, and fast seven days, you will again hear greater things than these."

Then I awoke, and my body shuddered violently, and my 14 soul was troubled, so that it fainted. But the angel who 15 came and talked with me held me fast, and strengthened me and set me on my feet. And on the second night it came to 16

5:2–16

pass that Phaltiel, the captain of the people, came to me and said to me.

17 "Where have you been and why is your face so sad? Or do you not know that Israel has been intrusted to you in the
18 land of their exile? Get up therefore and eat some bread, so that you may not forsake us, as a shepherd leaves his flock in the power of wicked wolves."

19 Then I said to him,

"Go away from me, and do not come near me for seven days, and then you can come to me."

And he listened to what I said, and went away from me.
20 So I fasted for seven days, wailing and lamenting, just
21 as the angel Uriel commanded me. And it came to pass after seven days that the thoughts of my mind were very painful to me again. And my soul received the spirit of
22 understanding again, and I began again to utter words be-
23 fore the Most High, and said,

"Sovereign Lord, from all the forests on the earth and
24 from all its trees you chose one vine, and from all the lands in the world you chose for yourself one garden, and from all
25 the flowers in the world you chose for yourself one lily, and from all the depths of the sea you filled yourself one river, and of all the cities that have been built you consecrated
26 Zion to yourself, and of all the birds that have been created you named for yourself one dove, and of all the cattle that
27 have been formed you provided for yourself one sheep, and of all the peoples that have multiplied you got yourself one people, and you gave to this people that you desired a law
28 that was approved by all. And now, Lord, why have you given this one up to the many, and after preparing one root above the others have you scattered your only one among
29 the many? And those who opposed your promises have
30 trampled on those who believed your agreements. For if

you really hate your people it ought to be punished with your own hands."

And it came to pass when I had uttered these words that 31 the angel who had come to me on a previous night was sent to me. And he said to me, 32

"Listen to me, and I will instruct you; attend to me, and I will tell you more."

And I said, 33

"Speak, my lord."

And he said to me,

"Are you so very much distracted over Israel, or do you love him more than his Maker does?"

And I said, 34

"No, sir, but I spoke from grief, for my heart pains me every hour, while I strive to understand the way of the Most High, and to inquire into what his decree apportions."

And he said to me, 35

"You cannot."

And I said,

"Why, sir, then why was I born? And why did not my mother's womb become my grave, so that I might not see the trouble of Jacob, and the exhaustion of the posterity of Israel?"

And he said to me, 36

"Count up for me those that have not yet come, and gather the scattered raindrops for me, and make the withered flowers green again for me, and open the closed 37 chambers for me, and bring out for me the winds shut up in them, or show me the picture of a voice, and then I will show you the mark you ask to see."

And I said, 38

"Sovereign Lord, who is there who can know these things

39 except he whose dwelling is not with men? But I am foolish, and how can I speak of these things about which you have asked me?"

40 And he said to me,

"Just as you cannot do one of these things that were mentioned, so you cannot find out my judgment, or the end of the love that I have promised my people."

41 And I said,

"But behold, sir, you protect those who are alive at the end, but what will those who were before us do, or we, or those who come after us?"

42 And he said to me,

"I will compare my judgment to a crown; just as there is no slowness on the part of those who are last, there is no swiftness on the part of those who are first."

43 And I answered and said,

"Could you not have created at one time those who have been created, and those who are now, and those who are to be, so that you might show your judgment sooner?"

44 And he answered me and said,

"The creation cannot make more haste than the Creator, and the world cannot at one time hold all who have been created in it."

45 Then I said,

"How could you say to your slave that you would surely make the creation created by you alive all together? If therefore they are all to live at once, it can support them all at once now."

46 And he said to me,

"Ask a woman's womb and say to it, 'If you bring forth ten children, why do so at intervals?' Ask it therefore to produce ten at once."

47 And I said,

"Of course it cannot, but can do it only in time."

And he said to me, 48

"And I have made the earth the womb for those who are at intervals engendered in it. For just as an infant cannot 49 bear, or as one who is old cannot do it any more, so I have organized the world that I created."

And I asked him and said, 50

"Since you have now shown me the way, I will speak before you. For is our mother, of whom you have told me, still young, or is she now approaching old age?"

And he answered me and said, 51

"Ask a woman who bears children, and she will tell you. For if you say to her, 'Why are those whom you have borne 52 lately not like those whom you bore before but smaller in stature?' she herself will tell you, 'Those who were born in 53 the vigor of youth are of one kind, and those who were born in old age, when the womb was failing, are of another.' So you too must consider that you are smaller in 54 stature than those who were before you, and those who come 55 after you will be smaller than you, for the creation is already growing old, as it were, and past the strength of youth."

And I said, 56

"I beseech you, sir, if I have found favor in your sight, show your slave by whom you will visit your creation."

And he said to me, [6

"As for the beginning of the world of the earth, before the outlets of the world were fixed, and before the assembled winds blew, and before the voices of the thunders sounded, 2 and before the lightning flashes shone, and before the foundations of Paradise were laid, and before the beautiful 3 flowers were seen, and before the moving forces were established, and before the innumerable companies of angels were gathered, and before the heights of the air were raised 4

5:48–6:4

aloft, and before the dimensions of the firmaments were
5 named, and before Zion was appointed his footstool, and
before the years of the present were discovered, and before
the wiles of present-day sinners were cut off, and those
6 who had treasured the faith were sealed; even then I considered it, and these things were made through me, and
through no other, just as their end also shall come through
me, and through no other."

7   And I answered and said,
"What will mark the parting of the times? Or when will
the end of the first or the beginning of the second be?"

8   And he said to me,
"From Abraham to Abraham, for from him sprang Jacob
and Esau, but Jacob's hand held Esau's heel from the
9 beginning. For Esau is the end of this age, and Jacob is the
10 beginning of the one that follows. For the beginning of a
man is his hand, and the end of a man in his heel. Between
the heel and the hand look for nothing else, Ezra!"

11   Then I answered and said,
"O Sovereign Lord, if I have found favor in your sight,
12 show your slave the end of your signs, some part of which
you showed me the other night."

13   And he answered and said to me,
"Rise to your feet, and you will hear a very loud voice.
14 And if the place where you stand is violently shaken,
15 you must not be terrified when it speaks, for what it says
is about the end, and the foundations of the earth will
16 understand that the speech concerns them; they will
tremble and quake, for they know that at the end they must
be changed."

17   And it came to pass that, when I heard, I rose to my feet
and listened, and, behold, a voice was speaking, and the
18 sound of it was like the noise of many waters. And it said,

6:5–18

"Behold, the days are coming, and it shall be, when I begin to draw near to visit those who live on the earth, and 19 when I begin to require their wrongdoing from those who have done it, and when the humiliation shall be complete, and when the age which is beginning to pass away shall be 20 sealed, I will perform these signs: the books will be opened before the face of the firmament, and they shall all see it together; and infants a year old shall talk, and women with 21 child will bring forth untimely infants at three or four months, and they will live and dance, and sown ground 22 will suddenly appear unsown, and full storehouses will suddenly be found empty, and the trumpet will sound, and 23 when all men hear it, they will suddenly be terrified. And 24 it will come to pass at that time that friends will make war on their friends like enemies, and the earth and those who live on it will be greatly terrified, and the sources of the springs will stop, so that for three hours they will not run. And it shall be that whoever shall have survived all these 25 things that I have foretold to you shall himself be saved and shall see my salvation and the end of my world. And they 26 will see the men who were taken up, who from their birth have not tasted death, and the heart of the earth's inhabitants will be changed and converted to a different spirit. For evil will be destroyed and deceit will be abolished, 27 but faith will flourish, and corruption be conquered, and 28 truth, which has been without fruit so long, will be disclosed."

And it came to pass, while he talked with me, that behold, 29 little by little the place where I stood was moved upon itself. And he said to me, 30

"I have come to show you these things and things to come, this night. If therefore you will pray again and fast 31

6:19-31

again for seven days, I will again declare to you even greater
32 things than these by day. For your voice has surely been
heard before the Most High, for the Mighty One has seen
your uprightness, and has remarked your purity, which you
33 have maintained from your youth. And because of this he
sent me to show you all these things and to say to you, 'Be-
34 lieve and do not fear; and do not be in haste to engage in
idle speculations over the former times, so that you may not
have to hasten in the last times.' "

35   And it came to pass after this that again I wept and
fasted seven days as before, to complete the three weeks,
36 as I had been told. And it came to pass on the eighth night
that my heart was again troubled within me, and I began
37 to speak before the Most High. For my spirit was greatly
38 excited and my soul was distressed. And I said,

    "O Lord, at the beginning of the creation you surely
spoke, and said on the first day, 'Let heaven and earth be
39 made,' and your word performed the work. Then the spirit
was hovering, and darkness and silence were all around; the
40 sound of man's voice you had not yet heard. Then you
ordered a ray of light to be brought out of your storehouses,
41 so that your works might then appear. Again, on the second
day, you created the spirit of the firmament, and commanded it to divide and make a division between the waters,
so that one part might go up and one part remain below.
42 On the third day you commanded the waters to be gathered
together in the seventh part of the earth, but six parts you
dried up and kept them so that some of them might be
43 planted and cultivated and serve before you. For your word
44 went forth, and the work was immediately done. For suddenly there came forth fruit in immeasurable abundance,
and of manifold appeal to the taste, and flowers of inimitable
hues, and odors of unfathomable fragrance. These were

6:32–44

made on the third day. But on the fourth day you com- 45
manded the brightness of the sun to come into being, the
light of the moon, and the order of the stars, and you com- 46
manded them to serve man who was still to be formed. But 47
on the fifth day you ordered the seventh part, where the
water was gathered, to bring forth living things, birds and
fish, and it was done, the mute, lifeless water producing liv- 48
ing creatures, as it was commanded, so that nations might
tell of your wondrous works because of it. Then you pre- 49
served two living creatures; one you named Behemoth, and
the other you named Leviathan, and you separated them 50
from each other, for the seventh part, where the water was
gathered together, could not hold them both. And you 51
gave Behemoth one part, which had dried up on the third
day, to live in, in which there are a thousand mountains;
but to Leviathan you gave a seventh part that is moist; and 52
you preserved them to be devoured by whomsoever you
please, and when you please. But on the sixth day, you 53
commanded the earth to create before you cattle and wild
animals and reptiles, and over them Adam, whom you ap- 54
pointed leader over all the works that you had made, and
from him we are all descended whom you have chosen to
be your people. I have said all this before you, Lord, be- 55
cause you have said that it was for our sakes that you made
this first-born world. But as for the rest of the nations which 56
are sprung from Adam, you have said that they are nothing
and are like spittle, and you have compared their abundance to a drop in a bucket. And now, Lord, behold, these 57
nations that are counted as nothing rule over us and devour
us. But we, your people, whom you called your first-born, 58
only-begotten, chosen and beloved, are delivered into their
hands. If it was for our sakes that the world was created, 59

6:45-59

why do we not possess the world as our inheritance? How
long shall this be?"

7] And it came to pass, when I had finished saying these
words, that the angel was sent to me who had been sent to
2 me on the former nights, and he said to me,

"Get up, Ezra, and hear the words which I have come
to say to you."

3 And I said,

"Speak, my lord."

And he said to me,

"Suppose a sea lies in a broad expanse, so that it is wide
4 and vast, but the entrance to it is located in a narrow space,
5 so that it is like a river; if anyone is determined to reach the
sea, to see it or master it, how can he reach the broad water
6 unless he passes through the narrows? Another illustra-
tion: Suppose a city is built and located on level ground,
7 and is full of all good things, but the approach to it is narrow
and precipitous so that there is fire on the right hand and
8 deep water on the left, and there is only one path lying between them, that is, between the fire and the water, so that
9 the path can support the steps of only one man. Now if that
city is given to a man as an inheritance, if the heir does not
pass through the danger that lies before it, how can he receive his inheritance?"

10 And I said,

"True, sir."

And he said to me,

11 "Israel's destiny is like that. For I made the world for
their sakes, and when Adam transgressed my statutes, what
12 has now happened was decreed; and the ways of entering
this world were made narrow, grievous, and toilsome, and
few and evil, full of dangers and burdened with great hard-
13 ships. But the approaches to the greater world are broad

7:1-13

and safe and produce the fruit of immortality. Unless 14
therefore the living have really entered these narrow and
fruitless experiences, they cannot obtain the things that are
destined for them. But now why are you disturbed, though 15
you are to perish? And why are you so moved, though you
are mortal? And why do you not take into consideration 16
what is future, but only what is present?"

And I answered and said, 17

"Sovereign Lord, you have ordained in your law that the
upright shall possess these things, but the ungodly shall
perish. So the upright can endure straitened circum- 18
stances in the hope of ample ones, but those who have done
wickedly endure the straitened circumstances and will not
see the ample ones."

And he said to me, 19

"You are not a better judge than God, or more intelligent than the Most High! For let the many that exist 20
perish, rather than that the Law of God which has been set
before them be disregarded. For God strictly commanded 21
those who came, at their coming, as to what they should
do to live, and what they should observe to escape being
punished. But they disobeyed and opposed him, and they 22
devised foolish thoughts and conceived wicked wiles, and 23
went so far as to say that the Most High did not exist, and
they ignored his ways, and scorned his law, and denied his 24
agreements, and had no faith in his statutes, and did not
complete his work. Therefore, Ezra, the empty have 25
emptiness, and the full, fulness. For behold the time will 26
come, and it will be that when the signs come which I have
foretold to you, the city that appears as a bride will appear,
and the land which is now hidden will be seen. And who- 27
ever is delivered from the evils I have predicted will see my
wonders. For my son the Christ will be revealed with those 28

7:14–28

who are with him, and he will make glad those who are
29 left, in four hundred years. And it will be after those years
that my son Christ will die, and all who draw human breath.
30 And the world will be turned into its ancient silence for
seven days, as it was in the first beginning, so that no one
31 will be left. And it will be after seven days that the world
which is not yet awake will be wakened, and what is cor-
32 ruptible will perish. And the earth will give up those who
are asleep in it, and the dust those who are silent in it, and
the chambers will give up the souls that have been com-
33 mitted to them. And the Most High will be revealed on his
judgment seat, and pity will pass away, and long-suffering
34 be withdrawn, and judgment alone will remain, and truth
35 will stand, and faithfulness be strong, and work will be
rewarded, and its wages appear, and uprightness will awake
[36] and iniquity will not sleep. And the lake of torment will appear, and over against it will be a place of rest; the furnace
of the Pit will appear, and over against it the paradise of joy.
[37] Then the Most High will say to the heathen that have been
raised up, 'See and understand whom you have denied, or
whom you have refused to serve, or whose commands you
[38] have scorned. Look at this side and at that; on this side,
joy and rest, and on that, fire and torment.' So he will speak
[39] to them on the Day of Judgment; a day that has no sun
[40] or moon or stars, or cloud, or thunder, or lightning, or wind
[41] or water or air, or darkness or evening or morning, or summer or heat or winter or frost or cold, or hail or rain or dew,
[42] or noon or night, or dawn or sunshine or brightness or light,
only the splendor of the glory of the Most High, by which all
[43] will begin to see what is destined for them. For it will last as
[44] though for a week of years. This is my judgment and its arrangement; and to you alone have I shown this."
[45]   And I answered,

7:29–[45]

"I said then, Lord, and I say now, blessed are those who live and keep your commandments! But about those for [46] whom I prayed, who is there of those who live who has not sinned, or who is there that is born who has not transgressed your agreement? And now I see that the world to come will [47] bring joy to few but torment to many. For an evil heart [48] has grown up in us, which has alienated us from these commands, and has led us off to corruption and the ways of death, and shown us the paths of perdition, and removed us far from life, and that, not just a few, but almost all who have been created!"

And he answered me and said,   [49]

"Listen to me, and I will instruct you, and I will admonish you a second time. It was on this account that the Most [50] High made not one world but two. For because you have [51] said that the upright are not many but few, and the ungodly abound, hear the answer to this. If you have a very few [52] precious stones, will you increase their number with lead and clay?"

And I said,   [53]

"Lord, how can that be?"

And he said to me,   [54]

"Not only that, but ask the earth and she will tell you; intreat her, and she will inform you. For you must say to [55] her, 'You produce gold and silver and copper and also iron and lead and clay. But silver is more abundant than gold, [56] and copper than silver, and iron than copper, lead than iron, and clay than lead. So consider which things are pre- [57] cious and to be desired, what is abundant, or what is rare?'"

And I said,   [58]

"Sovereign Lord, what is plentiful is cheaper, for what is more rare is more precious."

And he answered me and said,   [59]

7:[46]–[59]

"Consider with yourself what you have thought, for he who has what is hard to get rejoices more than he who has [60] what is plentiful. It is so with the judgment that I have promised; for I will rejoice over the few who will be saved, because it is they who have made my glory to prevail more now, and through whom my name has now been honored. [61] And I will not grieve over the great number of those who perish, for they are the ones who are now like vapor, and counted as flame and smoke; they have burned and glowed and gone out."

[62] And I answered and said,

"O earth, why have you brought forth, if the understand-[63] ing is made out of dust like other creatures! For it would have been better if the dust itself had not been born, so that [64] the intelligence might not have sprung from it. But now the intelligence grows with us, and it is on this account that we are tormented, because we must perish, and we know it! [65] Let the human race lament, and the wild beasts rejoice; let all who are born lament, but the four-footed creatures and [66] the cattle be glad. For they are much better off than we, for they do not look for a judgment, and they do not know of any torment or salvation promised to them after death. [67] But what benefit is it to us that we are preserved alive but [68] cruelly tormented? For all who are born are involved in iniquities and full of sins and weighed down with offenses. [69] And if we were not to come to judgment after death, perhaps it would have been better for us."

[70] And he answered me and said,

"When the Most High made the world, and Adam and all who came from him, he first prepared the judgment and the [71] things that belong to the judgment. And now understand from your own words, for you said that the intelligence [72] grows with us. So those who live on the earth will be tortured on this account because, though they had intelligence, they did iniquity, and though they received commandments, they did not keep them, and though they had obtained the Law, they broke it. What will they have to say [73] then at the judgment, or how will they answer in the last times? For how long the Most High has shown long-suffer- [74] ing to those who inhabit the world, and not for their sakes, but for the sake of the times that he has fixed!"

Then I answered and said, [75]

"If I have found favor in your sight, Sovereign, show this also to your slave; whether after death as soon as each one of us gives up his soul, we shall be faithfully kept at rest until those times come when you begin to renew the creation, or shall be tortured at once."

And he answered me and said, [76]

"I will show you that also; but you must not associate with those who have shown scorn, or count yourself among those who are tortured. For you have a treasure of works [77] laid up with the Most High, but it will not be shown to you until the last times. For about death, the teaching is: When [78] the final sentence goes forth from the Most High that a man is to die, when the soul departs from the body to return again to him who gave it, first of all it prays to the glory of the Most High; if it was one of those who scorned and did [79] not observe the way of the Most High, and of those who have despised his law, and of those who hate those who fear God, such spirits shall not enter dwellings but wander about [80] thenceforth in torment, always grieving and sad, in seven ways: The first way is that they have scorned the Law of [81] the Most High. The second way is that they can no longer [82] make a good repentance, so that they may live. The third [83] way is that they will see the reward destined for those who have believed the agreements of the Most High. The fourth [84]

7:[73]–[84]

way is that they will consider the torment destined for them
[85] in the last days. The fifth way is that they will see that the
dwelling-places of the others are guarded by angels in pro-
[86] found silence. The sixth way is that they will see that some
of them will pass over to be tormented henceforth. The
[87] seventh way, which is worse than all the ways that have
been mentioned, is that they will waste away in shame and
be consumed in disgrace, and wither with fear, at seeing the
glory of the Most High before whom they sinned while they
lived, and before whom they are destined to be judged in
the last times.

[88]   "But of those who have observed the ways of the Most
High, this is the order, when they shall be separated
[89] from this fragile jar. In the time when they lived in it,
they carefully served the Most High, though they were
in danger every hour, so as to keep the Law of the Law-
[90] giver perfectly. Therefore this is the teaching about them:
[91] First of all, they see with great rapture the glory of him who
[92] takes them up, for they will rest in seven orders. The first
order is that they have striven with much toil to conquer the
wicked thought that was formed with them, so that it should
[93] not lead them away from life to death. The second order
is that they see the labyrinth in which the souls of the un-
[94] godly wander, and the punishment that awaits them. The
third order is that they see the testimony that he who
formed them has borne to them, because when they were
alive they faithfully observed the Law which was given
[95] them. The fourth order is that they understand the rest
which they now enjoy, gathered in their chambers, in great
quietness, watched over by angels, and the glory that awaits
[96] them in the last days. The fifth order is that they exult that
they have now escaped what is corruptible and will possess
the future as their inheritance, and besides perceive the nar-

7:[85]–[96]

rowness and toilsomeness from which they have been freed
and the spaciousness they are destined to receive and enjoy
in immortality. The sixth order is that it is shown to them [97]
how their face is destined to shine like the sun, and how they
are to be made like the light of the stars, and be incorrupti-
ble thenceforth. The seventh order, which is greater than all [98]
those that have been mentioned, is that they will exult boldly, and that they will trust confidently, and rejoice fearlessly,
for they hasten to see the face of him whom they served in
life, and from whom they are to receive their reward when
they are glorified. These are the orders of the souls of the [99]
upright, as henceforth proclaimed, and the above ways of
torture are those which those who would not give heed will
henceforth suffer."

And I answered and said, [100]

"Then will time be given the souls after they are separated
from the bodies, to see what you have told me of?"

And he said to me, [101]

"They have freedom for seven days, to see on the seven
days the things you have been told, and afterward they will
be gathered in their dwellings."

And I answered and said, [102]

"If I have found favor in your sight, show me, your slave,
further, whether on the Day of Judgment the upright will
be able to intercede for the ungodly, or to beseech the Most
High on their behalf, fathers for sons, or sons for parents, [103]
brothers for brothers, relatives for their kinsmen, and friends
for those who are most dear to them."

And he answered me and said, [104]

"Since you have found favor in my sight, I will show you
this also. The Day of Judgment is final and shows to all the
stamp of truth. Just as now a father cannot send his son
or a son his father or a master his slave or a friend his dearest

[105] friend to be sick for him, or sleep or eat or be cured, so no
one can pray for another then, or lay a burden on another,
for they must all bear everyone his own iniquity or uprightness then."

36   And I answered and said,
"How then do we now find that first Abraham prayed for
the men of Sodom, and Moses for our forefathers who sinned
37 in the desert, and Joshua after him for Israel in the days of
38 Achan, and Samuel in the days of Saul, and David for the
39 plague, and Solomon for those in the sanctuary, and Elijah
for those who received the rain, and for one who was dead,
40 that he might live, and Hezekiah for the people in the days
41 of Sennacherib, and many others for many? So if now, when
corruption has increased and wrong has multiplied, the upright have prayed for the ungodly, why will it not be so then
also?"

42   And he answered me and said,
"The present world is not the end, and its glory is not lasting; therefore those who were strong prayed for the weak.
43 But the Day of Judgment will be the end of this world, and
the beginning of the immortal world to come, in which cor-
44 ruption has passed away, immorality is ended, unbelief
is abolished, uprightness has increased, and truth has ap-
45 peared. So no one will then be able to pity one who is
condemned in the judgment, or harm one who is victorious."

46   And I answered and said,
"This is my first and last word: for it would have been
better for the earth not to have produced Adam, or when
47 it had produced him compelled him not to sin. For what
good is it to all men to live in sorrow and expect punishment
48 after death? O Adam, what have you done? For although
it was you who sinned, the fall was not yours alone, but also

7:[105]–48

ours, for we are descended from you. For what good does 49
it do us if the eternal world is promised to us, but we have
done deeds that bring death? And that an imperishable 50
hope is proclaimed to us, but we have miserably failed?
And that safe and healthy habitations are reserved for us, 51
but we have lived wickedly? And that the glory of the Most 52
High is going to protect those who have lived purely, but we
have walked in the most wicked ways? And that a Paradise 53
will be revealed the fruit of which endures uncorrupted, which
contains plenty and healing, but we cannot enter it, for we 54
have lived in unseemly ways? And that the faces of those 55
who have practiced abstinence will shine brighter than the
stars, but our faces will be blacker than darkness? For when 56
we were alive and committed iniquity, we did not consider
what we were to suffer after death."

And he answered and said, 57

"This is the meaning of the battle that every man born
on earth must fight, that, if he is beaten, he will suffer what 58
you have said, but if he is victorious, he will receive what I
say. For this is the way of which Moses spoke, when he was 59
alive, saying to the people, 'Choose life for yourself, so that
you may live!' But they would not believe him or the 60
prophets after him, or yet me who have spoken to them,
so there will be not so much grief at their destruction as joy 61
over those who have been persuaded of salvation."

And I answered and said, 62

"I know, sir, that the Most High is now called merciful,
because he has mercy on those who have not yet come into
the world, and gracious, because he is gracious to those who 63
turn to his Law, and long-suffering, because he is long- 64
suffering to those who have sinned as his creatures, and 65
bountiful, because he had rather give than exact, and of 66
great mercy, because he multiplies mercies more and more

7:49–66

to those who are alive and those who have passed away and
67 those who are to be, for if he did not multiply them, the
68 world with those who live in it would not be made alive, and
a giver, for if he did not give in his goodness, so that those
who have committed iniquities might be relieved of them,
69 not one ten-thousandth of mankind could have life; and a
judge, for if he did not pardon those who were created by
70 his word, and erase a multitude of offenses, there would
probably be left only very few of the innumerable multitude."

8]   And he answered me and said,
"The Most High made this world for the sake of many,
2 but the world to come, for the sake of few. But I will tell
you a parable, Ezra. Just as, if you ask the earth, it will tell
you that it produces much more soil from which earthen-
ware is made, but little dust from which gold comes, that is
3 the way with the present world; many have been created,
but few will be saved."

4   And I answered and said,
"Then drink down understanding, my soul, and devour
5 wisdom, my heart! For not of your own will you came, and
against your will you go, for you have been given only a
6 short time to live. O Lord above us, if you will only allow
your slave to pray before you, and would give us seed for the
heart and cultivation of the understanding so that fruit may
be produced, by which a corruptible being, who bears the
7 image of man, may live! For you stand alone, and we are
8 one creation of your hands, as you have said. And when
you bring to life a body formed in the womb, and provide
its members, what you have created is preserved in fire and
water, and for nine months what you have formed endures
9 your creation which has been created in it. But that which
preserves and that which is preserved are both preserved by

your preserving. And when the womb gives up what has been created in it, you have commanded that from the 10 members themselves, that is from the breasts, milk, the fruit of the breasts, be given, so that what has been formed 11 may be nourished for a time. And afterward you develop it in your mercy. You nourish it in your uprightness, and 12 instruct it through your Law, and bring it up in your wisdom. You put it to death as your creation, and make it live 13 as your work. If then you lightly destroy him who was 14 formed with such pains, at your command, why was he made at all? And now I will speak out: About all man- 15 kind you know best; but it is about your people that I am grieved, and it is for your inheritance that I mourn, and 16 about Israel that I am sad, and about the posterity of Jacob that I am disturbed. Therefore I will begin to pray 17 before you for myself and for them, for I see the failings of us who live in the land and I have heard of the strictness of 18 the judgment that is to come. Therefore hear my voice, and 19 consider my words, and I will speak before you."

The beginning of the words of the prayer of Ezra, before he was taken up. And he said,

"Lord, who inhabit eternity, whose are the highest heav- 20 ens, and whose upper chambers are in the air, whose throne 21 is immeasurable, and whose glory is beyond comprehension, before whom the hosts of angels stand trembling, and at 22 your command are changed to wind and fire, whose word is sure and whose utterances are certain, whose command is mighty and whose orders are terrible, whose look dries up 23 the depths, and whose indignation melts the mountains, and whose truth endures forever, hear, Lord, the prayer 24 of your slave, and listen to the petition of your creature, and heed my words; for as long as I live I must speak, and as 25 long as I have my reason I must answer. Do not look at the 26

8:10–26

sins of your people, but at those who have served you in
27 truth! And do not notice the pursuits of the ungodly, but
those who have observed your agreements under torture.
28 And do not think of those who have behaved wickedly in
your sight, but remember those who have willingly ac-
29 knowledged your fear. And do not will the destruction
of those who have the ways of cattle, but have regard for
30 those who have so finely taught your Law. And do not be
indignant at those who are deemed worse than beasts, but
31 love those who have always trusted in your glory. For we
and our forefathers have followed ways that bring death,
but it is because of us sinners that you are called merciful.
32 For if you desire to have pity on us, you will be called merci-
33 ful, for we have no deeds of uprightness to show. For the
upright, who have many good deeds laid up with you, will
34 receive their reward in consequence of their own deeds. For
what is man, that you are indignant at him, or what is a cor-
35 ruptible race, that you are so bitter toward it? For in truth
there is no one among those who were ever born who has not
acted wickedly, or among those who have grown up who has
36 not sinned. For in this, Lord, your uprightness and goodness
will be declared, if you have mercy on those who have no
stock of good deeds."

37   And he answered me and said,
"Some things you have said well, and it will come to pass
38 in accordance with your words. For indeed I will not think
about the forming of those who have sinned, or their death
39 or judgment or destruction, but I will rejoice over the
fashioning of the upright, over their pilgrimage also, and
40 their salvation and the reward they will receive. So it is as
41 I have said. For just as the farmer sows many seeds upon
the ground, and plants a multitude of plants, and yet not
all that was sown will be saved in due time, and not all that

were planted will take root, so those who are sown in
the world will not all be saved."

And I answered and said,   42

"If I have found favor before you, I will speak. For if the   43
farmer's seed does not come up, because it has not received
your rain in season, or if it has been spoiled by an excess of
rain, it perishes; but man, who was formed by your hands   44
and is called your image, because he is made like you—for
whose sake you formed everything—do you compare him
to the farmer's seed? No, Lord above us, but spare your   45
people and have pity on your inheritance, for you pity your
own creation."

And he answered me and said,   46

"The present for those who are now, and the future for
those who shall be. For you are far from able to love what   47
I have created more than I. But you have often counted
yourself among the ungodly. Never! But for this you will   48
be commended before the Most High, because you humbled   49
yourself, as was fitting, and did not count yourself among
the upright, so as to glorify yourself too much. For those   50
who inhabit the world in the last times will be afflicted with
many great miseries, because they have walked in great
pride. But you must think of yourself and ask about the   51
glory of those who are like yourself. For it is for you that   52
Paradise is opened, the tree of life is planted, the age to
come is prepared, plenty is provided, a city is built, a rest is
ordained, good deeds completed, wisdom perfected beforehand. The root of evil is sealed up from you, for you sick-   53
ness is extinct, and death has departed; Hades has fled, and
corruption has gone into oblivion; sorrows have passed   54
away, and the treasure of immortality is finally displayed.
So do not ask any more questions about the great number   55
of those who perish. For though they had received liberty,   56

8:42-56

they scorned the Most High and despised his Law, and
57 forsook his ways. Moreover they trampled upon his saints
58 and said in their hearts that there was no God, though they
59 knew well that they must die. For just as the things I have
spoken of await you, so the thirst and torment which are
prepared await them. For the Most High did not wish man
60 to perish, but those who were created have themselves defiled the name of him who made them, and proved ungrate-
61 ful to him who prepared life for them. Therefore my judg-
62 ment is now drawing near, but I have not revealed it to all
men, but only to you and a few like you."

And I answered and said,

63 "Behold, Lord, you have revealed to me the great number
of signs which you are going to perform in the last days,
but you have not revealed to me at what time you will do
this."

9] And he answered me and said,

"Measure it carefully within yourself, and it will be that
when you see that a certain part of the signs which have
2 been foretold have passed, then you will understand that it
is the very time when the Most High is to visit the world
3 that was made by him. So when there shall appear in the
world earthquakes, the tumult of peoples, plots of the
4 heathen, wavering of leaders, and confusion of princes, then
you will understand that it was of these things that the Most
High spoke from the days that were of old, from the be-
5 ginning. For just as with everything that has happened
in the world, the beginning is plain and the end manifest,
6 so also are the times of the Most High; the beginnings are
signalized by wonders and mighty works, and the end by
7 acts and signs. And it will be that everyone who will be
saved, and who is able to escape by reason of his deeds or
8 his faith, by which he believed, will survive the dangers I

have foretold, and will see my salvation in my land, and
within my borders which I have consecrated to myself from
eternity. Then those who have now neglected my ways will   9
be amazed, and those who have rejected them with contempt will abide in torment. For as many as failed to   10
acknowledge me in their lifetime, though they received my
benefits, and as many as disdained my Law, while they still   11
had freedom, and while an opportunity to repent was still
open to them, did not understand but scorned it, these   12
must recognize it after death, through torment. So you must   13
no longer be curious as to how the ungodly will be punished,
but ask how the righteous will be saved, to whom that age
belongs and for the sake of whom it was made."

I answered and said,   14

"I said before, and say now, and will say again, there are   15
more that perish than that will be saved, as a wave is greater   16
than a drop of water."

And he answered me and said,   17

"As is the field, so is the seed, and as are the flowers, so are
the colors, and as is the work, so is it judged, and as is the
farmer, so is the threshing-floor. For there was a time in
the ages of eternity, when I was preparing for those who now   18
are, before the world was made for them to live in, and   19
no one opposed me then, for there was no one else; but now
those who have been created in this world which is provided
with an unfailing table and an inexhaustible pasture, have
become corrupt in their characters. So I considered my   20
world, and, behold, it was lost; and my universe, and, behold, it was in danger, because of the devices of those who
had come into it. And I saw, and spared them, not very   21
greatly, and saved myself one grape out of a cluster, and
one plant out of a forest. So let the multitude perish, that   22
were born in vain, but let my grape be saved, and my

9:9–22

23 plant, because with much labor I have perfected them. But
24 if you will let seven days more pass but not fast in them, but
go to a flowery field, where no house is built, and eat only of
the flowers of the field, and taste no meat and drink no
25 wine, but only flowers, and will pray to the Most High continually, I will come and talk with you."

26 So I went as he told me, to the field called Ardat, and I
sat there among the flowers, and ate the wild plants, and
27 the food they afforded satisfied me. And it came to pass
after seven days that as I lay on the grass my heart was
28 troubled as it had been before. Then my mouth was
opened, and I began to speak before the Most High, and
said,

29 "O Lord, you surely showed yourself to our forefathers
in the desert when they came out of Egypt and went into
30 the desert, which was untrodden and unproductive, and
you surely said, 'Israel, hear me, and mark my words, pos-
31 terity of Jacob. For behold, I sow my Law in you, and it
will bring forth fruit in you, and you will be glorified
32 through it forever.' But our forefathers who received the
Law did not keep it, and did not observe the statutes, yet
the fruit of the Law did not perish, for it could not, because
33 it was yours; but those who had received it perished, because they had not kept what had been sown in them.
34 And, behold, it is the rule that when the earth has received
seed, or the sea a ship, or any dish food or drink, and when
it comes about that what was sown or what was launched
35 or what was put in is destroyed, they are destroyed, but the
things which contained them remain. But with us it has
36 not been so; we who received the Law will perish because we
37 sinned, along with our heart which received it; but the Law
does not perish, but abides in its glory."
38 When I said this to myself, I lifted up my eyes and saw

a woman at my right, and behold, she was weeping and
wailing aloud, and was deeply grieved at heart, and her
clothes were torn, and she had ashes on her head. And I 39
dismissed the thoughts I had been thinking, and turned to
her and said to her, 40
"Why do you weep, and why are you grieved at heart?"
And she said to me, 41
"Let me weep over myself, my lord, and continue to
mourn, for I am greatly embittered in spirit and deeply
afflicted."
And I said to her, 42
"What has happened to you? Tell me."
And she said to me, 43
"Your servant was barren and had no child, though I had
a husband for thirty years. And every day and hour, those 44
thirty years, I prayed to the Most High, night and day.
Then after thirty years it came about that God heard your 45
servant, and looked on my affliction and gave heed to my
distress and gave me a son. And I rejoiced greatly over
him, I and my husband and all my neighbors, and we paid
great honor to the Mighty One. And I brought him up with 46
great care. And it came about, when he was grown up, that 47
I proceeded to take a wife for him, and made a marriage
feast.
"And it came about that when my son entered his wed- [10
ding chamber, he fell down and died. And we all over- 2
turned the lights, and all my neighbors rose up to comfort
me, and I was quiet until evening the second day. And it 3
came about, when they had all stopped comforting me, to
quiet me, that I got up in the night, and fled, and came to
this field, as you see. And now I plan not to return to the 4
city, but to stay here, and I will not eat or drink, but mourn
and fast continually until I die."

9:39–10:4

5   Then I broke off the reflections with which I was still occupied, and answered her in anger and said,

6   "You most foolish of all women, can you not see our sor-
7   row, and what has happened to us? For Zion, the mother
8   of us all, is afflicted with grief and in deep humiliation. Now lament bitterly, for we are all lamenting, and be sad, for we
9   are all sad, but you sorrow for just one son. For ask the earth, and she will tell you that it is she who ought to mourn
10   over so many who have come into being upon her. And from the beginning all have been born of her and others will come, and, behold, almost all of them go to perdition,
11   and the most of them are destined to destruction. Who therefore ought to mourn more, if not she, who has lost such a multitude, rather than you, who sorrow for only one?
12   But if you say to me, 'My lamentation is not like the earth's, for I have lost the fruit of my womb, which I bore with pain
13   and brought forth with sorrow; but it is with the earth after the manner of the earth; the multitude that is now in it goes
14   as it came'; then I say to you, 'As you brought forth with pain, so the earth also has from the beginning given her
15   fruit, man, to him who made her.' So keep your sorrow to yourself, and bear bravely the misfortunes that have
16   overtaken you. For if you accept the judgment of God, you will receive your son back in due time, and be praised
17   among women. So go into the city to your husband."
18   And she said to me,
     "I will not do it, or enter the city, but I will die here."
19   Then I proceeded to speak to her further, and said,
20   "Do not do that, but let yourself be persuaded because of the misfortunes of Zion, and be comforted because of the
21   sorrow of Jerusalem. For you see that our sanctuary has been laid waste, and our altar torn town, and our temple
22   destroyed, and our harp is brought low, and our song is

10:5–22

silenced, and our rejoicing has ceased, and the light of our lamp is put out, and the chest of our agreement is plundered, and our sacred things are polluted, and the name by which we have been called is profaned, our children are abused, and our priests are burned, and our Levites have gone into captivity, and our girls are defiled, and our wives are ravished, and our upright men are carried off, and our little ones are exposed, and our young men are enslaved, and our strong men are made weak. And worst of all is the seal 23 of Zion, for she is now sealed up from her glory, and delivered into the hands of those who hate us. So shake off 24 your great sadness and lay aside your many sorrows, so that the Mighty One may become gracious to you, and the Most High may give you rest, and relief from your troubles."

And it came to pass, as I spoke to her, that her face suddenly shone exceedingly and the look of her countenance 25 flashed like lightning, so that I was too greatly frightened to go near her, and wondered what it could mean. And 26 behold, she suddenly gave a loud and fearful cry, so that the earth shook at the sound. And I looked, and behold the 27 woman no longer appeared to me, but a city was being built and a place of huge foundations showed itself; and I was afraid, and cried aloud and said,

"Where is the angel Uriel, who came to me at first? For 28 it was he who brought me into this great bewilderment; my end has become corruption, and my prayer a reproach!"

And as I said this, behold, the angel who had come to me 29 at first, came to me, and saw me; and, behold, I lay there 30 like a corpse, and I had lost my reason, and he took my right hand, and steadied me, and helped me to my feet, and said to me,

"What is the matter with you, and why are you troubled, 31

10:23-31

and why are your understanding and the thinking of your mind confused?"

32 And I said,
"Because you utterly abandoned me. I did as you told me, and went out to the field, and behold, I looked, and I saw what I cannot describe."

33 And he said to me,
"Stand up like a man, and I will instruct you."

34 And I said,
"Speak, my lord, only do not abandon me, so that I may
35 not die in vain. For I have seen what I did not know, and
36 I heard what I do not understand. Is my mind deceived,
37 or my soul dreaming? Now therefore I beseech you to explain to your slave about this confusion."

38 And he answered me and said,
"Listen to me, and I will teach you, and tell you about the things of which you are afraid, for the Most High has
39 revealed many secrets to you. For he has seen your rectitude, and that you have sorrowed continually for your
40 people and lamented bitterly over Zion. This then is the
41 meaning of the vision: The woman who appeared to you a little while ago, whom you saw mourning and began to com-
42 fort, but whom you then saw not in the form of a woman,
43 but she appeared to you as a city that was being built, and as to what she told you about the misfortune of her son,
44 this is the explanation: The woman that you saw, whom
45 you now see as a city that is built, is Zion! And as for her telling you that she was barren for thirty years, that was because there were three thousand years when no offering was
46 yet offered in her; and it came to pass that after three thousand years Solomon built the city and offered sacrifices; it was then that the barren woman bore a son.
47 And as for her telling you that she brought him up with

10:32–47

care, that was the period of residence in Jerusalem. And as 48
for her saying to you, 'As my son was going into the marriage chamber, he died,' and that misfortune had overtaken her, that was the fall of Jerusalem that has taken
place. And, behold, you saw her face and how she mourned 49
for her son, and you began to comfort her for what had
happened. And now the Most High seeing that you are 50
deeply grieved, and are whole-heartedly distressed for her,
has shown you the splendor of her glory and the charm of
her beauty. It was on this account that I told you to stay 51
in the field where no house was built, for I knew that the 52
Most High was going to reveal these things to you. That 53
was why I told you to go into the field, where there was no
foundation of a building, for no work built by man could 54
stand in the place where the city of the Most High was to be
revealed. So do not be afraid, or terrified at heart, but go in, 55
and see the splendor and greatness of the building, as far as
the sight of your eyes can see. And afterward you will hear 56
as much as the hearing of your ears can hear. For you are 57
more blessed than many, and you have been called by the
Most High as few have been. But tomorrow night you must 58
stay here, and the Most High will show you in dreams those 59
visions of what the Most High is going to do in the last days
to those who live on the earth."

So I slept that night and the following one, as he had
commanded me. And it came to pass on the second night [11
that I had a dream, and behold, there came up out of the
sea an eagle, with twelve feather-covered wings and three
heads. And I looked, and behold he spread his wings over 2
the whole earth, and all the winds of heaven blew upon him,
and the clouds gathered about him. And I looked, and out 3
of his wings grew additional wings, and they became small,
dwarfish wings. But his heads were resting; the middle 4

head was greater than the other heads, but it was resting
5 like them. And I looked, and behold, the eagle flew with
his wings, to reign over the earth, and over those who live
6 on it. And I saw that everything under heaven was subject
to him, and no one opposed him, nor any creature that was
7 on the earth. And I looked and, behold, the eagle rose upon
his talons, and uttered his voice to his wings, saying,

8   "Do not all watch at once, sleep each in his own place,
9 and watch by turns; but let the heads be reserved for the
last."

10   And I looked, and behold, the voice did not come from
11 his heads but from the midst of his body. And I counted his
additional wings, and behold, there were eight of them.
12 And I looked, and behold, on the right side, one wing arose
13 and it reigned over the whole earth. And it came to pass,
after it had reigned, that it came to an end, and disappeared,
so that even the place where it had been could not be seen.
Then the second arose and reigned, and it ruled a long
14 time. And it came to pass, after it had reigned, that it also
15 came to an end, so that it disappeared like the first. And
behold a voice was heard, saying to it,

16   "Listen, you who have ruled the earth so long, I make this
17 proclamation to you before you begin to disappear: No one
after you will rule as long as you have ruled, or even half
as long!"

18   Then the third wing raised itself up, and ruled like the
19 former ones, and it also disappeared. And so it fell to all
the wings, one by one to be emperor, and then to disappear
20 again. And I looked, and behold, in due time, the additional wings on the right side raised themselves up, in order
to be emperor, and there were some of them who succeeded
21 but immediately disappeared, and some of them raised
22 themselves up, but did not remain emperor. And afterward

11:5–22

I looked, and behold, the twelve wings and two little wings disappeared, and nothing was left on the eagle's body ex- 23 cept the three heads that were resting and six little wings. And I looked, and behold, from the six little wings two 24 separated, and stayed under the head that was on the right side; but four stayed in their places. And I looked, 25 and behold, these four additional wings planned to raise themselves up and be emperors. And I looked, and behold, 26 one raised itself up, and immediately disappeared; and a second, and it disappeared more quickly than the first. 27 And I looked, and behold, the two that were left also 28 planned to reign; but while they were planning it, behold, 29 the one of the resting heads that was in the middle awoke, for it was greater than the other two heads; and I saw how 30 the two heads were united with it; and behold, the head 31 turned with the ones that were with it, and it ate up the additional wings which planned to reign. Moreover, this 32 head made itself master of the whole earth, and ruled very oppressively over its inhabitants, and it had more power over the world than all the wings that had gone before. And 33 afterward I looked, and behold, the middle head suddenly disappeared, just as the wings had done. But the two 34 heads remained, and they also reigned over the earth and over its inhabitants. And I looked, and behold, the head 35 on the right side ate up the one on the left.

Then I heard a voice saying to me,   36
"Look before you, and think about what you see."

And I looked, and behold, what seemed to be a lion 37 rose out of the forest roaring, and I heard how he uttered a man's voice to the eagle, and spoke saying,

"Listen, and I will speak to you. The Most High says to 38 you, 'Are you not all that is left of the four animals that I 39 made to reign in my world, so that through them the end

11:23–39

40 of my times might come? And you are the fourth to come, and you have conquered all the animals that are past, and you have held the world in subjection in great terror, and the whole earth with harsh oppression, and you have lived
41 so long in the world with deceit; and you have not judged
42 the earth with truth. You have persecuted the meek and hurt the peaceable, you have hated those who tell the truth, and loved liars, and you have destroyed the dwellings of the fruitful, and torn down the walls of those who did you no
43 harm. And your insolence has reached the Most High and
44 your pride the Mighty One. And the Most High has looked at his times, and behold, they are ended, and his ages are
45 completed! Therefore you will surely disappear, you eagle, and your dreadful wings, and your wicked additional wings, and your malignant heads, and your cruel talons, and your
46 whole worthless body, so that the whole earth may be freed from your violence, and be refreshed and relieved, and hope for the justice and mercy of him who made her.''

12] And it came to pass, while the lion was saying these words
2 to the eagle, that I looked, and behold, the head that had been left disappeared, and the two wings which had gone over to it lifted themselves up to reign, and their reign was
3 short and full of uproar. And I looked, and behold, they also disappeared, and the whole body of the eagle was burned, and the earth was panic-stricken.

Then, because of great disturbance of mind and great fear, I awoke, and I said to my spirit,
4 "Behold, you have brought this upon me, because you
5 try to search out the ways of the Most High! Behold, I am still weary in mind and very weak in my spirit, and there is not the least strength left in me, because of the great fear
6 which I felt this night. So now I will intreat the Most High to strengthen me to the end.''

11:40–12:6

And I said,   7

"Sovereign Lord, if I have found favor in your sight, and
if I am counted upright by you beyond many, and if my
prayer has indeed come up before your face, strengthen me,   8
and show your slave the meaning and explanation of this
dreadful vision, so as to comfort my soul fully. For you have 9
thought me worthy to be shown the end of the times and the
last of them."

And he said to me,   10

"This is the meaning of this vision that you have seen: As   11
for the eagle that you saw rising from the sea, it is the fourth
kingdom that appeared in a vision to your brother Daniel.
But it was not explained to him as I now explain it to you   12
or have explained it. Behold, the days are coming when a   13
kingdom will rise on the earth, and it will be more terrible
than all the kingdoms that were before it. Moreover, twelve   14
kings will reign over it, one after another. But the second   15
who is to reign will rule longer than the twelve. This is   16
the meaning of the twelve wings that you saw. And as for   17
your hearing a voice that spoke, that came not from his
heads but from the middle of his body, this is the meaning:
In the midst of the time of the kingdom no small struggles   18
will arise, and it will be in danger of falling, but it will not
fall then, but will regain its former power. And as for your 19
seeing eight additional wings springing from his wings, this
is the meaning: For eight kings will rise in it, whose times   20
will be short and whose years will be fleeting, and two of   21
them will fall when the middle of its time draws near; but
four will be preserved for the time when the time of its end
begins to approach; but two will be kept until the end. And   22
as for your seeing the three heads resting, this is the meaning: In its last days the Most High will raise up three kings, 23
and they will renew many things in it, and will distress the

12:7–23

24 earth and those who live in it, with greater oppression
than all who were before them. That is why they are called
25 the eagle's heads. For it is they that will bring his wicked-
26 ness to a head and will bring him to his end. And as for
your seeing the greater head disappear—one of them will
27 die in his bed, but in torment. But as for the two who were
28 left, the sword will devour them. For the sword of one of
them will devour the one who was with him, but he too will
29 fall by the sword in the last days. And as for your seeing two
additional wings crossing over to the head on the right side,
30 this is the meaning: It is these that the Most High has kept
for the eagle's end, for their reign was short and full of dis-
31 turbance, as you saw. And as for the lion that you saw
roused roaring out of the forest, and speaking to the eagle,
and rebuking him for his wickedness and all his words that
32 you have heard, he is the Anointed One, whom the Most
High has kept until the end of the days, who will spring from
the posterity of David and come and talk with them. He will
charge them with their ungodliness and rebuke them for
their wickedness, and reproach them to their faces with
33 their transgressions. For first he will set them alive before
his judgment seat, and when he has rebuked them, he will
34 destroy them. But my people who remain he will mercifully
set free, who remain in my borders, and he will make them
glad until the end comes, the Day of Judgment, of which I
35 told you at the beginning. This is the dream that you had,
36 and this is its meaning. But you alone were worthy to know
37 the secret of the Most High. So write all that you have seen
38 in a book, and put it in a secret place, and teach them to the
wise among your people, whose hearts you know can receive
39 and keep these secrets. But you must stay here seven days
more, so that you may be shown whatever it pleases the
Most High to show you."

12:24–39

Then he departed from me. And it came about that when 40
all the people had heard that the seven days had passed and
I had not returned to the city, they all gathered together,
from the least to the greatest, and came to me and spoke to
me saying,

"How have we sinned against you, and what harm have 41
we done you, that you have entirely abandoned us, and
stay in this place? For of all the prophets, you alone are 42
left to us, like a grape cluster out of the vintage, and like
a lamp in a dark place, and like a safe harbor for a ship
in a storm. Are not the evils that have befallen us enough? 43
So if you abandon us, how much better it would have been 44
for us if we too had been burned in the burning of Zion!
For we are no better than those who died there." And they 45
wept aloud.

And I answered them and said,

"Have courage, Israel, and do not be sorrowful, you 46
house of Jacob. For you are remembered before the Most 47
High, and the Mighty One will never forget you. For I have 48
not abandoned you or withdrawn from you, but I came to
this place to pray over the desolation of Zion, and to ask for
mercy in view of the degradation of our sanctuary. And 49
now go home, every one of you, and when these days are
over, I will come to you."

And the people went back to the city, as I told them to 50
do. But I stayed in the field for seven days, as he had com- 51
manded me, and I ate only of the flowers of the field; my
food was vegetables in those days.

And it came about after seven days that in the night I [13
dreamed a dream, and behold a wind arose from the sea, 2
so that it stirred up all its waves. And I looked, and behold, 3
the wind brought out of the heart of the sea something like
the figure of a man, and this man flew with the clouds of

12:40–13:3

heaven, and wherever he turned his face to look, everything
4 that was seen by him trembled, and wherever the voice
went from his mouth, all who heard his voice melted as wax
5 melts when it feels the fire. And after that I looked, and
behold, an innumerable multitude of men was gathered
together from the four winds of heaven, to make war upon
6 the man who had come up out of the sea. And I looked, and
behold, he carved himself out a great mountain, and flew
7 up upon it. But I sought to see the region or place from
8 which the mountain had been carved, and I could not. And
after that I looked, and behold, all who had gathered
together against him, to fight with him, were much afraid,
9 but dared to fight. And behold, when he saw the onset of
the multitude that approached, he did not raise his hand,
10 or hold a sword, or any weapon of war, but I saw only how
he sent out of his mouth what looked like a flood of fire, and
out of his lips a flaming breath, and from his tongue he sent
11 forth a storm of sparks. These were all mixed together, the
flood of fire, and the flaming breath, and the mighty storm,
and it fell upon the onset of the multitude which was ready
to fight, and burned them all up, so that suddenly there was
nothing to be seen of the countless multitude but the dust
of their ashes and the smell of smoke. When I saw it, I was
12 amazed. Afterward I saw this man come down from the
mountain, and call to him another multitude that was
13 peaceable. Then many people came to him, some joyful,
some sorrowful, some in fetters, some bringing offerings.

Then in an excess of fear I awoke, and besought the Most
High, and said,
14 "You have shown your slave these wonders from the beginning, and have thought me worthy to have my prayer
15 heard by you. Now show me further the meaning of this
16 dream! For as I think of it in my mind, alas for those who

13:4–16

will be left in those days, and alas much more for those
who are not left! For those who are not left will be sad, 17
since they know what is reserved for the last days, but 18
cannot attain them. But alas for those who are left, too, for 19
this reason, for they must experience great dangers and
much distress, as these dreams show. Yet it is better, for all 20
the danger, to attain these things, than to pass from the
world like a cloud, and not to see what will happen at the
end."

And he answered me and said,

"I will tell you the meaning of the vision, and I will reveal 21
to you the things of which you speak. As for what you say 22
about those who are left, this is the meaning: He who oc- 23
casions the danger at that time will guard those who are
exposed to danger, who have works, and faith in the Almighty. So you must understand that those who are left are 24
more blessed than those who have died. This is the mean- 25
ing of the vision: As for your seeing a man come up from the
heart of the sea, he is the one whom the Most High has kept 26
a long time, through whom he will redeem his creation; and
he will organize those who are left. And as for your seeing 27
wind and fire and storm issue from his mouth, and as for his 28
not holding a sword or a weapon of war, but destroying the
onset of the multitude that came to subdue him, this is
the meaning: Behold, the days are coming when the Most 29
High is going to deliver those who are on the earth, and 30
amazement will come upon those who live on the earth, and 31
they will plan to make war one upon another, city upon city
and place upon place, people upon people, and kingdom
upon kingdom. And it will come about, when this happens, 32
that the signs will occur which I showed you before, and
my Son will be revealed, whom you saw as a man coming
up. And it will come about, when all the nations hear his 33

13:17-33

voice, that every man will leave his country and the wars
34 that they have with one another, and a countless multitude
such as you saw will be gathered together, wishing to
35 come and subdue him. But he will stand on the top of
36 Mount Zion. And Zion will come and be revealed to all
men, made ready and built, like the mountain that you
37 saw carved out without hands. And my Son will charge the
heathen who have come with their ungodliness (this was
38 symbolized by the storm), and will upbraid them to their
face with their evil thoughts and the tortures with which
they are to be tortured (which were symbolized by the
flame), and he will destroy them without effort by the Law
39 (which is symbolized by the fire). And as for your seeing
him gather about himself another multitude that was peace-
40 able, these are the ten tribes that in the days of King Hoshea
were carried away from their own land into captivity, whom
Shalmaneser, king of Assyria, made captives, and carried
beyond the river; they were carried off to another country.
41 But they formed this plan among themselves, to leave the
heathen population, and go to a more distant region, where
42 the human race had never lived, so that there perhaps they
might keep their statutes, which they had not kept in their
43 own country. And they went in by the narrow passages
44 of the Euphrates River. For the Most High then did wonders for them, for he held back the sources of the river until
45 they had passed over. But it was a long journey of a year
and a half to that country, and that country is called Arza-
46 reth. There they have lived until the last time, and now,
47 when they are about to come again, the Most High will hold
back the sources of the river again, so that they can cross
over. It is on that account that you saw the multitude
48 gathered together in peace. But those also who are left of
your people, who are found within my holy borders, will

13:34-48

live. Therefore it will be that when he destroys the multi- 49
tude of the nations that are gathered together, he will protect the people that remain, and then he will show them 50
many, many wonders."

And I said, 51

"Sovereign Lord, show me this—why I saw a man come
up from the heart of the sea."

And he said to me, 52

"Just as no one can seek out or know what is in the depth
of the sea, so no one on earth can see my Son, or those who
are with him, except at the time of his Day. This is the 53
meaning of the dream that you had. And you alone have
been enlightened about these things, because you have for- 54
saken your own affairs and devoted yourself to mine, and
have sought after my Law, for you have devoted your life 55
to wisdom and called understanding your mother. That is 56
why I have shown you this, for there is reward with the
Most High! For it will be that after three more days I will
say other things to you, and declare weighty and wonderful
matters to you."

Then I went away and walked in the field, greatly glorify- 57
ing and praising the Most High for the wonders that he does
from time to time, and because he directs the times and the 58
things that take place in the times. And I stayed there three
days.

And it came to pass on the third day, as I sat under an [14
oak, behold, a voice came from a bush in front of me, and
said,

"Ezra, Ezra!"

And I said, 2

"Here I am, sir!"

And I rose to my feet, and he said to me, 3

"I revealed myself visibly in the bush, and talked with

4 Moses, when my people was in slavery in Egypt, and I sent
him, and led my people out of Egypt, and brought them to
5 Mount Sinai, and kept him with me many days, and told
him many wonderful things, and showed him the secrets
of the times, and the end of the times, and commanded him,
saying,

6 " 'These words you must publish openly, and those you
7, 8 must keep secret.' And now I tell you, the signs that I have
shown you, and the dreams that you have had, and the
meaning of them that you have heard, lay up in your heart!
9 For you will be taken up from among men, and henceforth
you will live with my Son and those who are like you, until
10 the times are ended. For the world has lost its youth, and
11 the times are beginning to grow old. For the life of the
world is divided into twelve parts, and nine parts and half
12 of the tenth part are already past, and there are left two
13 parts and half of the tenth part. Now therefore put your
house in order, and warn your people, comfort the humble
among them, and teach those who are wise, and now re-
14 nounce the life that perishes, and dismiss from your mind
mortal considerations, and throw off the burdens of human
15 existence, and lay aside your weak nature, and put away
your perplexities, and hasten to escape from these times.
16 For worse evils are still to come than those you have seen
17 happen. For the more the world grows weak with age, the
18 more evils will increase upon those who live in it. Truth
will more and more retire, and falsehood draw near. For
the eagle that you saw in your vision is already hastening to
come."

19   And I answered and said,
20   "Let me speak before you, sir! For behold, I will go away,
as you have commanded me, and I will warn the people
who are now living; but who will warn those who are still

14:4–20

to be born? For the world lies in darkness, and those who
live in it have no light; for your Law is burnt, and so no one 21
knows what has been done by you or what is going to be
done. But if I have found favor before you, impart to me 22
the holy Spirit, and I will write all that has happened in the
world since the beginning, which were written in your Law,
so that men can find the path, and those who wish to live
in the last times may live."

And he answered me and said,   23

"Go, gather the people together, and tell them not to look
for you for forty days. But you must prepare for yourself 24
many writing tablets, and take with you Seraiah, Dabria,
Shelemiah, Elkanah, and Asiel, who are able to write
swiftly. And you are to come here, and I will light the lamp 25
of understanding in your heart, and it will not be put out
until the things you are to write are finished. And when 26
you have finished, some things you shall publish and some
you shall hand down secretly to the wise. At this hour tomorrow you shall begin to write."

And I went as he commanded me, and gathered all the 27
people together, and said,

"Israel, hear these words. Our forefathers lived in Egypt 28,29
as strangers at first, and they were delivered from there,
and received the Law of life, which they did not observe, 30
which you also transgressed after them. Then land was 31
given you to possess in the country of Zion, but you and your
forefathers acted unrighteously and did not observe the ways
which the Most High commanded you to keep; and, as he 32
is an upright judge, he took from you what he had given you
in his own time. And now you are here, and your brothers 33
are in the interior. If therefore you will rule your mind and 34
instruct your heart, you will be preserved while you live,
and obtain mercy after death. For after death will come 35

14:21-35

the judgment, when we will live again, and then the
names of the upright will appear and the deeds of the un-
36 godly will be disclosed. But let no one come near me now,
or look for me for forty days."

37 Then I took the five men, as he commanded me, and
38 we went to the field, and stayed there. And it came to pass
the next day that a voice called me, and said,

"Ezra, open your mouth, and drink what I give you to
drink."

39 And I opened my mouth, and, behold, a full cup was
offered me. It was full of what looked like water, but the
40 color of it was like fire. And I took it, and drank, and when
I had drunk it, my heart gushed forth understanding, and
wisdom grew in my breast, for my spirit retained its
41 memory, and my mouth opened and was no longer closed.
42 Moreover, the Most High gave understanding to the five
men, and they wrote what was said, one after another, in
letters that they did not know. And they stayed forty days;
43 they wrote in the daytime, and ate their bread at night; but
44 I spoke by day and was not silent at night. In forty days
45 ninety-four books were written. And it came to pass, when
the forty days were over, that the Most High spoke to me
and said,

"Publish the twenty-four books that you wrote first, for
46 the worthy and the unworthy to read, but keep the seventy
books that were written last, to hand down to the wise men
47 among your people, for in them is the source of understanding, and the spring of wisdom, and the stream of knowl-
48 edge." And I did so, [in the seventh year, in the sixth week,
after five thousand years of the creation, and three months
and twelve days.

Then Ezra was caught up, and taken to the land of those
who were like him, after he had written all this. And he was

called the scribe of the knowledge of the Most High forever
and ever.]

(*The oriental versions end with this bracketed conclusion, which
is absent from the Latin.*)

"Behold, speak in the hearing of my people the words of [15
prophecy which I will put in your mouth," says the Lord,
"and have them written on paper, for they are trustworthy 2
and true. Do not fear what they imagine against you, or let 3
the unbelief of those who oppose you trouble you. For all 4
unbelievers will die in their unbelief.

"Behold," says the Lord, "I will bring evils upon the 5
whole world, the sword and famine and death and destruction. For wickedness has spread over the whole earth, and 6
their harmful doings are complete. Therefore," says the 7
Lord, "I will not be silent any longer about their ungodly 8
acts which they impiously commit, or endure them in their
wicked practices. Behold, innocent and upright blood cries
to me, and the souls of the upright cry out continually. I 9
will certainly avenge them," says the Lord, "and all innocent blood I will require of them for myself. Behold, my 10
people is led to slaughter like a flock; I will not suffer them
to live in the land of Egypt any longer, but I will bring them 11
out with a strong hand and an outstretched arm, and I will
strike Egypt with plague as I did before, and destroy all its
land. Let Egypt lament, and its foundations, for the 12
plague of punishment and correction that the Lord will
bring upon it. Let the farmers who cultivate the soil lament, 13
for their grain will fail, and their trees will be destroyed
by blight and hail and a fearful star. Alas for the world 14
and those who live in it! For the sword and their destruc- 15
tion have drawn near, and nation will rise against nation to
fight, with swords in their hands. For there will be incon- 16
stancy among men; they will grow strong, one party against

15:1-16

another, and have no regard for their king or the chief of
17 their princes, in their strength. For a man will want to enter
18 a city, and will not be able. For because of their pride, the
cities will be in confusion, the houses will be wiped out, men
19 will be afraid. A man will not have pity on his neighbor,
when it comes to making an attack on their houses with the
sword, and plundering their property, because of hunger
for bread, and because of great distress.

20   "Behold, I will call together," says God, "all the kings of
the earth, to fear me, from the sunrise and from the south,
from the east and from Lebanon, to turn and give back
21 what they have given them. For as they have done unto this
day to my chosen, I will do, and will pay it back into their
22 laps." This is what the Lord God says: "My right hand
will not spare the sinners, and my sword will not cease from
23 those who shed innocent blood on the earth." And a fire
went forth from his wrath, and consumed the foundations
24 of the earth and the sinners like burnt straw. "Alas for those
who sin, and do not keep my commandments," says the
25 Lord; "I will not spare them. Begone, you rebellious sons,
26 do not pollute my sanctuary." For the Lord knows all who
offend against him, therefore he has given them up to die
27 and to be killed. For now disasters have come upon the whole
world, and you will stay among them, for God will not deliver you, because you have sinned against him.

28   Behold, a dreadful vision, appearing from the east!
29 And the nations of Arabian serpents will come out with
many chariots, and from the day they set out, their hissing
will be carried over the earth, so that all who hear them will
30 fear and tremble. The Carmonians will come out frantic
with anger, like wild boars from the forest, and they will
come in great strength, and engage them in battle, and will
31 lay waste a part of the land of Assyria with their teeth. And

15:17-31

afterward the serpents, mindful of their origin, will prevail, and if they conspire in great strength and turn to pursue them, they also will be thrown into confusion and be 32 silenced by their strength, and turn and flee. And from the 33 land of Assyria a waylayer will beset them and destroy one of them, and fear and trembling will come upon their army, and indecision upon their kings.

Behold, clouds from the east, and from the north to the 34 south, and their appearance is very dreadful, full of wrath and storm; and they will strike against one another, and will 35 shed an abundance of stars upon the earth, and their own star, and there will be blood from the sword up to a horse's belly and a man's thigh and a camel's hock, and there will 36,37 be great fear and trembling on the earth, and those who witness that wrath will shudder, and trembling will seize them. And, after that, heavy rainstorms will come from the 38 the south and the north, and another part from the west. And winds from the east will grow strong, and will reveal 39 it, and the cloud that he raised in his wrath, and the star will be driven violently from the east to the south and west to produce destruction. And great clouds will rise, huge and 40 angry, with the star, to destroy all the earth and its inhabitants, and they will pour over every deep and height a dreadful star, fire and hail and flying swords and floods 41 of water, so that all the fields and streams will be filled with the abundance of those waters. And they will break down 42 cities and walls and mountains and hills and forest trees and grass in the meadows and their grain. And they will 43 cross over steadily to Babylon and destroy her. They will 44 come to her and surround her and pour out the star and all its wrath upon her, and the dust and smoke will go up to heaven, and they will all lament her, round about her. And 45 those who survive will serve those who have destroyed her.

15:32–45

46 And you, Asia, partner of the beauty of Babylon, and the
47 glory of her person, alas for you, poor wretch, because you
have become like her; you have ornamented your daughters
in immorality to please and glory in your lovers, who have
48 always desired you! You have imitated that hateful adul-
teress in all her deeds and devices. Therefore, God says,
49 "I will send misfortunes upon you, widowhood, poverty,
famine, the sword, pestilence, to lay waste your houses
50 and bring them to destruction and death. And the glory of
your strength will dry up like a flower, when the heat that is
51 directed upon you rises. And you will grow weak like a poor
creature beaten with stripes and wounds, so that you cannot
52 receive your heroes and lovers. Would I act against you
53 with such zeal," says the Lord, "if you had not always killed
my chosen, exulting and clapping your hands, and speak-
54 ing over their dead bodies, drunk as you were? So adorn the
55 beauty of your face! A prostitute's wages will be in your
56 lap, so you will receive your recompense. As you shall do
to my chosen," says the Lord, "so God will do to you, and he
57 will deliver you to misfortunes. And your children will die
of hunger, and you will fall by the sword, and your cities
will be destroyed and all your people in the country will fall
58 by the sword, and those who are in the mountains will
perish with hunger, and will eat their own flesh and drink
their own blood in their hunger for bread and thirst for
59 water. Unhappy beyond others, you will come and endure
60 fresh afflictions. And as they pass by they will crush the unprofitable city, and destroy a part of your land, and do away
with a portion of your glory, as they return from the de-
61 struction of Babylon. And you will be demolished by them
62 like stubble, and they will be like fire to you. And they will
devour you and your cities, your land and your mountains,
63 all your forests and fruit trees they will burn with fire. They

15:46–63

will carry your sons away as captives, and take your wealth as plunder, and spoil the beauty of your face."

Alas for you, Babylon and Asia! Alas for you, Egypt and [16 Syria! Put on sackcloth and haircloth, and bewail your sons 2 and lament them, for your destruction is at hand. The 3 sword has been sent upon you, and who is there to turn it aside? A fire has been sent upon you, and who is there to put 4 it out? Misfortunes have been sent upon you, and who is 5 there to drive them away? Can one drive off a hungry lion 6 in a forest, or put out a fire in the stubble, when it has once begun to burn? Can one turn back an arrow shot by a 7 strong archer? If the Lord God sends misfortunes, who can 8 turn them back? When fire goes out from his wrath, who is 9 there to put it out? When he lightens, who will not fear? 10 When he thunders, who will not shudder? When the Lord 11 threatens, who will not be utterly destroyed at his presence? The earth trembles to its foundations, the sea is stirred to 12 its depths, and its waves are thrown into confusion, and its fish also, at the presence of the Lord, and the glory of his might. For his right arm that bends the bow is strong, his 13 arrows that he shoots are sharp; they will not miss when they begin to be shot to the ends of the earth. Behold, disasters 14 are shot forth, and they will not return until they come upon the earth. A fire is lighted, and will not be put out, until it 15 consumes the foundations of the earth. Just as an arrow shot 16 by a strong archer does not come back, so the disasters which shall be shot at the earth will not turn back. Alas for 17 me! Who will deliver me in those days?

It is the beginning of sorrows, when there will be great 18 mourning; the beginning of famine, when many will perish; the beginning of wars, when powers will fear; the beginning of disasters, when all will tremble. What will they do in these circumstances, when disasters come? Behold, famine 19

16:1-19

and pestilence and distress and anguish are sent as scourges
20 to correct men. But in spite of all these things they will not
turn from their wickedness, or ever remember the scourges.
21 Behold, grain will be so cheap on the earth that they will
think they are sure of peace, and then disasters will spring up
22 on the earth—the sword, famine, and great disorder. For
many who live on the earth will die of hunger, and the rest
23 who survive the famine the sword will destroy. And the
dead will be thrown out like dung, and there will be no one
to comfort them; for the earth will be left desolate, and its
24 cities will be torn down. There will be nobody left to culti-
25 vate the ground and sow it. The trees will bear fruit, but
26 who will gather it? The grapes will ripen, but who will
tread them? For there will be a great deserting of the land
27 here and there. For one man will long to see another, or to
28 hear his voice. For ten will be left, out of a city, and two, out
of a field, who have hidden in the thick woods and the clefts
29 of the rocks. Just as in an olive orchard, three or four
30 olives may be left on each tree, or when the grapes are
gathered in a vineyard, some clusters are left by those who
31 search the vineyard carefully, so in those days three or four
will be left by those who search their houses with the sword.
32 And the earth will be left desolate, and its fields will be given
up to briars, and all its roads and paths will grow thorns,
33 because no sheep will go along them. Girls will grieve, because they have no bridegrooms, women will grieve because
they have no husbands, their daughters will grieve because
34 they have no help. Their bridegrooms will be destroyed
in war, and their husbands will die of hunger.

35 But listen to these things, and understand them, you
36 slaves of the Lord! Behold, it is the word of the Lord; receive it, do not disbelieve the things of which the Lord
37 says, "Behold, disasters are approaching and they are not

16:20–37

delayed." Just as a woman with child, in the ninth month, 38
when the hour of her delivery draws near, two or three hours
before it, is seized with agonizing pains about her womb,
and when the child comes forth from the womb it will not
delay for a moment, so these disasters will not delay in com- 39
ing upon the earth, and the world will groan and pains will
envelop it.

"Hear my word, my people, prepare for battle, and in the 40
midst of these disasters be like strangers in the earth; let him 41
who sells do it as though he would have to flee; and let him
who buys do it as though he would lose it; let him who 42
trades do it as though he would get no profit; and let him
who builds build as though he were not going to live in
what he builds; let him who sows do it as though he were not 43
to reap, and let him who prunes do it as though he were not
to gather the grapes; let those who marry do it as though 44
they were not to have sons, and those who do not marry as
though they were widowed. Because those who toil, toil in 45
vain, for strangers will gather their fruits, and plunder their 46
property, and overthrow their houses and take their sons
captive, for they produce their children for captivity and
famine. And those who do business do it to be plundered; 47
the more they adorn their cities and their houses and their
possessions and their persons, the angrier I will be with them 48
for their sins," says the Lord. Just as a respectable and virtu- 49
ous woman abhors a prostitute, so uprightness will abhor 50
wickedness, when she adorns herself, and will accuse her to
her face, when he comes who is to defend him who seeks out
every sin on the earth.

Therefore do not be like her or her works. For behold, 51,52
in a little while, wickedness will be removed from the earth,
and uprightness will reign over us. Let no sinner say he 53
has not sinned, for he will burn fiery coals upon the head

16:38–53

of him who says, "I have not sinned before God and his
54 glory." Behold, the Lord knows all the doings of men, and
55 their devices, and their thoughts and their hearts. When he
said, "Let the earth be made," it was made, and "Let the
56 heaven be made," it was made. At his command the stars
were established, and he knows the number of the stars.
57 He searches the deep and its treasuries; he has measured
58 the sea and what it holds. He has shut up the sea in the
midst of the waters, and by his command he has hung the
59 earth upon the water. He has stretched the heaven like an
60 arch and based it upon the waters. He has put springs of
water in the desert, and lakes upon the tops of the mountains, so as to send rivers from the heights so that the earth
61 might drink. He formed man, and put a heart in the
midst of his body, and imparted to him breath and life and
62 understanding, and the breath of Almighty God, who created all things and searches out things hidden in secret
63 places. He certainly knows your devices, and what you
think in your hearts. Alas for sinners and those who want to
64 hide their sins! Because the Lord will closely examine all
65 their doings, and prove you all guilty. And you will be put
to shame when your sins are brought out into the sight of
men, and your iniquities rise up to accuse you on that day.
66 What will you do? Or how will you hide your sins in the
67 presence of God and his angels? Behold, God is the judge;
fear him. Give up your sins, and forget your iniquities, and
never practice them again; then God will lead you forth
and deliver you from all distress.

68 For behold, the hot anger of the great multitude is
kindled over you, and some of you they will carry off and
69 make you eat what is sacrificed to idols. And those who
give them their consent they will hold in derision and con-
70 tempt and trample on them. For there will be disturbances

here and there, and in near-by cities a great uprising
against those who fear the Lord. They will be like madmen, 71
sparing no one, in plundering and pillaging those who still
fear the Lord. For they will pillage and plunder their 72
property, and drive them out of their houses. Then will 73
appear the testing of my chosen, like gold which is tested by
fire.

"Listen, my chosen," says the Lord. "Behold, the days 74
of persecution are here, and I will deliver you from them.
Do not fear or doubt, for God is your guide. And you who 75,76
keep my commandments and precepts," says the Lord God,
"let not your sins drag you down, or your wickedness prevail
over you. Alas for those who are bound by their sins and 77
covered with their wickedness, as a field is overgrown with
woods, and its grain so covered with thorns that no one can
get through. It is shut out, and left to be consumed by 78
fire."

16:71-78

THE BOOK OF TOBIT

The author of this skillfully constructed and charming piece of religious fiction has adapted and combined the story of Ahikar (of which Aramaic papyri of the fifth century B.C. have been found in Egypt), the story of the grateful dead (of which there is an early version in Cicero, De divinatione *1.27*), and the Egyptian tractate of Khons, which told how a demon was cast out of a princess. It is possible that our book was intended as a corrective to the story of Khons. The sustained tension, certain of the narrative techniques, and even the pious objectives of Tobit are reminiscent of Hellenistic romance, but the characterization is superior and the piety more deeply felt and contagious. The personages engage our sympathy as human beings, and their religious devotion is intimate and humane. The prayers they offer follow the patterns of public ritual, but they are genuinely moving cries of the heart. Tobit is probably to be dated to the beginning of the second century B.C. The new emergence of individuality and of personal religion and the fusion of elements from disparate sources which it illustrates are characteristic phenomena of the Hellenistic age, in the west as well as the east.

The three great manuscripts of the Greek Bible differ in their texts of Tobit. The present translation follows tradition in presenting the text of the Vaticanus and Alexandrinus; the Sinaiticus may represent an older text.

THE BOOK OF TOBIT

1} THE STORY OF TOBIT, THE SON OF TOBIEL, the son of Hananiel, the son of Aduel, the son of Gabael, of the stock of Asael, of the tribe of Naphtali,

2 who in the days of Shalmaneser, king of Assyria, was carried into captivity from Thisbe, which is to the south of Kedesh Naphtali in Galilee above Asher.

3 I, Tobit, walked all the days of my life in ways of truth and uprightness. I did many acts of charity for my brothers and my nation who were taken to the land of the Assyrians,

4 to Nineveh, with me. And when I was in my own country, in the land of Israel, when I was young, the whole tribe of my forefather Naphtali revolted from the house in Jerusalem, which had been chosen from all the tribes of Israel for all the tribes to offer sacrifice in, and in which the temple of the dwelling of the Most High had been dedicated and built for all ages.

5 So all the tribes which had revolted with it would offer
6 sacrifice to the heifer Baal. But I alone went many a time to Jerusalem for the festivals, as the Scripture commands all Israel in an everlasting decree, taking with me the first fruits and the tenth parts of my crops and my first shearings, and I would give them to the priests, the sons of Aaron, at the
7 altar. A tenth part of all my produce I would give to the sons of Levi, who officiated at Jerusalem, and another tenth I would sell, and go and spend the proceeds in Jerusalem
8 each year, and a third tenth I would give to those to whom it was fitting to give it, as Deborah my grandmother had instructed me—for I was left an orphan by my father.

9 When I became a man, I married Hannah, who was of
10 the stock of our family, and by her I had a son, Tobias. And when I was carried into captivity to Nineveh, all my
11 brothers and relatives ate the food of the heathen, but I

kept myself from eating it, because I remembered God with 12
all my heart. And the Most High gave me favor and stand- 13
ing with Shalmaneser, and I became his buyer. I made a 14
journey to Media, and deposited ten talents of silver with
Gabael, the brother of Gabrias, in Ragae, in Media. But 15
when Shalmaneser died, his son Sennacherib became king
in his place, and the highways were unsafe, so that I could
no longer travel to Media.

In the times of Shalmaneser I used to do many acts of 16
charity for my brothers. I would give my bread to the
hungry and my clothes to the naked, and if I saw one of my 17
people dead and thrown outside the wall of Nineveh, I
would bury him. And if Sennacherib the king killed anyone 18
who had come as a fugitive from Judea, I buried them
secretly, for he killed many in his anger, and their bodies
were looked for by the king and could not be found. But 19
one of the Ninevites went and informed the king about me,
that I was burying them, and I hid, and when I learned that
I was being sought for, to be put to death, I was frightened
and escaped. Then all my property was seized, and nothing 20
was left me but my wife Hannah and my son Tobias.

Before fifty days had passed, his two sons killed him, and 21
fled into the mountains of Ararat, and Esarhaddon his son
became king in his place. He appointed Ahiqar, my brother
Hanael's son, to have charge of all the accounting of his
kingdom and all its administration. And Ahiqar asked for 22
me, and I went to Nineveh. Ahiqar was cupbearer and
keeper of the signet and had charge of administration and
of the accounts; Esarhaddon appointed him second to himself, and he was my nephew.

When I reached my home and my wife Hannah was re- [2
stored to me, and Tobias my son, at the Harvest Festival,
which is the feast of the Seven Weeks, a good dinner was

1:12–2:1

2 prepared for me, and I sat down to eat. And I saw the abundance of food, and I said to my son,

"Go and bring any poor man of our brothers whom you can find, who remembers the Lord, and I will wait for you."

3 And he came back and said,

"Father, one of our race has been strangled and thrown out in the bazaar!"

4 Then before I tasted anything I rushed out and brought
5 him into a room until the sun set. Then I returned and
6 washed myself and ate my food in sadness; and I remembered the prophecy of Amos, as he said,

Your feasts will be turned into sorrow,
And all your good cheer into lamentation.

7 And I wept aloud.

And when the sun was set, I went and dug a grave and
8 buried him. And my neighbors laughed at me and said, "He is not yet afraid of being put to death for doing this. He ran away, and here he is burying the dead again."

9 That same night, after I had buried him, I returned, and as I was ceremonially defiled, I lay down to sleep by the
10 wall of the courtyard, with my face uncovered, And I did not know that there were sparrows in the wall above me, and, as my eyes were open, the sparrows' droppings fell into my eyes and produced white films on them; and I went to the physicians, and they could not help me. But Ahiqar supported me for two years, until he went to Elymais.

11 Then my wife Hannah found employment at women's
12 work, and sent the work back to its owners, and they paid
13 her wages, and gave her a kid besides. But when she came home to me, the kid began to bleat. And I said to her,

"Where did this kid come from? Is it stolen? Give it back to its owners, for we have no right to eat anything that is stolen."

But she said to me,   14
"It was given me as a gift, in addition to my wages."
But I would not believe her, and told her to give it back
to its owners, and I blushed for her. Then she answered
and said to me,
"And where are your charities? Where is your uprightness? Of course you know everything!"
Then I was grieved, and wept, and I prayed sorrowfully, [3
and said,
"Lord, you are upright, and all your doings and all your   2
ways are mercy and truth, and you always judge truly and
justly. Remember me and look upon me; do not take   3
vengeance on me for my sins and my ignorant acts, and for
those of my forefathers, which they committed in your
sight, for they disobeyed your commands. You have given   4
us up to pillage and captivity and death, and made us a
proverb and a reproach among all the nations among
whom we have been scattered. And now your judgments   5
which are many are right, in exacting from me for my sins
and those of my forefathers, because we did not keep your
commandments, for we have not walked uprightly before
you. So now deal with me according to your pleasure;   6
command my spirit to be taken from me, so that I may be
released and return to dust, for I had rather die than live,
because I have had to listen to false reproaches, and have
felt great sorrow. Command me to be released from this
distress and taken to my everlasting place of abode; do not
turn your face away from me."
On that very day, it happened to Sarah, the daughter of   7
Raguel, in Ecbatana in Media, that she too was reproached
by her father's maids, because she had been married to   8
seven husbands, and the wicked demon Asmodeus had killed

them before they had been with her as is customary with wives. They said to her,

"Do you not know that you strangle your husbands? You have already had seven, and you have not borne the name 9 of one of them. Why do you torment us? If they are dead, go after them! May we never see son or daughter of yours!"

10 When she heard these things, she was deeply hurt, and wished to hang herself, but she said,

"I am my father's only child; if I do this, it will disgrace him, and I will bring his old age down to the grave in sorrow."

11 And she prayed by her window, and said,

"Blessed are you, O Lord, my God, and blessed be your holy and honored name forever; may all your works bless 12 you forever. And now, Lord, I turn my face and my eyes 13 to you; command me to be released from the earth and to 14 hear reproach no more. You know, Lord, that I am inno- 15 cent of any sin with man; I have never defiled my name, or the name of my father, in the land of my captivity. I am my father's only child; he has no other child to be his heir. He has no brother near him or nephew whom I should keep myself to marry. I have already lost seven husbands; why must I live any longer? And if it is not your pleasure to kill me, command that some regard be had for me, and some pity be shown me, and that I no more may have to listen to reproach."

16 And the prayer of both of them was heard in the presence 17 of the glory of the great Raphael, and he was sent to cure them both; for Tobit, to remove the white films, and to give Sarah, the daughter of Raguel, to Tobit's son Tobias, as his wife, and to bind Asmodeus, the wicked demon, be- cause Tobias was entitled to possess her. So at the same

3:9–17

time, Tobit went into his house, and Sarah, the daughter
of Raguel, came down from her upstairs room.

On that day Tobit remembered the money that he had [4
deposited with Gabael in Ragae in Media. And he said to 2
himself,

"I have asked for death; why should I not call my son
Tobias, to explain to him before I die?"

So he called him, and said, 3

"My boy, when I die, bury me, and do not neglect your
mother; provide for her as long as you live; do what is
pleasing to her, and do not grieve her in anything. Remem- 4
ber, my boy, that she faced many dangers for you before
your birth, and when she dies, bury her beside me in one
grave. All your life, my boy, remember the Lord, our God; 5
do not consent to sin and transgress his commands. Act
uprightly all your life, and do not walk in the ways of wrongdoing.

"For if you do right, prosperity will attend your under- 6
takings. To all who act uprightly, give charity from your
property, and do not let your eye begrudge what you give
to charity. Do not turn your face away from any poor man,
and God's face will not be turned away from you. Give to 7
charity in proportion to what you have; if you have little, 8
do not be afraid to give sparingly to charity, for then you 9
will lay up a good treasure for yourself against a day of adversity; for charity will save you from death, and keep you 10
from going down into darkness. Charity is a good offering 11
in the sight of the Most High for all who give it.

"My boy, beware of any immorality. First, take a wife 12
who is of the stock of your forefathers; do not marry an alien,
who does not belong to your father's tribe, for we are the
sons of the prophets. Remember, my boy, that Noah, Abraham, Isaac, and Jacob, our forefathers of old, all married

wives from among their kindred, and were blessed in their
13 children, and their posterity will possess the land. Now, my
boy, love your kindred, and do not disdain your brothers
and the sons and daughters of your people and refuse to
marry one of them. For such disdain leads to ruin and great
distress, and worthlessness brings loss and great want, for
14 worthlessness is the mother of famine. The wages of any
man who works for you, you must not retain overnight, but
you must pay him immediately. If you serve God, you will
be rewarded. Take care, my boy, in all that you do, and be
15 well disciplined in all your conduct. Do not do to anyone
else what you hate. Do not drink wine to the point of intoxi-
cation; drunkenness must not go with you on your way.
16 Give some of your bread to the hungry and of your clothes
to the naked. Give all your surplus to charity, and do not let
17 your eye begrudge what you give to charity. Scatter your
bread on the graves of the upright, but do not give to
sinners.
18 "Ask advice of every wise man, and do not think lightly
19 of any useful advice. Always bless the Lord God, and ask
him to make your ways straight and your paths and plans
prosper. For no heathen nation possesses understanding,
but the Lord gives all good things, and he humbles whoever he pleases, as he chooses.

"Now, my boy, remember my commands; do not let them
20 be blotted from your mind. And now I must inform you
of the ten talents of silver that I deposited with Gabael, son
21 of Gabrias, in Ragae in Media. Do not be afraid, my boy,
because we have become poor. You are well off, if you fear
God and refrain from any sin, and do what is pleasing in his
sight."

5] Then Tobias answered and said to him,

"Father, I will do all that you have commanded me. But how can I get the money, when I do not know him?" 2

So he gave him the receipt, and said to him, 3

"Seek out a man to go with you, and I will pay him wages, as long as I live; so go and get the money."

And he went to look for a man, and found Raphael, who 4 was an angel, though Tobias did not know it. And he said 5 to him,

"Can I go with you to Ragae in Media, and do you know that region?"

And the angel said to him, 6

"I will go with you, for I know the way, and I have stayed with our brother Gabael."

And Tobias said to him, 7

"Wait for me, and I will tell my father."

And he said to him, 8

"Go, and do not delay."

And he went in and said to his father,

"Here I have found a man who will go with me."

And he said,

"Call him to me, so that I may find out what tribe he belongs to and whether he is a reliable man to go with you."

So he called him, and he came in, and they greeted each 9 other. And Tobit said to him, 10

"Brother, to what tribe and to what family do you belong? Inform me."

And he said to him, 11

"Are you in search of a tribe and family, or a hired man to go with your son?"

And Tobit said to him,

"I only want to learn your connections and your name, brother."

And he said, 12

5:2-12

"I am Azariah, the son of Hananiah the older, one of your kinsmen."

13 And he said to him,

"Welcome, brother! Do not be angry with me for trying to learn your tribe and your family; you are a kinsman of mine, and come of a fine, good lineage. For I came to know Hananiah and Jathan, the sons of Shemaiah the older, when we used to travel to Jerusalem together to worship and offer our first-born cattle and the tenths of our produce, for they did not go astray when our brothers did; you come of

14 a fine stock, brother. But tell me what wages I am to give you; a drachma a day and your expenses and my son's?

15 And I will add to your wages besides, if you come back safe and sound."

16 So they agreed on these terms. And he said to Tobias, "Get ready for the journey, and farewell."

So his son made his preparations for the journey, and his father said to him,

"Go with this man, and God who lives in heaven will prosper your journey, and let his angel go with you,"

And they both went out to start, and the boy's dog followed them.

17 And his mother Hannah wept, and she said to Tobit,

"Why have you sent our child away? Is he not our walk-

18 ing-stick when he goes in and out before us? Do not let money be added to money, but let it be as dirt in compari-

19 son with our child. For while the Lord lets us live, that is enough for us."

20 And Tobit said to her,

"Do not be troubled, my sister. He will come back safe

21 and sound, and your eyes will see him. For a good angel will go with him, and he will have a prosperous journey, and will come back safe and sound."

5:13-21

So she stopped crying. 22

And they went on their way and came toward evening to [6 the river Tigris and there they spent the night. And the boy 2 went to wash himself, and a fish jumped out of the river and would have swallowed the boy. But the angel said to him, 3 "Take hold of the fish!"

And the boy seized the fish and threw it up on the land. And the angel said to him, 4

"Cut the fish up, and take its heart and liver and gall and keep them safe."

And the boy did as the angel told him, and they cooked 5 the fish and ate it. And they both traveled on until they drew near Ecbatana. And the boy said to the angel, 6

"Brother Azariah, what are the liver and heart and gall of the fish good for?"

And he said to him, 7

"As for the heart and the liver, if anyone is troubled with a demon or an evil spirit, you must make a smoke of them before the man or the woman, and they will be troubled no more. And as for the gall, if you rub it on a man who has 8 white films over his eyes, he will be cured."

When they approached Ragae, the angel said to the boy, 9,10

"Brother, we will stop today with Raguel, for he is your relative. He has an only daughter, named Sarah. I am going to tell him to give her to you in marriage, for you have a 11 right to have her, for you are her only relative, and she is 12 beautiful and sensible. So now if you will listen to me, I will speak to her father, and when we come back from Ragae, we will perform the marriage. For I know that by the law of Moses Raguel cannot marry her to anyone else under pain of death, for it is your right and no one else's to possess her."

Then the boy said to the angel, 13

5:22–6:13

"Brother Azariah, I have heard that this girl has been given in marriage to seven husbands and they all perished
14 in the bridal chamber. Now I am my father's only child, and I am afraid that if I go in, I will die like the others, for a demon is in love with her, and he harms only those who approach her. So I am afraid that I would die and bring my father's and my mother's life to the grave in sorrow over me; and they have no other son to bury them."

15 And the angel said to him,

"Don't you remember the commands your father gave you, about your taking a wife from your own relatives? Now you must listen to me, brother, for she must be your wife, and don't be concerned about the demon, for she will be
16 given to you tonight to be your wife. And when you go into the bridal chamber, you must take some of the ashes of the incense, and put on them some of the heart and the liver of
17 the fish, and make a smoke, and the demon will smell it and will flee and never come back. And when you go up to her, you must both rise up and cry out to the merciful God, and he will save you and have mercy on you. Have no fear, for she was destined for you from the beginning, and you will save her, and she will go home with you, and I suppose you will have children by her."

When Tobias heard this, he loved her, and he became deeply attached to her.

7] When they arrived at Ecbatana, they went to the house of Raguel, and Sarah met them and welcomed them, and
2 they greeted her, and she took them into the house. And Raguel said to Edna his wife,

"How much this young man resembles my cousin Tobit!"
3 And Raguel asked them,
"Where are you from, brothers?"
And they said to him,

6:14–7:3

"We belong to the sons of Naphtali who are in captivity in Nineveh."

And he said to them, 4

"Do you know our kinsman Tobit?"

And they said,

"We do."

And he said to them,

"Is he well?"

And they said, 5

"He is alive and well."

And Tobias said,

"He is my father!"

Then Raguel sprang up and kissed him, and he wept, 6 and blessed him, and said to him, 7

"You are the son of that fine, good man!"

And when he heard that Tobit had lost his eyesight, he was grieved, and wept, and his wife Edna and his daughter 8 Sarah wept too. And they welcomed them warmly, and they slaughtered a ram from the flock, and set food before them in abundance.

Then Tobias said to Raphael,

"Brother Azariah, speak about the things you talked of on our journey, and let that matter be settled."

So he communicated the matter to Raguel, and Raguel 9 said to Tobias,

"Eat, drink and be merry, for you have the right to take 10 my child. But I must reveal the truth to you. I have given 11 my child to seven husbands, and whenever they approached her, they died the same night. Still, for the present be merry."

And Tobias said,

"I will eat nothing here until you make a binding agreement with me to do this."

7:4-11

12 Then Raguel said,

"Take her at once according to the ordinance; you are her relative, and she belongs to you; and the merciful God will give you the greatest prosperity."

13 And he called in his daughter Sarah, and he took her by the hand and gave her to Tobias to be his wife, and said,

"Here, take her according to the law of Moses, and take her back to your father."

14 And he gave them his blessing. And he called in Edna his wife, and he took a scroll and wrote an agreement, and they
15 put their seals to it. Then they began to eat.

16 Then Raguel called Edna his wife aside and said to her,

"My sister, get the other bed chamber ready, and take her into it."

17 And she did as he told her, and took her into it, and she wept. And she let her daughter weep on her shoulder, and she said to her,

18 "Courage, my child! The Lord of heaven and earth show you favor instead of this grief of yours! Courage, my daughter!"

8] When they had finished supper, they took Tobias in to her.
2 And as he went, he remembered what Raphael had said, and took the ashes of the incense and put the heart and the liver
3 of the fish on them and made a smoke. And when the demon smelled the smoke, he fled to the farthest parts of Up-
4 per Egypt, and the angel bound him there. When they were both shut in together, Tobias got up from the bed and said,

"Get up, my sister, and let us pray that the Lord will have mercy upon us."

5 And he began to say,

"Blessed are you, God of our forefathers, and blessed be your holy and glorious name forever. Let the heavens and
6 all your creation bless you. You made Adam and gave him

his wife Eve as a helper and support, and from them came
the human race. You said, 'It is not good that the man
should be alone; let us make him a helper like himself.'
Now, Lord, it is not because of lust that I take my sister   7
here, but in truth. Have mercy on me, and let me grow old
with her."

And she said "Amen" with him; and they both slept all 8, 9
night.

And Raguel got up and went and dug a grave, for he said,
"Perhaps he will die too."   10

Then Raguel went into his house and said to his wife 11,12
Edna,

"Send one of the maids and let them see whether he is
alive, and if he is not, let us bury him without letting anyone
know."

And the maid opened the door and went in, and found   13
them both asleep. And she came out and told them that he 14
was alive. Then Raguel blessed God, and said,   15

"Blessed are you, O God, with every pure and holy bless- 16
ing! Let your saints and all your creation bless you, and
let all your angels and your chosen people bless you forever.
You are blessed because you have had mercy on two only   17
children; Lord, show them mercy; grant that they may live
to the end in health, with gladness and mercy."

Then he ordered his servants to fill up the grave. And he 18,19
made them a marriage feast that lasted fourteen days. And 20
Raguel swore to him before the days of the marriage feast
were over that he must not leave until the fourteen days of
the marriage feast were past, and then he should take half   21
of Raguel's property and return in safety to his father. "The
rest," he said, "will be yours when I and my wife die."

And Tobias called Raphael and said to him,   [9
"Brother Azariah, take with you a servant and two   2

camels, and go to Gabael, in Ragae in Media, and get me
3 the money and bring him to the marriage feast. For Raguel
4 has sworn that I must not leave, and my father is counting
the days, and if I delay long, he will be greatly grieved."

5 So Raphael went and spent the night with Gabael, and
gave him the receipt, and he brought out the bags with their
6 seals unbroken, and gave them to him. And they got up
early in the morning together, and came to the marriage
feast; and Tobias blessed his wife.

10] Now his father Tobit was counting each day. And when
the days required for the journey were past and they did not
2 come back, he said,

"Is it possible that they have been disappointed? Or is
Gabael perhaps dead, and there is no one to give him the
money?"

3, 4 And he was greatly distressed. And his wife said to him,
"The child has perished; that is why he has taken so
long."

And she began to bewail him, and said,

5 "Do I not care, my child, because I let you go, you light
of my eyes?"

6 And Tobit said to her,
"Be quiet, have no concern; he is all right."

7 And she said to him,
"Be quiet, do not deceive me; my child has perished."

And every day she would go down the road by which he
had left, and in the daytime she refused to eat, and through
the night she never ceased to bewail her son Tobias until the
fourteen days of the marriage feast, which Raguel had sworn
he must spend there, were over.

Then Tobias said to Raguel,
"Let me go, for my father and my mother are giving up
all hope of ever seeing me again."

9:3–10:7

But his father-in-law said to him,   8
"Stay with me, and I will send to your father, and they
will explain to him about you."

And Tobias said,   9
"No, send me to my father."

Then Raguel got up and gave him his wife Sarah and half 10
of his property, slaves and cattle and money. And he blessed 11
them as he let them go, and said,

"The God of heaven will give you prosperity, my children, before I die."

And he said to his daughter,   12
"Respect your father-in-law and your mother-in-law,
they are now your parents. Let me hear a good report of
you."

And he kissed her. And Edna said to Tobias,
"May the Lord of heaven bring you back safely, dear
brother, and grant that I may see your children by my
daughter Sarah, so that I may be glad before the Lord.
Here I solemnly intrust my daughter to you; do not hurt
her feelings."

After that, Tobias set off, praising God, because he had [11
prospered him on his journey, and he blessed Raguel and his
wife Edna.

He went on until they approached Nineveh. And   2
Raphael said to Tobias,

"Do you not know, brother, how you left your father?
Let us run ahead, before your wife, and get the house ready. 3
But take the gall of the fish in your hand."   4

So they went, and the dog went along after them.

And Hannah sat looking down the road for her boy.   5
And she saw him coming, and she said to his father,   6

"Here comes your son, and the man who went with him!"

And Raphael said,   7

8 "I know that your father will open his eyes; so you rub the gall on his eyes, and he will feel the sting and will rub them, and remove the white films, and he will see you."

9 And Hannah ran to meet them and fell on her son's neck and said to him,

"Now that I have seen you, my child, I am ready to die."

10 And they both wept. And Tobit came out to the door,
11 and he stumbled, and his son ran up to him and he took hold of his father and sprinkled the gall on his father's eyes, saying,

"Courage, father!"

12 And when his eyes began to smart, he rubbed them,
13 and the white films scaled off from the corners of his eyes.
14 And when he saw his son, he fell on his neck and wept, and said,

"Blessed are you, O God, and blessed is your name for-
15 ever, and blessed are all your holy angels. For though you have flogged me, you have had mercy on me; here I can see Tobias, my son."

And his son went in rejoicing, and told his father the wonderful things that had happened to him in Media.

16 So Tobit went out rejoicing to meet his daughter-in-law, at the gate of Nineveh. And those who saw him go were
17 amazed, because he had received his sight. And Tobit gave thanks before them, because God had had mercy on him. And when Tobit came up to Sarah his daughter-in-law, he blessed her, saying,

"Welcome, daughter! Blessed is God, who has brought you to us, and blessed are your father and your mother."

And there was rejoicing among all his brothers in
18 Nineveh. And Ahiqar and Nasbas his nephew came,
19 and Tobias' marriage feast was held for seven days, with great gladness.

11:8–19

Then Tobit called his son Tobias and said to him,   {12
"My child, see to the wages of the man who went with
you, for we must give him more."

And he said to him,   2
"Father, I can afford to give him half of what I brought
back, for he has brought me back to you safe and sound,   3
and he cured my wife and he brought me the money, and
besides he has cured you."

And the old man said,   4
"It is due him."

And he called the angel and said to him,   5
"Accept half of all that you brought back."

Then he called them both and said to them in private,   6
"Bless God and give thanks to him. Ascribe majesty to
him, and before all the living acknowledge how he has dealt
with you. It is a good thing to bless God and exalt his name,
declaring God's works and doing them honor, so do not be
slow to give him thanks. It is wise to keep a king's secret, but   7
the works of God should be gloriously revealed. Do good,
and evil will not overtake you. Prayer is good if accom-   8
panied with fasting, charity, and uprightness. A little with
uprightness is better than much with wickedness. It is better
to give to charity than to lay up gold. For charity will save   9
a man from death; it will expiate any sin. Those who give
to charity and act uprightly will have their fill of life; but   10
those who commit sin are the enemies of their own lives.
I will not conceal anything from you; as I said, it is wise to   11
keep a king's secret, but the works of God should be gloriously revealed. So now, when you and your daughter-in-law   12
Sarah prayed, I brought the remembrance of your prayer
before the Holy One. And when you buried the dead, I was
still with you. And when you did not shrink from getting up   13
and leaving your dinner to go and lay out the dead, your

12:1-13

14 good deed did not escape me, but I was with you. So God
15 sent me to cure you and your daughter-in-law Sarah. For I
am Raphael, one of the seven holy angels, who offer up the
prayers of God's people and go into the presence of the glory
of the Holy One!"

16 And they were both confounded, and fell on their faces,
17 for they were terrified. And he said to them,

"Do not be afraid; peace be with you. Bless God forever.
18 For not through any favor on my part but by the will of
19 God I came to you. Therefore bless him forever. All these
days that I appeared to you, I did not eat or drink, but you
20 beheld a vision. Now give thanks to God, for I must go up
to him who sent me, and you must write all that has happened on a scroll."

21,22 And when they got up, they no longer saw him. And they
acknowledged the great, wonderful doings of God, and how
the angel of the Lord had appeared to them.

13] Then Tobit wrote a prayer of rejoicing, and said,
"Blessed be God who lives forever, and blessed be his kingdom,

2 For he flogs, and he has mercy,
He takes men down to Hades, and he brings them up,
And there is no one who can escape his hand.

3 Give thanks to him, Israelites, before the heathen,
For he has scattered you among them.

4 Show his majesty there;
Exalt him in the presence of every living being,
For he is our Lord and God,
He is our father forever.

5 He will flog us for our wrongdoing,
And he will show mercy again and gather us from all the
heathen
Wherever you are scattered.

If you turn to him with all your heart,   6
And with all your soul, to act truly in his sight,
Then he will turn to you,
And he will not hide his face from you.
See how he will deal with you,
And give him thanks with your full voice.
Bless the Lord of Righteousness
And exalt the King of the Ages.
In the land of my captivity I give him thanks,
And I show his might and his majesty to a nation of
    sinners:
'Turn to him, you sinners, and do what is right in his sight;
Who knows but he will be pleased with you, and show you
    mercy?'
I exalt my God,   7
My soul exalts the king of heaven,
And exults in his majesty.
Let all men speak and give him thanks in Jerusalem.   8
O Jerusalem, the holy city,   9
He will flog you for the doings of your sons,
And again he will have mercy on the sons of the upright.
Give thanks to the Lord in goodness,   10
And bless the King of the Ages,
That his tent may be rebuilt in you with joy.
May he make glad in you those who are captives,
And the miserable may he love in you,
To all generations, forever.
Many nations will come from afar to the name of the Lord   11
    God,
Bearing gifts in their hands, gifts for the king of heaven.
Generations of generations will bring you exultation.
Cursed be all who hate you!   12
Blessed forever shall be all who love you.
Rejoice and exult in the sons of the upright,   13

13:6-13

For they will be gathered together, and they will bless
the Lord of the upright.

14 Blessed are those who love you!
They will rejoice in your peace.
Blessed are those who grieved over all your stripes,
For they will be glad about you, when they see all your
glory,
And they will rejoice forever.

15 Let my soul bless God, the great King,

16 For Jerusalem will be built of sapphire and emerald,
And her walls of precious stones,
And her towers and battlements of pure gold;

17 And the streets of Jerusalem will be paved with beryl and
ruby and stones of Ophir,

18 And all her lanes shall say 'Hallelujah,' and shall utter
praise, saying, 'Blessed be God, who has raised you up
forever.' "

14:2] And Tobit ended his thanksgiving. He was fifty-eight
years old when he lost his sight, and eight years later he recovered it; and he gave to charity and continued to fear

3 the Lord his God and to give thanks to him. And when
he had grown very old, he called his son and his son's sons
to him and said to him,

"My child, take your sons; here I have grown old and

4 will soon depart this life. Go to Media, my child, for I firmly believe what Jonah the prophet said about Nineveh,
that it will be destroyed, but in Media there will be peace,
rather than here, for a while, and that our brothers will be
scattered from the good land over the earth, and Jerusalem
will be desolate, and the house of God in it will be burned

5 down, and will be desolate for a time; and then God will
have mercy on them again, and bring them back to their
land; and they will build the house, though not as it was
before, until the times of that age are passed. And afterward

13:14–14:5

they will return from the places of their captivity and rebuild Jerusalem in splendor, and the house of God will be
rebuilt in it gloriously, for all generations forever, as the
prophets said of it. And all the heathen will turn to fear the 6
Lord God in truth, and they will bury their idols, and all   7
the heathen will bless the Lord. And his people will thank
God, and the Lord will uplift his people, and all who love
the Lord God in truth and uprightness will rejoice and show
mercy to our brothers. And now, my child, leave Nineveh,   8
for what the prophet Jonah said will surely happen. But   9
keep the law and the ordinances, and be merciful and upright, so that you may prosper. Bury me properly and my   10
wife beside me. And do not live any longer in Nineveh.
My child, see what Haman did to Ahiqar, who had brought
him up—how he plunged him from light into darkness and
how he requited him! Yet Ahiqar was saved and the other
was recompensed and disappeared in darkness himself.
Manasseh gave to charity, and escaped the fatal snare which
Haman set for him, but Haman fell into the trap and perished. See, my children, what charity can do, and how up-   11
rightness can save!"

As he said this, he breathed his last there in his bed. He
was a hundred and fifty-eight years old; and they gave him
a splendid funeral.

When Hannah died, he buried her beside his father.   12
Then Tobias went back with his wife and his sons to
Ecbatana, to Raguel his father-in-law. And he reached an   13
honored old age, and he gave his father-in-law and his
mother-in-law splendid funerals, and he inherited their
property and his father Tobit's. And he died in Ecbatana   14
in Media, at the age of a hundred and twenty-seven. But   15
before he died he heard of the destruction of Nineveh, which
Nebuchadnezzar and Ahasuerus had captured. So before
he died he rejoiced over Nineveh.

14:6-15

THE BOOK OF JUDITH

By opening his story with a statement that Nebuchadnezzar ruled over the Assyrians in Nineveh when, as every literate reader would know, Nebuchadnezzar ruled over Babylonians in Babylon, the author of Judith virtually gives notice that his work is a fiction. The first portion is obviously influenced by Herodotus' classic account of the apparently irresistible advance of a huge oriental host against a spiritual elect; the telltale "earth and water" (3.7) has come through from the Greek to the Hebrew to the Greek. The deliverance of the spiritual elect, after a stipulated wait of five days, when it had been cut off from water follows a similar story in the Lindian Chronicle. Instead of the goddess Athena the agent of deliverance here is the virtuous Judith. The central episode of her encounter with Holofernes breathes the atmosphere of Greek romance. There is an inevitable incongruity when a heroine of Greek romance is transformed into a stark Jael. But the story maintains its tension to the end, and deserves the popularity it has always enjoyed.

The conjuncture of history into which such an encouraging example of fortitude against overwhelming odds and of the efficacy of dietary observance would fit is the struggle against Antiochus Epiphanes recounted in the Books of the Maccabees. It may be significant that the heroine's name is the feminine of Judah, which was the name of the Maccabean hero. And no king before Antiochus would have insisted on recognition of his own divinity, as Nebuchadnezzar is here (3.8) reported to have done.

THE BOOK OF JUDITH

1] IN THE TWELFTH YEAR OF THE REIGN OF
Nebuchadnezzar, who ruled over the Assyrians in the
great city of Nineveh, in the days when Arphaxad ruled
2 over the Medes in Ecbatana, Arphaxad built around Ecbatana walls of hewn stones four and a half feet wide
and nine feet long. He built the walls a hundred and five
3 feet high and seventy-five feet wide, and at the gates he built
towers a hundred and fifty feet high, with foundations ninety
4 feet wide; and he made its gates, gates that rose to a height
of a hundred and five feet, and were sixty feet wide, so that
his host of warriors could march out and his infantry could
5 form. So in those days King Nebuchadnezzar made war on
King Arphaxad in the Great Plain; this plain is on the
6 borders of Ragae. He was joined by all the inhabitants of
the hill country and all who lived along the Euphrates and
Tigris and Hydaspes, and on the plains of Arioch, king of
Elymais, and many nations joined the army of the Chaldeans.

7 Then Nebuchadnezzar, king of Assyria, sent to all the inhabitants of Persia and to all who lived toward the west, who
were settled in Cilicia and Damascus and the Lebanon and
8 the Antilebanon, and to all who lived along the seacoast,
and to the inhabitants of Carmel and Gilead that were
heathen, and to Upper Galilee and the great plain of
9 Esdraelon, and to all that were in Samaria and its towns,
and beyond Jordan as far as Jerusalem and Betane and
Chelous and Kadesh, and the river of Egypt, Tahpanhes
10 and Raamses and all the land of Goshen, until you pass
Tanis and Memphis, and to all who lived in Egypt, until you
11 reach the borders of Ethiopia. But all the inhabitants of
the land paid no attention to the command of Nebuchadnezzar, king of Assyria, and would not go with him to the

war, for they were not afraid of him, but regarded him as just a single man, and they sent his messengers back disappointed and in disgrace.

Then Nebuchadnezzar was very angry with that whole 12 country, and he swore by his throne and his kingdom that he would certainly take vengeance upon all the regions of Cilicia, Damascus, and Syria, and kill with the sword all the inhabitants of the land of Moab and the Ammonites and all Judea and everybody in Egypt, until you come to the coasts of the two seas. So in the seventeenth year he made 13 war on King Arphaxad, and he overcame him. and put Arphaxad's whole army and all his cavalry and all his chariots to flight, and he took possession of his cities and 14 reached Ecbatana and and took its towers and plundered its bazaars and turned its glory into shame. Then he took 15 Arphaxad captive among the mountains of Ragae, and struck him down with his spears and utterly destroyed him. unto this day. Then he returned with the spoils and all 16 his motley army, a very great body of soldiers, and there he and his army took their ease and feasted for a hundred and twenty days.

In the eighteenth year of his reign, on the twenty-second [2 day of the first month, it was proposed in the palace of Nebuchadnezzar, king of Assyria, to take vengeance on all the land, just as he had said. He called together all his 2 ministers and all his nobles and set before them his secret purpose and fully related all the wickedness of the land with his own lips, and they decreed that all who had not obeyed 3 the command the king had uttered should be destroyed. When he had completed his plan, Nebuchadnezzar, king of 4 Assyria, summoned Holofernes, the general of his army, who was second to himself, and said to him,

"Thus says the Great King, the Lord of all the earth: 5

1:12-2:5

When you go from my presence, you must take with you men confident in their strength to the number of a hundred and twenty thousand infantry and twelve thousand

6 mounted men, and you must go out to attack all the western country, because they have disobeyed the command that I

7 uttered. You must call upon them to prepare earth and water, in token of submission, for I will go against them in my anger and I will cover the whole face of the earth with the feet of my army and I will give them up to them to

8 plunder, and their ravines will be filled with their wounded, and every brook and dashing river will be filled with their

9 dead, and I will send them as captives to the ends of all the

10 earth. But you must go and take all their frontiers for me in advance, and they must give themselves up to you, and you must hold them for me till the day of their punish-

11 ment. But as for those who disobey, your eye must not spare them, but you must give them up to be slain and

12 plundered in all your land. For as surely as I am alive, by the power of my kingdom, I have spoken and I will do

13 this with my hand. You must not transgress any of your lord's commands, but you must carry them out in full, as I have ordered you to do; you must not put off doing them."

14 So Holofernes left his master's presence and called in all the marshals and generals and officers of the Assyrian army,

15 and he mustered picked soldiers, as his master had ordered him to do, to the number of a hundred and twenty thousand

16 and twelve thousand mounted archers, and he marshaled

17 them as a great army is marshaled. He took camels and asses and mules, an immense number, for their transport, and sheep and cattle and goats without number to provision

18 them, and food in abundance for every man, beside a great

19 deal of gold and silver from the king's palace. And he set

off with his entire army to go ahead of King Nebuchadnezzar and to cover the whole face of the land toward the west with their chariots and horsemen and picked foot soldiers, and there went out with them a motley host like 20 locusts, like the dust of the earth; they could not be counted, they were so many.

They marched three days' journey from Nineveh, to the 21 edge of the plain of Bectileth, and they encamped opposite Bectileth, near the mountain that is to the north of Upper Cilicia. And he took his whole army, his infantry and 22 cavalry and chariots, and moved into the mountainous country and ravaged Put and Lud and plundered all the 23 sons of Rassis and the sons of Ishmael who lived along the desert, to the south of the country of Cheleon. Then he 24 crossed the Euphrates and passed through Mesopotamia and tore down all the high-walled towns on the river Abron, until you come to the sea. He took possession of the frontiers 25 of Cilicia, and cut down all who resisted him, and went as far as the southern frontiers of Japheth, facing Arabia. He encircled all the sons of Midian, burning their tents and 26 plundering their flocks. He went down into the plain of 27 Damascus during the wheat harvest and set all their fields on fire and destroyed their flocks and herds and plundered their cities and devastated their lands and smote all their young men with the edge of the sword.

So fear and horror of him fell on all the inhabitants of the 28 seacoast who were in Sidon and Tyre and those who lived in Sur and Ocine and all who lived in Jamnia, and the inhabitants of Azotus and Ascalon were exceedingly afraid of him. So they sent messengers and said in peaceful terms, [3

"Here we servants of Nebuchadnezzar the Great King 2 lie before you; use us as you please. Our dwellings and all 3 our land and every wheatfield, our flocks and herds and all

2:20–3:3

4 our tent-folds lie before you; use them as you please. Our
cities and their inhabitants are your slaves; come and treat
them as you see fit."

5 So the men went to Holofernes and and told him all these
6 things. And he went down to the seacoast with his army and
put garrisons in the high-walled towns and took picked men
7 from them for allies, and the people and all the country
round welcomed him with garlands and dances and music.
8 And he broke down all their frontier landmarks and cut
down their groves, and he succeeded in destroying all the
gods of the country, in order that all the nations should
worship Nebuchadnezzar alone, and that all their tongues
and tribes should call upon him as god.

9 Then he came toward Esdraelon, near Dothan, which is
10 opposite the main ridge of Judea, and they pitched their
camp between Geba and Scythopolis, and he remained
there a whole month, in order to gather together all the
transport of his army.

4] Then the Israelites who lived in Judea heard all that
Holofernes, the commander-in-chief of Nebuchadnezzar,
king of Assyria, had done to the heathen, and how he had
2 plundered all their temples and destroyed them, and they
were dreadfully afraid of him and disturbed about Jeru-
3 salem and the temple of the Lord their God. For they had
recently come back from their captivity, and all the people
of Judea had gathered together not long before, and the
sacred dishes and the altar and the temple had been con-
4 secrated after their profanation. So they sent into all the
borders of Samaria and to Cona and Bethhoron and Bel-
main and Jericho and to Choba and Aesora and the valley
5 of Salem and occupied in advance all the summits of the
high mountains and fortified the villages that were on them
and stored up food in preparation for war, for their fields

had lately been reaped. And Joakim the high priest, who 6
was in Jerusalem at that time, wrote to the inhabitants of
Bethulia and Betomesthaim which is opposite Esdraelon facing the plain near Dothan, telling them to seize the passes 7
of the mountains, because through them Judea could be
entered, and it was easy to prevent any from approaching,
as the way was narrow, with room for two men at most.

So the Israelites did as they were ordered by Joakim 8
the high priest and the council of all the people of Israel who
live in Jerusalem. And every man of Israel cried to God 9
with great earnestness, and they humbled themselves with
great sincerity. They and their wives and their children and 10
their cattle and every visitor and hired man and slave put
sackcloth on their loins. And every man and woman of 11
Israel who lived in Jerusalem, with their children, fell down
before the temple and threw ashes on their heads and spread
out their sackcloth before the Lord. And they covered the
altar with sackcloth and cried earnestly in concert to the 12
God of Israel praying that he would not permit their children to be plundered and their wives to be pillaged and the
cities they had inherited to be destroyed, and the sanctuary
to be profaned and reviled, to the delight of the heathen.
Then the Lord heard their voice and regarded their afflic- 13
tion. The people continued to fast for several days all over
Judea and Jerusalem before the sanctuary of the Lord Almighty. And Joakim the high priest and all the priests who 14
officiated before the Lord and ministered to the Lord offered
the continual burnt offering and the vows and the freewill
offerings of the people with sackcloth upon their loins and 15
ashes upon their miters, and they cried to the Lord with all
their might to look with favor upon all the house of Israel.

Then Holofernes, the commander-in-chief of the As- [5
syrian army, was told that the Israelites had prepared

4:6–5:1

for war, and had closed the passes of the mountains and fortified every mountain top and put barricades in the level
2 country, and he was exceedingly angry, and he summoned all the princes of Moab and the generals of Ammon and all
3 the governors of the seacoast, and said to them,

"Tell me, you Canaanites, what is this people that occupies the mountain country, and what cities do they inhabit? How large is their army, and in what does their power or strength lie? What king has risen over them as leader of
4 their army, and why have they alone of all the inhabitants of the west refused to come and meet me?"

5 Then Achior, the commander of all the Ammonites said to him,

"Now let my lord hear what is said by the mouth of your servant, and I will tell you the truth about this nation which inhabits this mountain region near you; nothing false shall
6 proceed from your servant's mouth. This nation is de-
7 scended from the Chaldeans. In former times they lived for a while in Mesopotamia, because they would not follow the gods of their forefathers who were in the country of the
8 Chaldeans. But they left the ways of their ancestors and worshipped the God of heaven, a god whom they had come to know, and their parents drove them out from the presence of their gods, and they fled to Mesopotamia and lived there
9 a long time. Then their God told them to leave the place where they were living and go to the land of Canaan. So they settled there and grew rich in gold and silver and very
10 many cattle. Then they went down into Egypt, for a famine spread over the face of the land of Canaan, and they stayed there until they were grown up. There they became a great
11 multitude; their nation could not be counted. The king of Egypt took measures against them and took advantage of them, making them work at making bricks; they degraded

5:2-11

them and made them slaves. Then they cried to their God, 12
and he afflicted all the land of Egypt with incurable plagues;
and the Egyptians drove them out from among them. God 13
made the Red Sea dry up before them, and he set them on 14
the road to Sinai and Kadesh Barnea, and they drove out
all the inhabitants of the desert and lived in the country of 15
the Amorites, and they were so strong that they destroyed all
the people of Heshbon, and they crossed the Jordan and
took possession of all the mountain region. They drove out 16
before them Canaanite and Perizzite and Jebusite, and
Shechem and all the Gergesites and they settled there for a
long time. As long as they did not sin against their God, 17
they prospered, for God who hates wrongdoing was with
them. But when they abandoned the way he had deter- 18
mined for them, they were utterly destroyed through many
wars and carried off as captives to a country that was not
their own, and the Temple of their God was leveled to the
ground, and their cities were taken by their enemies. Now 19
they have turned to their God and have come back from
their dispersion that they suffered and they have taken
possession of Jerusalem where their sanctuary is, and they
have settled in the mountain region, for it was unoccupied.
Now, your Majesty, if there is any fault of ignorance in this 20
nation, and they are sinning against their God, and we perceive that they are guilty of this offense, then we can go up
and defeat them. But if there is no disobedience to law in 21
their nation, then my lord must pass by them, or their Lord
will protect them and their God defend them, and we shall
be disgraced in the eyes of the whole earth."

When Achior finished saying these things, all the people 22
who stood around about the tent objected, and the officers
of Holofernes and all the inhabitants of the seacoast and of
Moab advised putting him to death, "For," they said, "we 23

5:12–23

must not be afraid of the Israelites, for behold they are
24 a people with no strength or might in real warfare. So
now we must advance and they will be devoured by all
your army, Lord Holofernes."

6] When the disturbance made by the men around the
council had ceased, Holofernes, the commander-in-chief of
the Assyrian army, said to Achior and all the Moabites
before all the body of heathen,

2 "And who are you, Achior, and you mercenaries of
Ephraim, that you should act the prophet among us as you
have done today, and tell us not to make war upon the
people of Israel, because their God will protect them? What
3 god is there except Nebuchadnezzar? He will put forth his
strength and destroy them off the face of the earth, and their
God will not save them, but we who are his slaves will strike
them down as one man, and they will not withstand the
4 might of our horses. For with them we will consume them,
and their mountains will be drunk with their blood and
their plains will be filled with their dead bodies. The track
of their feet will not stand before us but they will utterly
perish, says King Nebuchadnezzar, the Lord of the whole
earth, for he said the words he had spoken would not be in
vain.

5 "But you, Achior, you hireling of Ammon, who have said
these things in the time of your inquity, you shall not see my
face again from this day until I take vengeance on the nation
6 of those that came out of Egypt. Then the sword of my
army and my host of servants will pierce your sides and you
7 will fall among their wounded when I return. Now my
slaves will take you into the mountains and put you in one
8 of the hill cities, and you will not perish until you are de-
9 stroyed with them. If you hope in your heart that they will
not be taken, your face must not be downcast; I have spoken

and none of the things that I have said will fail to be fulfilled."

Then Holofernes ordered his slaves who were standing 10 by in his tent to seize Achior and take him away to Bethulia and turn him over to the Israelites. And his slaves seized 11 him and took him out of the camp into the plain and brought him out of the midst of the plain into the hilly country and reached the springs which were below Bethulia. When the men of the town saw them, they caught up their 12 weapons and came out of the town to the crest of the hill and all the slingers prevented them from coming up, hurling stones upon them. So they slipped under the hill and 13 bound Achior and left him lying at the foot of the hill, and went off to their master.

Then the Israelites went down from their town and came 14 upon him. And they unbound him and took him back to Bethulia and brought him before the magistrates of their town, who in those days were Uzziah, the son of Micah, of 15 the tribe of Symeon, and Chabris, the son of Gothoniel, and Charmis, the son of Melchiel. They assembled all the elders 16 of the city, and all their young men and their women hurried together to the meeting, and they put Achior in the midst of all their people, and Uzziah asked him what had happened. And he answered and told them what had hap- 17 pened in the council of Holofernes, and all that he had said in the presence of the leaders of the Assyrians, and how Holofernes had boasted against the house of Israel. Then 18 the people fell down and worshiped God, and cried out,

"Lord God of Heaven, look down on their arrogance and 19 take pity on the humiliation of our nation, and look this day upon the face of those who are consecrated to you."

Then they consoled Achior and praised him highly, 20 and Uzziah took him from the meeting to his house and 21

6:10–21

gave a banquet for the elders, and they called upon the God
of Israel for help all that night.

7]   The next day Holofernes ordered all his army and all
his people who had come to his support to move against
Bethulia and to seize the mountain passes and to make war
2 on the Israelites. And every able-bodied man of them
moved that day; their strength was a hundred and seventy
thousand infantry and twelve thousand calvary, besides the
baggage and the footmen among them, a very great multi-
3 tude. They encamped in the valley near Bethulia, by the
spring, and they spread in breadth over Dothaim as far as
Belbaim and in length from Bethulia to Cyamon which faces
Esdraelon.

4   But the Israelites, when they saw their great numbers,
were greatly troubled and said to one another,
     "These people will lick up the face of the whole country,
and neither the high mountains nor the valleys nor the hills
will bear their weight."

5   And each one took up his weapons and they kindled fires
on their towers and stayed on guard all that night.

6   On the second day Holofernes led out all his cavalry be-
7 fore the Israelites who were in Bethulia, and he recon-
noitered the approaches to their city and located the springs
of water and seized them and set guards of soldiers over
them, and returned to his army.

8   Then all the rulers of the sons of Esau and all the leaders
of the people of Moab and the commanders of the seacoast
came to him and said,

9   "Let our master listen to what we have to say, in order
10 that there may not be any disaster to your army. For these
people of the Israelites do not rely on their spears, but on
the mountain heights in which they live, for it is not easy
11 to reach the tops of their mountains. So now, master, do not

fight against them in battle array, and not a man of your army will fall. Remain in your camp, and keep every man 12 of your force safe, and let your servants take possession of the spring of water that flows from the foot of the mountain, for 13 from it all the inhabitants of Bethulia get their water. Then thirst will destroy them, and they will surrender their town. We and our people will go up to the neighboring mountain summits to prevent anyone from getting out of the town. And they and their wives and their children will be con- 14 sumed with hunger, and before the sword is drawn against them they will be laid low in the streets where they live. So 15 you will repay them with evil because they rebelled and did not receive you peaceably."

Their words pleased Holofernes and all his attendants, 16 and he gave orders to do as they said. And the camp of the 17 sons of Ammon moved along with five thousand of the Assyrians, and they encamped in the valley and seized the water supply and the springs of the Israelites. And the sons 18 of Esau and the sons of Ammon went up and encamped in the mountainous country opposite Dothaim, and they sent some of them southward and eastward toward Akraba, near Chus, on the Brook Mochmur. The rest of the army of the Assyrians encamped in the plain, and they covered the whole face of the country, and their tents and their baggage train encamped in a great multitude, and they made a very great host.

Then the Israelites cried out to the Lord their God, for 19 their courage failed, because all their enemies had sur- rounded them and there was no way to escape from the midst of them. The whole army of Assyria, their infantry 20 and chariots and cavalry, remained in a circle around them for thirty-four days, and all the buckets of water of all the inhabitants of Bethulia failed, and their cisterns were empty, 21 and they had not a full supply of water to drink for one day,

22 for they measured it out to them to drink. Their little children were disheartened, and the women and the young men fainted with thirst and fell down in the streets of the town and in the roadways through the gates, and there was no strength left in them any longer.

23 Then all the people, the young men, the women, and the children, gathered together against Uzziah and the rulers of the town, and they cried aloud and said before all the elders,

24 "May God be judge between you and us, for you have done us a great wrong in not making peace with the As-

25 syrians. Now we have no one to help us, but God has sold us into their hands, to be laid low before them with thirst

26 and utter destruction. Now call them in and surrender the whole town to the people of Holofernes and to all his army

27 to be plundered. It is better for us to be plundered by them, for we shall become slaves and and our lives will be preserved, and we shall not see our babies die before our

28 eyes, and our wives and children expire. We call to witness against you heaven and earth, and our God, the Lord of our forefathers; let him not do what we have said today."

29 Great lamentation arose from all of them alike in the midst of the meeting, and they cried aloud to the Lord God.

30 Then Uzziah said to them,

"Courage, brothers! Let us hold out five days longer; by that time the Lord our God will show us his mercy, for he

31 will not utterly forsake us. But if these pass and no help

32 comes to us, I will do as you say." So he dismissed the people to their respective stations, and they went away to the walls and towers of their town, and sent their wives and children home, and there was great depression in the town.

8] In those days news of it came to Judith the daughter of

Merari, the son of Ox, the son of Joseph, the son of Oziel, the son of Elkiah, the son of Ananias, the son of Gideon, the son of Raphaim, the son of Ahitub, the son of Elijah, the son of Hilkiah, the son of Eliab, the son of Nathanael, the son of Salamiel, the son of Sarasadai, the son of Israel. Her hus- 2 band Manasseh belonged to her tribe and family, and he had died in the days of the barley harvest. For as he was 3 overseeing the men who were binding sheaves on the plain, the heat affected his head, and he threw himself upon his bed and died in his town Bethulia, and they buried him with his forefathers in the field that is between Dothaim and Balamon. Judith had been a widow and remained in her 4 house for three years and four months. She built herself a 5 tent on the top of her house, and she wore sackcloth next to her skin and her widow's mourning. She fasted all the 6 days of her widowhood except the day before the sabbath and the sabbath and the day before the new moon and the new moon, and the feasts and the joyful celebrations of the house of Israel. She was very beautiful and fair to see, and 7 her husband Manasseh had left her gold and silver, and male and female slaves, and cattle and lands, and she lived on them. There was nobody who spoke ill of her, for she 8 feared God with all her heart.

She heard the wicked words the people had spoken 9 against the governor because they fainted for lack of water, and Judith heard all the things that Uzziah said to them, how he swore to them that he would surrender the town to the Assyrian at the end of five days, and she sent her maid 10 who was in charge of all that she had and summoned Chabris and Charmis, the elders of her town. They came to 11 her, and she said to them,

"Listen to me, rulers of the inhabitants of Bethulia, for the thing is not right that you have said before the people today,

8:2-11

and have confirmed with this oath that you have sworn between God and you, saying that you will surrender the town
to our enemies, unless the Lord turns and helps us within
12 that time. Now who are you, who have tried God today,
and who set yourselves up in place of God among the sons
13 of men? You investigate the Lord Almighty, and will never
14 learn anything. You cannot sound the depth of a man's
mind, and you cannot grasp the thoughts of his understanding. How can you examine God, who made all these things,
and understand his mind and perceive his thought? No, no,
15 do not provoke the Lord our God. For if he does not wish
to help us within these five days, he has power to protect us
within whatever time he pleases, or to destroy us before our
16 enemies. But you must not treat the counsels of the Lord our
God as pledged, for God is not like a man, to be threatened,
17 or like a son of man, to be cajoled. Therefore let us wait
for the deliverance that comes from him, and call upon him
18 to help us, and he will hear our cry, if it pleases him. For
there has not arisen in our age nor is there today a tribe or
family or people or town of our stock that worships gods
19 made with hands, as they did in former times, because of
which our forefathers were given up to the sword and to be
20 despoiled and fell in a great disaster before our enemies. We
have known no other god than him, and so we hope that he
21 will not neglect us, nor any of our nation. For if we are
taken, all Judea will be taken, and our sanctuary will be
plundered, and he will hold our blood responsible for the
22 profanation of it, and the slaughter of our brothers and the
capture of the land and the desolation of our inheritance he
will bring back upon our heads among the heathen wherever we are in slavery, and we will become an offense and a
23 reproach in the sight of our masters. For our slavery will
not develop into favor, but the Lord our God will turn it

8:12–23

into disgrace. Now, brothers, let us set an example to our 24
brothers, for their lives depend on us, and the sanctuary and
the temple and the altar rest upon us. Notwithstanding all 25
this, let us give thanks to the Lord our God, who is making
trial of us as he did of our forefathers also. Remember how 26
he dealt with Abraham, and how he dealt with Isaac, and
what happened to Jacob in Syrian Mesopotamia, when he
was keeping the sheep of his uncle Laban. For he has not 27
tried us with fire, as he did them, to search their hearts, and
he has not taken vengeance upon us, but the Lord scourges
those who come near him, to instruct them."

Then Uzziah said to her, 28

"All that you have said, you have spoken with a pure
heart, and there is no one who can oppose your words. For 29
today is not the first time that your wisdom has been displayed, but from the beginning of your life all the people
have known your good sense, for what your mind designs is
good. But the people were exceedingly thirsty and they 30
compelled us to do as we told them we would, and to put
ourselves under an oath, which we cannot break. Now pray 31
for us, for you are a devout woman, and the Lord will send
rain to fill our cisterns, and we will not faint any more."

Then Judith said to them, 32

"Listen to me, and I will do something that will go down
to the sons of our nation for endless generations. You must 33
stand at the gate tonight, and I will go out with my maid,
and before the days are over after which you said you would
surrender the town to our enemies, the Lord will deliver
Israel by my hand. But you must not inquire about my act, 34
for I will not tell you what I am going to do until it is done."

Then Uzziah and the rulers said to her, 35

"Farewell, and the Lord God go before you, to take
vengeance upon our enemies." And they returned from the 36
tent and went to their posts.

8:24–36

9]   But Judith fell upon her face and put ashes on her head, and she stripped off the sackcloth that she had put on, and just as the incense offering of that evening was being offered in Jerusalem in the house of God, Judith cried aloud and said,

2   "Lord God of my father Symeon, in whose hand you put a sword to take vengeance on the aliens who had loosened a maiden's headdress to defile her and stripped her thigh to shame her, and profaned her womb to disgrace her; for you

3 said, 'It must not be done,' yet they did it. So you gave up their rulers to be killed, and their bed, which was ashamed of the deceit they had practiced, to be stained with blood, and you struck down slaves upon princes and princes upon

4 their thrones, and you gave up their wives to plunder and their daughters to captivity and all their spoils to be divided among your beloved sons, who were very zealous for you and abhorred the pollution of their blood and called on you

5 for help. O God, my God, listen to a widow like me. For you made what preceded those things, and those things, and what followed them, and you design the present and the

6 future, and what you meditate comes to pass. The things you plan present themselves and say, 'Here we are.' For all your ways stand ready, and you judge with foreknowledge.

7 For here the Assyrians are multiplied in their might, they are exalted over horse and rider, they glory in the arm of the foot soldiers, they place their hope in shield and spear and bow and sling, and do not know that you are a lord that

8 crushes wars. The Lord is your name; break their strength with your might, and shatter their force in your anger, for they plan to profane your sanctuary, to pollute the tent where your glorious name rests, to strike down the horn of

9 your altar with the sword. Look at their arrogance, direct your anger upon their heads, put in the hand of a widow like

10 me the strength to do what I have planned. With my de-

ceitful lips strike down the slave with the ruler and the ruler
with his servant, break down their state with a woman's
hand. For your strength is not in numbers nor your might 11
in the strong, but you are the God of the lowly, the helper
of the inferior, the champion of the weak, the protector of
the neglected, the savior of the despairing. Yes, God of my 12
father, and God of the inheritance of Israel, Lord of the
heavens and the earth, creator of the waters, king of all your
creation, hear my prayer and make my deceitful words the 13
wound and stripe of those who have planned such cruelty
against your agreement and your consecrated house, and
Mount Zion and the house your sons possess. Make your 14
whole nation and every tribe to know and understand that
you are God, the God of all power and might, and that the
nation of Israel has no protector but you."

It came to pass, when she had ceased calling on the God [10
of Israel and had finished saying all these things, that she rose 2
from her prostrate position and called her maid, and went
down into the house, where she lived on the sabbaths and
on her feast days, and she took off the sackcloth which she 3
had put on and she took off her widow's mourning and
washed herself with water and anointed herself with rich
ointment, and braided her hair and put on a headdress and
she dressed herself in festal attire which she used to wear
when her husband Manasseh was alive. She took sandals 4
for her feet, and put on her anklets and bracelets and rings
and earrings and all her ornaments and made herself very
beautiful to attract the eyes of any men who might see her.
Then she gave her maid a leather bottle of wine and a jar 5
of oil, and she filled a bag with parched grain and figs and
pure bread, and she packed all her dishes and had her carry
them.

Then they went out to the gate of the town of Bethulia 6

9:11–10:6

and they found Uzziah standing at the gate with Chabris
7 and Charmis, the elders of the town. When they saw her,
and that her face was altered and her dress changed, they
admired her beauty very greatly, and they said to her,

8 "May the God of our forefathers win you favor and fulfil
your designs, to the gratification of the sons of Israel and the
exaltation of Jerusalem."

9 And she worshiped God, and said to them,

"Order them to open the gate of the town for me, and I
will go out to carry out the things of which you talked with
me."

Then they ordered the young men to open the gate for her
10 as she had said, and they did so. And Judith went out, she
and her maid with her; and the men of the town watched
her until she had gone down the mountain and had gone
through the valley and they could see her no more.

11 They went straight on through the valley, and an out-
12 post of the Assyrians met her; and they took her into custody
and asked her,

"To what people do you belong and where do you come
from, and where are you going?"

And she said,

"I am a daughter of the Hebrews, and I am escaping from
their presence because they are going to be given to you to
13 devour. I am going to the presence of Holofernes, the commander-in-chief of your army, to give him a true report, and
I will show him a way by which he can go and become master of all the hilly country without losing from his men one
living body or spirit."

14 When the men heard her words and observed her face,
they regarded it as wonderfully beautiful, and they said to
her,

15 "You have saved your life by hurrying to come down to

the presence of our lord. So now go to his tent, and some of us will escort you until they deliver you into his charge. But 16 if you stand before him, have no fear in your heart but report to him what you have said, and he will treat you well."

Then they chose a hundred men of their number and had 17 them escort her and her maid, and they conducted them to the tent of Holofernes.

And they ran together from the whole camp, for the news 18 of her coming had spread among the tents, and they came and gathered about her as she stood outside the tent of Holofernes, waiting until they told him about her. And they 19 wondered at her beauty, and admired the Israelites, judging by her, and they said to one another,

"Who can despise these people, when they have such women among them? For it is not right to leave one man of them alive, for if we let them go they will be able to beguile the whole earth."

Then those who reclined with Holofernes and all his at- 20 tendants came out and took her into the tent. Now Holo- 21 fernes was resting on his bed, under the canopy, which was woven of purple and gold and emeralds and precious stones. And they told him about her, and he came forward into the 22 space before the tent, with silver lamps preceding him. But 23 when Judith came before him and his attendants, they all wondered at the beauty of her face, and she fell on her face and made obeisance to him, and his slaves raised her up.

Then Holofernes said to her, [11

"Take courage, lady, do not be afraid in your heart, for I never hurt anyone who has chosen to serve Nebuchadnezzar, the king of the whole earth. And now, if your peo- 2 ple that inhabit the hilly country had not slighted me, I would not have raised my spear against them. But they have brought this upon themselves. Now tell me why you 3

10:16–11:3

have escaped from them and come to us, for you have come
to save yourself. Take courage, for you shall live tonight
4 and henceforth. No one will hurt you but everybody will
treat you well, as they treat the slaves of my lord, King
Nebuchadnezzar."

5   And Judith said to him,
"Accept the words of your slave, and let your maidservant
speak before you, and I will declare nothing false to my
6 lord tonight. If you follow out the words of your maidservant, God will fully carry out the matter with you, and
7 my lord will not fall short of his designs. For by the life of
Nebuchadnezzar, king of the whole earth, and by the might
of him who has sent you to correct every soul, not only do
men serve him because of you, but also the wild animals and
cattle and wild birds, through your might, shall live under
8 the sway of Nebuchadnezzar and all his house. For we have
heard of your wisdom and the cleverness of your mind, and
the whole earth has been told that you are the only man in
the whole kingdom who is competent, and able in knowl-
9 edge and wonderful in the arts of war. Now as to what
Achior said in your council, we have heard his words, for the
men of Bethulia saved him, and he told them all that he had
10 said before you. Therefore, my lord and master, do not disregard what he said, but treasure it in your heart, for it is
true; for our nation cannot be punished, the sword cannot
11 prevail against them, unless they sin against their God. And
now, that my lord may not be defeated and disappointed,
death is about to fall upon them, for a sin has overtaken
them by which they will anger their God, when they shall
12 do what they should not. When food failed them, and all
their water grew scanty, they planned to resort to their
cattle and resolved to consume all that God by his laws
13 had forbidden them to eat. The first fruits of the wheat,

11:4–13

and the tenths of the wine and the oil which they had consecrated and reserved for the priests who stand before the face of our God in Jerusalem, which none of the people is permitted even to touch with their hands, they decided to consume. They have sent men to Jerusalem, because those 14 who live there have also done this, to bring them permission from the senate. The result will be that when the answer 15 reaches them and they do this, on that day they will be delivered up to you to be destroyed. So when I, your slave, 16 learned all this, I made my escape from their presence, and God sent me to perform things with you at which the whole earth, as many as shall hear of them, shall be astonished. For your slave is devout and serves the God of 17 heaven night and day. Now I will stay with you, my lord, and every night your slave will go out into the valley and I will pray to God and he will tell me when they have committed their sins. And I will come and report it to you also 18 and you shall go out with your whole army, and not one of them will oppose you. I will lead you through the heart of 19 Judea until you face Jerusalem, and I will set your throne in the midst of her, and you shall drive them like sheep that have no shepherd, and no dog shall so much as growl at you; for this was told me to give me foreknowledge; it was declared to me, and I was sent to tell you."

Her words pleased Holofernes and all his attendants, and 20 they wondered at her wisdom and said,

"There is not such a woman from one end of the earth to 21 the other, for beauty and intelligence."

And Holofernes said to her, 22

"God did well to send you before the people, to put strength in our hands, and bring destruction upon those who have slighted my lord. You are beautiful, and you speak 23 well, for if you do as you have said, your God shall be my

11:14–23

God, and you shall live in the house of King Nebuchadnezzar and be renowned over the whole earth."

12]   Then he commanded them to bring her in where his
silver dishes were, and gave orders that they should set some
of his own food before her, and that she should drink his
2 wine. But Judith said,

"I cannot eat them, for it might give offense, but I will
be supplied with the things I have brought with me."

3   Holofernes said to her,

"If what you have with you gives out, where can we get
more like it to give you?"

4   And Judith said to him,

"As surely as you are alive, my lord, your slave will not
use up the things I have with me before the Lord carries out
by my hand the things he has resolved upon."

5   So Holofernes' attendants brought her into the tent, and
she slept until midnight. And toward the morning watch
6 she got up, and sent to Holofernes, saying,

"Now let my lord give orders that your slave be permitted to go out to pray."

7   And Holofernes ordered his bodyguards not to hinder
her. And she remained in the camp three days, and at night
she went out into the valley of Bethulia and washed herself
8 at the spring in the camp. And when she came up from the
water, she prayed the Lord God of Israel to make her way
9 straight so that she might raise up the sons of his people.
Then she went in clean and stayed in the tent until she had
her food toward evening.

10   It happened that on the fourth day Holofernes gave a
banquet for his slaves only, and invited none of those on
11 duty. And he said to Bagoas, the eunuch who had charge
of all he had,

"Go now, and persuade this Hebrew woman who is in

12:1–11

your charge, to come to us and eat and drink with us. For 12
it is a disgrace to our dignity if we let such a woman go with
out having her company, for if we do not draw her to us she
will laugh at us."

So Bagoas went out from the presence of Holofernes and 13
went in to her and said,

"This beautiful maidservant must not hesitate to come to
my lord and to be honored in his presence and to drink wine
and be merry with us, and to become today like a daughter
of the Assyrians who wait in the house of Nebuchadnezzar."

Then Judith said to him,   14

"And who am I, to refuse my lord? For I will make haste
to do everything that is pleasing in his sight, and this will
be my boast to the day of my death."

And she got up and dressed herself beautifully with all 15
her feminine finery, and her slave went and spread fleeces
on the ground for her before Holofernes, which she had received from Bagoas for her daily use, so that she might re-
cline on them and eat.

So Judith went in and lay down, and Holofernes' mind 16
was amazed at her and his heart was stirred, and he was
exceedingly desirous of intimacy with her, for he had been
watching for an opportunity to deceive her ever since he had
seen her.

And Holofernes said to her,   17
"Drink now, and be merry with us."

And Judith said,   18
"Certainly I will drink, my lord, for my life means more
to me today than in all the days since I was born."

Then she took what her slave had prepared, and ate and 19
drank before him. And Holofernes was delighted with her, 20
and he drank a very great deal of wine, more than he had
ever drunk on one day since he was born.

12:12–20

13] But when evening came on, his slaves hastened to withdraw. And Bagoas went out to the tent and closed it, and
dismissed the attendants from his master's presence, and
they went off to their beds, for they were all tired, because
2 the banquet had been so long. But Judith was left alone in
the tent, with Holofernes prostrate upon his bed, for he was
3 drenched with wine. Judith had told her slave to stand outside her bed chamber and wait for her to come out, as usual;
for she had said that she would go out to offer her prayer;
and she had told Bagoas the same thing.

4 So they all went out from his presence, and there was no
one, small or great, left in the bed chamber. And Judith
stood beside his bed and said in her heart,

"Lord, God of all power, look favorably at this hour upon
5 the works of my hands for the exaltation of Jerusalem. For
now is the time to help your inheritance and to carry out
my undertaking for the destruction of the enemies who have
risen up against us."

6 And she went up to the rail of the bed, which was at
7 Holofernes' head, and took down from it his scimitar, and
she went close to the bed and grasped the hair of his head,
and said

"Give me strength, Lord, God of Israel, today!"

8 And she struck him on the neck twice, with all her might,
9 and severed his head from his body. Then she rolled his
body off the bed, and pulled the canopy down from the
pillars, and after a little while she went out and gave Holo-
10 fernes' head to her maid, and she put it in her bag of food,
and they both went out together as they were accustomed
to do, to offer their prayer. They passed through the camp
and skirted that valley, and went up the mountain to Bethulia and came to its gates.

13:1-10

And Judith called from a long way off to the watchmen, 11
at the gates,

"Open, open the gate! God, our God is with us, to show
his strength in Israel, and his might against our enemies,
as he has done today."

And it happened that when her townmen heard her 12
voice, they hastened down to the gate of their town, and
called the elders of the town together. And they all ran to- 13
gether, small and great, for it seemed strange to them that
she should come, and they opened the gate and welcomed
them, and they kindled a fire for light, and gathered about
them. And she said to them in a loud voice, 14

"Praise God, praise him! Praise God who has not withdrawn his mercy from the house of Israel, but has shattered
our enemies by my hand this very night!"

Then she took the head out of the bag and showed it, 15
and she said to them,

"Here is the head of Holofernes, the commander of the
army of Assyria, and here is the canopy under which he lay
in his drunkenness. For the Lord has struck him down by a
woman's hand. And as surely as the Lord lives, who pro- 16
tected me on the way I went, my face deceived him to his
destruction, and he committed no sin with me, to pollute
and disgrace me."

All the people were greatly astonished, and they bowed 17
down and worshiped God, and said under a common impulse,

"Blessed are you, our God, who have brought to nought
the enemies of your people today."

And Uzziah said to her, 18

"Blessed are you, my daughter, beyond all the women
on earth in the sight of the Most High God, and blessed is
the Lord God, who created the heavens and the earth, who
guided you to strike the leader of our enemies on the head.

13:11-18

19 Your hope shall never disappear from the minds of men
20 when they remember the strength of God. May God make
this an eternal glory to you and reward you with blessings,
because on account of the affliction of our nation you did
not spare your own life, but you anticipated our calamity,
going straight on before our God."

And all the people said,

"Be it so! Be it so!"

14] Then Judith said to them

"Listen to me, brothers. Take this head and hang it on
2 the battlement of your wall. And when the day breaks, and
the sun rises on the earth, you must take up your weapons,
each of you, and every valiant man go out of the town, and
you must put a captain over them as though you were going
down on the plain against the outpost of the Assyrians, but
3 you must not go down. Then they will take up their arms
and go into their camp and awaken the officers of the
Assyrian army; and they will hurry to the tent of Holofernes,
and they will not find him. Then fear will fall upon them
4 and they will flee before you. And you and all who inhabit
all the borders of Israel must follow them up and destroy
5 them as they go. But before you do this, bring Achior the
Ammonite to me, so that he may see and recognize the man
who despised the house of Israel and who sent him to us as
though to his death."

6 Then they summoned Achior from the house of Uzziah.
And when he came and saw the head of Holofernes in the
hand of a man in the gathering of people, he fell on his face
7 and his spirit failed. And when they raised him up, he fell
at Judith's feet, and made obeisance to her, and said,

"Blessed are you in every tent of Judah, and in every
8 nation those who hear your name will be alarmed. Now tell
me all that you have done in these days."

So Judith related to him in the presence of the people all

that she had done from the day that she went out of the
town until the time she was speaking to them. And when   9
she stopped speaking, the people uttered a great shout and
gave a joyful cry in their town. And when Achior saw all   10
that the God of Israel had done, he believed in God with all
his heart, and accepted circumcision and was adopted into
the household of Israel, and remained so unto this day.

When the dawn came, they hung Holofernes' head from   11
the wall, and every man took up his weapons and they went
out in companies toward the approaches to the mountain.
But when the Assyrians saw them, they sent word to their   12
officers, and they went to the generals and colonels and all
their officers. And they came to the tent of Holofernes and   13
said to him who had charge of all that he had,

"Wake our lord up, for these slaves have dared to come
down against us to battle, so that they may be utterly destroyed."

Then Bagoas went and knocked at the curtain of the tent,   14
for he supposed that he was sleeping with Judith. When no   15
one answered, he drew the curtain aside and and went into
the bed chamber, and found him thrown down dead upon
the step, and his head had been cut off and was gone. And   16
he cried out aloud, with lamentation and groaning and a
great shout, and tore open his clothing. And he went into   17
the tent where Judith stayed, and could not find her, and
he rushed out to the people and shouted,

"The slaves have deceived us; one Hebrew woman has   18
brought disgrace upon the house of Nebuchadnezzar, for
here is Holofernes lying on the ground, and his head is not
on his shoulders."

But when the leaders of the Assyrian army heard these   19
words, they tore open their shirts and their souls were dreadfully dismayed, and they raised an exceedingly loud crying
and shouting in the midst of the camp. And when the men [15

14:9–15:1

in the tents heard it, they were amazed at what had hap-
2 pened, and fear and trembling came upon them, and not
a man waited to face his comrade, but streaming out under
a common impulse they fled by every way of the plain and
3 of the hilly country. Those who had encamped in the hilly
country around Bethulia also turned and fled. Then the
Israelites, every soldier among them, streamed after them.
4 And Uzziah sent men to Betomasthaim and Bebai and
Chobai and Kola and all the borders of Israel, to tell of what
had been accomplished, and to order them all to stream out
5 after their enemies to destroy them. And when the Israelites heard, under a common impulse they all fell upon
them, and cut them in pieces as far as Chobai. Those of
Jerusalem and of all the hilly country also came, for
they had been told what had happened to the camp of their
enemies, and those in Gilead and in Galilee fell upon their
flank with great slaughter until they passed Damascus and
6 its borders. The remaining inhabitants of Bethulia fell upon
the Assyrian camp and pillaged it, and were made very rich.
7 And the Israelites when they returned from the slaughter
took possession of what remained, and the villages and ham-
lets in the hilly country and in the plain got a great quantity
of spoil, for there was a very great amount of it.
8 Then Joakim, the high priest, and the senate of the Israelites who lived in Jerusalem came to witness the blessings
which the Lord had conferred upon Israel and to see Judith
9 and greet her. And when they went to see her, they all
blessed her with one accord, and said to her,

"You are the exaltation of Jerusalem, you are the great
10 glory of Israel, you are the great boast of our nation. You
have done all this with your hand; you have done Israel
good, and God is well pleased with it. The Omnipotent
Lord bless you forever."

And all the people said,

15:2-10

"Be it so!"

And all the people plundered the camp for thirty days; 11 and they gave Judith the tent of Holofernes and all his silver dishes and his beds and his bowls and all his furniture, and she took them and put them on her mule, and she harnessed her wagons and piled them on them.

And all the women of Israel came to see her, and they 12 blessed her and made a dance in her honor, and she took branches in her hands and gave them to the women that were with her, and they crowned themselves with olive, 13 she and the women with her, and she went before all the people in the dance, leading all the women, and all the men of Israel in their armor, with garlands and with songs on their lips. And Judith began this thanksgiving before all [16 Israel, and all the people loudly sang this song of praise. And Judith said, 2

"Begin to play unto my God with tambourines,
 Sing unto my Lord to the sound of cymbals,
 Raise hymn and praise for him,
 Exalt his name, and call upon it,
 For the Lord is a God that shatters wars, 3
 For he brought me into his camp, in the midst of the people,
 Rescuing me from the hands of my pursuers.
 Assyria came from the north out of the mountains, 4
 He came with the myriads of his host,
 Their multitude blocked up the torrents,
 And their cavalry covered the hills.
 He said he was going to burn up my borders, 5
 And kill my young men with the sword,
 And throw my babies upon the ground,
 And take my children as spoils,
 And my girls as plunder.

6   The Lord Almighty brought them to nought
    By the hand of a woman.

7   For their champion did not fall at the hands of young men,
    The sons of the Titans did not strike him down,
    Nor the tall giants set upon him,
    But Judith, the daughter of Merari,
    Made him faint with the beauty of her face.

8   For she took off her widow's mourning,
    To lift up those who were in distress in Israel.
    She anointed her face with ointment,
    And arranged her hair in a headdress,
    And put on a linen dress to deceive him.

9   Her sandal ravished his eye,
    And her beauty captivated his soul.
    The scimitar passed through his neck.

10 Persians shuddered at her daring,
    And Medes were daunted at her boldness.

11 Then my oppressed people cried out,
    My weak people were terrified and cowered down,
    They lifted up their voices and turned to flee.

12 The sons of their maidservants stabbed them,
    And wounded them like runaways' children;
    They perished before the army of my Lord.

13 I will sing to my God a new song;
    Lord, you are great and glorious,
    Wonderfully strong, unconquerable.

14 Let all your creation serve you,
    For you but spoke, and they were created,
    You sent forth your Spirit, and it formed them,
    And there is no one that can resist your voice.

15 For mountains will be moved from their foundations like
        waters,
    And rocks will melt like wax before you,

But to those who fear you
You will continue to show mercy.
For any sacrifice for a fragrant odor is a small thing,   16
And any fat for a whole burnt offering is insignificant in
    your sight,
But he that fears the Lord is great forever.
Alas for the heathen that rise up against my nation.   17
The Lord Almighty will take vengeance on them in the
    day of judgment,
To apply fire and worms to their bodies,
And they will feel them and wail forever."

When they reached Jerusalem, they worshiped God, and   18
when the people were purified, they offered their whole
burnt offerings and their freewill offerings and their gifts.
And Judith dedicated to God all the dishes of Holofernes,   19
which the people had given her, and the canopy which she
had taken for herself from his bed chamber she gave as a gift
to God; and the people continued to celebrate in Jerusalem   20
before the sanctuary for three months, and Judith stayed
with them.

After those days everyone traveled back to his own in-   21
heritance, and Judith returned to Bethulia and remained
on her estate, and she was famous all over the land in her
time. Many men desired to marry her, but no man had   22
relations with her, all her life long, from the day Manasseh
her husband died and was gathered to his people. She be-   23
came greater and greater and she grew old in her husband's
house until she was a hundred and five. She set her maid
free, and died in Bethulia, and they buried her in the cave
of her husband Manasseh. And the house of Israel mourned   24
for her for seven days. Before she died she divided her property among all the nearest relations of her husband Manasseh and her own nearest relatives. No one could terrify the   25
Israelites in Judith's days, nor for a long time after she died.

16:16–25

THE ADDITIONS TO THE BOOK OF ESTHER

The Old Testament Book of Esther is, like Judith, a romantic story of how a Jewess saved her threatened people by charming a powerful enemy, but it is far less permeated with piety; the name of God does not occur in it. The six pieces presented here, which are included in the Greek text at appropriate points (as indicated in the marginal numeration), particularly the prayers attributed to Esther and the acknowledgment of divine help attributed to Mordecai, look as if they had been added in order to amend the secular tone of the book. The fuller text may, as some scholars hold, represent a different and equally ancient recension of the story. Even aside from the additions the Greek and Hebrew texts of Esther differ. Protestant scholars generally tend to the opinion that the additions were written in Greek, Catholics that they were translated from the more authentic Hebrew recension. The colophon in the last verse indicates that the translation of the book, apparently newly written, was brought to Egypt in the fourth year of the reign of Ptolemy and Cleopatra. Only one royal couple so named reached a fourth year of rule, and the date indicated is therefore 114 B.C.

THE ADDITIONS TO THE
BOOK OF ESTHER

11:2] IN THE SECOND YEAR OF THE REIGN OF
Artaxerxes the Great, on the first day of Nisan, Mordecai the son of Jair, the son of Shimei, the son of Kish,
3 of the tribe of Benjamin, had a dream. He was a Jew, and
lived in the city of Susa, an important man, in attendance
4 at the royal court; he was one of the captives that Nebuchadnezzar, king of Babylon, had brought from Jerusalem,
with Jeconiah, king of Judah. And this was his dream:
5 behold, noise and tumult, thunders and earthquake, uproar
6 on the earth. And here came two great dragons, both ready
7 to wrestle, and they uttered a great roar. And at their
roar every nation made ready for war, to fight against the
8 nation of the upright. And behold, a day of darkness and
gloom, affliction and anguish, distress and great tumult,
9 upon the earth. And the whole upright nation was troubled,
10 fearing their own hurt, and they prepared to perish; and
they cried out to God. And at their cry there arose as
though from a tiny spring, a great river, with abundant
11 water; light came, and the sun rose, and the humble were
exalted and consumed the glorious.

12 When Mordecai, who had had this dream, and had seen
what God had resolved to do, awoke, he kept it in his mind,
and all day sought by all means to understand it.

12] Now Mordecai took his rest in the court with Gabatha
and Tharra, the two royal eunuchs who kept watch in the
2 court. He overheard their reflections, and inquired into
their designs, and found out that they were preparing to
lay hands on King Artaxerxes, and he informed the king
3 about them. And the king examined the two eunuchs, and
4 when they confessed, they were led off to execution. And
the king wrote a memorandum about this matter, and Mor-
5 decai also wrote about it. And the king ordered Mordecai

to be in attendance at the court, and he made him presents
because of it. But Haman, the son of Ammedatha, a Bou-   6
gaean, was in high honor with the king, and he set out to
injure Mordecai and his people, because of the two royal
eunuchs.

(Esther 1:1—3:13 follows here in the Greek.)

And this is the copy of the letter: [13

"The Great King, Artaxerxes, to the rulers of a hundred
and twenty-seven provinces, from India to Ethiopia, and
to the subordinate governors, writes thus: Having become   2
ruler of many nations, and come to have dominion over the
whole world, I desire, not because I am elated by the pre-
sumption of power, but behaving always with mildness and
moderation, to insure that my subjects shall live in unbroken
tranquillity, and in order to make my kingdom peaceable
and open for travel in all its extent, to re-establish the peace
which all men desire. When I asked my counselors how   3
this end might be accomplished, Haman, who excels among
us in soundness of judgment, and is distinguished for his unfailing loyalty and steadfast fidelity, and has attained the
second rank in the kingdom, pointed out to us, that among   4
all the nations of the world there is scattered an ill-disposed
people, with laws contrary to those of every nation, which
continually disregards the royal ordinances, so that the unifying of our realm, directed by us with the best intentions,
cannot be effected. Understanding therefore that this na-   5
tion, and it alone, stands in constant opposition to all men,
perversely following a strange manner of life and laws, and
ill-disposed to our administration, doing all the harm it
can, so that our rule may not be made secure, we have   6
decreed that the persons designated in the letters sent to you
by Haman, who is in charge of our administration, and is a
second father to us, shall all, with their wives and children,

12:6–13:6

be destroyed, root and branch, by the sword of their enemies, without pity or mercy, on the fourteenth day of
7 the twelfth month, Adar, of this present year; so that they who all along have been disaffected, may in a single day go down through violence to Hades, and leave our government secure and undisturbed for the future."

(*Esther 3: 14—4: 17 follows here in the Greek.*)

8 And she besought the Lord, calling to mind all the doings of the Lord, and said,

9 "Lord, you King, who rule over all, for all is in your power, and there is no one who can oppose you when you
10 choose to save Israel, for you made heaven and earth,
11 and every wonderful thing under heaven, and you are Lord of all, and there is no one who can resist you, who
12 are the Lord; you know all things; you know, Lord, that it was not in insolence or arrogance or vainglory that I did
13 this, and refused to bow down to this proud Haman, for I would have been willing to kiss the soles of his feet, to save
14 Israel. But I did it so as not to set the glory of man above the glory of God, and I will bow down to no one but you,
15 my Lord, and I will not do it in pride. Now, Lord God and King, God of Abraham, spare your people, for they are looking at us to consume us, and they desire to destroy the in-
16 heritance that has been yours from the beginning. Do not be indifferent to your portion, which you ransomed for your-
17 self from the land of Egypt. Hear my prayer, and have mercy on your heritage; turn our mourning into feasting, so that we may live, and sing praise to your name, Lord; do not destroy the mouth of those who praise you."

18 And all Israel cried out with all their might, for death was before their eyes.

14] Then Esther, the queen, overwhelmed with deadly
2 anxiety, fled to the Lord; she took off her splendid clothing

13:7–14:2

and put on garments of distress and mourning, and instead
of the rarest perfumes, she covered her head with ashes and
dung, and she abased her body utterly, and every part that
she delighted to adorn she covered with her tangled hair.
And she prayed to the Lord and said,   3

"My Lord, our King, you stand alone; help me who
am alone, and have no helper but you; for my danger is in   4
my hand. Ever since I was born, I have heard in the tribe   5
of my family that you, Lord, took Israel from among all the
nations, and our forefathers from among all their ancestors
for an everlasting possession, and that you did for them all
that you promised. But now we have sinned before you, and   6
you have handed us over to our enemies, because we glori-   7
fied their gods; you are upright, Lord. And now they are   8
not satisfied that we are in bitter captivity but they have
made an agreement with their idols to abolish what your   9
mouth has ordained, and destroy your possession, and stop
the mouths of those who praise you and quench the glory
of your house, and your altar, and open the mouths of the   10
heathen to praise unreal gods, so that a mortal king may
be magnified forever. Lord, do not give up your scepter   11
to those who have no being, and do not let them mock at
our fall, but turn their plan against themselves, and make
an example of the man who has begun this against us. Re-   12
member, Lord; make yourself known in this time of our affliction and give me courage, king of the gods and holder of
all dominion. Put eloquent speech in my mouth, before this 13
lion, and change his heart to hate the man who is fighting
against us, so that there may be an end of him, and of those
who support him. But save us by your hand, and help me,   14
who stand alone, and have no one but you, Lord. You know   15
everything, and you know that I hate the splendor of the
wicked, and abhor the bed of the uncircumcised and of any

14:3-15

16 alien. You know what I am forced to do—that I abhor the symbol of my proud position, which is placed upon my head on the days when I appear in public; I abhor it like a filthy
17 rag, and never wear it in private. Your slave has not eaten at Haman's table, and I have not honored the king's feast,
18 or drunk the wine of the libations. Your slave has had no joy from the day I was brought here until now, except in
19 you, Lord God of Abraham. O God, whose might is over all, hear the voice of the despairing, and save us from the hands of evil-doers, and save me from what I fear."

15] And it came to pass on the third day, when she had ceased to pray, that she took off the clothes in which she had wor-
2 shiped, and dressed herself in splendor. When she was magnificently clad, she invoked the aid of the all-seeing God
3 and Savior, and took with her her two maids; on one she
4 leaned languishingly, while the other followed her, carrying
5 her train. She was radiant with her perfect beauty, and her face was happy as it was lovely, but her heart was in an
6 agony of fear. When she had gone through all the doors, she stood before the king. He was seated on his royal throne, clad in all his magnificence, and covered with gold and
7 precious stones; he was an awe-inspiring sight. And he raised his face, burning with splendor, and looked at her with the fiercest anger; and the queen fell down and turned pale and fainted, and she collapsed upon the head of the maid who went before her.

8 Then God changed the king's spirit to mildness, and in great anxiety he sprang from his throne and caught her in his arms, until she came to herself, and he reassured her with soothing words, and said to her,

9 "What is it, Esther? I am your brother. Courage,
10 you shall not die, for our command is only for the people; come near."

14:16–15:10

Then he lifted the gold scepter and laid in upon her neck,   11
and he embraced her and said,   12
"Tell me!"
And she said to him,   13
"I saw you, my lord, like an angel of God, and my mind
was dismayed with awe at your splendor; you are wonder-   14
ful, my lord, and your face is full of graciousness."
But as she spoke, she fell fainting; and the king was   15,16
troubled, and all his train tried to reassure her.

(*Esther 5:3—8:12 follows here in the Greek.*)

Of this letter the following is a copy: [16
"The Great King, Artaxerxes, sends greeting to the rulers
of countries in a hundred and twenty-seven provinces, from
India to Ethiopia, and to those who are loyal to our rule.
The more frequently they are honored by the excessive   2
favor of their benefactors, the prouder many men become,
and not only seek to injure our subjects, but, in their inabil-   3
ity to bear prosperity, they undertake designs against their
own benefactors, and not only uproot gratitude from among   4
men, but intoxicated by the boasts of foolish men they suppose they will escape the evil-hating justice of the ever all-
seeing God. And often many of those who occupy places   5
of authority have by the persuasiveness of the friends who
have been intrusted with the conduct of affairs, been made
accomplices in the shedding of innocent blood, and been involved in irremediable disasters, when such men by the   6
specious fallacies of their vicious natures beguile the sincere
good will of their sovereigns. And what has been impiously   7
accomplished by the baneful conduct of those who exercise
authority unworthily, you can see not so much from the
venerable histories which have come down to us, as from the
scrutiny of matters close at hand. And in order to make our   8
kingdom in the future tranquil and peaceful for all men, we   9

15:11–16:9

will change our attitude, and always decide the matters that fall under our notice with more considerate attention.

10 For Haman, the son of Hammedathi, a Macedonian, an alien indeed from the Persian blood, and widely removed
11 from our kindliness, being entertained as a guest by us, enjoyed the humanity that we extend to every nation to such a degree that he was called our father, and was continually bowed down to by all, as a person second only to the royal
12 throne. But he in his unbearable arrogance designed to
13 deprive us of our kingdom, and to compass the death of our preserver and perpetual benefactor Mordecai, and of Esther, our blameless partner in the kingdom, together with their whole nation, demanding with intricate deceptions
14 and intrigues that they be destroyed. For he thought by these means that he would find us deserted and would transfer the domination of the Persians to the Macedonians.
15 But we find that the Jews, who were consigned to annihilation by this thrice sinful man, are no evil-doers but are gov-
16 erned by most just laws, and are sons of the Most High, Most Mighty Living God, who has directed the kingdom for us and for our forefathers with most excellent guidance.
17 Therefore please pay no further attention to the letters sent
18 you by Haman, the son of Hammedathi, because the very man who was active in this has been hung with all his house at the gates of Susa, for God, who governs all things, has speedily inflicted on him the punishment he deserved.
19 Therefore put up the copy of this letter publicly every-
20 where, and let the Jews live under their own laws, and reinforce them, so that on the thirteenth day of the twelfth month, Adar, on that very day they may defend themselves against those who assail them at the time of their afflic-
21 tion. For God, who governs all things, has made this day a joy to them instead of proving the destruction of the

16:10–21

chosen race. So you must observe it as a notable day among 22
your commemorative festivals, with all good cheer, so that 23
both now and hereafter it may mean preservation to us and
to the loyal Persians, but to those who plot against us it
may serve as a reminder of destruction. But any city or 24
country without exception, which shall fail to act in accordance with this, shall be utterly destroyed in wrath with
fire and sword; it will be made not only impassable for men,
but also hateful to wild animals and birds for all time.

*(This is followed in the Greek by 8:13—10:3, where the Hebrew
Esther ends. The Greek version adds the following:)*

[10

And Mordecai said, 4
"This came from God. For I remember the dream 5
that I had about these things; for none of them has failed
to be fulfilled. As for the tiny spring that became a river, 6
when light came, and the sun shone and there was an
abundance of water, the river is Esther, whom the king
married and made queen. And I and Haman are the two 7
dragons. And those who gathered to destroy the name of 8
the Jews are the heathen. And my nation, which cried out 9
to God and was saved, is Israel; for the Lord has saved his
people, the Lord has delivered us from all these evils, and
God has wrought great signs and wonders, such as never
happened among the heathen. That is why he made two 10
lots, one for the people of God and one for all the heathen,
and these two lots came to the hour and time and day when 11
God should judge among all the nations. And God remembered his people, and he acquitted his inheritance. So these 12
days in the month of Adar, on the fourteenth and fifteenth 13
of that month, will be observed by them with assembling
together and joy and gladness before God from generation
to generation, forever, among his people Israel."

16:22–10:13

11】 In the fourth year of the reign of Ptolemy and Cleopatra, Dositheus, who said he was a priest and Levite, and Ptolemy his son, brought in (to Egypt) this preceding letter of Purim, which they said was true, and had been translated by Lysimachus the son of Ptolemy, one of the residents of Jerusalem.

THE WISDOM OF SOLOMON

This book is the most important in the Apocrypha for the development of theology, and at the same time, significantly, it affords the best example of the fusion of Greek and Hebrew ideas. The book seems to be a composite, with the break at the end of chapter 10. The first part contains first a mass of eschatological teaching on the destiny of the righteous and the wicked, and then the extended praise of Wisdom which gives the book its name. Wisdom is much more definitely hypostatized than it is in Proverbs or Ecclesiasticus, and in some respects approaches the conception of the logos. *The second part is apparently intended to admonish the Jews of Egypt against the dangers of materialism, skepticism, and idolatry—animal worship in particular is ridiculed—and to recall them to their ancestral faith. The first part appears to be a translation from Hebrew; here the emergence of Greek philosophical connotations in the Greek substitutes of Hebrew words which carried no such connotations is especially interesting. The second part is apparently an original composition in Greek. Since the Greek style of the whole work is consistent, with peculiar errors common to both parts, it has been ingeniously and plausibly suggested that the translator made the first part an introduction to his own inferior composition. There are significant echoes of Wisdom in various New Testament writers. Paul in particular seems to have known it well, and there are traces also in the authors of Ephesians, Hebrews, and I Peter. The probable date of Wisdom is the first century* B.C.

THE WISDOM OF SOLOMON

1] LOVE UPRIGHTNESS, YOU WHO JUDGE THE
       LAND,
    Think of the Lord with goodness,
And seek him with sincerity of heart.

2 For he is found by those who do not try him,
And is manifested to those who do not disbelieve him.

3 For crooked reasonings separate from God,
And when his power is tested, it exposes fools.

4 For wisdom cannot enter a deceitful soul,
Or live in a body in debt to sin.

5 For the holy spirit of instruction will flee from deceit,
And will rise and leave at unwise reasoning,
And be put to confusion at the approach of wrong.

6 For wisdom is a kindly spirit,
And will not acquit a blasphemer of what he says,
For God is a witness of his heart,
And a truthful observer of his mind,
And a hearer of his tongue.

7 For the spirit of the Lord fills the world,
And that which embraces all things knows all that is said.

8 Therefore no one who utters what is wrong will go unob-
    served,
Nor will justice, in its investigation, pass him by.

9 For there will be an inquiry into the designs of the ungodly,
And the sound of his words will reach the Lord,
To convict him of his transgressions.

10 For a jealous ear hears everything,
And the sound of grumbling is not hidden.

11   So beware of useless grumbling,
And spare your tongue from slander;
For no secret word goes for naught,
And a lying mouth destroys the soul.

Do not invite death by the error of your life,   12
Or incur destruction by the work of your hands;
For God did not make death,   13
And he does not enjoy the destruction of the living.
For he created everything to exist,   14
And the generative forces of the world are wholesome,
And there is no poisonous drug in them,
And the kingdom of Hades is not on earth.
For uprightness is immortal.   15
   But ungodly men by their acts and words have sum- 16
     moned him,
They thought him their friend, and softened,
And made an agreement with him,
For they are fit to belong to his party.

For they did not reason soundly, but said to themselves, [2
"Our life is short and miserable,
And there is no cure when man comes to his end,
And no one has been known to return from Hades.
For we were born at a venture,   2
And hereafter we shall be as though we had never existed,
Because the breath in our nostrils is smoke,
And reason is a spark in the beating of our hearts;
When it is quenched, the body will turn to ashes,   3
And the spirit will dissolve like empty air.
And in time our name will be forgotten,   4
And no one will remember what we have done,
And our life will pass away like the traces of a cloud,
And be scattered like mist
Pursued by the sun's rays
And overcome by its heat.
For our life is a fleeting shadow,   5
And there is no way to recall our end,
For it is sealed up and no one can bring it back.

1:12–2:5

6 So come, let us enjoy the good things that exist,
And eagerly make use of the creation as we did in our
youth.

7 Let us have our fill of costly wine and perfumes,
And let us not miss the spring flowers.

8 Let us crown ourselves with rosebuds before they wither;

9 Let none of us miss his share in our revelry;
Everywhere let us leave the signs of our gladness;
For this is our portion and this our lot.

10 Let us oppress the upright poor;
Let us not spare the widow,
Or respect the venerable gray head of the aged.

11 But let our strength be our law of uprightness,
For weakness is proved useless.

12 Let us lie in wait for the upright, for he inconveniences us
And opposes our doings,
And reproaches us with our transgressions of the Law,
And charges us with sins against what we have been
taught;

13 He professes to possess knowledge of God,
And calls himself a child of the Lord;

14 We have found him a reproof of our thoughts,
He is wearisome to us even to see,

15 For his life is not like others,
And his ways are strange.

16 He considers us counterfeit,
And avoids our ways as unclean.
He calls the end of the upright happy,
And boasts that God is his father.

17 Let us see whether what he says is true,
And let us test what will happen at his departure.

18 For if the upright man is a son of God, he will help him,
And save him from the hands of his adversaries.

2:6–18

Let us test him with insults and torture,   19
So that we may learn his patience,
And prove his forbearance.
Let us condemn him to a shameful death,   20
For he will be watched over, from what he says!"

   So they reasoned, but they went astray,   21
For their wickedness blinded them,
And they did not know God's secrets,   22
Or hope for the reward of holiness,
Or recognize the prize of blameless souls.
For God created man for immortality,   23
And made him the image of his own eternity,
But through the devil's envy death came into the world,   24
And those who belong to his party experience it.

   But the souls of the upright are in the hand of God,   [3
And no torment can reach them.
In the eyes of foolish people they seemed to die,   2
And their decease was thought an affliction,
And their departure from us their ruin,   3
But they are at peace.
For though in the sight of men they are punished,   4
Their hope is full of immortality,
And after being disciplined a little, they will be shown   5
   great kindness.
For God has tried them,
And found them worthy of himself.
He has tested them like gold in a furnace,   6
And accepted them like the sacrifice of a whole burnt
   offering.
They will shine out, when he visits them,   7
And spread like sparks among the stubble.
They will judge nations and rule peoples,   8
And the Lord will reign over them forever.

2:19–3:8

9   Those who trust in him will understand the truth,
And those who are faithful will cling to him in love,
For his chosen will find favor and mercy.

10 But the ungodly will be punished according to their
reasonings,
For they disregarded what was right and turned away from
the Lord,

11 For the man who makes light of wisdom and instruction is
wretched,
And there is nothing in their hope, and their labors are unprofitable,
And what they do is useless.

12 Their wives are silly,
And their children bad;
There is a curse on their birth.

13 For happy is the barren woman who is undefiled,
Who has not experienced a sinful union;
She will have fruit when God examines men's souls.

14 And happy is the eunuch who has not transgressed the
Law with his hand,
Nor imagined wicked things against the Lord,
For special favor shall be shown him for his faith,
And a more delightful share in the Lord's sanctuary.

15 For good work brings renown,
And the root of understanding is unerring.

16 But the children of adulterers will not grow up,
And the offspring of an illicit union will disappear.

17 For if they are long-lived, they will be thought of no account,
And, at the last, their old age will be unhonored.

18 If they die early, they will have no hope
Or comfort on the day of decision.

19 For the fate of an unrighteous generation is hard.

3:9-19

It is better to be childless but virtuous, [4
For in the memory of virtue there is immortality,
For it is recognized by both God and men;
When it is present, men imitate it, 2
And they long for it when it is gone.
And it marches in triumph, wearing a wreath forever,
Victorious in the contest for prizes that are undefiled.
But the numerous brood of the ungodly will be unprofit- 3
able,
And with its base-born slips will not strike its roots deep,
Or establish a secure foundation.
For though it flourishes with branches for a while, 4
It stands insecurely and will be shaken by the wind,
And uprooted by the force of the winds.
The twigs will be broken off before they are grown, 5
And their fruit will be useless, not ripe enough to eat,
And good for nothing.
For children born of unlawful slumbers 6
Will be witnesses to their parents' guilt when they are ex-
amined.
But an upright man, if he dies before his time, will be at 7
rest,
For an honored old age does not depend on length of time, 8
And is not measured by the number of one's years,
But understanding is gray hair for men, 9
And a blameless life is old age.
Because he pleased God well, he was loved by him, 10
And while living among sinners he was taken up.
He was caught up, so that wickedness might not alter his 11
understanding,
Or guile deceive his soul.
For the spell of wickedness obscures what is good, 12
And the instability of desire perverts the innocent mind.

4:1-12

13 Being perfected in a little while he has fulfilled long years,
14 For his soul pleased the Lord;
   Therefore he hurried from the midst of wickedness.
   The peoples saw yet did not perceive
   Or take such a thing to heart,
15 For favor and mercy are with his chosen,
   And he watches over his saints.
16 But an upright man who has fallen asleep will condemn
      the ungodly who are still alive,
   And youth that is soon perfected, the great age of the un-
      righteous.
17 For they see the wise man's end,
   And do not perceive what the Lord's purpose about him
      was,
   And for what he kept him safe;
18 They see, and make light of him;
   But the Lord will laugh them to scorn.
19 And afterward they will become a dishonored corpse,
   And be insulted among the dead forever;
   He will burst them open, dumb and swollen,
   And will shake them from their foundations,
   And they will be utterly dried up,
   And they will suffer anguish,
   And the memory of them will perish.
20 They will come like cowards at the reckoning-up of their
      sins,
   And their transgressions will convict them to their face.
5] Then the upright man will stand with great boldness
   Face to face with his oppressors
   And with those who set his labors at nought.
2 They will be dreadfully dismayed at the sight,
   And amazed at the unexpectedness of his deliverance.
3 They will talk to themselves in repentance,

4:13–5:3

And in their distress of mind they will groan and say,
"This is the man we fools once laughed at,   4
And made a byword of reproach.
We thought his life was madness,
And his end dishonored.
How did he come to be reckoned among the sons of God,   5
And why is his lot among the saints?
Then we must have wandered from the true way,   6
And the light of uprightness did not light us,
And the sun did not rise upon us.
We were full of paths of lawlessness and destruction,   7
And traveled through trackless deserts,
But we did not recognize the Lord's road.
What good did our arrogance do us?   8
And what have wealth and ostentation done for us?
They have all passed away like a shadow,   9
And like a messenger running by;
Like a ship crossing the billowing water,   10
And when it is gone there is no track to be found
Or path of its keel in the waves;
Or as when a bird flies through the air,   11
It leaves no sign of its passage;
The light air, whipped by the beat of its wings,
And torn apart by the force of its speed,
Is traversed as its wings move,
And afterward no sign of its passage is found there.
Or as when an arrow is shot at a mark,   12
The air is pierced and immediately returns to itself,
So that its course is unknown;
So we also, as soon as we were born, ceased to be,   13
And had no sign of virtue to show,
But were consumed in our wickedness.
For the ungodly man's hope is like chaff carried by the 14
   wind,

5:4-14

And like hoarfrost driven away by a storm,
It is dissipated like smoke before the wind,
And passes by like the memory of a stranger who stays but
  a night.

15 But the upright live forever,
And their reward is with the Lord,
And the Most High takes care of them.

16 Therefore they will receive the glorious kingdom,
And the beautiful diadem from the Lord's hand,
For he will cover them with his right hand,
And shield them with his arm.

17 He will take his jealousy for his armor,
And will make creation his weapons to repulse his foes.

18 He will put on uprightness for a corselet,
And wear unfeigned justice for a helmet.

19 He will take holiness for an invincible shield,

20 And sharpen his stern anger for a sword;
And with him the world will go to war against the madmen.

21 Well-aimed flashes of lightning will fly,
And will leap to the mark from the clouds, as from a well-
  bent bow,

22 And from a catapult hailstones full of wrath will be hurled.
The water of the sea will be angry with them,
And the rivers will roll relentlessly over them.

23 A mighty wind will oppose them,
And winnow them like a tempest.
And lawlessness will lay waste the whole earth,
And wrongdoing overturn the thrones of princes.

6] Listen therefore, kings, and understand:
Learn this, judges of the ends of the earth;

2 Pay attention, rulers of the people,
Who boast of multitudes of nations;

3 For your dominion was given you from the Lord,

And your sovereignty from the Most High.

He will examine your works and inquire into your plans;

For though you are servants of his kingdom, you have not 4
judged rightly,

Or kept the Law,

Or followed the will of God.

He will come upon you terribly and swiftly, 5

For a stern judgment overtakes those in high places.

For the humblest man may be forgiven through mercy, 6

But the mighty will be mightily tested,

For the Lord of all will show no partiality, 7

And will not respect greatness,

For it was he who made small and great,

And he takes thought for all alike,

But a rigorous inquiry is in store for the powerful. 8

My words are addressed to you, therefore, you monarchs, 9

So that you may learn wisdom and not go astray;

For those who observe holy things in holiness will be made 10
holy,

And those who are taught them will have a defense to offer;

So desire my words, 11

Long for them, and you will be instructed.

Wisdom is bright and unfading, 12

And she is easily seen by those who love her,

And found by those who search for her.

She forestalls those who desire her, by making herself 13
known first.

The man who rises early to seek her will not have to toil, 14

For he will find her sitting at his gates.

For to think of her is the highest understanding, 15

And the man who is vigilant for her sake will soon be free
from care.

For she goes about in search of those who are worthy of her, 16

And she graciously appears to them in their paths,
And meets them in every thought.

17   For the truest beginning of her is the desire for instruc-
         tion,
And concern for instruction is love of her,

18   And love for her is the observance of her laws,
And adherence to her laws is assurance of immortality,

19   And immortality brings men near to God;

20   So the desire for wisdom leads to a kingdom.

21   If therefore you take pleasure in thrones and scepters,
         monarchs of the people,
Honor wisdom, so that you may reign forever.

22   But what wisdom is and how she came to be, I will declare,
And I will not hide these secrets from you,
But I will trace her out from the beginning of creation,
And make the knowledge of her clear,
And I will not pass by the truth;

23   I will not travel with futile envy,
For it cannot associate with wisdom.

24   The multitude of the wise is the salvation of the world,
And a prudent king is the stability of his people.

25   So be instructed by my words and you will be benefited.

7]   I too am a mortal man, like all men,
And a descendant of that first-formed man, who sprang
         from the earth;

2   And I was shaped into flesh in my mother's womb,
Solidified in blood in ten months
From man's seed and the pleasure of marriage.

3   And when I was born I breathed in the common air,
And fell on the kindred earth,
Giving the same first cry as all the rest.

4   I was carefully wrapped up and nursed,

5   For no king has any other beginning of existence;

6:17–7:5

But all men have one entrance upon life, and the same way 6
of leaving it.

Therefore I prayed, and understanding was given me; 7
I called, and the spirit of wisdom came to me.

I preferred her to sceptres and thrones, 8
And I thought wealth of no account compared with her.

I did not think a priceless stone her equal, 9
For all the gold, in her presence, is just a little sand,
And silver is no better than mud, before her.

I loved her more than health and good looks, 10
And I preferred her even to light,
And her radiance is unceasing.

But all blessings came to me along with her, 11
And uncounted wealth is in her hands.

And I rejoiced over them all, because wisdom ruled them, 12
For I did not know that she was their mother.

I learned honestly, and I share ungrudgingly, 13
I will not hide her wealth away,

For it is an unfailing treasure for men, 14
And those who get it make friends with God,
Being commended to him by the gifts that come from her
discipline.

May God grant to me to speak properly, 15
And to have thoughts worthy of what he has given;
For it is he that guides wisdom
And directs the wise.

For in his hand are we and our words, 16
All understanding and knowledge of trades.

For it is he that has given me unerring knowledge of what 17
is,
To know the constitution of the world and the working of
the elements;

The beginning and end and middle of periods of time, 18

7:6–18

The alternations of the solstices and the changes of the
seasons,

19 The cycles of the years and the positions of the stars,
20 The natures of animals, and the dispositions of wild beasts,
The powers of spirits and the designs of men,
The varieties of plants and the virtues of roots;

21 All that was secret or manifest I learned,
22 For wisdom, the fashioner of all things, taught me.
For there is in her a spirit that is intelligent, holy,
Unique, manifold, subtle,
Mobile, clear, undefiled,
Distinct, beyond harm, loving the good, keen,

23 Unhindered, beneficent, philanthropic,
Firm, sure, free from care,
All-powerful, all-seeing,
And interpenetrating all spirits
That are intelligent, pure, and most subtle.

24 For wisdom is more mobile than any motion,
And she penetrates and permeates everything, because she
is so pure;

25 For she is the breath of the power of God,
And a pure emanation of his almighty glory;
Therefore nothing defiled can enter into her.

26 For she is a reflection of the everlasting light,
And a spotless mirror of the activity of God,
And a likeness of his goodness.

27 Though she is one, she can do all things,
And while remaining in herself, she makes everything new.
And passing into holy souls, generation after generation,
She makes them friends of God, and prophets.

28 For God loves nothing but the man who lives with wisdom.
29 For she is fairer than the sun,
Or any group of stars;

7:19-29

Compared with light, she is found superior;
For night succeeds to it,   30
But evil cannot overpower wisdom.
For she reaches in strength from one end of the earth to the   [8
    other,
And conducts everything well.
  I loved her and sought after her from my youth up,   2
And I undertook to make her my bride,
And I fell in love with her beauty.
She glorifies her high birth in living with God,   3
For the Lord of all loves her.
For she is initiated into the knowledge of God,   4
And is a searcher of his works.
But if the possession of wealth is to be desired in life,   5
What is richer than wisdom, which operates everything?
And if understanding works,   6
Who in all the world is a greater craftsman than she?
And if a man loves uprightness,   7
Her labors are virtues;
For she teaches self-control and understanding,
Uprightness and courage;
Nothing in life is more useful to men than these.
But if a man longs for much experience,   8
She knows antiquity and can forecast the future,
She understands the tricks of language and the solving of
    riddles;
She knows the meaning of signs and portents,
And the outcomes of seasons and periods.
So I decided to bring her to live with me,   9
Knowing that she would give me good counsel,
And encouragement in cares and grief.
Because of her I will have glory among the multitude,   10
And honor with the elders, though I am young,

7:30–8:10

11 I will be found keen in judgment,
    And I will be admired in the presence of monarchs.
12 When I am silent, they will wait for me to speak,
    And when I speak, they will pay attention,
    And if I talk at some length,
    They will put their hands over their mouths.
13 Because of her, I will have immortality,
    And leave an everlasting memory to those who come after
        me.
14 I will govern peoples, and nations will be subject to me.
15 Dread sovereigns will be frightened when they hear of me;
    Among the people I will appear good and in war brave.
16 When I enter my house, I will find rest with her,
    For intercourse with her has no bitterness,
    And living with her no grief,
    But gladness and joy.
17 When I considered these things with myself,
    And reflected in my mind
    That in kinship with wisdom there is immortality,
18 And in her friendship there is pure delight,
    And unfailing wealth in the labors of her hands,
    And understanding in the experience of her company,
    And glory in sharing in her words,
    I went about seeking how to win her for myself.
19 I was a well-formed child,
    And a good soul fell to me,
20 Or rather, I was good and entered an undefiled body.
21 But I perceived that I could not win her unless God gave
        her to me
    (And this too came of understanding, to know from whom
        the favor came).
    I appealed to the Lord and besought him,
    And said with all my heart:

8:11–21

"God of my forefathers and merciful Lord,   [9

Who created all things by your word,

And by your wisdom formed man   2

To rule over the creatures you had made,

And manage the world in holiness and uprightness,   3

And pass judgment in rectitude of soul,

Give me the wisdom that sits by your throne,   4

And do not reject me as unfit to be one of your servants.

For I am your slave and the son of your maidservant,   5

A man weak and short-lived,

And inferior in my understanding of judgment;

For even if one among the sons of men is perfect,   6

If the wisdom that comes from you is lacking, he will count

    for nothing.

You have chosen me out to be king of your people,   7

And to be judge of your sons and daughters;

You told me to build a sanctuary on your holy mountain,   8

And an altar in the city where you dwell,

A copy of the holy tent which you prepared in the be-

    ginning;

And with you is wisdom, which knows your works,   9

And was present when you made the world,

And understands what is pleasing in your sight,

And what is in accord with your commands.

Send her forth from the holy heavens   10

And dispatch her from your glorious throne,

To be with me and toil,

And so that I may know what is pleasing to you.

For she knows and understands all things,   11

And she will guide me with good sense in my actions,

And will guard me with her splendor.

Then my doings will be acceptable,   12

And I will judge your people uprightly,

And be worthy of the throne of my father.

13 For what man can know the counsel of God,
Or who can decide what the Lord wills?

14 For the calculations of mortals are timid,
And our designs are likely to fail,

15 For a perishable body weighs down the soul,
And its earthy tent burdens the thoughtful mind.

16 We can hardly guess at things upon the earth,
And we have hard work finding the things that are just at hand,
But who has tracked out the things in heaven?

17 And who has learned your counsel unless you gave him wisdom,
And sent your holy spirit from on high?

18 So the paths of those who were on the earth were straightened,
And men were taught the things that please you,
And were saved by wisdom."

10] It was she that protected the first-formed father of the world,
In his loneliness, after his creation,
And rescued him from his transgression,

2 And gave him strength to master all things.

3 And when an unrighteous man abandoned her in his anger,
He perished in his fratricidal rage.

4 When the earth was deluged because of him, wisdom again saved
The upright man, steering him with a cheap piece of wood.

5 It was she that when the nations were confused, in their wicked conspiracy,
Recognized the upright man, and preserved him blameless before God,

9:13–10:5

And kept him steadfast against having pity on his child.

When the ungodly were perishing, she saved an upright   6
  man,
Who fled from the fire that descended on the Five Towns;
To their wickedness a smoking waste   7
Still bears lasting witness,
As do trees that bear fruit that never ripens,
And a pillar of salt that stands as a memorial of an un-
  believing soul.

For because they passed wisdom by,   8
They were not only made incapable of recognizing what
  was good,
But also left behind them to life a memorial of their folly,
So that their faults could not pass unnoticed.

But wisdom delivered those who served her from their   9
  troubles.

An upright man, who was a fugitive from a brother's   10
  wrath,
She guided in straight paths;
She showed him God's kingdom,
And gave him knowledge of holy things;
She made him prosper in his toils
And increased the fruit of his labors;

When those who oppressed him were covetous, she stood   11
  by him,
And made him rich.

She protected him from his enemies,   12
And kept him safe from those who lay in wait for him,
And decided his hard contest in his favor,
So that he should know that godliness is stronger than any-
  thing.

When an upright man was sold, she did not abandon him, 13
But delivered him from sin;

10:6–13

She went down into the pit with him,
14 And she did not leave him in prison,
Until she brought him the scepter of a kingdom,
And power over those who lorded it over him;
She showed that they were false who had blamed him,
And she gave him everlasting honor.

15   She delivered from a nation of oppressors
A holy people and a blameless race;

16 She entered the soul of a servant of the Lord,
And withstood awe-inspiring kings with portents and signs;

17 She paid to holy men a reward for their toils,
She guided them along a wonderful way,
And became a shelter for them in the daytime,
And a flame of stars at night.

18 She brought them over the Red Sea,
And led them through deep waters.

19 But their enemies she overwhelmed,
And cast them up from the bottom of the deep.

20 Therefore the upright despoiled the ungodly,
And they sang, Lord, of your holy name,
And praised with one accord your defending hand.

21 For wisdom opens the mouth of the dumb,
And makes the tongues of babes speak plainly.

11}   She made their doings prosper by means of a holy
prophet.

2 They traveled through an uninhabited desert,
And pitched their tents in trackless places.

3 They withstood their enemies and repulsed their foes.

4 They grew thirsty and called upon you,
And water was given them out of a rocky cliff,
And a cure for their thirst out of the hard stone.

5 For the means by which their enemies were punished
Benefited them in their time of need.

10:14–11:5

Instead of the fountain of an ever flowing river,   6
Stirred up with filthy blood,
As a rebuke for the decree to kill the babes,   7
You gave them plenty of water, in a way unlooked for,
Showing through their thirst at that time   8
How you punished their adversaries.
For when they were tried, although they were only disci-   9
     plined in mercy,
They learned how the ungodly were tormented, when they
     were judged in wrath.
For these you tested like a father, warning them,   10
But those you examined like a stern king, condemning
     them.
Whether absent or present, they were harassed alike;   11
For a double grief seized them,   12
And groaning over the memory of the past.
For when they heard that through their punishments   13
The others were benefited, they felt it was the Lord.
For the man who had long before been cast forth and ex-   14
     posed, and whom they had rejected with scorn,
As events resulted, they admired,
When they felt thirst in a different way from the upright.
But for the foolish fancies of their unrighteousness,   15
Misled by which they worshiped unreasoning reptiles
     and worthless vermin,
You sent a multitude of unreasoning creatures upon them
     to punish them,
So that they should know that a man is punished by the   16
     things through which he sins.
For your all-powerful hand, which created the world out   17
     of formless matter,
Did not lack means to send upon them a multitude of
     bears, or bold lions,

11:6-17

18 Or newly created wild animals, unknown before, and full
   of rage,
   Either puffing out a fiery breath,
   Or scattering a roar of smoke,
   Or flashing dreadful sparks from their eyes,
19 Which could not only have destroyed them utterly by the
   harm they did,
   But have made them die of fright at the very sight of them.
20 Why, without these, they might have been felled by a
   single breath,
   Being pursued by justice,
   And scattered by the breath of your power.
   But you ordered everything by measure and number and
   weight.
21 For it is always yours to have great strength,
   And who can withstand the might of your arm?
22 For in your sight the whole world is like what turns the
   scale in a balance,
   And like drop of dew that comes down on the earth in the
   morning.
23 But you have mercy on all men, because you can do all
   things,
   And you overlook men's sins to lead them to repent,
24 For you love all things that exist,
   And abhor none of the things that you have made;
   For you would never have formed anything if you hated it.
25 And how could anything have endured, if you had not
   willed it,
   Or what had not been called forth by you have been preserved?
26 But you spare all, because they are yours, Lord, lover of life,
12] For your imperishable spirit is in all things.
2   Therefore you correct little by little those who go astray,

11:18–12:2

And you admonish them by reminding them of the things
    through which they sin;
So that they may escape from their wickedness and believe
    in you, Lord.
For those who long ago inhabited your holy land   3
You hated for acting most hatefully,   4
Practicing enchantments and unholy rites,
Merciless killing of children,   5
And cannibal feasting on human flesh and blood.
Initiates from the midst of a pagan brotherhood,   6
And parents who were murderers of helpless lives,
You determined to destroy by the hands of our forefathers,
So that the land which you prized above all others   7
Might receive a worthy colony of God's children.
But even these, as being men, you spared,   8
And you sent wasps as forerunners of your host,
To destroy them little by little.
Not that you were unable to make the upright defeat the   9
    ungodly in battle,
Or to destroy them at one blow with terrible wild animals
    or a stern command,
But in judging them little by little you gave them oppor-   10
    tunity to repent,
For you were not ignorant that their origin was evil,
And their wickedness inborn,
And that their manner of thought would never change.
For they were a race accursed from the beginning,   11
And it was not through fear of any man that you left them
    unpunished for their sins.
For who can say, "What have you done?"   12
Or who can oppose your judgment?
And who can accuse you of the destruction of the nations
    which you made?

12:3–12

Or who will come to stand before you as the avenger of
    unrighteous men?

13 For neither is there any god but you, who care for all men,
To show that you do not judge unrighteously,

14 Nor will any king or monarch be able to face you about
    those whom you have punished.

15 But since you are upright, you conduct all things uprightly,
Considering it inconsistent with your power
To condemn the man who does not deserve to be punished.

16 For your strength is the beginning of uprightness
And the fact that you are Lord of all makes you spare all.

17 For when men disbelieve in the perfection of your power,
    you display your strength,
And in the case of those that know, you rebuke their rash-
    ness.

18 But you, being master of your strength, judge us with fair-
    ness
And govern us with great forbearance.
For the power is at your command, whenever you wish it.

19   By such deeds you taught your people
That the upright man must be humane,
And you made your sons be of good hope,
Because you give repentance for sins,

20 For if you punished with such care and indulgence
Those who were the enemies of your servants, and deserved
    death,
Giving them time and opportunity to escape from their
    wickedness,

21 With what exactness you have judged your sons,
To whose forefathers you gave oaths and agreements
    promising them good!

22   So when you discipline us, you flog our enemies ten
    thousand fold,

So that when we judge we may reflect on your goodness,
And when we are judged we may look for mercy.
Therefore you tormented through their own abominable 23
practices
Those who lived wickedly, in a life of folly,
For they went astray far beyond the ways of error, 24
Accepting as gods the lowest and basest of animals,
Being deceived like foolish babies.
Therefore you sent your judgment in mockery of them, 25
As though to unreasoning children.
But those who cannot be admonished by mockeries of cor- 26
rection,
Will experience a judgment worthy of God.
For because through what they suffered they became in- 27
dignant
At those whom they considered gods, being punished by
means of them,
They saw and recognized as the true God him whom they
had before refused to know.
Therefore the very height of condemnation overtook them.
For all men are foolish by nature, and had no perception [13
of God,
And from the good things that were visible they had not
the power to know him who is,
Nor through paying attention to his works did they recog-
nize the workman,
But either fire, or wind, or swift air, 2
Or the circle of the stars, or rushing water,
Or the heavenly luminaries, the rulers of the world, they
considered gods.
And if through delight in their beauty they supposed that 3
these were gods,
Let them know how far superior is the Lord of these.

12:23–13:3

For the originator of beauty created them;
4 But if it was through awe at their power and operation,
Let them conclude from them how much mightier he who
  formed them is.
5 For from the greatness and beauty of what is created,
The originator of them is correspondingly perceived.
6 But yet little blame attaches to these men,
For perhaps they just go astray
In their search for God and their desire to find him;
7 For living among his works they search
And believe the testimony of their sight, that what they see
  is beautiful.
8 But again, even they are not to be excused;
9 For if they had power to know so much
That they could try to make out the world,
Why did they not sooner find the Lord of all this?
10   For they are miserable, and their hopes are set on the
        dead,
Who have called the works of men's hands gods,
Gold and silver, the subject of art,
And likenesses of animals,
Or useless stone, worked by some ancient hand.
11 But if some carpenter saws down a tree he can handle,
And skilfully strips off all its bark,
And shaping it nicely
Makes a dish suited to the uses of life,
12 And burns the chips of his work
To prepare his food, and eats his fill;
13 But the worst of them, which is good for nothing,
A crooked piece, full of knots,
He takes and carves to occupy his spare time,
And shapes it with understanding skill,
He makes it a copy of a human form,

13:4-13

Or makes it like some common animal,   14
Smearing it with vermilion, and painting its surface red,
And coating every blemish in it;
And making an abode for it worthy of it,   15
He fixes it on the wall, and fastens it with iron.
So he plans for it, so that it will not fall down,   16
For he knows that it cannot help itself;
For it is only an image and needs help.
But he prays to it about his property and his marriage and   17
    his children,
And is not ashamed to speak to a lifeless thing,
And appeals to something that is weak, for health,   18
And asks something that is dead, for life,
And supplicates what is itself utterly inexperienced, for aid,
And something that cannot even take a step, about a
    journey,
And he asks strength for gain and business and success in   19
    what he undertakes
From something whose hands are most feeble.
        Again, a man setting out on a voyage, and about to [14
            travel over wild waves,
Calls upon a piece of wood more unsound than the ship
    that carries him.
For it was designed through the desire for gain,   2
And wisdom was the craftsman that built it.
And your providence, Father, pilots it,   3
For you give a way even in the sea,
And a safe path through the waves,
Showing that you can save from anything,   4
So that even without skill a man may go to sea.
But it is your will that the works of your wisdom should   5
    not be idle;
Therefore men trust their lives to even the smallest plank,

13:14–14:5

And cross the flood on a raft and get safely over.

6 For in the beginning, when the haughty giants perished,
The hope of the world took refuge on a raft,
And steered by your hand left to the world a generating germ.

7 For blessed is wood through which uprightness comes,

8 But what is made with hands is accursed, along with the man who made it,
Because he shaped it, and what was perishable was called a god.

9 For the ungodly man and his ungodliness are equally hateful to God.

10 For what is done must be punished with the man who did it.

11 Therefore there will be an examination of the idols of the heathen,
For, although part of God's creation, they became an abomination,
And snares to the souls of men,
And a trap for the feet of the foolish.

12 For the devising of idols is the beginning of fornication,
And the invention of them is the corruption of life.

13 For they did not exist from the beginning, and they will not last forever;

14 For through the vanity of men they came into the world,
And therefore a speedy end for them was designed.

15 For a father afflicted with untimely grief
Made a likeness of his child, that had been quickly taken from him,
And presently honored as a god him who was once a dead man,
And handed down to his subjects mysteries and rites.

16 Then the ungodly practice, strengthened by time, came to be observed as law,

And by the orders of monarchs carved images were worshiped.

And when men could not honor them in their presence, 17
because they lived far away,

They imagined how they looked, far away,

And made a visible image of the king they honored,

So as by their zeal to flatter the absent one as though he
were present.

But the ambition of the artist stimulated 18

Even those who did not know the subject to intensified
worship;

For he, perhaps wishing to gratify someone in authority, 19

Elaborated the likeness by his art into greater beauty;

And the multitude, attracted by the charm of his work- 20
manship,

Now regarded as an object of worship the one whom they
had recently honored as a man.

And this proved an ambush for man's life, 21

Because men in bondage to misfortune or royal authority

Clothed stick and stones with the Name that cannot be
shared with others.

And then it was not enough for them to go astray about 22
the knowledge of God,

But though living in a great war of ignorance,

They call such evils peace.

For neither while they murder children in their rites nor 23
celebrate secret mysteries,

Nor hold frenzied revels with alien laws

Do they keep their lives or marriages pure, 24

But one man waylays another and kills him, or grieves him
by adultery.

And it is all a confusion of blood and murder, theft and 25
fraud,

14:17-25

Depravity, faithlessness, discord, perjury,

26 Clamor at the good, forgetfulness of favors,
Defilement of souls, confusion of sex,
Irregularity in marriage, adultery, and indecency.

27 For the worship of the unspeakable idols
Is the beginning and cause and end of every evil.

28 For they either rejoice in madness, or prophesy falsely,
Or live unrighteously, or readily forswear themselves.

29 For since they believe in lifeless idols,
They do not expect to be harmed for swearing wickedly.

30 But justice will overtake them for both matters,
Because they thought wickedly of God and gave heed to
   idols,
And because they swore unrighteously to deceive, in disregard of holiness.

31 For it is not the power of the gods men swear by,
But the penalty of those who sin
That always pursues the transgression of the unrighteous.

15] But you, our God, are kind and true,
You are long-suffering, and govern everything in mercy.

2 For even if we sin, we are yours, and know your might;
But we will not sin, for we know that we are accounted
   yours.

3 For to know you is perfect uprightness,
And to recognize your might is the root of immortality.

4 For no artful device of men has led us astray,
Nor the fruitless labor of scene-painters,
A figure smeared with varied colors,

5 The appearance of which leads to desire in fools,
And they long for the lifeless form of a dead image.

6 Lovers of evil and deserving of such hopes
Are those who make them and those who feel desire for
   them and those who worship them.

14:26–15:6

For a potter, molding the soft earth,   7
Laboriously shapes each object for our use;
Why, from the same clay he forms
Dishes to serve clean purposes,
And those of the opposite kind, all alike;
But of what use shall be made of either,
The potter is the judge.
And with misdirected toil he shapes a futile god out of the   8
    same clay,
And having shortly before sprung from the earth,
After a little goes to that from which he was taken,
When he is called upon to return the soul that was lent
    him.
But he is concerned, not because he will grow tired,   9
Nor because his life is short,
But he competes with gold- and silversmiths,
And copies those who mold brass,
And thinks it a glory that he can form counterfeits.
His heart is ashes, and his hope cheaper than dirt,   10
And his life more worthless than clay,
For he has not recognized the one who formed him,   11
And inspired him with an active soul,
And breathed into him the breath of life.
But they consider our existence play,   12
And life a lucrative fair,
For, they say, one must make money any way one can,
    even by evil.
For this man knows better than all others that he sins,   13
Producing from earthy material fragile dishes and carved
    images.
But most foolish, and more wretched than a baby's soul,   14
Are all those enemies of your people, who oppress them,
For they consider all the idols of the heathen gods,   15

15:7–15

Which can neither use eyes to see with,
Nor noses to inhale the air,
Nor ears to hear with,
Nor fingers on their hands to feel with,
And their feet are of no use to walk on.

16 For a man made them,
And one whose own spirit is borrowed formed them;
For no man can form a god like him;

17 For mortal as he is, what he makes with his lawless hands is
        dead;
For he is better than the things he worships,
For of the two, he has life, but they never had it.

18 Why, they worship even the most hateful animals;
For by comparison, they are worse than the other animals
        in their lack of intelligence;

19 Nor are they in their appearance as animals so beautiful
        as to be desired,
But they have escaped both the praise of God and his
        blessing.

16] Therefore they were punished as they deserved, by simi-
        lar animals,
And tormented with a multitude of vermin.

2 And instead of this punishment, you benefited your people,
And to satisfy the desire of their appetite, you prepared
        something with a strange taste—
Quails for food,

3 So that those others, when they desired food,
Because of the hideousness of the things sent among them,
Should lose even the smallest appetite,
While they, after being in want for a little while,
Should partake of something with a strange taste.

4 For it was necessary that an unescapable want should come
        upon those others for their tyrannical behavior,

15:16–16:4

But these should only be shown how their enemies were
tormented.

For when the terrible fury of wild animals came upon   5
them,

And they were perishing by the bites of wriggling snakes,
Your wrath did not continue to the uttermost,
But they were harassed for a little while to admonish them,   6
For they had a token of preservation to remind them of the
commandment of your law;

For the one who turned toward it was saved not because of   7
what he saw,

But because of you, who are the preserver of all.
And by this you persuaded our enemies   8
That you are the one who saves from every evil.
For they were killed by the bites of locusts and flies,   9
And no cure was found for their life,
For they deserved to be punished by such means.
But not even the teeth of venomous serpents could over-   10
come your sons,

For your mercy came to help them and healed them.
For it was to remind them of your oracles that they were   11
stung,

And they were quickly delivered,
To keep them from falling into deep forgetfulness
And becoming sundered from your kindness.
For it was no plant or plaster that cured them,   12
But your word, Lord, that heals all men.
For you have power over life and death,   13
And you take men down to the gates of Hades and bring
them up again.

A man may kill in his wickedness,   14
But the spirit once it is gone out he cannot bring back,
Nor can he release the imprisoned soul.

16:5–14

15   But it is impossible to escape your hand,
16   For ungodly men, refusing to know you,
      Were flogged with the strength of your arm,
      Pursued by unusual rains and hailstorms and relentless
          showers,
      And utterly consumed by fire.
17   For, strangest of all, on the water, which quenches every
          thing,
      The fire had the greater effect,
      For the universe is the champion of the upright:
18   For now the flame was quieted,
      So that it should not burn up the animals sent against the
          ungodly,
      But that they, when they saw it, might recognize that they
          were pursued by the judgment of God;
19   And again it blazed up in the midst of the water, with
          more than fiery power,
      To destroy the products of an unrighteous land.
20   Instead of these you gave your people angels' food,
      And untiringly supplied them with bread from heaven,
          ready to eat,
      Strong in all enjoyment and suited to every taste;
21   For your support manifested your sweetness toward your
          children,
      And the bread, responding to the desire of the man that
          took it,
      Was changed to what each one desired.
22   But snow and ice endured fire without melting,
      So that they should know that fire was destroying the crops
          of their enemies,
      Blazing in the hail,
      And flashing in the rain;

16:15-22

And that this again, in order that upright men might be fed, 23
Had forgotten its power.

For creation, serving you who made it, 24
Strains against the unrighteous, to punish them,
But relaxes on behalf of those who trust in you, to benefit
them.

Therefore even then, assuming all forms, 25
It served your all-sustaining bounty,
In response to the desire of those who were in need,
So that your sons, whom you have loved, Lord, might 26
learn
That it is not the production of the crops that supports
man,
But that it is your word that preserves those who believe in
you.

For what the fire could not destroy 27
Melted away when it was simply warmed by a fleeting
sunbeam,
So that it might be known that we must rise before the 28
sun to give you thanks,
And appeal to you at the rising of the light.

For the unthankful man's hope will melt like the wintry 29
hoarfrost,
And run off like useless water.

For your judgments are great and hard to set forth; [17
Therefore uninstructed souls went astray.

For when lawless men thought they were oppressing a holy 2
nation
They lay shut up under their roofs, exiled from the eternal
providence,
Prisoners of darkness and captives of the long night.

For when they thought they were hidden in their secret sins 3
By a dark veil of forgetfulness,

16:23–17:3

They were scattered, terribly frightened,
And appalled by specters.

4 For even the inner chamber that held them did not protect
them from fear,
But appalling sounds rung around them,
And somber ghosts appeared, with gloomy faces.

5 And no fire was strong enough to succeed in giving them
light,
Nor could the bright flames of the stars
Undertake to illumine that hateful night.

6 Only there shone on them
A fearful flame, of itself,
And though dreadfully frightened at that sight when it
could not be seen,
They thought the things they beheld still worse.

7 And the delusions of magic art were prostrate,
And their boasted wisdom suffered a contemptuous rebuke,

8 For those who claimed to drive away fears and troubles
from sick souls
Were sick themselves with ridiculous fear.

9 For if nothing alarming frightened them,
Yet scared by the creeping of vermin and the hissing of
reptiles

10 They died of fright,
Refusing to look even upon the air, which could not be
escaped on any side.

11 For wickedness is a cowardly thing, condemned by a witness of its own,
And being distressed by conscience, has always exag-
gerated hardships;

12 For fear is nothing but the giving up of the reinforcements
that come from reason,

17:4-12

And as the expectation of them from within is deficient, 13
It reckons its ignorance worse than the cause of the torment.
But they, all through the night, which was really powerless, 14
And came upon them from the recesses of a powerless Hades,
Sleeping the same sleep,
Were now driven by monstrous phantoms, 15
And now paralyzed by their soul's surrender;
For they were drenched in sudden, unlooked-for fear.
Then whoever was there fell down 16
And so was shut up and guarded in a prison not made of iron;
For whether a man was a farmer or a shepherd, 17
Or a laborer whose work was in a wilderness,
He was overtaken and suffered the unavoidable fate,
For they were all bound with one chain of darkness.
Whether there was a whistling wind, 18
Or a melodious sound of birds in spreading branches,
Or the regular noise of rushing water,
Or a harsh crashing of rocks thrown down, 19
Or the unseen running of bounding animals,
Or the sound of the most savage wild beasts roaring,
Or an echo thrown back from a hollow in the mountains,
It paralyzed them with terror.
For the whole world was bathed in bright light, 20
And occupied in unhindered work;
Only over them was spread a heavy night, 21
A picture of the darkness that was to receive them.
But heavier than the darkness were they to themselves.
But your holy ones enjoyed a very great light; [18

17:13–18:1

And the others, hearing their voices but not seeing their forms,

Thought them happy, because they had not suffered,

2 But they were thankful because the others, though they had before been wronged, did not hurt them,

And prayed to be separated from them.

3 Therefore you provided a blazing pillar

As guide on their unknown journey,

And an unharmful sun for their honorable exile.

4 For they deserved to be deprived of light and imprisoned in darkness

Who had kept your sons shut up,

Through whom the imperishable light of the Law was to be given to the world.

5 When they plotted to kill the babies of the holy ones,

Though one child had been exposed and saved,

To rebuke them you took from them a multitude of their children,

And destroyed them all together in a mighty flood.

6 That night was made known to our forefathers beforehand,

So that they should know certainly what oaths they had believed, and rejoice.

7 The preservation of the upright and the destruction of their enemies

Were expected by your people;

8 For in punishing their adversaries,

You called us to you and glorified us.

9 For in secret the holy children of good men offered the sacrifice,

And with one accord agreed to the divine law,

That they should share alike

The same blessings and dangers,

And were already beginning to sing the praises of their
 forefathers,

When there echoed back the discordant shout of their 10
 enemies,

And the piteous sound of lamentation for children spread
 abroad;

But slave was punished with master, with the same penalty, 11

And the commoner suffered the same as the king,

And all of them together under one form of death 12

Had countless corpses.

For those who were alive were not even enough to bury
 them,

For in one instant their most valued children were destroyed.

For though they disbelieved everything because of their 13
 enchantments,

When the first-born were destroyed, they acknowledged
 that the people was God's son.

For when gentle silence enveloped everything, 14

And night was midway of her swift course,

Your all-powerful word leaped from heaven, from the 15
 royal throne,

A stern warrior, into the midst of the doomed land,

Carrying for a sharp sword your undisguised command, 16

And stood still, and filled all things with death,

And touched heaven but walked upon the earth.

Then suddenly apparitions in dreadful dreams startled 17
 them,

And unlooked-for fears assailed them,

And one thrown here half-dead, another there, 18

Showed why they were dying,

For the dreams that had alarmed them warned them of it, 19

So that they should not perish without knowing why they
 suffered.

18:10–19

20 But the experience of death affected the upright also,
And a multitude were destroyed in the desert.
But the wrath did not continue long.

21 For a blameless man hurried to fight in their defense,
Bringing the great shield of his ministering,
Prayer and the propitiation of incense;
He withstood that wrath and put an end to the disaster,
Showing that he was a servant of yours;

22 But he overcame that anger not by bodily strength,
Nor by force of arms,
But by his word he subdued the chastiser,
When he appealed to the oaths and agreements given to
the forefathers.

23 For when the dead had already fallen on one another in
heaps,
He stood between and cut the wrath short
And cut off its way to the living.

24 For on his long robe was the whole world,
And the glories of the forefathers were in the carving of the
four rows of stones,
And your majesty was on the diadem upon his head.

25 Before these the destroyer gave way, and these he feared,
For that experience of wrath was enough by itself.

19] But, on the ungodly, pitiless anger came to the uttermost,
For he knew their future also beforehand,

2 That after permitting them to go away,
And sending them off in haste,
They would change their minds and pursue them.

3 For while they were still busy with their mourning,
And were lamenting beside the graves of the dead,
They involved themselves in another foolish design,
And pursued as runaways those whom they had driven
out with entreaties.

18:20–19:3

For the fate they deserved dragged them on to this end,   4
And made them forget what had happened,
So that they should make up the punishment that their
    torments lacked,
And your people should experience an incredible journey,   5
While they themselves should find a strange death.
For the whole creation in its own kind was reshaped anew,   6
In obedience to your commands,
So that your servants might be protected unharmed.
The cloud was seen that overshadowed the camp,   7
And the emergence of dry land where water had stood
    before,
An unobstructed road out of the Red Sea,
And a grassy plain out of the raging billow;
Through which those who were protected by your hand   8
    passed over as a nation,
Witnessing marvelous portents.
For they ranged like horses   9
And skipped like lambs,
Praising you, Lord, who had delivered them.
For they still remembered the things in their sojourning,   10
How instead of the birth of animals the earth brought
    forth gnats,
And instead of aquatic creatures the river vomited up a
    host of frogs.
But later they saw a new production of birds also,   11
When moved by appetite they asked for delicacies;
For quails came up from the sea to their relief.   12
    And those punishments came upon the sinners   13
Not without premonitory signs, in the violence of the
    thunders;
For they suffered justly through their own wickedness,
For they exhibited a more bitter hatred of strangers.

19:4-13

14 For some would not receive men who did not know them,
when they came to them,
But these men made slaves of strangers who showed them
kindness.

15 And not only so, but those others shall have some consideration
For the men they received with such hostility were aliens;

16 But these men, though they had welcomed them with
feasting,
Afflicted those who had already shared the same rights
with them, with dreadful labors.

17 And they were stricken with loss of sight too,
Like those others, at the upright man's door,
When, surrounded with yawning darkness,
Each one sought the way through his own doors.

18 For the elements changed in order with one another,
Just as on a harp the notes vary the character of the time,
Yet keep the pitch,
As one may accurately infer from the observation of what
happened;

19 For land animals were turned into water creatures,
And swimming things changed to the land;

20 Fire retained its power in water,
And water forgot its quenching property.

21 Contrariwise, flames did not wither the flesh
Of perishable animals that walked about among them,
Nor was the easily melting ice-like kind of immortal food
melted.

22 For in everything, you, Lord, magnified and glorified
your people,
And you did not neglect them, but stood by them at every
time and place.

19:14–22

ECCLESIASTICUS, OR THE WISDOM OF JESHUA SON OF SIRACH

This book is a wholesome reminder that even in the intertestamentary period not all men were strenuously involved in religious struggle. Its tone is secular, and it can be read almost as an essay of Montaigne is read. Ecclesiasticus presents the reflections of a learned and experienced man who is conscious of his own attainments. He is aware that the law of the Most High and his covenant must be recognized and is concerned for religious truth and observance, but his emphasis is on the worldly wisdom that comes from experience. For instance, as we read in 38.1–15, if a man is sick he should pray, cleanse his heart from sin, and offer sacrifice—but he must put himself in the hands of a physician, for God created physicians. There is a suggestion of an Attic atmosphere in Ecclesiasticus' concern for the orderly functioning of society, for specialization and competence among craftsmen. The familiar (if only from funeral services) eulogy of famous men (44.1 ff.) recognizes not only effective administrators, counselors, and orators, but also "such as found out musical tunes and recited verses in writing."

Ecclesiasticus is the only book in the Apocrypha whose author's name, something of his personality, and his date are known. At 50.27 he gives his name as Jeshua son of Sirach of Jerusalem, and he speaks of himself elsewhere also. He has much to say of the proper conduct and values of social intercourse and of the benefits and obligations of friendship. His code is enlightened self-interest. His opinion of women (25.15 ff.) is very low. In the Prologue his grandson and namesake tells us that he translated the book into Greek in Egypt at a date corresponding to 132 B.C. The book must then have been written by an upper-class Jerusalemite about 180 B.C. Hebrew fragments of the book found in the present century are not the original but a retranslation from the Greek. Considering that the book was written in Hebrew, the tone of Ecclesiasticus is more compelling evidence than the institution of gymnasia and the adoption of Greek dress for the assimilation of the Greek outlook in Jerusalem in the pre-Maccabean period.

ECCLESIASTICUS, OR THE WIS-
DOM OF JESHUA, THE
SON OF SIRACH

THE PROLOGUE

SINCE MANY GREAT THINGS HAVE BEEN communicated to us through the Law and the prophets, and the others who followed after them, for which we must give Israel the praise due to instruction and wisdom; and since not only must those who read become expert themselves but those who love learning must also be able to be useful to the uninitiated, both in speaking and in writing, my grandfather Jeshua, after devoting himself for a long time to the reading of the Law and the prophets and the other books of our forefathers, and after attaining considerable proficiency in them, was led to write on his own account something in the line of instruction and wisdom, so that lovers of learning and persons who become interested in these things might make still greater progress in living in accordance with the Law.

You are therefore invited to read it through, with favorable attention, and to excuse us for any failures we may seem to have made in phraseology, in what we have labored to translate. For things once expressed in Hebrew do not have the same force in them when put into another language; and not only this book, but the Law itself, and the prophecies, and the rest of the books, differ not a little in translation from the original.

For after I came to Egypt in the thirty-eighth year of the reign of King Euergetes, and spent some time there, I found a copy of it of no small educational value, and thought

223

it absolutely necessary that I should myself devote diligence and labor to the translation of this book, devoting long hours and expert knowledge in the intervening time to the task of completing the book and publishing it, for those also who, in the land where they are visiting, being already prepared in character to live in accordance with the Law, desire to advance in learning.

THE WISDOM OF SIRACH

1} ALL WISDOM COMES FROM THE LORD,
And remains with him forever.

2 The sand of the seas, and the drops of rain,
And the days of eternity—who can count them?

3 The height of the heavens, and the breadth of the earth,
And the deep, and wisdom—who can track them out?

4 Wisdom was created before them all,
And sound intelligence from eternity.

6 To whom has the source of wisdom been revealed?
And who knows her devices?

8 There is but one who is wise, a very terrible one,
Seated upon his throne;

9 The Lord himself created her;
He saw her and counted her,
And poured her out upon all he made;

10 Upon all mankind, as he chose to bestow her;
But he supplied her liberally to those who loved him.

11 To fear the Lord is a glory and a ground of exultation;
A joy, and a crown of ecstasy.

12 To fear the Lord delights the heart,
And brings gladness and joy and long life.

13 The man who fears the Lord will have a happy end,
And be blessed in the day of his death.

14 To fear the Lord is the source of wisdom,
And she was created with the faithful in the womb.

15 She has built her nest among men as a foundation from
eternity,
And among their posterity she will be held in trust.

16 To fear the Lord is to be satisfied with wisdom,
For she intoxicates them with her fruits.

17 She will fill all their houses with desirable things,
And their storehouses with her produce;

To fear the Lord is a crown of wisdom,   18
Making peace and healing health flourish.
He beheld her and counted her;
He rained down understanding and sound knowledge,   19
And increased the glory of those who possessed her.
To fear the Lord is the root of wisdom,   20
And her branches are long life.

Unrighteous anger can never be excused,   22
For the weight of a man's anger drags him down.
A patient man will control himself for a while,   23
And afterward joy will break out.
He will repress his words for a time,   24
And the lips of many will tell of his understanding.
In the storehouses of wisdom there are wise proverbs,   25
But godliness is a detestation to the irreligious.
If you desire wisdom, keep the commandments,   26
And the Lord will supply you with her liberally.
For to fear the Lord is wisdom and education,   27
And faith and meekness win his approval.
Do not disobey the fear of the Lord,   28
And do not approach it with a divided heart.
Do not be a hypocrite in the mouths of men,   29
And take heed to your own lips.
Do not exalt yourself, or you may fall,   30
And bring disgrace upon yourself;
And the Lord will reveal your secrets
And prostrate you before all the congregation,
Because you did not come to the fear of the Lord,
But your heart was full of deceit.

My child, if you come to serve the Lord,   [2
Prepare yourself to be tried.
Set your heart right and be firm,   2
And do not be hasty when things go against you;

3   Hold fast to him, and do not forsake him,
     So that you may be honored when your life ends.

4   Accept whatever happens to you,
     And be patient in humiliating vicissitudes.

5   For gold is tested with fire,
     And men who are approved must be tested in the furnace
        of humiliation.

6   Have faith in him, and he will help you;
     Make your ways straight, and put your hope in him.

7   You who fear the Lord, wait for his mercy,
     And do not turn aside, or you will fall.

8   You who fear the Lord, have faith in him,
     And you will not lose your reward.

9   You who fear the Lord, hope for his blessings,
     And for everlasting joy and mercy.

10   Look at the generations of antiquity and see,
     Who that put his trust in the Lord was ever put to shame?
     Or who that continued to fear him was ever forsaken?
     Or who that called upon him was overlooked by him?

11   For the Lord is merciful and has pity,
     And forgives sins and delivers in times of affliction.

12   Alas for cowardly hearts and palsied hands!
     And for a sinner who follows two paths!

13   Alas for a faint heart, for it does not believe;
     Therefore it will not be protected.

14   Alas for you, who have lost your steadfastness!
     What will you do when the Lord visits you?

15   Those who fear the Lord will not disobey his words,
     And those who love him will keep his ways.

16   Those who fear the Lord will seek his favor,
     And those who love him will be filled with the Law.

17   Those who fear the Lord will prepare their hearts,
     And will humble their souls before him.

2:3–17

"Let us fall into the Lord's hands, 18
And not into the hands of men."
For as his majesty is,
So is his mercy also.

Listen to me, your father, children, [3
And act in such a way that you may be preserved.

For the Lord has glorified the father above his children, 2
And he has established the rights of the mother over her
  sons.

He who provides for his father atones for his sins,
And he who shows his mother honor is like a man who lays 4
  up treasure.

He who provides for his father will be gladdened by his 5
  children,
And will be heard on the day that he prays.

He who shows his father honor will have a long life, 6
And he who listens to the Lord will refresh his mother, 7
And will serve his parents as his masters.

Honor your father in word and deed, 8
So that his blessing may attend you.

For a father's blessing establishes the houses of his chil- 9
  dren,
But a mother's curse uproots their foundations.

Do not glorify yourself by dishonoring your father, 10
For your father's disgrace is no glory to you.

For a man's glory arises from honoring his father, 11
And a neglected mother is a reproach to her children.

My child, help your father in his old age, 12
And do not grieve him, as long as he lives.

If his understanding fails, be considerate, 13
And do not humiliate him, when you are in all your
  strength.

Charity given to a father will not be forgotten, 14

And will build you up a further atonement for your sins.

15 When you are in trouble, you will be remembered;
    Like frost in sunshine your sins will melt away.

16 He who deserts his father is like a blasphemer,
    And he who angers his mother is cursed by the Lord.

17 My child, carry on your business in humility,
    And you will be loved by men whom God accepts.

18 The greater you are, the more you must practice humility,
    And you will find favor with the Lord.

20 For the Lord's power is great,
    And he is glorified by the humble-minded.

21 Do not seek for what is too hard for you,
    And do not investigate what is beyond your strength;

22 Think of the commands that have been given you,
    For you have no need of the things that are hidden.

23 Do not waste your labor on what is superfluous to your
        work,
    For things beyond man's understanding have been shown
        you.

24 For many have been led astray by their imagination,
    And a wicked fancy has made their minds slip.

26 It will go hard with an obstinate heart at the end,
    And the man who loves danger will perish through it.

27 An obstinate heart will be loaded with troubles,
    And the irreligious man will add one sin to another.

28 There is no cure for the misfortune of the proud,
    For a wicked plant has taken root in him.

29 An intelligent man's mind can understand a proverb;
    And a wise man desires a listening ear.

30 As water will quench a blazing fire,
    So charity will atone for sin.

31 He who returns favors is remembered afterward,
    And when he totters, he will find a support.

3:15-31

My child, do not defraud the poor man of his living, [4
And do not make the eyes of the needy wait.
Do not pain a hungry heart,
And do not anger a man who is in want.   2
Do not increase the troubles of a mind that is incensed, 3
And do not put off giving to a man who is in need.
Do not refuse a suppliant in his trouble,   4
And do not avert your face from the poor.
Do not turn your eyes away from a beggar,   5
And do not give anyone cause to curse you,
For if he curses you in the bitterness of his spirit,   6
His creator will hear his prayer.
Make yourself beloved in the congregation,   7
And bow your head to a great personage;
Listen to what a poor man has to say,   8
And give him a peaceful and gentle answer.
Rescue a man who is being wronged from the hand of the 9
    wrongdoer,
And do not be faint-hearted about giving your judgment.
Be like a father to the fatherless,   10
And take the place of a husband to their mother.
Then you will be like a son of the Most High,
And he will show you more than a mother's love.

Wisdom makes her sons exalted,   11
And lays hold of those who seek her.
Whoever loves her loves life,   12
And those who seek her early will be filled with joy.
Whoever holds her fast will win glory;   13
The Lord will bless every house he enters.
Those who serve her serve the Holy One,   14
And the Lord loves those who love her.
Whoever obeys her will judge the heathen,   15
And whoever attends to her will dwell in security.

4:1-15

16 If he trusts in her, he will possess her,
And his descendants will retain possession of her.

17 For at first she will go with him in devious ways,
She will bring fear and cowardice upon him,
And torment him with her discipline,
Until she can trust in his soul,
And test him with her judgments.

18 Then she will come straight back to him again, and make
him glad,
And reveal her secrets to him.

19 If he wanders off, she will forsake him,
And hand him over to his downfall.

20 Watch your opportunity and guard against evil,
And do not have to feel shame for your soul.

21 For there is a shame that brings sin,
And there is a shame that is glory and favor.

22 Show regard for no one at the expense of your soul,
And respect no one, to your own downfall.

23 Do not refrain from speaking when it is needed;
For wisdom is known through speech,

24 And instruction through the spoken word.

25 Do not contradict the truth,
But feel shame for your want of education.

26 Do not be ashamed to confess your sins,
And do not try to force back the current of a river.

27 Do not make yourself a bed for a fool,
And do not show partiality for a ruler;

28 Contend for the truth to the death,
And the Lord will fight for you.

29 Do not be rash in speech,
But slothful and slack in action.

30 Do not be like a lion at home,
And unreasonable with your servants.

4:16–30

Do not stretch your hand out to receive, 31
But close it when you should repay.

Do not set your heart on your money, [5
And do not say, "It is enough for me."
Do not follow your soul and your strength 2
And pursue the desires of your heart.
Do not say, "Who can have power over me?" 3
For the Lord will certainly take vengeance.
Do not say, "I sinned, and what happened to me?" 4
For the Lord is long-suffering.
As for atonement, do not be unafraid 5
To add one sin to another,
And do not say, "His mercy is great, 6
He will make atonement for the multitude of my sins."
For mercy and wrath are both with him,
And his anger will rest upon sinners.
Do not put off turning to the Lord, 7
And do not postpone it from day to day;
For the Lord's wrath will suddenly come forth,
And in the time of vengeance you will perish.

Do not set your heart on unrighteous gain, 8
For it will be of no benefit to you in the time of misfortune.
Do not winnow in every wind, 9
And do not follow every path;
That is what the deceitful sinner does.
Be steadfast in your understanding, 10
And let what you say be one.

Be quick to hear, 11
And make your reply with patience.
If you possess understanding, answer your neighbor, 12
But if you do not have it, keep your hand over your mouth!
Both glory and disgrace come from speaking, 13

4:31–5:13

And a man's tongue is his downfall.

14   Do not be known as a whisperer,
And do not set an ambush with your tongue,
For shame rests upon the thief,
And evil condemnation on the double-tongued.

15 Do not be ignorant in great matters or in small,

6] And do not prove an enemy instead of a friend;
For an evil name incurs disgrace and reproach;
So does a sinner who is double-tongued.

2   Do not exalt yourself in your soul's designs,
So that your soul may not be torn in pieces like a bull;

3 If you eat up your leaves, you will destroy your fruit,
And leave yourself like a dried-up tree.

4 A wicked heart will destroy its possessor,
And fill his enemies with malignant joy.

5 Sweet speech makes many friends,
And a polite tongue multiplies courtesy.

6 Let those who are at peace with you be many,
But let your advisers be one in a thousand.

7 If you make a friend, make one only after testing him,
And do not be in a hurry to confide in him.

8 There are friends who are so when it suits their convenience,
Who will not stand by you when you are in trouble.

9 And there are friends who turn into enemies,
And reveal quarrels to your discredit.

10 And there are friends who will sit at your table,
But will not stand by you when you are in trouble.

11 They will make themselves at home, as long as you are
     prosperous,
And will give orders to your servants;

12 If you come down in the world, they will take sides against
     you,
And hide themselves from your presence.

Separate yourself from your enemies,   13
And beware of your friends.
A faithful friend is a strong protection;   14
A man who has found one has found a treasure.
A faithful friend is beyond price,   15
And his value cannot be weighed.
A faithful friend is a life-giving medicine,   16
And those who fear the Lord will find it.
The man who fears the Lord will make genuine friend- 17
ships,
For to him his neighbor is like himself.

My child, from your youth up cultivate education,   18
And you will keep on finding wisdom until you are gray.
Approach her like a man who plows and sows,   19
And wait for her abundant crops.
For in cultivating her, you will toil but little,
And soon you will eat her produce.
She seems very harsh, to the undisciplined,   20
And a thoughtless man cannot abide her.
She will rest on him like a great stone to test him,   21
And he will not delay to throw her off.
For wisdom is what her name implies,   22
And to most men she is invisible.

Listen, my child, and accept my opinion,   23
And do not refuse my advice.
Put your feet into her fetters,   24
And your neck into her collar.
Put your shoulder under her and carry her,   25
And do not weary of her chains;
Come to her with all your heart,   26
And follow her ways with all your might.
Inquire and search, and she will be made known to you, 27
And when you have grasped her, do not let her go.

6:13–27

28 For at last you will find the rest she gives,
And you will find her turning into gladness.

29 Her fetters will become your strong defense,
And her collars a splendid robe.

30 She wears gold ornaments,
And her chains are purple thread;

31 You will put her on like a splendid robe,
And put her on your head like a victor's wreath.

32 My child, if you wish, you can be educated,
And if you devote yourself to it, you can become shewd.

33 If you love to hear, you will receive,
And if you listen, you will be wise.

34 Take your stand in the throng of elders;
Which of them is wise? Attach yourself to him.

35 Be willing to listen to every godly discourse,
And do not let any wise proverbs escape you.

36 If you see a man of understanding, go to him early,
And let your feet wear out his doorstep.

37 Think about the statutes of the Lord,
And constantly meditate on his commandments.
He will strengthen your mind,
And the wisdom you desire will be given you.

7] Do no evil, and evil will not overtake you.
Avoid what is wrong, and it will turn away from you.

2 My son, do not sow among the furrows of iniquity,

3 And you will not reap them seven fold.

4 Do not ask the Lord for pre-eminence,
Or the king for a seat of honor.

5 Do not justify yourself in the sight of the Lord,
Or show off your wisdom before the king;

6 Do not seek to be made a judge,
Or you may not be able to put down wrongdoing;
Or you may show partiality to a man of influence,

And put a stumbling block in the way of your own up-
    rightness.
Do not sin against the multitude of the city,   7
And do not throw yourself down in the throng.
Do not repeat a sin,   8
For with even one offense you are not innocent.
Do not say, "He will consider the number of my offerings,   9
And when I sacrifice to the Most High God, he will accept
    it."
Do not be discouraged about your prayers,   10
And do not fail to give to charity.
Do not laugh at a man when he is in bitterness of spirit;   11
For there is one who can humble and can exalt!
Do not sow a lie against your brother,   12
Or do such a thing to your friend.
Do not consent to utter any lie,   13
For the practice of it is not beneficial.
Do not indulge in idle talk in the throng of elders,   14
And do not repeat yourself when you pray.
Do not hate hard work,   15
Or farming, which was created by the Most High.
Do not be counted in the crowd of sinners;   16
Remember that wrath will not delay.
Humble your heart exceedingly,   17
For fire and worms are the punishment of the ungodly.
   Do not exchange a friend for an advantage,   18
Or a real brother for the gold of Ophir.
Do not fail a wise, good wife,   19
For her favor is worth more than gold.
Do not ill-treat a servant who does his work faithfully,   20
Or a hired man who is devoting his life to you.
Let your soul love an intelligent servant;   21
Do not defraud him of his freedom.

7:7-21

22 If you have cattle, look after them,
   And if they are profitable to you, keep them.
23 If you have children, discipline them,
   And from their youth up bend their necks.
24 If you have daughters, look after their persons,
   And do not look too favorably upon them.
25 If you give your daughter in marriage, you will have done
      a great thing,
   But bestow her on a man of understanding.
26 If you have a wife after your own heart, do not cast her out,
   But do not trust yourself to one whom you hate.
27 Honor your father with your whole heart,
   And do not forget the pangs of your mother.
28 Remember that it was of them you were born,
   And how can you requite them for what they have done
      for you?
29 Honor the Lord with all your soul,
   And revere his priests.
30 Love him who made you with all your strength,
   And do not forsake his ministers.
31 Fear the Lord and honor the priest,
   And give him his portion, as you were commanded,
   The first fruits, and the sin offering, and the gift of the
      shoulders,
   And the sacrifice of consecration, and the first fruits of holy
      things.
32 Stretch out your hand to the poor also,
   That your blessing may be accomplished.
33 A present pleases every man alive,
   And in the case of the dead, do not withhold your kindness.
34 Do not be wanting to those who weep,
   But mourn with those who mourn.
35 Do not hesitate to visit a man who is sick,

For you will be loved for such acts.
In all that you say remember your end,   36
And you will never commit a sin.

   Do not quarrel with a powerful man,   [8
Or you may fall into his hands.
Do not contend with a rich man,
Or he may outweigh you.   2
Gold has been the destruction of many,
And perverted the minds of kings.
Do not quarrel with a garrulous man,   3
And do not add fuel to the fire.
Do not make sport of an uneducated man,   4
Or you may dishonor your own forefathers.
Do not reproach a man when he turns from his sin;   5
Remember that we are all liable to punishment.
Do not treat a man with disrespect when he is old,   6
For some of us are growing old.
Do not exult over a man who is dead;   7
Remember that we are all going to die.
Do not neglect the discourse of wise men,   8
But busy yourself with their proverbs;
For from them you will gain instruction,
And learn to serve great men.
Do not miss the discourse of old men,   9
For they learned it from their fathers.
For from them you will gain understanding,
And learn to return an answer in your time of need.
Do not kindle the coals of a sinner,   10
Or you may be burned with the flame of his fire.
Do not start up before an insolent man,   11
So that he may not lie in ambush for what you say.
Do not lend to a man who is stronger than you,   12
Or if you do, act as though you had lost it.

13 Do not give surety beyond your means,
And if you give surety, regard it as something you will have
    to pay.

14 Do not go to law with a judge;
For in view of his dignity they will decide for him.

15 Do not travel with a reckless man,
So that he may not overburden you.
For he will do just as he pleases,
And you will perish through his folly.

16 Do not have a fight with a hot-tempered man,
And do not travel across the desert with him,
For bloodshed is as nothing in his eyes,
And where there is no help, he will strike you down.

17 Do not take counsel with a fool,
For he will not be able to keep the matter secret.

18 Do not do a secret thing before a stranger,
For you do not know what he will bring forth.

19 Do not open your heart to every man,
And do not accept a favor from him.

9] Do not be jealous about the wife of your bosom,
And do not teach her an evil lesson, to your own hurt.

2 Do not give your soul to a woman,
So that she will trample on your strength.

3 Do not meet a prostitute,
Or you may fall into her snares.

4 Do not associate with a woman singer,
Or you may be caught by her wiles.

5 Do not look closely at a girl,
Or you may be entrapped in penalties on her account.

6 Do not give yourself to prostitutes,
So that you may not lose your inheritance.

7 Do not look around in the streets of the city,
And do not wander about the unfrequented parts of it.

Avert your eyes from a beautiful woman, 8
And do not look closely at beauty that belongs to someone
  else.
Many have been led astray by a woman's beauty,
And love is kindled by it like a fire.
Do not ever sit at table with a married woman, 9
And do not feast and drink with her,
Or your heart may turn away to her,
And you may slip into spiritual ruin.
  Do not forsake an old friend, 10
For a new one is not equal to him.
A new friend is new wine;
When it grows old, you will enjoy drinking it.
Do not envy the glory of a sinner; 11
For you do not know what disaster awaits him.
Do not share in the satisfaction of ungodly men, 12
Remember that until death they will not be found upright.
Keep far from a man who has the power of life and death, 13
And you will have no suspicion of the fear of death.
If you do approach him, do not offend him,
So that he may not take away your life.
Understand that you are striding along among traps,
And walking on the city battlements.
As far as you can, guess at your neighbors, 14
And take counsel with those who are wise.
Let your discussion be with men of understanding, 15
And all your discourse about the Law of the Most High.
Make upright men your companions at table, 16
And your exultation be over the fear of the Lord.
It is for the skill of the craftsmen that a piece of work is 17
  commended,
And a ruler of the people must be wise in what he says.
A talkative man is dreaded in his city, 18
And a man who is rash in speech is hated.

9:8-18

10]   A wise judge will instruct his people,
And the rule of a man of understanding is well ordered.

2   Like the judge of a people are his officers,
And like the governor of a city are all who live in it.

3   An uneducated king ruins his people,
But a city becomes populous through the understanding
of its rulers.
Authority over the earth is in the hands of the Lord,

4   And in due time he will set over it one who will serve his
purpose.

5   A man's prosperity is in the hands of the Lord,
And he makes his glory rest on the person of the scribe.

6   Do not get angry with your neighbor for any misdeed,
And do not gain your end by acts of violence.

7   Pride is detested in the sight of the Lord and of men,
And injustice is wrong in the sight of both.

8   Sovereignty passes from one nation to another
Because of injustice and violence and greed for money.
Why are dust and ashes proud?

9   For while a man is still alive, his bowels decay;

10   There is a long illness—the doctor makes light of it;
A man is a king today, and dead tomorrow.

11   For when a man dies,
Reptiles, animals, and worms become his portion.

12   A man begins to be proud when he departs from the
Lord,
And his heart forsakes his Creator.

13   For pride begins with sin,
And the man who clings to it will rain down abomina-
tions.
For this reason, the Lord brings unheard-of calamities
upon them,
And overturns them utterly.

10:1–13

The Lord tears down the thrones of rulers, 14
And seats the humble-minded in their places.
The Lord plucks up nations by the roots, 15
And plants the lowly in their places.
The Lord overturns heathen countries, 16
And destroys them down to the foundations of the earth.
He takes some of them away, and destroys them, 17
And makes the memory of them cease from the earth.
Pride was not created for men, 18
Nor fierce anger for those who are born of women.
What is an honorable posterity? A human posterity! 19
What is an honorable posterity? Men who fear the Lord.
What is a base posterity? A human posterity!
What is a base posterity? Men who break the command-
ments.
Among his brothers, their leader is honored, 20
And those who fear the Lord are honored in his eyes.
Rich, and distinguished, and poor alike— 21
Their glory is the fear of the Lord. 22
It is not right to slight a poor man who has understanding, 23
And it is not proper to honor a sinful man.
Prince, judge, and ruler are honored, 24
But none of them is greater than the man who fears the
Lord.
Free men will wait on a wise servant, 25
And the intelligent man will not object.
Do not parade your wisdom when you are at work, 26
And do not commend yourself when you are in need;
It is better to work and have plenty of everything, 27
Than to go about commending yourself but in want of
bread.
My child, glorify your soul with meekness, 28
And show it such honor as it deserves.

10:14–28

29 Who can justify a man who sins against his own soul?
And who can honor a man who disgraces his own life?

30 A poor man is honored for his knowledge,
And a rich man is honored for his wealth.

31 If a man is honored in poverty, how much more will he
be in wealth?
And if a man is dishonored when he is rich, how much more
will he be when he is poor?

11] The wisdom of a humble person will lift up his head,
And make him sit among the great.

2 Do not praise a man for his good looks,
And do not detest a man for his appearance.

3 The bee is one of the smallest of winged creatures,
But what she produces is the greatest of sweets.

4 Do not boast of the clothes you wear,
And do not be uplifted when you are honored,
For the works of the Lord are marvelous,
And his doings are hidden from men,

5 Many sovereigns have had to sit on the ground,
While a man who was never thought of has assumed the
diadem.

6 Many rulers have been utterly disgraced,
And men of renown have been delivered into the hands of
others.

7 Do not find fault before you investigate,
First understand, and then rebuke.

8 Do not answer before you hear,
And do not interrupt in the middle of what is being said.

9 Do not quarrel about a matter that does not concern you,
And when sinners judge, do not sit in council with them.

10 My child, do not busy yourself about many things.
If you multiply your activities, you will not be held guiltless,

And if you pursue, you will not overtake,
And you will not escape by running away.
One man toils and labors and hurries,   11
And is all the worse off.
Another is slow, and needs help,   12
Lacks strength and has plenty of poverty,
Yet the eyes of the Lord look favorably on him,
And he lifts him up out of his low position   13
And lifts up his head,
And many wonder at him.
Good and evil, life and death,   14
Poverty and wealth, are from the Lord,
What the Lord gives stays by the godly,   17
And what he approves will always prosper.
One man grows rich by carefulness and greed,   18
And this will be his reward:
When he says, "Now I can rest,   19
And enjoy my goods,"
He does not know when the time will come
When he will die and leave them to others.

Stand by your agreement, and attend to it,   20
And grow old in your work.
Do not wonder at the doings of the sinner,   21
But trust in the Lord and stick to your work.
For it is easy in the Lord's eyes
Swiftly and suddenly to make a poor man rich.
The blessing of the Lord rests on the wages of the godly;   22
And he quickly makes his blessing flourish.
Do not say, "What do I need,   23
And from this time on what can benefit me?"
Do not say, "I have enough,   24
And from this time on how can I be injured?"
In prosperity one forgets misfortune,   25

11:11-25

26 For it is easy in the Lord's sight when a man dies
    To repay him according to his ways.

27 An hour of hardship makes one forget enjoyment,
    And when a man dies, what he has done is disclosed.

28 Count no one happy before his death,
    And a man will be known by his children.

29   Do not bring any and every man to your home,
    For a treacherous man has many wiles.

30 A proud man's heart is like a decoy partridge in a cage,
    And like a spy he looks for your downfall;

31 For he tries to entrap you, turning good into evil,
    And he finds fault with your favorite things.

32 A spark of fire kindles a whole heap of coals,
    And a sinful man lies in wait for blood.

33 Beware of an evil-doer, for he contrives wickedness,
    Or he will bring blame on you forever.

34 If you entertain a stranger, he will disturb and torment
        you,
    And he will estrange you from your home.

12]   If you do a kindness, know to whom you are doing it,
    And you will be thanked for your good deeds.

2   If you do a kindness to a godly man, you will be repaid,
    If not by him, yet by the Most High.

3   The man who persists in evil will not prosper,
    Nor the man who will not give to charity.

4   Give to the godly man, and do not help the sinner;

5   Do kindnesses to the humble-minded, and do not give to
        the ungodly;
    Hold back his bread, and do not give it to him,
    So that he may not come to control you with it;
    For you will experience twice as much evil
    For all the good you do him.

6   For the Most High hates sinners,

And will take vengeance on the ungodly.

Give to the good man, and do not help the sinner. 7

  A friend cannot be proved in prosperity, 8
Nor an enemy concealed in adversity.

When a man prospers, his enemies are grieved, 9
And when he is unfortunate, even his friend separates from
  him.

Never trust your enemy, 10
For his wickedness is like bronze that rusts;

Even if he acts humbly, and goes about bent over, 11
Look out for yourself, and be on your guard against him.

You must be to him like a man who wipes a mirror clean,
And you must make sure that it is not all covered with rust.

Do not place him at your side, 12
Or he may overthrow you and take your place.

Do not seat him at your right hand,
Or he may try to get your seat,

And you may at last learn the truth of what I say,
And be stung by my words.

Who pities a snake-charmer when he is bitten, 13
Or all those who have to do with wild animals?

In the same way who will pity a man who approaches a 14
  sinner,
And mingles with his sins?

He will stay with you for a while, 15
But if you fall, he will not hold out.

An enemy will speak sweetly with his lips, 16
But in his heart he will plan to throw you into a pit.

An enemy will shed tears with his eyes,
But if he gets a chance, he cannot get blood enough.

If misfortune overtakes you, you will find him there before 17
  you,
And while he is pretending to help you, he will trip you up.

12:7–17

18 He will shake his head, and clap his hands,
And whisper a great deal, and change his expression
toward you.

13]   The man who touches pitch will get his hands dirty,
And the man who associates with a proud person will become like him.

2   Do not lift a load that is too heavy for you,
And do not associate with a man stronger or richer than
you are.
What relation can an earthen pot have with a kettle?
The kettle knocks against it, and it is broken in pieces.

3   When a rich man does a wrong, he adds a threat;
When a poor man suffers a wrong, he must beg pardon.

4   If you can be useful, he makes you work for him,
And if you are in want, he abandons you.

5   As long as you have anything, he will live with you,
And will strip you bare, but he will feel no distress.

6   If he needs you, he will deceive you,
And smile upon you, and raise your hopes.
He will speak you fair and say, "Is there anything you
need?"

7   He will shame you with his food,
Until he has impoverished you again and again,
And finally he will mock you.
Afterward when he sees you he will pass you by,
And shake his head at you.

8   Take care not to be misled,
And humbled through your own folly.

9   When a leading man invites you, be retiring,
And he will invite you all the more.

10 Do not press upon him, or you may be pushed away;
But do not stand too far off, or you may be forgotten.

11 Do not aim to speak to him as an equal,

But do not believe all he says;
For he will test you with much conversation,
And will examine you with a smile.
He who does not keep to himself what is said to him is   12
   unmerciful;
And will not hesitate to hurt and to bind.
Keep them to yourself, and take great care,   13
For you are walking with your own downfall.
   Every creature loves its like,   15
And every man loves his neighbor.
All living beings gather with their own kind,   16
And a man associates with another like himself.
What companionship can a wolf have with a lamb?   17
Just as much as a sinner with a godly man.
What peace can there be between a hyena and a dog?   18
And what peace between a rich man and a poor one?
Wild asses are the prey of lions in the wilderness,   19
Just as the poor are pasture for the rich.
Humility is detestable to the proud,   20
Just as a poor man is detestable to a rich one.
When a rich man is shaken, he is steadied by his friends, 21
But when a poor man falls down, his friends push him
   away.
When a rich man falls, there are many to help him;   22
He tells secrets, and they justify him.
When a humble man falls, they add reproaches.
He speaks with understanding, but no place is made for
   him.
When a rich man speaks, everyone keeps silent,   23
And they extol what he says to the clouds.
When a poor man speaks, they say, "Who is that?"
And if he stumbles, they will help to throw him down.
Wealth is good if it carries with it no sin,   24
And poverty is called evil by the ungodly.

13:12–24

25   A man's disposition affects his appearance,
Both for good and for evil.

26   A cheerful face is a sign of a happy heart,
But it takes painstaking thought to compose proverbs!

14]   How happy is the man who makes no slip with his mouth,
And is not stabbed with sorrow for his sins!

2   Happy is the man whose heart does not condemn him,
And who has not given up hope.

3   Wealth does not become a niggardly man,
And what use is money to an envious man?

4   The man who withholds from himself amasses for others,
And others will enjoy his goods.

5   If a man is evil to himself, to whom will he be good?
For he will not take any pleasure in his own money.

6   There is nobody worse than the man who is grudging to
himself,
And that is the penalty of his wickedness.

7   If he does any good, he does it through forgetfulness,
And shows his wickedness in the end.

8   He is a wicked man who has an envious eye,
Turning away his face, and pretending not to see human
souls.

9   A covetous man's eye is never satisfied with what he gets,
And wicked injustice dries up the heart.

10   An evil eye begrudges bread,
And is in want of it at his own table.

11   My child, if you have any means, provide well for yourself,
And make suitable offerings to the Lord.

12   Remember that death will not delay,
And the agreement of Hades has not been shown to you.

13   Treat your friend well before you die,
And reach out and give to him as much as your strength
permits.

13:25–14:13

Do not miss your time of prosperity,   14
And do not let the good fortune that you desire escape you.
Will you not leave the fruit of your labors to someone else,   15
And the result of your toil to be cast lots for?
Give and take, and deceive your soul,   16
For there is no looking for luxury in Hades.
Human life grows old like a cloak,   17
For from the beginning the decree has read, "You will
    surely die."
Like the thick leaves on a flourishing tree,   18
Which drops some and puts forth others,
Are the generations of flesh and blood;
One dies, and another is born;
Everything made will decay and disappear,   19
And the man who has made it will depart with it.

Happy is the man who meditates on wisdom,   20
Who reasons with his understanding;
Who considers her ways in his mind,   21
And reflects on her secrets;
(Go after her like a hunter
And lie in wait by her ways!)   22
Who peers in at her windows,   23
And listens at her doorways;
Who lodges close to her house,   24
And fastens his pegs in her walls;
Who pitches his tent close beside her,   25
And finds comfortable lodgings;
Who puts his children under her shelter,   26
And spends the night under her branches;
He will be sheltered by her from the heat,   27
And will lodge in her splendors.

The man who fears the Lord will do this,   [15
And he who masters the Law will win her.

14:14–15:1

2 She will meet him like a mother,
   And receive him like a bride.

3 She will feed him with the bread of understanding,
   And give him the water of wisdom to drink;

4 He will lean on her, and not fall,
   And will rely on her, and not be disappointed.

5 She will exalt him above his neighbors,
   And open his mouth in the midst of the assembly;

6 He will find joy and a crown of gladness,
   And possess eternal renown.

7 Men with no understanding will not win her,
   And sinners will not see her.

8 She is far from pride,
   And liars give no heed to her.

9   Praise is not becoming on the lips of a sinner,
   For it was not sent him from the Lord.

10 For praise must be uttered in wisdom,
   And the Lord will make it prosper.

11 Do not say, "It was because of the Lord that I fell away,"
   For he will not do things that he hates.

12 Do not say, "It was he that led me astray,"
   For he has no need of a sinner.

13 The Lord hates anything abominable;
   And it is not loved by those who fear him.

14 It was he who made man in the beginning,
   And left him in the hands of his own decision;

15 If you will, you can keep the commandments,
   And acting faithfully rests on your own good pleasure.

16 He has set fire and water before you;
   Stretch out your hand for whichever you wish.

17 Life and death are before a man,
   And whichever he chooses will be given him.

18 For the wisdom of the Lord is great;

He is mighty in strength, and beholds all things.
His eyes rest on those who fear him,   19
And he knows everything man does.
He has not commanded anyone to be ungodly,   20
And he has given no one permission to sin.

Do not desire a multitude of unprofitable children,   [16
Nor delight in ungodly sons.
If they multiply, do not rejoice in them,   2
Unless the fear of the Lord is with them.
Do not put your trust in their lives,   3
And do not rely on their number;
For one is better than a thousand,
And to die childless than to have children that are un-
    godly.
For from one man of understanding, a city will be peopled,   4
But a tribe of lawless men will be destroyed.
Many such things my eyes have seen,   5
And mightier things than these my ears have heard.
In a gathering of sinners a fire is kindled,   6
And in a disobedient nation wrath burns.
He did not forgive the giants of old,   7
Who rebelled in their strength;
He did not spare the people among whom Lot was living,   8
Whom he detested for their pride.
He did not have mercy on the doomed nation,   9
Who were dispossessed for their sins;
Or on the six hundred thousand men on foot,   10
Who gathered against him in their obstinacy.
Why, if there is one stiff-necked man,   11
It is a wonder if he goes unpunished;
For both mercy and wrath are with him,
He is mighty in forgiveness, and yet pours out his wrath;   12
Great as is his mercy, so great is his correction also;

15:19–16:12

He will judge a man by his doings.

13   A sinner will not escape with his booty,
And the steadfastness of the godly man will not be disappointed.

14   He will make room for all mercy,
Yet what every man receives will be governed by what he has done.

17   Do not say, "I will be hidden from the Lord,
And on high who will remember me?
Among so many people I will not be noticed,
And what is my soul in a boundless creation?

18   Behold the heaven and the heaven of heavens,
The abyss and the earth shake when he inspects them;

19   Yes, the mountains and the foundations of the earth
Shake and tremble when he looks at them.

20   No mind can think about them,
And who can grasp his ways?

21   There are hurricanes which no man sees,
And the most of his doings are done in secret.

22   Who can declare his upright deeds,
Or who can endure them? For his agreement is far from me."

23   A man who is wanting in understanding thinks in this way,
And a senseless, misguided man has these foolish thoughts.

24   Listen to me, my child, and receive instruction,
And apply your mind to what I say;

25   I will disclose instruction by weight,
And declare knowledge with exactness.

26   When the Lord created his works in the beginning,
After he made them, he fixed their several divisions.

27   He organized his works in a system forever,
And their divisions for all their generations.
They do not grow hungry or tired,

And they do not stop working.
None of them crowds his neighbor aside,   28
And they never disobey his command.
After that, the Lord looked at the earth,   29
And filled it with his blessings.
He covered the face of it with every living creature,   30
And to it they return.

    The Lord created man out of the ground,   [17
And made him return to it again.
He set a limit to the number of their days,   2
And gave them dominion over what was on the earth.
He clothed them with strength like his own,   3
And made them in his own image.
He put fear of them in every living creature,   4
And made them masters of the wild animals and birds.
He gave them reason and speech and sight,   6
Hearing, and a mind for thought.
He filled them with the knowledge of understanding,   7
And showed them good and evil.
He put his eyesight in their minds   8
To show them the majesty of his works,
So that they would praise his holy hame   9
And declare the majesty of his works.
He gave them knowledge also,   11
And gave them a law of life as an inheritance.
He made an everlasting agreement with them,   12
And showed them his decrees.
Their eyes saw his glorious majesty,   13
And their ears heard the glory of his voice.
He said to them, "Beware of anything that is wrong,"   14
And he gave everyone of them commands about his neigh-
    bor.
    Their ways are always before him;   15

16:28–17:15

They cannot be hidden from his eyes.

17 For every nation he appointed a ruler,
But Israel is the Lord's own portion.

19 All their doings are as clear as the sun before him,
And his eyes rest continually upon their ways.

20 Their iniquities are not hidden from him,
And all their sins are before the Lord.

22 A man's charity is like a signet with him,
And a man's liberality he will preserve like the apple of his
eye.

23 Afterward he will rise up and requite them,
And pay back their recompense upon their heads.

24 But to those who repent he has given a way to return,
And he encourages those whose endurance fails.

25 Turn to the Lord, and forsake your sins;
Offer a prayer before him, and lessen your offense.

26 Draw near to the Most High, and turn away from iniquity,
And hate bitterly what he abhors.

27 Who will praise the Most High in Hades,
Compared with those who give him thanks while they still
live?

28 Thanksgiving from the dead perishes as though he were
not;
It is the man who is alive and well that should praise the
Lord.

29 How great is the mercy of the Lord,
And his forgiveness for those who turn to him!

30 For everything cannot exist in men,
For man is not immortal.

31 What is brighter than the sun? Yet it is eclipsed;
So flesh and blood devise evil.

32 He looks after the power of the very height of heaven,
But all men are only dust and ashes.

17:17–32

He who lives forever has created all things alike; [18

The Lord alone can be thought upright. 2

He has permitted no one to declare his works, 4
And who can track out his mighty deeds?

Who can compute the power of his majesty? 5
And who can in addition detail his mercies?

It is not possible to take from them or to add to them, 6
Or to track out the wonders of the Lord.

Where man ends, he begins, 7
And when man stops, will he be perplexed?

What is man, and of what use is he? 8
What is the good of him, and what is the evil?

The length of a man's days 9
Is great at a hundred years,

Like a drop of water from the sea, or a grain of sand, 10
Are a few years in the day of eternity.

Therefore the Lord has been patient with them, 11
And he has poured out his mercy upon them.

He sees and recognizes that their end is evil, 12
So he increases his forgiveness.

A man has mercy on his neighbor, 13
But the mercy of the Lord is for all mankind,
Reproving and training and teaching them,
And bringing them back as a shepherd does his flock.

On those who accept his training he has mercy, 14
And on those who eagerly seek his decrees.

My child, do not spoil your good deeds, 15
Or when you make any gift cause pain by what you say.

Does not the dew assuage the scorching heat? 16
So a word is more potent than a gift.

Why, is not a word better than a gift? 17
Both mark the charitable man;

A fool ungraciously abuses people, 18

18:1-18

And a present from a grudging man makes one cry his
eyes out.

19 Learn before you speak,
And take care of yourself before you get sick;

20 Examine yourself before you are judged,
And at the time of visitation you will find forgiveness.

21 Humble yourself before you fall sick,
And when you would sin, show repentance instead.

22 Let nothing prevent you from paying your vows in time,
And do not wait till you die to be justified.

23 Prepare yourself before you make a vow,
And do not be like a man who tests the Lord.

24 Think of his wrath in later days,
And the time of vengeance, when he turns away his face

25 Remember the time of famine in the time of plenty,
Poverty and want in the days of wealth.

26 Between morning and evening the situation changes,
And it all passes swiftly in the sight of the Lord.

27 A wise man is always reverent,
And in days of sin he is careful not to offend;

28 Every man of understanding recognizes wisdom,
And will thank the man who finds her.

29 Men skilled in the use of words compose cleverly themselves,
And pour forth apt proverbs.

30 Do not follow your impulses,
But restrain your longings.

31 If you give assent to the impulse of your heart,
It will make you a laughingstock to your enemies.

32 Do not indulge in too much luxury,
Do not be tied to its expense.

33 Do not be impoverished from feasting on borrowed money
When you have nothing in your purse.

18:19-33

A workman who is a drunkard will never get rich; [19
The man who despises little things will gradually fail;
Wine and women make men of understanding stand aloof; 2
And the man who is devoted to prostitutes is reckless.
Worms and decay will eventually possess him, 3
And the rash soul will be destroyed.
    The man who trusts people quickly is light-minded; 4
And he who sins offends against his own soul.
The man who is merry of heart will be condemned, 5
And he who hates loquacity has the less malice. 6
If you never repeat what you are told, 7
You will fare none the worse.
Before friend or foe do not recount it, 8
And unless it would be sinful of you, do not reveal it.
For someone has heard you and watched you, 9
And when the time comes he will hate you.
If you hear something said, let it die with you, 10
Have courage, it will not make you burst!
A fool to express a thought suffers such pangs 11
As a woman in childbirth suffers to bear a child.
Like an arrow sticking in the flesh of the thigh 12
Is a word in the heart of a fool.
    Question a friend; perhaps he did not do it; 13
Or if he did, so that he will not do it again.
Question your neighbor; perhaps he did not say it; 14
Or if he did, so that he may not repeat it.
Question a friend, for often there is slander, 15
And you must not believe everything that is said.
A man may make a slip without intending to— 16
Who has not sinned with his tongue?
Question your neighbor before you threaten him, 17
And leave room for the Law of the Most High.
    The fear of the Lord is the sum of wisdom, 20

19:1–20

And in all wisdom the Law is fulfilled.

22 The knowledge of wickedness is not wisdom,
And where the counsel of sinners is, there is no understanding.

23 There is a cunning that is detestable,
And there is a foolish man who is only deficient in wisdom.

24 A man who is inferior in understanding but fears God is better
Than one who abounds in prudence but transgresses the Law.

25 There is an exact kind of shrewdness that is wrong,
And there is a man who acts crookedly to gain a judgment.

26 There is a kind of villain that bends mournfully,
But inwardly is full of deceit.

27 He covers his face, and pretends to be deaf,
But when no one is looking, he will take advantage of you.

28 And though for lack of strength he may be prevented from sinning,
If he finds an opportunity, he will do you harm.

29 A man is known by his appearance,
And an intelligent man can be told by the expression of his face.

30 A man's clothes and a broad smile,
And the way he walks tell what he is.

20} There is a rebuke that is uncalled for,
And a time when the man who keeps silent is wise.

2 How much better it is to rebuke someone than to get angry,
For the man who makes full confession will be kept from failure.

4 Like a eunuch's craving to ravish a girl
Is the man who would do right by violence.

5 One man keeps silence and is considered wise;
While another is hated for his loquacity.

19:22–20:5

One man keeps silence because he has nothing to say;   6
And another keeps silence because he knows it is the time
   for it.

A wise man will keep silence till his time comes,   7
But a boaster and a fool miss the fitting time.

The man who talks excessively is detested,   8
And he who takes it on himself to speak is hated.

   There are advantages that come to a man in adversity,   9
And there are gains that result in loss.

There are gifts that will do you no good,   10
And there are gifts that are returned double.

There are humiliations for the sake of gaining glory,   11
And there are men who rise from low conditions.

One man buys much for little,   12
And yet pays for it seven times over.

A man who speaks wisely makes himself beloved;   13
But the pleasant speeches of fools are thrown away.

A present from a fool will do you no good,   14
For his eyes are not one but many.

He gives little but finds a great deal of fault,   15
And opens his mouth like a town-crier.
He will lend today and ask it back tomorrow;
Such a man is hateful.

The fool says, "I have not got a friend;   16
And I get no thanks for my good deeds."
Those who eat his bread are evil-tongued;
How many will laugh at him, and how often!   17

   A slip on the ground is better than a slip of the tongue;   18
So the fall of the wicked will come quickly.

A disagreeable man and an unseasonable story—   19
They will both be constantly on the lips of the uneducated.

A proverb on the lips of a fool will be refused,   20
For he will not utter it at the proper time.

21   One man is kept from sinning through poverty,
      So his conscience does not prick him when he goes to rest.

22   Another loses his own life from sheer embarrassment,
      And destroys it by his senseless expression.

23   Another out of embarrassment makes promises to his
          friend,
      And so makes him his enemy for nothing.

24   A lie is a bad blot in a man;
      It is continually found on the lips of the ignorant.

25   A thief is better than a habitual liar,
      But they are both doomed to destruction.

26   Dishonor is habitual with a liar,
      And his shame attends him continually.

27   A man who speaks wisely makes his way in the world,
      And a man of good sense pleases the great.

28   The man who cultivates the soil makes his heap high,
      And the man who pleases the great atones for wrongdoing.

29   Gifts and presents can blind the eyes of wise men,
      And avert reproofs like a muzzle on the mouth.

30   Hidden wisdom and concealed treasure—
      What is the use of either of them?

31   A man who conceals his folly is better
      Than a man who conceals his wisdom.

21]   My child, if you have sinned, do not do it again,
      And pray over your former sins.

2   Flee from sin as from the face of a snake;
      For if you approach it, it will bite you.
      Its teeth are lion's teeth,
      And destroy the souls of men.

3   All iniquity is like a two-edged sword;
      A blow from it cannot be healed.

4   Terror and violence lay waste riches;
      So the house of a proud man will be laid waste.

The prayer from a poor man's mouth reaches his ears,   5
And his judgment comes speedily.

A man who hates reproof is walking in the sinner's steps,   6
But he who fears the Lord will turn to him in his heart.

A man who is mighty in tongue is known afar off,   7
But a thoughtful man knows when he slips.

The man who builds his house with other men's money   8
Is like one who gathers stones for winter.

An assembly of wicked men is like tow wrapped together;   9
For their end is a blazing fire.

The way of sinners is made smooth with stones,   10
But at the end of it is the pit of Hades.

The man who keeps the Law controls his thoughts,   11
And wisdom is the consummation of the fear of the Lord.

The man who is not shrewd will not be instructed,   12
But there is a shrewdness that spreads bitterness.

A wise man's knowledge abounds like a flood,   13
And his counsel is like a living spring.

The heart of a fool is like a broken dish;
It will hold no knowledge.   14

If a man of understanding hears a wise saying,   15
He commends it, and adds to it;
A self-indulgent man hears it, and it displeases him,
And he throws it behind his back.

The discourse of a fool is like a burden on a journey;   16
But enjoyment is found on the lips of a man of understanding.

The utterance of a sensible man will be asked for in an   17
assembly,
And what he says they will think over in their minds.

To a fool wisdom is like a ruined house,   18
And the knowledge of a man without understanding is
words that will not bear investigation.

21:5-18

19   To the foolish man, instruction is fetters on his feet;
And handcuffs on his right hand.

20   A fool raises his voice when he laughs,
But a shrewd man will hardly even smile quietly.

21   To a sensible man instruction is like a gold ornament,
And like a bracelet on his right arm.

22   The foot of a fool is quick to enter a house,
But an experienced man waits respectfully before it.

23   A senseless person peeps into a house through the door,
But a cultivated man stands outside.

24   It is stupidity in a man to listen at a door;
But a man of sensibility it would overwhelm with disgrace.

25   The lips of strangers will talk of these things,
But the words of sensible men are weighed on the scales.

26   The minds of fools are in their mouths,
But the mouth of wise men is their mind.

27   When an ungodly man curses his adversary,
He curses his own soul.

28   A whisperer pollutes his own soul,
And will be hated in the neighborhood.

22]   A slothful man is like a filthy stone,
And everybody hisses at his disgrace.

2   A slothful man is like the filth of a dunghill;
Anyone who picks it up shakes out his hand.

3   It is a disgrace to be the father of an ignorant son,
And to have a daughter is a disadvantage.

4   A sensible daughter will get a husband of her own,
But one who brings disgrace is a grief to her father.

5   She who is bold disgraces her father and her husband,
And will be despised by both.

6   Unseasonable talk is music in a time of mourning;
But blows and discipline in wisdom are always in order.

7   The man who teaches a fool is gluing a potsherd together,

21:19-22:7

Or rousing a sleeper out of a deep sleep.

The man who lectures to a fool lectures to one who is doz-   8
ing,

And at the conclusion he will say, "What was it?"

Weep for one who is dead, for light has failed him;   11

And weep over a fool, for understanding has failed him.

Weep less bitterly over the dead, for he has gone to rest;

But the fool's life is worse than death.

The mourning for the dead lasts seven days,   12

But that for a fool or an ungodly man lasts all the days of
his life.

Do not talk much with a senseless man,   13

Or go to see a man of no understanding;

Beware of him, or you may have trouble,

And do not be dirtied when he shakes himself.

Avoid him, and you will find rest,

And you will not be wearied by his senselessness.

What is heavier than lead?   14

What can you call it but Fool?

Sand and salt and a lump of iron   15

Are easier to bear than a man without understanding.

A wooden girder fastened in a building   16

Is not loosened by an earthquake;

So a mind established on well-considered thought

Will not be afraid in an emergency.

A mind fixed on understanding thought   17

Is like a plaster ornament on a smooth wall.

Fences set up in the air   18

Will not stand against the wind;

So a cowardly heart with foolish thoughts

Will not stand against any fear.

The man who pricks the eye makes tears fall,   19

And the man who pricks the heart makes it show feeling.

22:8–19

20 The man who throws a stone at the birds scares them away,
   And the man who abuses a friend destroys a friendship.

21 Even if you draw the sword against your friend,
   Do not despair, for there is a way to repent;

22 If you open your mouth against your friend,
   Do not be afraid, for there is such a thing as reconciliation;
   But when it comes to abuse and arrogance and telling a
      secret and a treacherous blow—
   At such treatment any friend will take to flight.

23 Win your neighbor's confidence when he is poor,
   So that when he prospers you may be filled likewise.
   Stand by him in time of trouble,
   So that you may share his inheritance with him.

24 The vapor and smoke from the furnace precede the fire;
   So abuse precedes bloodshed.

25 I will not shrink from giving shelter to a friend,
   And I will not hide myself from him,

26 And if misfortune overtakes me on his account
   Everyone who hears of it will beware of him.

27 Who will set a guard over my mouth,
   And put a skilful seal upon my lips,
   So that I may not fall because of them,
   And my tongue may not destroy me?

23] O Lord, Father and Master of my life,
   Do not abandon me to their designs;
   Do not let me fall because of them.

2 Who will set scourges over my mind,
   And the discipline of wisdom over my heart,
   So that they may not spare me for my errors of igno-
      rance,
   And it may not pass over my sins,

3 So that my acts of ignorance may not become numerous,
   And my sins multiply,

                                    22:20–23:3

And I fall before my adversaries,
And my enemy rejoice over me?
O Lord, Father and God of my life, 4
Do not give me roving eyes,
And avert evil desire from me;
Let not sensual appetite and intercourse master me, 6
And do not give me up to a shameless mind.

Listen, my children, to the discipline of the mouth, 7
For he who observes it will not be taken captive.
It is through his lips that the sinner is caught, 8
And the abusive and the proud are tripped up by them.
Do not accustom your mouth to an oath, 9
And do not form the habit of uttering the name of the Holy
One;
For just as a servant who is constantly being questioned 10
Does not lack the marks of a blow,
So the man who constantly swears and utters the Name 11
Cannot be absolved from sin.
A man who swears a great deal will be filled with iniquity,
And the scourge will never leave his house.
If he offends, his sin rests upon him,
And if he disregards it, he sins doubly;
And if he has sworn needlessly, he is not justified,
For his house will be filled with misery.

There is a way of speaking that may be compared with 12
death;
It must not be found in the inheritance of Jacob.
For all this will be far from the godly,
And they will not wallow in sin.
Do not accustom your mouth to foul rudeness, 13
For that is sinful speech.
Remember your father and mother, 14
When you sit in council with the great,

23:4-14

Or you may forget yourself in their presence,
And seem like a fool through the habit you have formed,
So that you will wish you had never been born,
And curse the day of your birth.

15 A man who forms the habit of abusive speech
Will never be educated as long as he lives.

16 There are two kinds of men that multiply sins,
And a third that incurs wrath:
A spirit hot as a burning fire;
It cannot be quenched until it is consumed;
One who is a fornicator in his physical body;
He will not stop until the fire burns him up;

17 To the fornicator all bread is sweet;
He will not tire until he dies;

18 A man who goes astray from his own bed,
And says to himself, "Who can see me?
Darkness is around me, and the walls hide me;
So no one can see me; what risk do I run?
The Most High will not remember my sins."

19 The eyes of men are his only fear,
And he does not know that the eyes of the Lord
Survey all the ways of men,
And observe the secret places.

20 All things were known to him before they were created,
So was it also after they were completed.

21 Such a man will be punished in the streets of the city,
And caught where he least suspects it.

22 It is so also with a wife who leaves her husband,
And provides an heir by a stranger.

23 For, first, she disobeys the law of the Most High,
And, second, she wrongs her husband,
And, third, she commits adultery through her fornication,
And provides children by a stranger.

23:15-23

She will be brought before the assembly, 24
And her sin will be visited upon her children.

Her children will not take root, 25
And her branches will not bear fruit.

She will leave her memory for a curse, 26
And her reproach will not be blotted out,

And those who are left behind will know 27
That there is nothing better than the fear of the Lord,
And nothing more pleasant than observing the Lord's
    commandments.

Wisdom is her own recommendation, [24
And exults in the midst of her people.

She opens her mouth in the assembly of the Most High, 2
And in the presence of his might she utters her boast:

"I issued from the mouth of the Most High, 3
And covered the earth like a mist.

I lived on the heights, 4
And my throne was on the pillar of cloud.

I alone compassed the circuit of heaven, 5
And I walked in the depth of the abyss.

I owned the waves of the sea and the whole earth 6
And every people and nation.

Among all these I sought a resting-place; 7
In whose possession should I lodge?

Then the Creator of all gave me his command; 8
And he who created me made my tent rest,
And said, 'Pitch your tent in Jacob,
And find your inheritance in Israel.'

He created me from the beginning, before the world, 9
And I shall never cease.

I ministered before him in the holy tent, 10
And so I was established in Zion.

He made me rest likewise in the beloved city, 11

23:24–24:11

And I had authority over Jerusalem.

12 I took root in the glorified people,
In the portion of the Lord, and of his inheritance.

13 I was exalted like a cedar in the Lebanon,
Or a cypress in the mountains of Hermon;

14 I was exalted like a palm tree in Engadi,
Or like the rose bushes in Jericho;
Like a fine olive tree in the field;
I was exalted like a plane tree.

15 I gave forth a perfume like cinnamon and camel's thorn,
And I spread fragrance like choice myrrh;
Like galbanum, onycha, and stacte,
And like the smoke of frankincense in the tent.

16 I stretched out my branches like a terebinth,
My branches were glorious, graceful branches.

17 I made grace grow like a vine,
And my blossoms produced fame and wealth.

19 Come to me, you who desire me,
And fill yourselves with my produce.

20 For the memory of me is sweeter than honey,
And the possession of me, than the honeycomb.

21 Those who eat me will still be hungry,
And those who drink me will still be thirsty.

22 He who obeys me will not be put to shame,
And those who work with me will commit no sin."

23 All this is the book of the agreement of the Most High
God,
The Law which Moses ordained for us
As an inheritance for the congregations of Jacob;

25 Which fills men with wisdom like the Pishon,
And like the Tigris in the days of the new wheat;

26 Which overflows with understanding like the Euphrates,
And like the Jordan in harvest time;

24:12-26

Which makes instruction shine forth like light, 27
Like the Gihon in the days of the vintage.
Just as the first man did not know her perfectly, 28
The last one will not track her out.
For her thinking is fuller than the sea, 29
And her counsel than the great deep.
    I came out like a canal from the river, 30
And like a watercourse in a garden.
I said, "I will water my garden, 31
And drench my flower bed."
And behold, my canal became a river,
And my river became a sea.
I will again make instruction dawn like the daybreak, 32
And make it shine forth afar.
I will pour out teaching again like prophecy, 33
And leave it behind for endless generations.
Observe that I have not labored for myself only, 34
But for all who seek her out.
    In three things I show my beauty and stand up in [25
      beauty
Before the Lord and men;
Harmony among brothers, and friendship among neigh-
    bors,
And wife and husband suited to each other.
But three kinds of men my soul hates, 2
And I am greatly angered at their existence:
A poor man who is proud, and a rich man who lies,
And an old man who is an adulterer and lacks understand-
    ing.
    If you have not gathered in your youth, 3
How can you find anything in your old age?
How beautiful judgment is for hoary hair, 4
And the knowledge of what to advise for the elderly!

24:27–25:4

5 How beautiful is the wisdom of old men,
  And consideration and counsel in men of distinction.
6 Rich experience is the crown of old men,
  And their boast is the fear of the Lord.
7   Nine things I have thought of and considered happy:
  And I can mention a tenth with my tongue:
  A man who is happy in his children;
  One who lives to see his enemies fall;
8 Blessed is the man who lives with a wife of understanding;
  And the one who does not slip with his tongue;
  And the one who is not a slave to his inferior;
9 Blessed is the man who finds good sense;
  And the one who discourses to the ears of men who listen;
10 How great the man is who finds wisdom;
  But there is no one greater than the man who fears the
     Lord.
11 The fear of the Lord surpasses everything,
  To what can the man who possesses it be compared?
13   Any wound but a wounded heart!
  And any wickedness but the wickedness of a woman!
14 Any calamity but a calamity brought about by those who
     hate you;
  And any vengeance but the vengeance of your enemies!
15 There is no head higher than a snake's head,
  And no anger greater than an enemy's.
16 I had rather keep house with a lion and a serpent
  Than keep house with a wicked woman.
17 A woman's wickedness changes her looks,
  And darkens her face like a bear;
18 Her husband sits at table among his neighbors,
  And involuntarily groans bitterly.
19 Any malice is small to a woman's malice;
  May the lot of the sinner befall her!

25:5–19

Like a sandy climb to an old man's feet   20
Is a talkative wife to a quiet man.
Do not fall down before a woman's beauty,   21
And do not greatly desire her for a wife.
It means anger and impudence and great disgrace,   22
If a woman supports her husband.
A humbled mind and a downcast face,   23
And a wounded heart mean a wicked wife.
A woman who does not make her husband happy
Means palsied hands and paralyzed knees.
Sin began with a woman,   24
And because of her we all die.
Do not give water an outlet   25
Nor a wicked woman freedom to speak.
If she does not act as you would have her,   26
Cut her off from your person.

    Happy is the man who has a good wife!   [26
The number of his days is doubled.
A noble wife gladdens her husband,   2
And he lives out his years in peace.
A good wife is good fortune;   3
She falls to the lot of those who fear the Lord,
Whether rich or poor, he has a stout heart;   4
And always has a cheerful face.

    There are three things my heart is afraid of,   5
And a fourth person that I fear:
Town gossip, and the gathering of a mob,
And a false accusation—these are all worse than death.
It is heartache and sorrow when one wife is the rival of   6
    another,
And a tongue-lashing that exposes things to everybody.
A wicked woman is a chafing ox-yoke;   7
Taking hold of her is like grasping a scorpion.

8 A drunken woman gets very angry,
And does not even cover up her own shame.

9 A woman's immorality is revealed by her roving looks,
And by her eyelids.

10 Keep a close watch over a headstrong daughter,
For if she is allowed her liberty, she may take advantage
of it.

11 Keep watch over a roving eye,
And do not be surprised if it offends against you.

12 Like a thirsty traveler who opens his mouth
And drinks of any water that is near,
She will sit down before every tent peg,
And open her quiver to the arrow.

13 The grace of a wife delights her husband,
And her knowledge fattens his bones.

14 A silent wife is a gift from the Lord,
And a well-trained spirit is beyond estimation.

15 A modest wife is blessing after blessing,
And a self-controlled spirit no scales can weigh.

16 Like the sun rising on the Lord's loftiest heights,
Is the beauty of a good woman as she keeps her house in
order.

17 Like a lamp shining on the holy lampstand,
Is a beautiful face on a good figure.

18 Like gold pillars on silver bases
Are beautiful feet with shapely heels.

28 Over two things my heart is grieved,
And over a third anger overcomes me:
A soldier in poverty and want,
And men of understanding who are treated like dirt,
And the man who turns back from uprightness to sin—
The Lord will prepare a sword for him!

29 A merchant can hardly keep himself from doing wrong,

And a storekeeper cannot be acquitted of sin.
Many sin for the sake of gain,   [27
And the man who is intent on increasing what he has, has
   to shut his eyes.
A peg will stick between the joints of stones,   2
And between buying and selling, sin is ground out.
Unless a man earnestly holds on to the fear of the Lord,   3
His house will soon be overturned.
   When a sieve is shaken, the refuse remains in it;   4
So, when a man reasons, his filth remains.
The furnace tests the potter's dishes,   5
And the test of a man is in his reasoning.
Its fruit shows how a tree has been cultivated;   6
So does the expression of the thought of a man's mind.
Do not praise a man before you hear him reason,   7
For that is the way men are tested.
If you pursue what is right, you will overtake it,   8
And put it on like a splendid robe.
Birds roost with their own kind,   9
And truth comes back to those who practice it.
The lion lies in wait for his prey,   10
And so does sin for for those who do wrong.
The discourse of a godly man is always wise,   11
But the foolish man changes like the moon.
Among unintelligent people watch your opportunity to   12
   leave,
But among thoughtful people stay on.
The discourse of fools is offensive,   13
And their laughter is wanton sinfulness.
A profane man's talk makes your hair stand on end,   14
And their quarreling makes you stop your ears.
When arrogant men quarrel, there is bloodshed,   15
And their abuse of one another is dreadful to hear.

27:1-15

16 The man who tells secrets destroys confidence,
   And will not find a friend to his mind.

17 If you love your friend, keep faith with him,
   But if you tell his secrets, do not pursue him.

18 For sure as a man loses his dead,
   You have lost your neighbor's friendship,

19 And as you let a bird out of your hand,
   You have let your neighbor out, and you will never catch
      him.
   Do not go after him, for he is far away,

20 And has made his escape like a gazelle from a trap.

21 For you can bind up a wound,
   And be reconciled after abuse,
   But for the man who tells secrets there is no hope.

22 A man who winks his eye plots mischief,
   And no one can keep it from him.

23 Face to face with you he speaks sweetly,
   And will show respect for what you say;
   But afterward he will twist his lips,
   And make a stumbling block of your words.

24 I have hated many things, but found nothing like him,
   And the Lord hates him too.

25 The man who throws a stone into the air is throwing it on
      his own head,
   And a treacherous blow wounds both.

26 The man who digs a hole will fall into it,
   And the man who sets a trap will be caught in it.

27 If a man does wicked things, they will roll on him,
   And he will not know where they come from.

28 Mockery and abuse overtake arrogant men,
   And vengeance lies in wait for them like a lion.

29 Those who enjoy the downfall of the godly will be caught
      in a trap,

And pain will consume them before they die.
Wrath and anger are also detestable,   30
And the sinful man clings to them.
The man who takes vengeance will have vengeance taken [28
on him by the Lord,
And he will keep close watch of his sins.
Forgive your neighbor his wrongdoing;   2
Then your sins will be forgiven when you pray.
Shall one man cherish anger against another,   3
And yet ask healing from the Lord?
Does he have no mercy on a man like himself,   4
And yet pray for his own sins?
If he, though he is flesh and blood, cherishes anger,   5
Who will atone for his sins?
Remember your end and give up your enmity;   6
Think of death and destruction, and stand by the com-
mandments.
Remember the commandments, and do not be angry with   7
your neighbor;
Think of the agreement of the Most High, and overlook
men's ignorance.
Keep from quarreling, and you will reduce your sins,   8
For a passionate man kindles quarrels.
A sinful man creates dissension among friends,   9
And arouses enmity among those who are at peace.
The more fuel, the more the fire will burn,   10
And the more obstinate the quarrel, the more it will burn.
The stronger a man is, the greater is his anger,
And the richer he is, the haughtier will his wrath be.
A hurried dispute kindles a fire,   11
And a hasty quarrel means bloodshed.
If you blow on a spark, it will blaze,   12
And if you spit on it, it will be put out;
Yet both come out of your mouth.

27:30–28:12

13   Curse the whisperer and the deceitful man;
For he has destroyed many who were at peace.

14   A third person's tongue has stirred many up,
And removed them from one nation to another;
It has torn down strongly fortified cities,
And overthrown the houses of the great.

15   A third person's tongue has driven out noble women,
And robbed them of the fruit of their labors.

16   The man who listens to it will find no rest,
And will not live in peace.

17   The blow of a whip leaves a bruise,
But the blow of a tongue breaks the bones.

18   Many have fallen by the edge of the sword,
But not so many as have fallen by the tongue.

19   Happy is the man who is protected from it,
Who does not feel its anger,
Who does not bear its yoke,
And is not bound with its chains.

20   For its yoke is an iron yoke,
And its chains are brazen chains;

21   Its death is a cruel death,
And Hades is better than it.

22   It will not control godly men,
And they will not be burned in its fire.

23   Those who forsake the Lord will fall into it,
And it will burn at them and not be put out;
It will be sent upon them like a lion,
And ravage them like a leopard.

24   If you see to hedging your property in with thorns,
And shut up your silver and gold,

25   Make balances and scales to weigh your words,
And make a barred door for your mouth.

26   Take heed not to make a slip with it,
Or you will fall before someone lying in wait for you.

28:13–26

The man who shows mercy will lend to his neighbor, **[29**
And the man who takes him by the hand keeps the commandments.

Lend to your neighbor when he is in need, **2**
And pay your neighbor back again when it is time.

Keep your word and keep faith with him, **3**
And in every emergency you will find what you need.

Many consider a loan as a windfall, **4**
And bring trouble on those who help them.

A man will kiss another man's hands until he gets it; **5**
And speak humbly about his neighbor's money;
But when payment is due, he extends the time,
And answers indifferently,
And finds fault about the time of payment.

If a man succeeds, he will hardly get half of it, **6**
And he will consider that a windfall.

If he does not, the other has defrauded him of his money,
And needlessly made him his enemy;
He will pay him with curses and abuse,
And repay him with insults instead of honor.

Many refuse to lend, not from their wickedness, **7**
But they are afraid of being needlessly defrauded.

But be patient with a poor man, **8**
And do not make him wait for charity.

For the commandment's sake help the needy man, **9**
And, in view of his need, do not send him away unsatisfied.

Lose your money for the sake of a brother or a friend, **10**
And do not let it rust to ruin under a stone.

Lay up your treasure according to the commandments of **11**
the Most High,
And it will be more profitable to you than gold.

Store up gifts to charity in your storerooms, **12**
And it will deliver you from all harm.

29:1–12

13 Better than a mighty shield and a ponderous spear,
   It will fight for you against your enemy.

14 A good man will go surety for his neighbor,
   But the man who has lost his sense of shame will abandon
   him.

15 Do not forget the favor your surety has done you,
   For he has put himself in your place.

16 A sinner will disregard the service done him by his surety,

17 And an ungrateful man will forsake the man who saved
   him.

18 Going surety has ruined many prosperous men,
   And shaken them like an ocean wave.
   It has driven influential men out of their houses,
   And made them wander among foreign nations.

19 A sinner fails in acting as security,
   And the man who pursues profits falls into lawsuits.

20 Help your neighbor to the best of your ability,
   But take heed that you do not fall.

21 The basis of life is water and bread and clothing,
   And a house to cover one's nakedness.

22 The life of a poor man under a shelter of logs is better
   Than splendid fare in someone else's house.

23 Be contented with much or little,
   And you will not hear the reproach of being a stranger.

24 It is a miserable life to go from house to house;
   And where you are a stranger, you cannot open your
   mouth.

25 If you entertain others and give them drink, you will have
   no thanks,
   And besides that you will have bitter things to hear:

26 "Come in, stranger, set the table,
   And if you have anything with you, let me have it to eat."

27 "Get out, stranger, here is somebody more important;

29:13-27

My brother has come to be my guest; I need my house."
These things are trying to a man of sensibility: 28
The reproach of a household and the abuse of a creditor.

The man who loves his son will continually beat him,   [30
So that he may be glad at the end.

The man who disciplines his son will profit by him,   2
And boast of him among his acquaintances;
The man who teaches his son will make his enemy jealous,   3
And exult over him before his friends.

When his father dies, it is as though he were not dead,   4
For he leaves behind him one like himself.

In his lifetime he sees him and rejoices,   5
And in death he does not grieve.

He has left one to avenge him upon his enemies,   6
And to repay the kindness of his friends.

The man who spoils his son will have to bind up his   7
    wounds,
And his heart will tremble at every cry.

An unbroken horse turns out stubborn,   8
And a son left to himself grows up headstrong.

If you pamper your child, he will astonish you.   9
Play with him, and he will grieve you;
Do not laugh with him, so that you may not have to mourn   10
    with him
And gnash your teeth over him at last.

Do not allow him liberty in his youth;   11
Bruise his sides while he is a child,   12
So that he will not become stubborn and disobey you.

Discipline your son and take pains with him,   13
So that he will not distress you with his bad behavior.

    A poor man who is well and has a strong constitution is   14
        better off
Than a rich man who is afflicted in body.

29:28–30:14

15 Health and a good constitution are better than any
      amount of gold,
    And a strong body than untold riches.
16 There is no greater wealth than health of body,
    And there is no greater happiness than gladness of heart.
17 Death is better than a wretched life,
    And eternal rest than continual sickness.
18 Good things spread out before a mouth that is closed
    Are like piles of food laid on a grave.
19 What good is an offering of fruit to an idol?
    It can neither eat nor smell.
    That is the way with a man who is afflicted by the Lord:
20 He sees things with his eyes and groans
    Like a eunuch embracing a girl!
21   Do not give yourself up to sorrow,
    And do not distress yourself of your own accord.
22 Gladness of heart is a man's life.
    And exultant joy prolongs his days.
23 Be kind to yourself and comfort your heart,
    And put sorrow far from you;
    For sorrow has destroyed many,
    And there is no profit in it.
24 Envy and anger shorten a man's days,
    And worry brings on old age before its time.
25 A heart that is cheerful and good
    Will pay attention to the food he eats.
31]   Anxiety about wealth makes a man waste away,
    And his worry about it drives away his sleep.
 2 Wakefulness and worry banish drowsiness
    As a serious illness dispels sleep.
 3 A rich man toils to amass money,
    And when he stops to rest, he enjoys luxury;

A poor man toils for the want of a livelihood,   4
And if he stops to rest, he finds himself in want.

The man who loves gold cannot be called upright,   5
And the man who pursues profits will be led astray by
    them.

Many have been brought to their downfall because of gold   6
And have been brought face to face with ruin.

It is a stumbling block to those who are possessed by it,   7
And every foolish man is taken captive by it.

Happy is the rich man who is found blameless,   8
And does not go after gold;

Who is he?—that we may congratulate him,   9
For he has worked wonders among his people.

Who has been tested by it and found perfect?   10
He has a right to boast.

Who has been able to transgress and has not transgressed,
And to do wrong and has not done it?

His prosperity will be lasting,   11
And the congregation will talk of his charities.

Do you sit at a great table?   12
Do not gulp at it,
And do not say, "How much there is on it!"

Remember that an envious eye is wrong.   13
What has been created that is worse than the eye?
That is why it sheds tears on every face.

Do not reach out your hand wherever it looks,   14
And do not crowd your neighbor in the dish;

Be considerate of him of your own accord,   15
And be thoughtful in everything.

Eat like a human being what is served to you,   16
Do not champ your food, or you will be detested.

Be the first to leave off for good manners' sake,   17
And do not be greedy, or you will give offense.

31:4–17

18 Even though you are seated in a large company,
Do not be the first to help yourself.

19   How adequate a little is for a well-bred man!
He does not have to gasp upon his bed!

20 Healthy sleep results from moderation in eating;
One gets up in the morning, in good spirits.
The distress of sleeplessness and indigestion
And colic attend the greedy man.

21 If you are compelled to eat,
Get up in the middle of the meal and stop eating.

22 Listen to me, my child, and do not disregard me.
And in the end you will find my words true:
Be industrious in all your work,
And no disease will overtake you.

23 The man who is generous with his bread men's lips will
bless,
And their testimony to his goodness can be relied on.

24 The town will grumble at the man who is grudging with
his bread,
And their testimony to his niggardliness is correct.

25   Do not play the man about wine,
For wine has been the ruin of many.

26 The furnace proves the steel's temper by dipping it;
So wine tests hearts when proud men quarrel.

27 Wine is like life to men
If you drink it in moderation;
What life has a man who is without wine?
For it was created to give gladness to men.

28 An exhilaration to the heart and gladness to the soul
Is wine, drunk at the proper time and in sufficient quantity;

29 Bitterness to the soul is much drinking of wine
Amidst irritation and conflict.

31:18–29

Drunkenness increases the anger of a foolish man to his **30**
   injury,
Reducing his strength and causing wounds.
Do not rebuke your neighbor at a banquet, **31**
   And do not despise him in his mirth.
Do not say a reproachful word to him,
   And do not press him to repay you.
If they make you master of the feast, do not be uplifted; [**32**
   Behave like one of them among them.
Look after them, and then take your seat;
When you have performed your duties, take your place, **2**
   So that you may rejoice on their account,
   And be crowned with a wreath for your efficiency.
Speak, elder, for that is your part, **3**
   With sound understanding, and do not interfere with the
   music.
When there is to be entertainment, do not talk volubly, **4**
   And do not philosophize when it is inopportune.
A carbuncle signet in a gold setting **5**
   Is a musical concert at a banquet.
An emerald signet richly set in gold **6**
   Is the melody of music with the taste of wine.
Speak, young man, if you are obliged to, **7**
   And only if you are asked repeatedly.
Speak concisely; say much in few words; **8**
   Act like a man who knows more than he says.
When among great men do not act like an equal; **9**
   And when another man is speaking, do not talk much.
The lightning hastens before the thunder, **10**
   And approval opens the way for a modest man.
Leave in good season and do not bring up the rear; **11**
   Hurry home and do not linger.
Amuse yourself there, and do what you please, **12**
   But do not sin through proud speech.

31:30–32:12

13 For all these things bless your Maker,
Who makes you drink his blessings till you are satisfied.

14   The man who fears the Lord will accept his discipline,
And those who rise early to seek him will gain his approval.

15 The man who pursues the Law will get his fill of it,
But the hypocrite will be tripped up by it.

16 Those who fear the Lord will discern his judgment,
And will kindle upright acts like the light.

17 A sinful man will shun reproof,
And will find a legal decision to his liking.

18   A man of discretion will not neglect thought;
An alien or a proud man will not cower from fear;

19 Do nothing without consideration;
And when you do a thing, do not change your mind.

20 Do not walk in a path full of obstacles,
And do not stumble over stony ground.

21 Do not trust an untried way,

22 And guard against your children.

23 In every act have faith in yourself,
For that is the keeping of the commandments.

24 The man who has faith in the Law heeds the commandments,
And the man who trusts in the Lord will not fail.

33]   No evil will befall the man who fears the Lord
But in trial he will deliver him again and again.

2 A wise man will not hate the Law,
But the man who is hypocritical about it is like a ship in
a storm.

3 A man of understanding will trust in the Law,
And he trusts the Law as he would a decision by the sacred
lot.

4 Prepare what you have to say, and then you will be listened
to;
Knit your instruction together and give your answer.

32:13–33:4

The heart of a fool is a wagon wheel;   5
And his thought is like a turning axle.

A stallion is like a mocking friend;   6
He neighs under everyone who mounts him.

Why is one day better than another,   7
When the light of every day in the year is from the sun?

By the Lord's knowledge they have been separated,   8
And he has made the various seasons and festivals.

Some of them he has exalted and made sacred,   9
And some he has made ordinary days.

All men are from the ground,   10
And Adam was created out of earth.

In the wealth of his knowledge the Lord has distinguished   11
    them,
And made their ways different.

Some of them he has blessed and exalted,   12
And some he has made holy and brought near himself.

Some of them he has cursed and humbled,
And thrown down from their position.

Like clay in the hand of the potter—   13
For all his ways are guided by his good pleasure—
So men are in the hand of their Creator,
To be repaid as he decides.

As good is the opposite of evil,   14
And life the opposite of death,
So the sinner is the opposite of the godly man.

So look upon all the works of the Most High,   15
In pairs, one the opposite of the other.

I was the last to wake up,   16
Like one who gleans after the grape-gatherers;
By the blessing of the Lord I got ahead,
And like a grape-gatherer I filled my winepress.

Observe that I have not labored for myself only,   17

33:5–17

But for all who seek instruction.

18 Hear me, you leaders of the people,
And you rulers of the assembly, listen to me.

19   To a son or a wife, to a brother or a friend,
Do not give power over yourself as long as you live,
And do not give your money to someone else,
So that you may not change your mind and have to ask
    for it.

20 As long as you live and have breath in your body,
Do not sell yourself to anybody.

21 For it is better that your children should ask from you,
Then that you should look to the clean hands of your sons.

22 In all that you do retain control,
So that you will not put any stain upon your reputation.

23 When the days of your life reach their end,
At the time of your death distribute your property.

24   Fodder and a stick and loads for an ass,
Bread and discipline and work for a servant.

25 Put your slave to work, and you will have rest;
Leave his hands idle, and he will seek his liberty.

26 The yoke and the strap will bend his neck,
And racks and tortures are for a servant who is a wrong-
    doer.

27 Put him to work, so that he will not be idle,
For idleness teaches much evil.

28 Set him such work as is suited to him,
And if he does not obey, load him with fetters.

29 But do not be overbearing to anybody,
And do not do anything without consideration.

30   If you have a servant, regard him as yourself,
Because you have bought him with blood.

31 If you have a servant, treat him like a brother,
For you need him as you do your own life.

If you ill-treat him, and he leaves and runs away,
Where will you look for him?
   Vain and delusive are the hopes of a man of no under- [34
    standing,
And dreams give wings to fools!
Like a man who catches at a shadow, and chases the wind, 2
Is the man who is absorbed in dreams.
A vision of dreams is this against that, 3
The likeness of one face before another.
From an unclean thing what can be clean? 4
And from something false what can be true?
Divinations and omens and dreams are folly, 5
And fancies of the mind like those of a woman in travail.
Unless they are sent from the Most High as a warning, 6
Do not pay any attention to them,
For dreams have deceived many, 7
And setting their hopes on them has led to their downfall.
The Law must be observed without any such falsehoods, 8
And wisdom finds perfection in truthful lips.
   A well-taught man knows a great deal, 9
And a man of experience will discourse with understanding.
The man who has not been tested knows little, 10
But the man who has wandered far gains great ingenuity.
I have seen much in my travels, 11
And I understand more than I can describe;
I have often been in danger of death, 12
But I have been saved by these qualities.
The spirit of those who fear the Lord will live, 13
For their hope is in him who can save them.
The man who fears the Lord will have no dread, 14
And will not be afraid, for he is his hope.
Happy is the soul of the man who fears the Lord! 15
Whom does he regard? And who is his support?

34:1-15

16   The eyes of the Lord rest on those who love him,
A mighty shield, a strong support,
A shelter from the hot wind and the noonday heat,
A guard against stumbling and a defense against falling.

17   He lifts up the soul and gives light to the eyes,
And bestows healing, life, and blessing.

18   If a man offers a sacrifice that was wrongfully obtained,
     it is blemished,
And the gifts of sinful men are not acceptable.

19   The Most High is not pleased with the offerings of ungodly
men,
And a man cannot atone for his sins with a great number
of sacrifices.

20   The man who offers a sacrifice from the property of the
poor
Sacrifices a son before his father's eyes.

21   Scanty fare is the living of the poor;
The man who deprives them of it is a murderous man.

22   The man who takes away his neighbor's living murders
him,
And the man who deprives a hired man of his wages is
guilty of bloodshed.

23   One man builds and another tears down;
What do they gain but toil?

24   One man prays and another curses;
Which one's voice will the Lord listen to?

25   If a man washes himself after touching a corpse and then
touches it again,
What good has his bath done him?

26   That is the way with a man who fasts for his sins,
And goes and does the same things over.
Who will listen to his prayer?
And what has he gained by humiliating himself?

34:16-26

The man who keeps the Law will make many offerings; [35
He who gives heed to the commandments will offer a
   thanksgiving sacrifice,
The man who returns a kindness will offer a meal offering,   2
And the man who gives to charity will offer the sacrifice
   of praise.
Avoiding wickedness wins the Lord's approval,   3
And avoiding wrongdoing is atonement.
Do not appear before the Lord empty-handed,   4
For all these things must be done because they are com- 5
   manded.
The offering of an upright man enriches the altar,   6
And its fragrance reaches the Most High.
The sacrifice of an upright man is acceptable,   7
And the memory of it will not be forgotten.
Glorify the Lord with a generous eye,   8
And do not stint the first fruits of your hands.
In all your giving show a joyful face,   9
And dedicate your tithes with gladness.
Give to the Most High as he has given to you,   10
With a generous eye, and as your hand has found.
For the Lord is one who repays,   11
And he will repay you seven times over.
   Do not try to bribe him, for he will not accept it,   12
And do not rely on an ill-gotten sacrifice;
For the Lord is a judge,
And there is no partiality with him.
He will show no partiality against the poor,   13
But he will listen to the prayer of the man who is wronged.
He will not disregard the supplication of the orphan,   14
Or the widow, if she pours out her story.
Do not the widow's tears run down her cheeks,   15
While she utters her complaint against the man who has
   caused them to fall?

16 The man who serves God with good will is welcomed,
And his prayer reaches to the clouds.

17 The prayer of the humble pierces the clouds,
And until it reaches God, he will not be consoled.
He will not leave off until the Most High considers him,
And does justice to the upright, and passes judgment.

18 And the Lord will not delay,
Or be slow about them,
Until he crushes the loins of the unmerciful,
And takes vengeance on the heathen;
Until he destroys the multitude of the insolent,
And breaks the scepters of the unrighteous;

19 Until he repays a man for his doings,
And repays men's deeds according to their thoughts;
Until he judges the case of his people,
And makes them glad with his mercy.

20 Mercy is as beautiful in a time of trouble
As rain clouds in a time of drought.

36] Have mercy upon us, Lord God of all, and look upon us,

2 And cast fear of you upon all the heathen.

3 Raise your hand against alien peoples,
And let them see your might.

4 As you have been sanctified before them, in us,
May you be magnified before us, in them;

5 And let them know, as we have known,
That there is no god, Lord, but you.

6 Show signs again, and show other wonders,
Make your hand and your right arm glorious.

7 Arouse your anger and pour out your wrath,
Destroy the adversary and wipe out the enemy.

8 Hasten the time and remember your oath;
And let them relate your mighty acts.

9 Let him that would save himself be consumed in furious
fire,

And let those who harm your people meet destruction.
Crush the heads of the enemy's rulers,   10
Who say, "There is no one but ourselves!"
Gather all the tribes of Jacob,   11
And give them their inheritance, as it was of old.
Have mercy, Lord, on the people that has borne your   12
    name,
And on Israel, whom you compared to your first-born.
Have pity on the city of your sanctuary,   13
Jerusalem, the place where you rest.
Fill Zion with the celebration of your goodness,   14
And your people with your glory.
Bear witness to those whom you created in the beginning,   15
And fulfil the prophecies made in your name.
Give those who wait for you their reward,   16
And let men trust in your prophets.
Hear, Lord, the prayer of your suppliants,   17
With Aaron's blessing on your people,
And all the people on the earth will know
That you are the Lord, the eternal God.
    The stomach will eat any food,   18
Yet one food is better than another.
As the mouth tastes the meat of game,   19
An intelligent mind detects false words.
A perverse mind causes pain,   20
But an experienced man will pay him back.
A woman can receive any man,   21
Yet one girl surpasses another.
A woman's beauty gladdens one's countenance,   22
And exceeds every desire man has.
If mercy and meekness are on her lips,   23
Her husband is not like the sons of men.
The man who gets a wife enters upon a possession,   24

36:10–24

A helper like himself, and a pillar of support.

25 Where there is no hedge, a piece of property will be
    plundered,
    And where there is no wife, a man will wander about and
    groan.

26 For who will trust an active robber
    Who bounds from one city to another?
    So who will trust a man who has no nest,
    And spends the night wherever evening overtakes him?

37] Every friend will say, "I am your friend";
    But sometimes a friend is a friend only in name.

2 Is it not a sorrow like that for death itself
    When a companion and friend turns into an enemy?

3 O wicked thought! Why were you shaped
    To cover the earth with deceit?

4 There are companions who rejoice in their friends' happi-
    ness,
    But, when trouble comes, are against them.

5 There are companions who labor with a friend for their
    stomach's sake,
    Who will take up the shield in the face of war.

6 Do not forget your friend in your heart,
    And do not be unmindful of him in your wealth.

7 Every adviser praises good counsel,
    But some give advice in their own interests.

8 Be on your guard against advisers
    And first find out what is for their advantage—
    For they will take thought for themselves—
    Or they will cast the lot against you,

9 And say to you, "Your way is good,"
    And will stand over against you to see what will happen
    to you.

10 Do not consult with the man who looks suspiciously at you,

                                    36:25–37:10

And conceal your purpose from those who are jealous of
    you;
With a woman about her rival,   11
Or with a coward about a war;
With a merchant about business,
Or with a buyer about selling;
With an envious man about gratitude,
Or with a merciless man about kindliness;
With an idler about any piece of work,
Or with a man hired by the year about finishing his work;
With a lazy servant about a large undertaking;
Do not look to these for any advice.
But stay all the time with a godly man,   12
Who you know keeps the commandments;
Whose heart is at one with your heart,
And who will sorrow with you if you fail.
And hold fast the counsel of your own mind,   13
For you have nothing more to be depended on than it.
For a man's soul is sometimes wont to bring him news   14
Better than seven watchmen sitting high on a watchtower.
And, above all this, intreat the Most High   15
To direct your way in truth.
    Every undertaking begins with reason,   16
And consideration precedes every work.
If we trace the changes of the mind,   17
Four parts appear,   18
Good and evil, life and death.
But it is the tongue that continually rules them.
A man may be shrewd and the instructor of many,   19
And yet be unprofitable to himself.
A man skilful in his use of words may be hated;   20
He will fail to get any food.
For agreeableness has not been given him by the Lord,   21

37:11–21

Because he has been deprived of all wisdom.
A man may be wise for himself,

22 And the products of his understanding may be trustworthy
on his lips;

23 A wise man will instruct his own people,
And the products of his understanding will be trustworthy;

24 A wise man will be satisfied with blessing,
And all who see him will call him happy.

25 A man's life is numbered by days,
But the days of Israel are unnumbered.

26 The wise man will obtain the trust of his people,
And his name will live forever.

27 My child, test your soul while you live,
And see what hurts it, and do not give it that.

28 For not everything is good for everyone,
And not everybody enjoys everything.

29 Do not be insatiable about any luxury,
And do not be carried away with food,

30 For sickness comes with excessive eating,
And greediness leads to severe illness.

31 Many have died of greediness,
But the man who guards against it prolongs his life.

38} Show the physician due honor in view of your need of
him,
For the Lord has created him;

2 Healing comes from the Most High,
And he will receive presents from the king.

3 The skill of the physician exalts him,
And he is admired among the great.

4 The Lord has created medicines out of the earth,
And a sensible man will not refuse them.

5 Was not water made sweet by wood,
So that its strength might be shown?

And he has given men knowledge 6
So that he might be glorified for his wonderful works.
With them he cures and takes away pain, 7
The druggist makes a mixture of them. 8
His works will never end,
And from him peace spreads over the face of the earth.
    My child, do not be negligent when you are sick, 9
But pray to the Lord, and he will cure you.
Renounce wrongdoing and make your hands do right, 10
And cleanse your heart from every sin,
Offer a fragrant offering and a memorial sacrifice of fine 11
    flour,
And make your offering rich, as though you were no longer
    to live,
And leave room for the physician, for the Lord has created 12
    him,
And he must not desert you, for you need him.
There is a time when your welfare depends upon them, 13
For they too will pray the Lord 14
To guide them to bringing relief
And effecting a cure and restoration to health.
As for the man who sins in the sight of his Maker, 15
May he fall into the hands of the physician!
    My child, for the dead let your tears fall, 16
And like one who is suffering terribly begin your lament.
Wrap his body up fittingly,
And do not neglect his burial.
Weep bitterly and wail passionately 17
And show your grief as he may deserve,
For one day or perhaps two, to avert criticism;
Then be comforted for your sorrow.
For death comes of sorrow, 18
And sorrow of heart prostrates one's strength.

38:6–18

19 In misfortune grief will continue,
And the life of the poor saddens the heart.

20 But do not resign your heart to grief;
Dismiss it, but remember your end,

21 Do not forget it, for he will not come back;
You cannot help him, and you will harm yourself;

22 "Remember my judgment, for yours will be like it;
Mine today, and yours tomorrow!"

23 When the dead is at rest, let his memory rest,
And be comforted for him when his spirit departs.

24 A scribe attains wisdom through the opportunities of
leisure,
And the man who has little business to do can become wise.

25 How can the man who holds the plow become wise,
Who glories in handling the ox-goad?
Who drives oxen, and guides them at their work,
And whose discourse is with the sons of bulls?

26 He sets his mind on turning his furrows,
And his anxiety is about fodder for heifers.

27 It is so with every craftsman and builder,
Who keeps at work at night as well as by day.
Some cut carved seals,
And elaborate variety of design;
Another puts his mind on painting a likeness,
And is anxious to complete his work.

28 It is so with the smith sitting by his anvil,
And expert in working in iron;
The smoke of the fire reduces his flesh,
And he exerts himself in the heat of the furnace.
He bends his ear to the sound of the hammer,
And his eyes are on the pattern of the implement.
He puts his mind on completing his work,
And he is anxious to finish preparing it.

38:19-28

It is so with the potter, as he sits at his work,   29
And turns the wheel with his foot;
He is constantly careful about his work,
And all his manufacture is by measure;
He will shape the clay with his arm,   30
And bend its strength with his feet;
He puts his mind on finishing the glazing,
And he is anxious to make his furnace clean.

　　All these rely on their hands;   31
And each one is skilful in his own work;
Without them, no city can be inhabited,   32
And men will not live in one or go about in it.
But they are not sought for to advise the people,   33
And in the public assembly they do not excel.
They do not sit on the judge's seat,
And they do not think about the decision of lawsuits;
They do not utter instruction or judgment,
And they are not found using proverbs.
Yet they support the fabric of the world,   34
And their prayer is in the practice of their trade.

　　It is not so with the man who applies himself,   [39
And studies the Law of the Most High.
He searches out the wisdom of all the ancients,
And busies himself with prophecies;
He observes the discourse of famous men,   2
And penetrates the intricacies of figures.
He searches out the hidden meaning of proverbs,   3
And acquaints himself with the obscurities of figures.
He will serve among great men,   4
And appear before rulers.
He will travel through the lands of strange peoples,
And test what is good and what is evil among men.
He will devote himself to going early   5

38:29–39:5

To the Lord his Maker,
And will make his entreaty before the Most High.
He will open his mouth in prayer,
And make intreaty for his sins.

6   If the great Lord pleases,
He will be filled with the spirit of understanding,
He will pour out his wise sayings,
And give thanks to the Lord in prayer;

7   He will direct his counsel and knowledge,
And study his secrets.

8   He will reveal instruction in his teaching,
And will glory in the Law of the Lord's agreement.

9   Many will praise his understanding,
And it will never be blotted out.
His memory will not disappear,
And his name will live for endless generations.

10   Nations will repeat his wisdom,
And the congregation will utter his praise.

11   If he lives long, he will leave a greater name than a thousand,
And if he goes to rest, his fame is enough for him.

12   I have reflected further, and I will utter it,
And I am full as the full moon.

13   Listen to me, you holy sons, and bud
Like a rose that grows by a watercourse;

14   Exhale fragrance like a frankincense tree,
And blossom like a lily.
Give forth an odor and sing a song,
Bless the Lord for all his works.

15   Magnify his name,
And confess him with praise,
With songs on your lips and with lyres,
And this is what you are to say in your thanksgiving:

39:6–15

"The works of the Lord are all extremely good,   16
And every command of his will be obeyed in its proper
    season."
No one can say "What does this mean? Why is that?"   17
For in his good time they will all be searched out,
At his command the waters stood in a heap,
And the reservoirs of water at the word he uttered.
At his order all that he pleases is done,   18
And there is no one who can interfere with his saving
    power.
The doings of all mankind are before him,   19
And it is not possible to be hidden from his eyes.
From everlasting to everlasting he beholds them,   20
And nothing is marvelous to him.
No one can say, "What does this mean? Why is that?"   21
For everything has been created for its use.

    His blessing covers the land like a river,   22
And saturates the dry land like a flood.
As he turns fresh water into salt water,   23
So the heathen will experience his wrath.
To his people his ways are straight,   24
Just as they are stumbling blocks to the disobedient.
From the beginning good things have been created for   25
    the good,
Just as evils have been created for sinners.
The elements necessary for man's life   26
Are water and fire and iron and salt,
And wheat flour and milk and honey,
The blood of the grape, and olive oil and clothing.
All these things prove good to the godly,   27
Just as they turn into evils for the sinful.

    There are winds which have been created for vengeance,   28
And, when he is angry, they make their scourges strong;

39:16–28

When the consummation comes, they will pour out their
   strength,
And calm the anger of their Creator.

29 Fire and hail and famine and death—
These have all been created for vengeance.

30 The teeth of wild animals, and scorpions and vipers,
And the sword that drives the ungodly to destruction—

31 They will rejoice when he commands,
And be made ready on the earth for their functions.
And they will not disobey his word, at their proper times.

32 Therefore from the beginning I have become assured,
And have reached this conclusion and left it in writing:

33 The works of the Lord are all good,
And will supply every need when it arises,

34 And no one can say, "This is worse than that,"
For they will all prove good in their season.

35 So now sing praise with all your heart and voice,
And bless the name of the Lord.

40] Much occupation is appointed for every man,
And a heavy yoke rests on the sons of Adam
From the day they come out of their mother's womb
Until the day when they return to the mother of us all,

2 Their perplexities and anxiety of mind,
Their apprehension, and the day of their end!

3 From the man who sits on his splendid throne
To the one who is abased in dust and ashes,

4 From the man who wears purple and a crown
To the one who is clad in coarse linen,

5 There is wrath and envy and trouble and perplexity
And fear of death and anger and strife,
And when a man rests upon his bed,
His sleep at night confuses his knowledge.

6 He gets little or no rest,

And afterward in his sleep, he is like a watchman on duty,
Bewildered by the vision of his mind
Like a man who has escaped from the front of battle.
In the moment of his extremity he wakes up,   7
And wonders that his fear came to nothing.
It is so with all flesh, man and beast;   8
And with sinners seven times more;
Death and blood and strife and sword,   9
Misfortunes, famine and affliction and plague—
All these were created for the wicked,   10
And because of them the flood came.
All that comes from the earth returns to the earth,   11
And what comes from the waters turns back to the sea.
   All bribery and injustice will be blotted out,   12
But good faith will stand forever.
The property of unrighteous men will dry up like a river,   13
And explode like a clap of thunder in a rain.
As surely as an open-handed man is glad,   14
Transgressors will utterly fail.
The children of the ungodly will not put forth many   15
   branches;
They are unclean roots on a precipitous rock.
Sedge by any water or riverbank   16
Will be plucked up before any grass.
Kindness is like a garden of blessing,   17
And charity endures forever.
   The life of a self-supporting man or of a workman is   18
   made sweet,
But a man who finds a treasure is better off than both of
   them.
Children or the building of a city perpetuate a man's   19
   name,
But an irreproachable wife is counted better than both of
   them.

40:7–19

20 Wine and music delight the heart,
But the love of wisdom is better than both of them.

21 The flute and the lute make sweet melody,
But a pleasant tongue is better than both of them.

22 The eye desires grace and beauty,
But more than both of them the springing grain.

23 A friend and a comrade meet opportunely,
But a wife with her husband is better than both of them.

24 Brothers and help are for a time of trouble,
But charity is a better deliverer than both of them.

25 Gold and silver make a man stand firm,
But good counsel is more approved than both of them.

26 Money and vigor elate the mind,
But the fear of the Lord is better than both of them.
There is no flaw in the fear of the Lord,
And with it there is no need to seek for help.

27 The fear of the Lord is like a garden of blessing,
And covers a man better than any glory.

28 My child, do not lead a beggar's life;
It is better to die than to beg.

29 When a man looks to another man's table,
His existence cannot be considered life.
He pollutes his soul with another man's food,
But a man who is intelligent and well-instructed will be-
ware of it.

30 In a shameless man's mouth begging is sweet,
But it kindles a fire in his heart.

41] O death, how bitter is the remembrance of you
To a man at peace among his possessions,
To a man who is free from distractions and prosperous in
everything,
And is still vigorous enough to enjoy his food!

2 O death, your sentence is good
For a needy man of failing strength,

40:20–41:2

In extreme old age, and distracted about everything;
Who is contrary, and has lost his patience.
Do not fear the sentence of death;   3
Remember those who went before you and those who
    come after.
This is the sentence of the Lord upon all flesh and blood,
And how can you refuse what is the will of the Most High? 4
Whether it was ten or a hundred or a thousand years,
There is no reproach about life in Hades.

    The children of sinners are detestable children,   5
And live in the circles of the ungodly.
The possessions of the children of sinners will be lost,   6
And perpetual reproach will follow their posterity.
His children will blame an ungodly father   7
Because they are reproached on his account.
Alas for you, ungodly men,   8
Who have forsaken the law of the Most High God!
When you are born, you are born to a curse,   9
And when you die, a curse will be your lot.
Everything that springs from the earth will go back to the 10
    earth;
Just as surely the ungodly go from a curse to destruction.
Men grieve about their bodies,   11
But the name of sinners is not good and will be blotted out.
Take heed about your name, for you retain it longer   12
Than a thousand great stores of gold.
The days of a good life are numbered,   13
But a good name lasts forever.
Children, maintain instruction and be at peace;   14
Concealed wisdom and invisible treasure—
What is the use of either?
A man who hides his folly is better   15

41:3-15

Than a man who hides his wisdom.

16   Therefore regard what I say;
For not every kind of shame is it well to maintain,
And not everything is approved in good faith by all.

17 Be ashamed of a father and mother, for immorality,
And of a prince and a ruler, for a lie;

18 Of a judge and a magistrate, for an offense,
And of an assembly and the people, for disregard for the
    Law;
Of a partner and a friend, for unjust dealing,

19 And of the place where you are living, for theft;
Respect the truth of God and his agreement,
Be ashamed to lean on your elbow at table;
To be contemptuous about giving back what you have
    received;

20 And to keep silent before those who greet you;
To look at a woman who is a courtesan,

21 And to turn your face away from a relative;
To take someone's portion or present,
And to stare at a married woman;

22 To meddle with another man's maid,
(And do not stand over her bed);
To utter words of abuse before friends
(And after you make a gift do not add abuse);

23 To repeat what you have heard,
And to tell things that are secret.

24 Then you will be really modest,
And win the approval of everyone.

42]   Do not be ashamed of these things,
And do not show partiality, so as to sin:

2 Of the Law of the Most High and his agreement,
And of judgment, to punish the ungodly;

3 Of having a reckoning with a partner and fellow-travelers,

And of a present from what is inherited by your companions;

Of the accuracy of scales and weights, 4
And of the acquisition of much or little;
Of profit from dealing with merchants, 5
And of the careful training of children;
And of staining the side of a bad servant with blood.
It is well to put a seal on a wicked wife, 6
And where there are many hands, lock things up.
Whatever you hand over, let it be by number and weight; 7
And in giving and receiving, let everything be in writing.
Do not be ashamed to instruct the senseless and foolish, 8
Or an aged man who is charged with immorality.
Then you will be really instructed,
And approved in the eyes of every man alive.

A daughter is a secret cause of sleeplessness to her father, 9
And his concern for her robs him of his rest;
In her youth, for fear she will pass her prime,
And when she is married, for fear she will be hated;
When she is a girl, for fear she will be profaned, 10
And be with child in her father's house;
When she has a husband, for fear she will transgress;
And when she is married, for fear she will be childless.
Keep a close watch over a headstrong daughter, 11
For fear she will fill your enemies with malignant joy,
And make you the talk of the town and notorious among
the people,
And disgrace you before the multitude.
Do not look at anybody for her beauty, 12
And do not sit among women,
For as a moth comes out of clothing, 13
A woman's wickedness comes from a woman.
A man's wickedness is better than a beneficent woman, 14
Or a woman that disgraces you shamefully.

42:4–14

15   I will call to mind the doings of the Lord,
And recount the things that I have seen.
By the commands of the Lord his works are done;
16 The light-giving sun looks down on everything,
And his work is full of the glory of the Lord.
17 He has not permitted the saints of the Lord
To recount all his wonders,
Which the Lord, the Almighty, has firmly established,
So that the universe might stand fast through his glory.
18 He searches out the great deep and the human mind,
And he understands their designs;
For the Most High possesses all knowledge,
And looks upon the portent of eternity,
19 And declares the things that are past and the things that
    are to come,
And uncovers the tracks of hidden things.
20 No thought escapes him,
Not one word is hidden from him.
21 He has ordained the majesty of his wisdom,
For he is from everlasting to everlasting.
It cannot be increased or diminished,
And he has no need of any counselor.
22 How much to be desired are all his works,
And how sparkling they are to see.
23 All these things live and last forever,
With all their functions, and they are all obedient.
24 They are all in pairs, one facing another,
Not one of them is missing.
25 One confirms the good of the other,
And who can have too much of beholding his glory?
43]   The glory of the height is the firmament in its purity,
The sight of the heavens with the spectacle of their splendor.
2 The sun, when he appears, making proclamation as he goes
    forth,

Is a wonderful instrument, the work of the Most High;
At noonday he dries up the country,   3
And who can withstand his burning heat?
A man who blows a furnace works in the midst of heat,   4
But the sun three times as much, burning up the moun-
     tains.
He breathes out fiery vapors,
And shoots forth his beams, blinding men's eyes.
Great is the Lord who made him,   5
At whose command he hurries on his course.
The moon, too, he places in its position at its season,   6
To mark times and be an everlasting sign;
The moon gives the sign for the festival,   7
A light that wanes after reaching the full.
The month is named after her;   8
She increases marvelously as she changes,
An instrument of the hosts on high,
Shining in the firmament of the heavens.
The beauty of heaven is the glory of the stars,   9
A system giving light in the highest places of the Lord.
At the command of the Holy One they take their places as   10
     he decrees,
And they will not fail in their watches.
See the rainbow, and bless him who made it   11
Surpassingly beautiful in its brightness.
It curves over the heaven in a glorious circle,   12
The hands of the Most High have stretched it out,
By his command he brings the hurrying snow,   13
And makes swift the lightnings of his judgment;
Because of it, the storehouses are opened,   14
And the clouds fly out like birds.
In his majesty he makes the clouds thick,   15
And the hailstones are broken in pieces.

43:3–15

16 When he appears, the mountains shake.
    At his wish the south wind blows.

17 His voice in the thunder rebukes the earth;
    So do the hurricane from the north and the whirlwind.
    He sprinkles the snow like birds fluttering down,
    It comes down like locusts settling;

18 The eye is amazed at the beauty of its whiteness,
    And the mind is astonished at its raining.

19 He pours hoarfrost over the earth like salt,
    And, when it freezes, it becomes points of thorns.

20 The cold north wind blows,
    And the ice freezes on the water;
    It lodges on every pool of water,
    And the water puts it on like a breastplate.

21 It consumes the mountains and burns up the wilderness,
    And shrivels the green herbage like fire,

22 A mist coming quickly heals everything;
    The dew falling refreshes things after the heat.

23 By his counsel he has stilled the deep,
    And planted islands in it.

24 Those who sail the sea tell of its danger,
    And we wonder at what we hear with our ears.

25 There are strange and wonderful works in it,
    All kinds of living things, the whale creation.

26 Because of him his messenger prospers on his way,
    And through his command all things consist.

27 We may say more, but we will not reach the end,
    And the conclusion of what we have to say is: He is the
        whole.

28 Where can we find strength to glorify him?
    For he is greater than all his works.

29 The Lord is terrible and exceedingly great,
    And his power is wonderful.

43:16–29

Glorify the Lord and exalt him   30
As much as you can, for even then he will surpass it.
When you exalt him put forth all your strength;
Do not grow weary, for you will not reach the end.
Who has ever seen him, so that he can describe him?   31
And who can tell his greatness as it really is?
Many things greater than these still remain hidden,   32
For we have seen but few of his works.
For the Lord has made all things,   33
And he has given wisdom to the godly.

   Let us now praise distinguished men,   [44
Our forefathers before us.
They are a great glory to the Lord who created them;   2
They show his majesty from of old.
Men who exercised authority in their reigns,   3
And were renowned for their might!
They gave their counsel with understanding,
And brought men tidings through their prophecy—
Leaders of the people in deliberation and understanding, 4
Men of learning for the people,
Wise in their words of instruction;
Composers of musical airs,   5
Authors of poems in writing;
Rich men, endowed with strength,   6
Who lived in peace upon their lands—
All these were honored in their generation,   7
And were a glory in their day.
There are some of them who have left a name,   8
So that men declare their praise;
And there are some who have no memorial,   9
And have perished as though they had not lived,
And have become as though they had not been,
With their children after them.

43:30–44:9

10 Yet these were merciful men,
   And their uprightness has not been forgotten.

11 With their descendants it will remain,
   A good inheritance for their posterity.

12 Their descendants stand by the agreements,
   And their children also for their sakes;

13 Their posterity will endure forever,
   And their glory will not be blotted out.

14 Their bodies are buried in peace,
   But their name lives to all generations.

15 Peoples will recite their wisdom,
   And the congregation declare their praise!

16   Enoch pleased the Lord and was taken up from the
         earth,
   A pattern of repentance for all generations.

17 Noah was found perfect and upright;
   In the time of God's anger he was taken in exchange.
   On his account a remnant was left to the earth
   When the flood occurred.

18 Everlasting agreements were made with him,
   That all life should never be blotted out by a flood.

19   Abraham was the great father of a multitude of nations,
   And no one has been found equal to him in glory.

20 He observed the Law of the Most High,
   And entered into an agreement with him.
   He certified the agreement in his flesh,
   And, when he was tested, he proved faithful.

21 For that reason he assured him with an oath
   That nations would be blessed through his posterity,
   And that he would make him as numerous as the dust of
         the earth,
   And would raise his posterity as high as the stars,
   And that they should possess

44:10–21

From sea to sea,
And from the river to the end of the earth.
He guaranteed it to Isaac also in like manner, 22
Because of his father Abraham.
The blessing of all mankind and the agreement
He made to rest upon the head of Jacob. 23
He acknowledged him with his blessings,
And gave them to him as his inheritance.
And he divided his portions,
And distributed them among twelve tribes.

From his posterity he brought a man of mercy, [45
Who found favor in the sight of all mankind,
And was beloved by God and man—
Moses, whose memory is blessed.
He made him equal to his holy ones in glory, 2
And made him great in the fears of his enemies.
By his words he brought wonders to pass; 3
He made him glorious in the sight of kings.
He gave him commands for his people,
And showed him some of his glory.
Through faithfulness and meekness he sanctified him, 4
He chose him out of all mankind.
He made him hear his voice; 5
He brought him into the thick darkness,
And gave him his commandments face to face,
The law of life and knowledge,
To teach Jacob his agreement,
And Israel his decrees.

He exalted Aaron, a holy man like him, 6
Who was his brother, from the tribe of Levi.
He made him an everlasting ordinance, 7
And gave him the priesthood of the people.
He blessed him with stateliness,

And put on him a splendid robe;
8 He clothed him with glorious perfection,
And strengthened him with garments of authority,
The drawers, the robe, and the apron,
9 And he surrounded him with pomegranates,
With very many gold bells all around
To ring out as he walked,
To make their sound heard in the temple,
To remind the sons of his people;
10 With a holy garment, with gold and violet
And purple, a work of embroidery;
With the oracle of judgment, the decider of truth.
11 With twisted scarlet, the work of an artist;
With precious stones, engraved like signets,
In a setting of gold, the work of an engraver,
For a reminder, in carved letters,
Giving the number of the tribes of Israel;
12 With a gold crown upon his turban,
Engraved like a signet with "Sacredness":
A glorious distinction, a work of might,
The desire of the eyes, richly adorned.
13 Before him, there never were such beautiful things,
No alien will ever put them on,
But his sons alone
And their posterity forever.
14 His sacrifices will be wholly consumed
Twice every day perpetually.
15 Moses filled his hands,
And anointed him with sacred oil;
It became an everlasting agreement with him
And his posterity all the days of heaven,
To minister to him and act as priest
And bless the people in his name.

45:8-15

He chose him out of all the living 16
To offer sacrifice to the Lord,
Incense and fragrance for a memorial sacrifice,
To make atonement for your people.
In his commandments he gave him 17
Authority over the agreements about judgments,
To teach Jacob the decrees
And to enlightèn Israel with his law.
Strangers conspired against him, 18
And envied him in the desert;
The men with Dathan and Abiram,
And the company of Korah, in their wrath and anger.
The Lord saw it and was not pleased, 19
And they were destroyed by his fierce anger;
He executed signs upon them,
To devour them with his blazing fire.
And he increased Aaron's glory, 20
And gave him his inheritance;
He apportioned to him the very first of the first fruits;
He prepared the Presentation Bread in abundance,
For they are to eat the sacrifices of the Lord, 21
Which he gave to him and his posterity.
But he has no share in the land of the people, 22
And he has no portion among the people,
For he himself is your portion and your inheritance.
  Phineas, the son of Eleazar, is the third in glory, 23
For he was zealous for the fear of the Lord,
And stood fast, when the people turned away,
In the goodness and eagerness of his soul,
And made atonement for Israel.
Therefore an agreement of peace was established with him, 24
That he should be the leader of the saints and of his people,
That he and his posterity should possess

The dignity of the priesthood forever.

25 And an agreement was made with David,
The son of Jesse, of the tribe of Judah;
As the king's inheritance passes only from son to son,
The inheritance of Aaron is for his posterity.

26 May he give you wisdom of mind
To judge his people with uprightness
So that their prosperity may not come to an end,
But their glory may last through all their generations.

46] Joshua, the son of Nun, was mighty in war,
And the successor of Moses in prophesying.
He became, as his name describes him,
Great to save his chosen,
To take vengeance on the enemies that rose up against
them,
So that he might give Israel their possessions.

2 How glorious he was when he lifted up his hands,
And pointed his sword at the towns!

3 Before him who ever stood so fast?
For he carried on the wars of the Lord.

4 Was not the sun stayed by his hand,
And one day increased to two?

5 He called on the Most High Ruler,
When his enemies pressed upon him on all sides,
And the great Lord answered him

6 With hailstones of mighty power.
He made war burst upon that nation,
And at the descent he destroyed his opponents,
So that the heathen might recognize his armor,
And know that he fought in the sight of the Lord.
This champion was followed by one

7 Who in the days of Moses did an act of piety,
No other than Caleb, the son of Jephunneh,

Who stood opposed to the community,
And restrained the people from sin,
And quieted their wicked grumbling.
These two alone were preserved
Out of six hundred thousand people on foot　　8
To bring them into their possessions,
To a land running with milk and honey.
And the Lord gave Caleb strength,　　9
And it remained with him until he was old,
So that he climbed the heights of the land,
And his posterity obtained a heritage,
So that all the sons of Israel might see　　10
That it is good to follow after the Lord.

　The judges too, with their various names,　　11
All whose hearts did not fall into idolatry,
And who did not turn away from the Lord—
May their memory be blessed!
May their bones revive where they lie,　　12
And their names be transmitted
To the descendants of their renown.

　　There was Samuel, beloved by his Lord;　　13
A prophet of the Lord, he established the kingdom,
And anointed princes over his people.
By the Law of the Lord he judged the community,　　14
And the Lord showed regard for Jacob.
By his faithfulness he was proved a prophet,　　15
And he was known to be trustworthy through the words of
　his vision,
And he called upon the Lord, his Master,　　16
When his enemies pressed him on every side,
And he offered him a suckling lamb;
Then the Lord thundered from heaven,　　17
And made his voice heard with a loud noise,

46:8–17

18 And he wiped out the rulers of the Tyrians
And all the princes of the Philistines.

19 And before he fell asleep forever,
He called them to witness, before the Lord and his
anointed,
"From no human being have I taken his property,
Even as much as a pair of shoes,"
And no one accused him.

20 Even after he fell asleep he prophesied,
And showed the king his end,
And lifted his voice out of the earth
In prophecy, to blot out the wickedness of the people.

47] After him Nathan arose,
To prophesy in the days of David.

2 Just as the fat is separated from the offering,
David was separated from the Israelites.

3 He played with lions as though they were kids,
And with bears as though they were lambs of the flock.

4 In his youth did he not kill a giant,
And relieve the people of reproach,
When he lifted his hand with a stone in the sling,
And brought down the boasting of Goliath?

5 For he called on the Lord, the Most High,
And he gave strength to his right hand
To slay a mighty warrior,
And to exalt the strength of his people.

6 So they lauded him for his ten thousands,
And praised him for the blessings of the Lord,
When the glorious diadem was brought to him.

7 For he wiped out his enemies on every side,
And annihilated his adversaries the Philistines,
He crushed their strength, unto this day.
Over all that he did he gave thanks

46:18–47:7

To the Holy One, the Most High, with words of praise.   8
He sang praise with his whole heart,
And he loved his Maker.
He placed singers before the altar,   9
To make sweet melody with their voices.
He gave dignity to the festivals,   10
And set the seasons in order throughout the year,
While they praised God's holy name,
And the sanctuary rang with it from early morning.
The Lord took away his sins,   11
And exalted his strength forever,
And gave him the agreement about the kings,
And a glorious throne in Israel.
   After him arose his wise son,   12
Who lived in wide borders because of him;
Solomon reigned in days of peace,   13
And God gave him rest on every side,
So that he might erect a house in his name,
And provide a sanctuary forever.
How wise you became in your youth,   14
And how full of understanding, like a river!
Your soul covered the earth,   15
And you filled it with puzzling proverbs.
You name reached distant islands,   16
And you were loved for your peaceful sway.
For your songs and proverbs and figures,   17
And your expositions, the countries wondered at you.
Through the name of the Lord God,   18
Who is called the God of Israel,
You gathered gold like tin,
And accumulated silver like lead.
You laid your flanks beside women,   19
And were brought into subjection by your body.

47:8–19

20 You brought a stain upon your fame,
And polluted your posterity,
So that you brought wrath upon your children,
And they were grieved at your folly,

21 So that the sovereignty was divided,
And a disobedient kingdom arose out of Ephraim.

22 But the Lord will not forsake his mercy,
And he will not prove false to any of his words,
Nor will he blot out the descendants of his chosen,
Nor destroy the posterity of him who loved him.
For he gave Jacob a remnant,
And David a root sprung from him.

23 So Solomon rested with his forefathers,
And left behind him one of his own children,
"The people's folly," a man wanting in understanding,
Rehoboam, who by his counsel made the people revolt.
And there was Jeroboam, the son of Nebat, who made
Israel sin,
And showed Ephraim a sinful way.

24 Their sins became so exceedingly many
That they dislodged them from their land.

25 For they sought out every kind of wickedness,
Until vengeance should come upon them.

48] Then the prophet Elijah arose like fire,
And his word burned like a torch;

2 He brought a famine upon them,
And made them few by his zeal,

3 By the word of the Lord he shut up heaven;
In the same way, he brought down fire three times.

4 How glorified you were, Elijah, in your wonderful acts,
And who can glory like you?

5 You who raised one who was dead, from death,
And from Hades, by the word of the Most High;

47:20–48:5

Who brought kings down to destruction, 6
And distinguished men from their beds.
Who heard rebukes at Sinai, 7
And judgments of vengeance at Horeb;
Who anointed kings to exact retribution, 8
And prophets to succeed him;
Who were taken up in a whirlwind of fire, 9
In a chariot with fiery horses;
Who, it is written, is to come in rebuke at the appointed 10
    time,
To quiet anger before it becomes wrath,
To turn the heart of the father to his son,
And to reform the tribes of Jacob.
Happy are those who saw you, 11
And those who fell asleep in love;
For we will surely live.

When Elijah was sheltered by the whirlwind, 12
Elisha was filled with his spirit.
In all his days he was not shaken by any ruler
And no one overmastered him.
Nothing was too wonderful for him, 13
And when he had fallen asleep, his body prophesied.
In his life he did signs, 14
And after his death he worked wonders.
For all this the people did not repent, 15
And did not forsake their sins,
Until they were carried away captive from their land,
And scattered over all the earth.
And the people were left very few in number,
But a prince remained in the house of David.
Some of them did what was right, 16
And some of them sinned more and more.

Hezekiah fortified his city, 17

And brought water into the midst of it;
He dug the sheer rock with iron,
And built wells for water.

18 In his days Sennacherib came up,
And sent the commander, and departed.
And he raised his hand against Zion,
And uttered great boasts in his arrogance;

19 Then their hearts and hands were shaken,
And they suffered like women in travail.

20 Then they called upon the Lord, who is merciful,
Spreading out their hands to him,
And the Holy One heard them speedily from heaven,
And delivered them by the hand of Isaiah.

21 He struck the camp of the Assyrians,
And his angel wiped them out.

22 For Hezekiah did what pleased the Lord,
And was strong in the ways of his forefather David,
Which the prophet Isaiah commanded,
Who was great and faithful in his prophetic vision.

23 In his days the sun went back,
And prolonged the life of the king.

24 Through the spirit of might he foresaw the future,
And comforted those who mourned in Zion.

25 He revealed the things that were to be, forever,
And the hidden things, before they came to pass.

49] The memory of Josiah is like a blending of incense
Carefully prepared by the perfumer;
Everyone finds it sweet as honey to the taste,
And like music at a banquet.

2 He succeeded in converting the people,
And abolished the wicked abominations.

3 He made his heart right with the Lord,
In the days of wicked men he encouraged godliness.

48:18–49:3

Except David and Hezekiah and Josiah,   4
They all sinned greatly,
For they forsook the Law of the Most High.
The kings of Judah failed utterly,
For they gave their strength to others,   5
And their glory to a foreign nation.
They set fire to the city chosen for the sanctuary,   6
And made her streets desolate,
For the sake of Jeremiah; for they had misused him;   7
Though he was consecrated before his birth to be a
    prophet,
To root up and injure and ruin,
Likewise to build and to plant.

It was Ezekiel who saw the glorious vision,   8
Which he showed him upon the chariot borne by the
    winged creatures.
For he remembers his enemies with rain,   9
And to do good to those who make their paths straight.
And may the bones of the Twelve Prophets revive out of   10
    their place,
For they comforted Jacob,
And delivered them with their confident hope.

How shall we magnify Zerubbabel?   11
For he was like a signet on the right hand;
So was Jeshua, the son of Jozadak,
For they in their days rebuilt the house,   12
And raised a temple holy to the Lord,
Prepared for everlasting glory.
The memory of Nehemiah also is lasting,   13
For he raised up for us the walls which had fallen,
And set up barred gates,
And rebuilt our houses.

49:4-13

14   No one was ever created on earth like Enoch,
For he was taken up from the earth;
15   Nor was a man ever born like Joseph,
The leader of his brothers, the support of the people;
And his bones were cared for.
16   Shem and Seth were greatly honored above other men,
But above every living thing was Adam in his creation.

50]   It was Simon, the son of Onias, the great priest,
Who in his lifetime repaired the house,
And in his days strengthened the sanctuary.
2   He laid the foundation for the height of the double wall,
The lofty substructure for the temple inclosure.
3   In his days a water cistern was hewed out,
A reservoir in circumference like the sea,
4   He took thought for his people to keep them from calamity,
And fortified the city against siege.
5   How glorious he was, surrounded by the people,
As he came out of the sanctuary!
6   Like the morning star among the clouds,
Like the moon when it is full;
7   Like the sun shining forth upon the sanctuary of the Most
High;
Like the rainbow, showing itself among glorious clouds,
8   Like roses in the days of first fruits,
Like lilies by a spring of water,
Like a sprig of frankincense, on summer days,
9   Like fire and incense in the censer,
Like a dish of beaten gold,
Adorned with all kinds of precious stones;
10   Like an olive putting forth its fruit,
And like a cypress towering among the clouds.
11   When he assumed his glorious robe,
And put on glorious perfection,

49:14–50:11

And when he went up to the holy altar,
He made the court of the sanctuary glorious.
And when he received the portions from the hands of the 12
 priests,
As he stood by the hearth of the altar,
With his brothers like a wreath about him,
He was like a young cedar on Lebanon,
And they surrounded him like the trunks of palm trees,
All the descendants of Aaron in their splendor, 13
With the Lord's offering in their hands,
Before the whole assembly of Israel;
And when he finished the service at the altars, 14
To adorn the offering of the Most High, the Almighty,
He stretched out his hand to the cup, 15
And poured out some of the blood of the grape;
He poured it out at the foot of the altar,
A fragrant odor unto the Most High, the King of All.
Then the descendants of Aaron shouted; 16
They sounded the trumpets of beaten work;
They made a great sound heard,
For a reminder, before the Most High.
Then all the people made haste together, 17
And fell upon their faces on the ground,
To worship their Lord,
The Almighty, the Most High.
The singers too praised him with their voices; 18
They made sweet music in the fullest volume.
And the people intreated the Lord Most High, 19
With prayer before him who is merciful,
Until the worship of the Lord should be finished,
And they completed his service.
Then he came down and lifted his hands 20
Over the whole assembly of the descendants of Israel,

50:12–20

To pronounce the blessing of the Lord with his lips,
And to exult in his name.

21 And they prostrated themselves a second time,
To receive the blessing from the Most High.

22   Now bless the God of all,
Who in every way does great things;
Who exalts our days from our birth,
And deals with us according to his mercy.

23 May he give us gladness of heart,
And may there be peace in our days
In Israel, and through the days of eternity.

24 May he intrust his mercy to us,
And let him deliver us in our days.

25   With two nations my soul is vexed,
And the third is no nation;

26 They who live on the mountain of Samaria, and the
     Philistines,
And the foolish people that live in Shechem.
     Instruction in understanding and knowledge

27 Has Jeshua, son of Sirach, son of Eleazar, of Jerusalem,
Written in this book,
Who poured forth wisdom from his mind.

28 Happy is he who concerns himself with these things,
And he that lays them up in his mind will become wise.

29 For if he does them, he will be strong for all things,
For the light of the Lord is his path.

51]   I will give thanks to you, Lord and King,
And praise you as God my Savior.
I give thanks to your name,

2 For you have been my protector and helper,
And have delivered my body from destruction,
And from the snare of a slanderous tongue.
From lips that utter lies,

50:21-51:2

And before those who stood by,
You were my helper and delivered me,   3
In the greatness of your mercy and of your name,
From the gnashing of teeth when I was about to be de-
    voured,
From the hand of those who sought my life,
From the numerous troubles that I had,
From choking fire all around me,   4
And from the midst of a flame which I had not kindled,
From the depth of the heart of Hades,   5
And from the unclean tongue and the lying speech.
An unrighteous tongue uttered slander to the king;   6
My soul drew nigh to death,
And my life was near to Hades beneath;
They surrounded me on every side, and there was no one 7
    to help me;
I looked for the help of men, and there was none.
Then I remembered your mercy, Lord,   8
And your work which has been from of old,
For you deliver those who wait for you,
And save them from the hand of their enemies.
And I sent up my supplication from the earth,   9
And prayed for deliverance from death.
I besought the Lord, the father of my lord,   10
Not to forsake me in my days of trouble,
At the time when there is no help against the proud.
I said, "I will praise your name continually,   11
And praise you with thanksgiving."
And my prayer was heard,
For you saved me from destruction,   12
And delivered me from my emergency.
Therefore I will give thanks to you and praise you,
And bless the name of the Lord.

51:3–12

13 When I was very young, before I went on my wander-
          ings,
    I sought wisdom expressly in my prayer;
14 In front of the temple I asked for her,
    And I will search for her unto the end.
15 From her flower as from her ripening grape,
    My heart delighted in her.
    My foot trod in uprightness;
    From my youth I followed her steps.
16 I bowed my ear a little and received her,
    And found much instruction for myself.
17 I made progress in her;
    And to him who gave me wisdom I will give glory.
18 For I resolved to practice her,
    And I was zealous for the good, and I shall not be disap-
          pointed.
19 My soul grappled with her,
    And in the fulfilment of the Law I was very strict.
    I spread out my hands to heaven above,
    And lamented my ignorance of her.
20 I directed my soul to her,
    And through purification I found her.
    I gained my purpose with her from the beginning;
    Therefore I will not be forsaken.
21 My heart was stirred to seek her;
    Therefore I obtained a good possession.
22 The Lord gave me the power to speak as my reward,
    And I will praise him with it.
23   Come to me, you who are untaught,
    And pass the night in the house of instruction.
24 Why do you say you are wanting in these things,
    And that your souls are very thirsty?
25 I opened my mouth and said,

Get her for yourselves without money,
Put your neck under her yoke,   26
And let your soul receive instruction.
She is to be found close by.
See with your own eyes that I have worked but little,   27
And yet found myself much repose.
Get some instruction with a great sum in silver,   28
And you will gain much gold with it.
Let your soul delight in his mercy,   29
And may you not be disappointed for praising him.
Finish your work in time,   30
And in his own time he will give you your reward.

51:26–30

THE BOOK OF BARUCH

Baruch son of Neriah was companion and secretary to the prophet Jeremiah, and it was natural for apocryphal writings to be fathered on him. The present book purports to have been sent by Baruch in 582 B.C. from exile in Babylonia to Jerusalem along with a sum of money to support the worship in the Temple—when in fact the Temple was in ruins and the priests scattered. The book is a composite. The first section (1.1–3.8) is devoted to praise, confession, and prayer; the second (3.9–4.4) prescribes cultivation of wisdom; and the third (4.5–5.9) consists of two odes of comfort and cheer. In style and spirit Baruch is the Apocrypha's closest approach to Old Testament prophecy. Echoes of Daniel indicate a date later than 164 B.C.

The Letter of Jeremiah, which is appended to Baruch in the Vulgate but put after Lamentations in the Septuagint, is mainly an admonition against idolatry. It was doubtless inspired by the actual letter in Jeremiah 29.1–23 in which the prophet advises the exiles to settle down, marry, "And seek the peace of the city whither I have caused you to be carried away captive." Whereas Baruch is a translation from Hebrew, the Letter may have been composed in Greek. Its date is hardly earlier than the first century B.C.

THE BOOK OF BARUCH

1] THESE ARE THE WORDS OF THE BOOK THAT
Baruch the son of Neriah, the son of Mahseiah, the
son of Zedekiah, the son of Hasadiah, the son of Hil-
2 kiah, wrote in Babylon, in the fifth year, on the seventh day
of the month, at the time when the Chaldeans took Jeru-
3 salem and burned it with fire. And Baruch read the words
of this book in the hearing of Jeconiah, the son of Jehoiakim,
king of Judah, in the hearing of all the people who came
4 to hear the book read, and in the hearing of the nobles,
and the princes, and in the hearing of the elders, and in the
hearing of all the people, small and great—in fact, of all who
5 lived in Babylon, by the River Sud. Then they wept, and
6 fasted, and prayed before the Lord; and they raised money,
7 each one giving what he could, and they sent it to Jerusalem, to Jehoiakim the high priest, the son of Hilkiah, the
son of Shallum, and to the priests, and to all the people that
8 were found with him in Jerusalem, when he took the plate
of the house of the Lord that had been carried away from
the temple, to return it to the land of Judah—the silver
dishes which Zedekiah the son of Josiah, king of Judah, had
9 made, after Nebuchadnezzar, king of Babylon, had carried
off Jeconiah and the officers and captives and nobles and
the common people from Jerusalem, and taken him to Baby-
10 lon. And they said,
"Here we send you money, so buy with the money burnt
offerings and sin offerings and incense and prepare a grain
offering, and offer them upon the altar of the Lord our God,
11 and pray for the life of Nebuchadnezzar, king of Babylon,
and for the life of Belshazzar his son, that their days may be
12 like the days of heaven, upon the earth. And the Lord will
give us strength, and he will give sight to our eyes, and we
will live under the shadow of Nebuchadnezzar, king of

Babylon, and under the shadow of Belshazzar his son,
and we will serve them for a long time and find favor in
their sight. Pray for us to the Lord our God, for we have 13
sinned against the Lord our God, and to this day the anger
of the Lord and his wrath have not turned away from us.
So read this scroll, which we send to you, to make your 14
confession in the house of the Lord, on festival days and on
days of assembly. And you shall say,   15
   " 'Uprightness belongs to the Lord our God, but confusion of face, as on this day, befits us, the men of Judah,
and the residents of Jerusalem, and our kings and our 16
officials, and our priests and our prophets, and our forefathers; for we have sinned before the Lord, and disobeyed 17,18
him, and we have not obeyed the voice of the Lord our God,
so as to follow the commands of the Lord which he set before
us. From the day when the Lord brought our fathers out 19
of the land of Egypt, until today, we have been disobedient
to the Lord our God, and we have been neglectful, in not
obeying his voice. And misfortunes have attended us, and 20
the curse has come upon us which the Lord agreed upon
with Moses his servant, on the day when he brought our
forefathers out of the land of Egypt, to give us a land that
ran with milk and honey, as they have this day. And we did 21
not obey the voice of the Lord our God, expressed in all
the words of the prophets whom he sent to us, but we fol- 22
lowed each one the design of his own wicked heart so as to
serve other gods, and do what was evil in the eyes of the
Lord our God. So the Lord made good his word which he [2
uttered against us, and against our judges who judged Israel,
and against our kings and against our officials and against
the men of Israel and Judah. Nowhere under heaven have 2
such calamities occurred as he has brought upon Jerusalem,
as it was written in the Law of Moses, so that one of us ate 3

1:13–2:3

the flesh of his son, and another of us ate the flesh of his
4 daughter. He has made us subject to all the kingdoms
around us, to be a reproach and a desolation among all the
5 peoples about us, where the Lord has scattered them. They
were brought low and not raised up, because we had sinned
against the Lord our God, in not obeying his voice.

6 " 'Uprightness belongs to the Lord our God, but confusion of face befits us and our forefathers, as it does this day.
7 All the calamities with which the Lord threatened us have
8 overtaken us. Yet we have not besought the Lord by turning away, each of us, from the designs of his wicked heart.
9 And the Lord has watched for these calamities and has
brought them upon us, for the Lord is upright in all his
10 doings which he has commanded us to imitate. Yet we have
not obeyed his voice and followed the Lord's commands,
which he has set before us.

11 " 'And now, Lord God of Israel, who brought your people out of Egypt with a strong hand and with portents and
wonders, and with great power and an uplifted arm, and
12 made yourself such a name as yours is today, we have
sinned, we have been ungodly, we have done wrong, Lord
13 our God, in the face of all your ordinances. Let your anger
be turned away from us, for few of us are left, among the
14 heathen, where you have scattered us. Listen, Lord, to our
prayer and our petition, and for your sake deliver us, and
grant us favor in the eyes of those who have led us into
15 captivity, so that the whole earth may know that you are
the Lord our God, for Israel and his descendants are called
16 by your name. Lord, look down from your holy dwelling,
and think about us. Turn your ear to us, Lord, and hear us;
17 open your eyes and see; for the dead, who are in Hades,
whose breath has been taken from their bodies, cannot
18 ascribe glory and uprightness to the Lord, but the soul that

2:4-18

grieves greatly, that goes about bent over and sick, with failing sight—the soul that hungers will ascribe glory and uprightness to you, Lord. For it is not for the upright acts 19 of our forefathers and of our kings that we present our prayer for pity before you, O Lord our God. For you have inflicted 20 your anger and your wrath upon us, just as you promised through your servants the prophets to do, when you said, "Thus says the Lord: Bow your shoulders and work for 21 the king of Babylon, and stay in the land which I gave to your forefathers. But if you will not obey the voice of the 22 Lord, and serve the king of Babylon, I will put an end to the 23 sound of joy and the sound of gladness, the voice of bridegroom and the voice of bride, in the towns of Judah and in Jerusalem, and the whole country will become untrodden and uninhabited."

" 'But we did not obey your voice and serve the king of 24 Babylon, and you made good your words that you had spoken through your servants the prophets, that the bones of our kings and the bones of our forefathers should be taken out of their places, and behold they are thrown out 25 to the heat by day and to the frost by night; and they perished in great misery, by famine and the sword and expulsion. And the house that was called by your name 26 you have made as it is today, because of the wickedness of the house of Israel and of the house of Judah. Yet you have 27 dealt with us, O Lord our God, with all your forbearance and all your great compassion, as you promised through 28 your servant Moses to do, when you commanded him to write the Law before the sins of Israel, and said,

" ' "Unless you obey my voice, this great buzzing multi- 29 tude will surely turn into a small number among the heathen where I will scatter them. For I know that they will not 30 listen to me, for they are a stiff-necked people. But in the

2:19–30

land to which they are carried away they will come to them-
31 selves, and they will know that I am the Lord their God.
32 I will give them minds and ears to listen, and they will
praise me in the land to which they are carried away, and
33 they will remember my name, and they will turn from their
obstinacy and their wicked doings, for they will remember
what befell their forefathers who sinned in the sight of
34 the Lord. Then I will restore them to the land that I swore
to give to their forefathers, Abraham and Isaac and Jacob,
and they will possess it; and I will multiply them, and they
35 will not be despised. And I will make an everlasting agreement with them that I shall be their God and they shall be
my people. And I will never again remove my people
Israel from the land which I have given them."

3) "'O Lord Almighty, God of Israel, the soul in anguish and
2 the wearied spirit cry out to you. Listen, Lord, and have
3 mercy, for we have sinned in your sight. For you abide for-
4 ever, and we perish forever. O Lord Almighty, God of
Israel, hear the prayer of the dead in Israel, and of the sons
of those who sinned in your sight, who did not obey the voice
of the Lord their God, so that calamities have pursued us.
5 Do not remember the iniquities of our forefathers, but re-
6 member your power and your name at this time, for you are
7 the Lord our God, and we will praise you, O Lord. For you
have put your fear into our hearts for this reason, that we
should call upon your name, and we will praise you in our
exile, for we have put out of our hearts all the iniquity of
8 our forefathers, who sinned in your sight. Here we are today
in exile, where you have scattered us, to be reproached and
cursed and condemned for all the iniquities of our forefathers who rebelled against the Lord our God.'"

9 Hear the commandments of life, O Israel;
Listen, and learn wisdom.

2:31–3:9

Why is it, Israel, that you are in the land of your enemies, 10
That you have grown old in a strange land,
That you have been polluted with the dead,
That you are counted among those in Hades?   11
You have forsaken the spring of wisdom.   12
If you had walked in the way of God,   13
You would have lived in peace forever.
Learn where wisdom is, where strength is,   14
Where understanding is, so that you may at the same
    time learn
Where length of days and life are,
Where there is light for the eyes, and peace.
Who can find her location,   15
And who can get into her storehouses?
Where are the rulers of the heathen,   16
And those who master the animals of the earth,
Who have their sport with the wild birds,   17
And lay up silver and gold,
In which men trust,
And have property without end;
Who work in silver and anxious care,   18
And whose works defy investigation?
They have vanished and gone to Hades,   19
And others have taken their places.
A younger generation has seen the light   20
And settled on the earth,
But they have not learned the way to knowledge,
Nor understood its paths,   21
Nor laid hold of it.
Their sons have strayed far out of their way;
It was never heard of in Canaan,   22
Or seen in Teman;
The sons of Hagar, who seek for understanding on the 23
    earth,

3:10–23

The merchants of Merran and Teman,
The story-tellers and the searchers for understanding
Have not found the way to wisdom,
Or remembered its paths.

24 O Israel, how great is the house of God,
And how vast the region that he possesses!

25 It is great, it has no end;
It is immeasurably high.

26 There were born the giants, famous of old,
Tall in stature, expert in war.

27 God did not choose them
Or give them the way of knowledge.

28 So they perished, because they had no understanding;
They perished through their own folly.

29 Who ever went up to heaven and got her,
And brought her down from the clouds?

30 Who ever crossed the sea and found her,
And will buy her with fine gold?

31 No one knows the way to her,
Or concerns himself with the path to her.

32 But he who knows all things knows her,
He has discovered her through his understanding.
He who created the earth forever,
Filled it with four-footed creatures;

33 He who sends forth the light, and it goes;
He called it, and it obeyed him in fear;

34 The stars shone in their watches, and were glad;
He called them, and they said, "Here we are!"
They shone with gladness for him who made them.

35 He is our God;
No other can be compared with him!

36 He found out the whole way to knowledge,
And has given it to Jacob his servant
And to Israel, whom he loved.

3:24-36

After that, she appeared on the earth   37
And mingled with men.

This is the book of the commandments of God,   [4
And the Law, that will endure forever.
All those who hold fast to it will live,
But those who forsake it will die.

Come back, Jacob, and take hold of it;   2
Approach the radiance from her light.

Do not give your glory to another,   3
And your benefits to an alien people.

Blessed are we, Israel,   4
Because we know the things that please God.

Have no fear, my people,   5
For the memorial of Israel;

You have been sold to the heathen,   6
Not to be destroyed,
But because you had angered God
You were handed over to your adversaries.

For you provoked him who made you   7
By sacrificing to demons, and not to God.

You forgot the everlasting God, who had brought you up,   8
And you grieved Jerusalem, that had reared you,

For she saw the anger that has come upon you from God,   9
and said,

"Listen, you women who live in Zion.
God has brought great sorrow upon me.

For I have witnessed the capture of my sons and daughters,   10
Which the Everlasting has brought upon them.

For I nursed them in gladness,   11
But I have sent them away with weeping and sorrow.

Let no one exult over a widow like me,   12
Forsaken by so many;
I have been left desolate because of the sins of my children,

3:37–4:12

Because they turned away from the Law of God.

13 But they would not learn his ordinances,
Or walk in the ways of God's commands,
Or follow the paths of correction in his uprightness.

14 Let the women who live in Zion come,
And remember the taking captive of my sons and daughters,
Which the Everlasting has brought upon them.

15 For he brought a nation from far away against them,
A ruthless nation, of strange speech,
Who had no respect for an old man
And no pity for a child,

16 And they led the widow's beloved sons away,
And left the lonely woman bereft of her daughters.

17 "But how can I help you?

18 For he who has brought these calamities upon you
Will deliver you from the hands of your enemies.

19 Go, my children, go,
For I am left desolate.

20 I have taken off the clothing of peace,
And put on the sackcloth of my supplication;
I will cry out to the Everlasting all my days.

21 Have courage, my children, cry out to God,
And he will save you from subjection, from the hands of
your enemies;

22 For I have set on the Everlasting my hope that he will save
you,
And joy has come to me from the Holy One for the mercy
Which will soon come to you, from your everlasting
Savior.

23 For I sent you out with sorrow and weeping,
But God will give you back to me with joy and gladness
forever.

4:13-23

For just as the women who live in Zion have just now seen 24
your deportation,
So they will soon see your deliverance come from your
God,
Which will come upon you with the great glory and splen-
dor of the Everlasting.
My children, endure patiently the anger that has come 25
upon you from God,
For your enemy has overtaken you;
But you will soon witness his destruction,
And put your feet upon their necks.
My luxurious ones have traveled rough roads, 26
They have been taken away like a flock carried off by ene-
mies.
Have courage, my children, and cry out to God, 27
For you will be remembered by him who brought this
upon you.
For as the thought once came to you to go astray from God, 28
You must return and seek him with tenfold fervor.
For he who has brought these calamities upon you 29
Will bring you everlasting joy with your deliverance."
Take courage, Jerusalem, 30
For he who named you will comfort you.
Those who did you harm and rejoiced at your fall will 31
be miserable;
The towns which enslaved your children will be miserable; 32
She who received your sons will be miserable.
For as she rejoiced at your fall, 33
And was glad of your ruin,
So she shall be grieved at her own desolation.
And I will take away her exultation in her great popula- 34
tion,
And her boasting will be turned to sorrow.

4:24–34

35 For from the Everlasting fire will descend upon her for many days,
And she will be a habitation of demons for a long time.

36 Look away eastward, Jerusalem,
And see the gladness that is coming to you from God.

37 See, your sons are coming, whom you sent away,
They are coming, gathered from east to west, at the command of the Holy One,
Rejoicing in the glory of God.

5] Take off the clothes of your sorrow and your harsh treatment, Jerusalem,
And put on forever the beauty of the glory that is from God.

2 Put on the cloak of the uprightness that is from God,
Put on your head the headdress of the glory of the Everlasting.

3 For God will show your splendor to all that is under heaven.

4 For your name will forever be called by God
The Peace of Uprightness and the Glory of Godliness.

5 Arise, Jerusalem, and stand upon the height,
And look away to the east,
And see your children gathered from the setting of the sun to its rising, at the command of the Holy One,
Rejoicing that God has remembered them.

6 For they went forth from you being led away on foot by their enemies,
But God will bring them in to you
Carried aloft in glory, like a royal throne.

7 For God has ordained that every high mountain and the everlasting hills shall be made low,
And the valleys filled up to make level ground,
So that Israel may go safely, to the glory of God.

4:35–5:7

And the woods and every fragrant tree have shaded Israel, 8
at God's command,

For God will lead Israel with joy, by the light of his glory, 9
With the mercy and uprightness that come from him.

THE LETTER OF JEREMIAH

A copy of a letter which Jeremiah sent to the captives {6
who were to be taken to Babylon by the king of Babylon, to
report to them as he had been commanded by God.

Because of the sins which you have committed in the 2
sight of God, you will be taken to Babylon as captives by
Nebuchadnezzar, king of Babylon. So when you reach 3
Babylon, you will stay there for many years, and for a long
time, seven generations; but afterward I will bring you away
from there in peace. Now in Babylon you will see gods made 4
of silver and gold and wood, carried on men's shoulders,
inspiring fear in the heathen. So beware of becoming just 5
like the foreigners, and being filled with awe at them, when
you see the throng before and behind them worshiping
them, but say in your heart, "Lord, we must worship you." 6
For an angel is with you, and he cares for your lives. 7

For their tongues are polished by a carpenter, and they 8
are gilded and silvered, but they are deceptions and cannot
speak. And as though for a girl fond of ornament, they 9
take gold and make crowns for the heads of their gods, and 10
sometimes the priests secretly withdraw gold and silver
from their gods and lavish it upon themselves, and give 11
some of it even to the prostitutes upon the housetop. And
they adorn them with clothes, like men, these gods of silver,
gold, and wood, though they cannot save themselves from 12
being corroded with rust. When they have dressed them in
purple clothing, they wipe their faces because of the dust 13

14 from the house which lies thick upon them. He carries a
scepter like a local human judge, though he cannot destroy
15 anyone who sins against him. He holds a dagger in his right
hand and an ax, but he cannot save himself from war and
16 robbers. Therefore it is manifest that they are not gods, so
you must not stand in awe of them.

17 For just as a man's dish is useless when it is broken, so are
their gods, when they have been set down in their houses.
Their eyes are full of dust raised by the feet of those who
18 come in. And just as the courtyard doors are shut upon a
man who has offended against a king, as though sentenced
to death, the priests close their houses securely with doors
and locks and bars, so that they will not be plundered by
19 robbers. They burn lamps, and more than they themselves
20 need, though their gods can see none of them. They are
just like one of the beams of the house, but men say their
hearts are eaten out, and when vermin from the ground de-
21 vour them and their clothing, they do not perceive it; their
22 faces are blackened by the smoke from the temple. Bats,
swallows, and birds light on their bodies and on their heads;
23 so do cats also. Therefore you may be sure they are not
gods, so you must not stand in awe of them.

24 As for the gold which they wear for ornament, they will
not shine unless someone wipes off the rust; for even when
25 they were being cast, they did not feel it. They are bought
26 at great cost, but there is no breath in them. As they have
no feet, they are carried on men's shoulders, thus exposing
27 their own disgrace to men. Even those who attend them
are ashamed, because if one of them falls on the ground, it
cannot get up by itself. And if someone sets it up, it cannot
move of itself, and if it is tipped, it cannot straighten itself
28 up; but gifts are offered to them as if they were dead. What
is sacrificed to them their priests sell and use the proceeds of;

6:14-28

and in like manner their wives preserve some of them, but give none of them to the poor or the helpless. A woman in 29 her sickness or in childbed can touch their sacrifices. Therefore, being assured from these facts that they are not gods, you must not stand in awe of them.

For how can they be called gods? For women set the 30 tables for gods of silver, gold, and wood; and in their temples 31 the priests sit apart with their clothes torn open, and their heads and beards shaved and their heads uncovered, and 32 they howl and shout before their gods as some do at a wake over a dead man. The priests take some of their clothes from 33 them and put them on their wives and children. And if 34 they experience any injury or any benefit from anyone, they cannot repay it; they cannot set up a king, or put one down. In like manner, they cannot bestow wealth or 35 money; if someone makes a vow to them and does not fulfil it, they will not exact it. They cannot save a man from 36 death, nor rescue the weak from the strong. They cannot 37 restore a blind man's sight, they cannot deliver a man who is in distress. They cannot take pity on a widow, or do good 38 to an orphan. These things made of wood and plated with 39 gold or silver are like stones from the mountain, and those who attend them will be put to shame. Why then should 40 anyone think them gods, or call them so?

Besides, even the Chaldeans themselves dishonor them, for when they see a dumb man, who cannot speak, they 41 bring him to Bel and pray that he may speak—as though Bel were able to understand. Yet they cannot perceive this 42 and abandon them, for they have no understanding themselves. And the women with ropes on, sit by the wayside, 43 burning chaff for incense, and when one of them is dragged off by one of the passers-by and lain with, she derides her companion, because she has not been as much desired as

6:29–43

44 herself, and has not had her rope broken. Everything that
is done to them is a deception. So why should anyone think
them gods, or call them so?

45 They are made by carpenters and goldsmiths; they can
46 be nothing but what the craftsmen wish them to be. The
very men who make them cannot last long; then how can
47 the things that are made by them be gods? For they have
only deceptions and reproach for those who come after.

48 For when war or calamity overtakes them, the priests consult together as to where they can hide themselves and
49 their gods. How therefore can one fail to see that they are
not gods, since they cannot save themselves from war or dis-
50 aster? For since they are made of wood and covered with
gold or silver, it will eventually be found out that they are
51 a deception. It will be evident to all the heathen and their
kings that they are not gods at all but the work of men's
52 hands, and that there is no work of God in them. Who then
can be ignorant that they are not gods?

53 For they cannot set up a king over a country, or give men
54 rain; they cannot decide a case, or give relief to a man who is
wronged; for they have no power; for like crows they are be-
55 tween heaven and earth. For when a temple of wooden
gods, or gilded or silvered ones, catches fire, their priests
flee and save themselves, but they themselves are burnt in
56 two like beams. They can offer no resistance to a king or
any enemies. Why then should anyone believe or suppose
that they are gods?

57 Gods made of wood, silvered or gilded, cannot save them-
58 selves from thieves or robbers, and the gold and silver on
them, and the clothes they have on, those who are strong
enough will strip from them and carry off, and they will
59 not be able to help themselves. So it is better to be a king
who can show his courage, or a household dish, that serves

6:44-59

its owner's purpose, than such false gods; or even a house door that keeps what is in the house safe, than such false gods; or a wooden pillar in a palace, than such false gods. For sun, moon, and stars shine, and when they are sent to 60 perform a service, they obey; in like manner lightning, 61 when it flashes, is widely visible, and in the same way the wind blows in every land; and when God commands the 62 clouds to spread over the whole world, they carry out his order. And the fire sent from above to consume mountains 63 and forests does as it is ordered. But these cannot be compared with them in their manifestations or their powers. Therefore you must not think that they are gods, or call 64 them so, since they are unable to decide cases or to benefit men. So as you know that they are not gods, you must not 65 stand in awe of them.

For they can neither curse kings nor bless them; they can- 66,67 not show portents in the heavens before the nations, or shine like the sun, or give light like the moon. The wild animals 68 are better than they are, for they can flee to cover and help themselves. So in no way is it evident to us that they are 69 gods; therefore you must not stand in awe of them.

For just as a scarecrow in a cucumber bed gives no pro- 70 tection, their wooden, gilded, and silvered gods give none. In like manner, their wooden, gilded, and silvered gods are 71 like a white thorn in a garden, on which every bird settles; and like a corpse, thrown out into the darkness. From the 72 purple and fine linen that rot upon them, you can tell that they are not gods; and they will finally be consumed themselves, and be despised in the land. An upright man who 73 has no idols is far better, for he will be far above reproach.

6:60–73

THE STORY OF SUSANNA

The story of Daniel naturally attracted embellishments, and the Story of Susanna is the first of three additions found in the Greek but not in the Hebrew Bible. It is placed at the beginning of the book because Daniel is still a youth in the story. The calumniation of a virtuous lady's innocence, its dramatic vindication, and the turning of the tables on the calumniators can be accepted on its own merits as an admirably told and edifying folk tale. But it may have been put to use to reinforce the juristic principle that the two witnesses which Scripture requires for condemnation must be examined separately. The date of Susanna is probably early first century B.C. The text commonly used for translation is that of Theodotion, which is somewhat fuller than the Septuagint text.

THE STORY OF SUSANNA

1
2 THERE ONCE LIVED IN BABYLON A MAN
named Joakim. He married a wife named Susanna,
the daughter of Hilkiah, a very beautiful and pious
3 woman. Her parents also were upright people and in-
4 structed their daughter in the Law of Moses. Joakim was
very rich, and he had a fine garden adjoining his house; and
the Jews used to come to visit him because he was the most
distinguished of them all.

5 That year two of the elders of the people were appointed
judges—men of the kind of whom the Lord said,
"Lawlessness came forth from Babylon, from elders who
were judges, who were supposed to guide the people."

6 These men came constantly to Joakim's house, and all
7 who had cases to be decided came to them there. And it
happened that when the people left at midday, Susanna
8 would go into her husband's garden and walk about. So the
two elders saw her every day, as she went in and walked
9 about, and they conceived a passion for her. So their
thoughts were perverted and they turned away their eyes,
so as not to look up to heaven or consider justice in giving
10 judgment. They were both smitten with her, but they could
11 not disclose their pain to each other, for they were ashamed
to reveal their passion, for they desired to have relations
12 with her, and they watched jealously every day for a sight
13 of her. And they said to one another,
"Let us go home, for it is dinner-time."

14 So they went out of the garden and parted from one another; then they turned back and encountered one another.
And when they cross-questioned one another as to the explanation, they admitted their passion. Then they agreed
together upon a time when they would be able to find her
alone.

Now it happened, as they were watching for an opportu- 15
nity, that she went in one day as usual with no one but her
two maids, and wished to bathe in the garden, as it was very
hot. And there was no one there except the two elders who 16
had hidden themselves and were watching her. And she 17
said to her maids,

"Bring me olive oil and soap, and close the doors of the
garden, so that I can bathe."

And they did as she told them, and shut the doors of the 18
garden, and went out at the side doors to bring what they
had been ordered to bring, and they did not see the elders,
for they were hidden. And when the maids went out, the 19
two elders got up and ran to her and said,

"Here the doors of the garden are shut, and no one can 20
see us, and we are in love with you, so give your consent and
lie with us. If you do not, we will testify against you that 21
there was a young man with you, and that was why you dismissed your maids."

And Susanna groaned and said, 22

"I am in a tight place. For if I do this, it means my death;
but if I refuse, I cannot escape your hands. I had rather not 23
do it and fall into your hands than commit sin in the Lord's
sight!"

Then Susanna gave a loud scream, and the two elders 24
shouted against her. And one of them ran and opened the 25
garden doors. And when the people in the house heard the 26
shouting in the garden, they rushed through the side doors
to see what had happened to her. And when the elders told 27
their story, her slaves were deeply humiliated, for such a
thing had never been said about Susanna.

The next day, when the people came together to her 28
husband, Joakim, the two elders came, full of their wicked
design to put Susanna to death. And they said before the 29
people,

15–29

"Send for Susanna, the daughter of Hilkiah, Joakim's wife."

30 And they did so. And she came, with her parents and her
31 children, and all her relatives. Now Susanna was accus-
32 tomed to luxury and was very beautiful. And the lawbreak-
ers ordered her to be unveiled, for she was wearing a veil,
33 so that they might have their fill of her beauty. And the
34 people with her and all who saw her wept. And the two
elders stood up in the midst of the people and laid their
35 hands on her head, and she wept and looked up to heaven,
36 for her heart trusted in the Lord. And the elders said,

"As we were walking by ourselves in the garden, this
woman came in with two maids, and shut the doors of the
37 garden and dismissed her maids, and a young man, who had
38 been hidden, came to her, and lay down with her. And we
were in the corner of the garden, and when we saw this
39 wicked action, we ran up to them, and though we saw them
together, we could not hold him, because he was stronger
40 than we, and opened the doors and rushed out. But we laid
hold of this woman and asked her who the young man was;
and she would not tell us. This is our testimony."

41 Then the assembly believed them, as they were elders of
the people and judges, and they condemned her to death.
42 But Susanna uttered a loud cry, and said,

"Eternal God, you who know what is hidden, who know all
43 things before they happen, you know that what they have
testified to against me is false, and here I am to die when
I have done none of the things they have so wickedly
charged me with."

44,45 And the Lord heard her cry, and as she was being led
away to be put to death, God stirred up the holy spirit of a
46 young man named Daniel, and he loudly shouted,

"I am clear of the blood of this woman."

47 And all the people turned to him and said,

"What does this mean, that you have said?"

And he took his stand in the midst of them and said,   48

"Are you such fools, you Israelites, that you have condemned a daughter of Israel without any examination or ascertaining of the truth? Go back to the place of trial. For   49
these men have borne false witness against her."

So all the people hurried back. And the elders said to   50
him,

"Come, sit among us and inform us, for God has given you the right to do so."

And Daniel said to them,   51

"Separate them widely from one another, and I will examine them."

And when they were separated from each other, he called   52
one of them to him, and said to him,

"You ancient of wicked days, how your sins have overtaken you, that you committed before, making unjust decisions, condemning the innocent and acquitting the guilty,   53
although the Lord said, 'You shall not put an innocent and upright man to death.' So now, if you saw this woman,   54
tell us, Under which tree did you see them meet?"

He answered,

"Under a mastic tree."

And Daniel said,   55

"You have told a fine lie against your own life, for already the angel of God has received the sentence from God, and he will cut you in two."

And he had him removed and ordered them to bring in   56
the other. And he said to him,

"You descendant of Canaan and not of Judah, beauty has beguiled you, and desire has corrupted your heart! This is   57
how you have been treating the daughters of Israel, and they yielded to you through fear, but a daughter of Judah

58 would not endure your wickedness. So now tell me, Under which tree did you catch them embracing each other?"

And he said,

"Under a liveoak tree."

59 And Daniel said to him,

"You have also told a fine lie against your own life! For the angel of God is waiting with his sword to saw you in two, to destroy you both."

60 And the whole company uttered a great shout and
61 blessed God who saves those who hope in him. And they threw themselves upon the two elders, for Daniel had convicted them out of their own mouths of having borne false
62 witness, and treated them as they had wickedly planned to treat their neighbor; they obeyed the Law of Moses and killed them. And innocent blood was saved that day.

63 And Hilkiah and his wife praised God for their daughter Susanna and so did Joakim her husband and all her rela-
64 tives, because she had done nothing immodest. And from that day onward, Daniel had a great reputation in the eyes of the people.

THE SONG OF THE THREE CHILDREN

Daniel 3.23 reads: "And these three men, Shadrach, Meshach, and Abednego, fell down bound in the midst of the burning fiery furnace." Then, with nothing said about what happened to the three "children," the text continues: "Then Nebuchadnezzar the king was astonished and rose up in haste, and spake, and said unto his counsellors, Did we not cast three men bound into the midst of the fire?" The present addition fills the gap between vv. 23 and 24. The first part is a long prayer of Azariah (the Hebrew name of Abednego) confessing his people's sin and imploring mercy, but not deliverance from the fiery furnace. The latter part is a splendid, formally constructed, hymn of thanksgiving, with a recurring refrain like that in Psalm 136. It has little relevance to the situation. Perhaps the prayer reflects the dark days at the beginning of the Maccabean uprising, and the hymn of thanksgiving the triumph. The dates are not too far from the date of Daniel, which is 164 B.C.

THE SONG OF THE THREE CHILDREN

ND THEY WALKED ABOUT IN THE MIDST
of the fire, singing hymns to God and blessing the
1 Lord. And Azariah stood still and uttered this
prayer; in the midst of the fire he opened his mouth and said,

2 "Blessed are you, Lord God of our forefathers, and worthy
of praise!
Your name is glorified forever!

3 For you are upright in all that you have done;
All your works are true, and your ways straight,
And all your judgments are true.
The sentences that you passed were just

4 In all that you have brought upon us,
And upon Jerusalem, the Holy City of our forefathers.
For in truth and justice you have brought all these things
upon us because of our sins.

5 For we have sinned and done wrong in forsaking you,

6 We have sinned grievously in everything, and have dis-
obeyed your commands;
We have not observed them or done
As you commanded us to do, for our own good.

7 All that you have brought upon us, and all that you have
done to us,
You have done in justice.

8 You have handed us over to enemies without law, to hateful rebels,
And to a ruthless king, the most wicked ruler in all the
world,

9 Yet we cannot open our mouths.
Shame and disgrace have overtaken your slaves and your
worshipers.

For the sake of your name, do not surrender us utterly;   10
Do not cancel your agreement,
And do not withdraw your mercy from us,   11
For the sake of Abraham whom you loved,
And for the sake of Isaac, your slave,
And for the sake of Israel, your holy one,
To whom you spoke, and promised   12
That you would make their descendants as many as the
    stars of heaven,
Or the sand that is on the seashore.
For, Master, we have become fewer than all the heathen,   13
And we are humiliated everywhere, because of our sins.
And now there is no prince, or prophet, or leader,   14
No burnt offering, or sacrifice, or offering, or incense;
No place to make an offering before you, or to find mercy.
But may we be accepted through a contrite heart and a   15
    humble spirit,
As though it were through whole burnt offerings of rams   16
    and bulls,
And through tens of thousands of fat lambs.
So let our sacrifice rise before you today,
And fully follow after you,
For those who trust in you will not be disappointed.
So now we follow you with all our hearts; we revere you   17
And seek your face. Do not disappoint us,   18
But deal with us in your forbearance
And your abundant mercy.
Deliver us in your wonderful way,   19
And glorify your name, Lord;
May all who do your slaves harm be disgraced;
May they be put to shame and lose all their power and   20
    might,
And may their strength be broken.
Let them know that you are the Lord God alone,   21

10–21

Glorious over the whole world."

22 Now the king's servants who threw them in never ceased
feeding the furnace fires with naptha, pitch, tow, and fag-
23 gots, and the flame streamed out above the furnace for forty-
24 nine cubits (seventy-three feet). It even spread, and burned
25 up those Chaldeans whom it found about the furnace. But
the angel of the Lord came down to join Azariah and his
companions in the furnace, and drove the fiery blaze out of
26 the furnace, and made the middle of the furnace as though
a moist wind was whistling through it, and the fire did not
touch them at all, or harm or trouble them.

27 Then all three, as with one mouth, praised, glorified, and
blessed God in the furnace, and said,

28 "Blessed are you, Lord God of our forefathers,
      And to be praised and greatly exalted forever.

29 And blessed is your glorious, holy name,
      And to be highly praised and greatly exalted forever.

30 Blessed are you in the temple of your holy glory,
      And to be highly praised and greatly glorified forever.

31 Blessed are you who sit upon winged creatures, and look
            into the depths,
      And to be praised and greatly exalted forever.

32 Blessed are you on your kingly throne,
      And to be highly praised and greatly exalted forever.

33 Blessed are you in the firmament of heaven,
      And to be praised and glorified forever.

34 Bless the Lord, all you works of the Lord,
      Sing praise to him and greatly exalt him forever.

35 Bless the Lord, you heavens,
      Sing praise to him and greatly exalt him forever.

36 Bless the Lord, you angels of the Lord,
      Sing praise to him and greatly exalt him forever.

37 Bless the Lord, all you waters above the heaven,

Sing praise to him and greatly exalt him forever.
Bless the Lord, all you powers,   38
 Sing praise to him and greatly exalt him forever.
Bless the Lord, sun and moon;   39
 Sing praise to him and greatly exalt him forever.
Bless the Lord, you stars of heaven,   40
 Sing praise to him and greatly exalt him forever.
Bless the Lord, all rain and dew,   41
 Sing praise to him and greatly exalt him forever.
Bless the Lord, all you winds,   42
 Sing praise to him and greatly exalt him forever.
Bless the Lord, fire and heat,   43
 Sing praise to him and greatly exalt him forever.
Bless the Lord, cold and warmth,   44
 Sing praise to him and greatly exalt him forever.
Bless the Lord, dews and snows,   45
 Sing praise to him and greatly exalt him forever.
Bless the Lord, nights and days,   46
 Sing praise to him, and greatly exalt him forever.
Bless the Lord, light and darkness,   47
 Sing praise to him and greatly exalt him forever.
Bless the Lord, ice and cold,   48
 Sing praise to him and greatly exalt him forever.
Bless the Lord, frosts and snows,   49
 Sing praise to him and greatly exalt him forever.
Bless the Lord, lightnings and clouds,   50
 Sing praise to him and greatly exalt him forever.
Let the earth bless the Lord,   51
 Let it sing praise to him and greatly exalt him forever.
Bless the Lord, you mountains and hills,   52
 Sing praise to him and greatly exalt him forever.
Bless the Lord, all things that grow on the earth,   53
 Sing praise to him and greatly exalt him forever.
Bless the Lord, seas and rivers,   55

38–55

Sing praise to him and greatly exalt him forever.
54 Bless the Lord, you springs,
    Sing praise to him and greatly exalt him forever.
56 Bless the Lord, you whales and all the things that move in
    the waters,
    Sing praise to him and greatly exalt him forever.
57 Bless the Lord, all you wild birds,
    Sing praise to him and greatly exalt him forever.
58 Bless the Lord, all you animals and cattle,
    Sing praise to him and greatly exalt him forever.
59 Bless the Lord, you sons of men,
    Sing praise to him and greatly exalt him forever.
60 Bless the Lord, O Israel,
    Sing praise to him and greatly exalt him forever.
61 Bless the Lord, you priests of the Lord.
    Sing praise to him and greatly exalt him forever.
62 Bless the Lord, you slaves of the Lord,
    Sing praise to him and greatly exalt him forever.
63 Bless the Lord, spirits and souls of the upright,
    Sing praise to him and greatly exalt him forever.
64 Bless the Lord, you who are holy and humble in heart,
    Sing praise to him and greatly exalt him forever.
65 Bless the Lord, Hananiah, Azariah, and Mishael,
    Sing praise to him and greatly exalt him forever.
    For he has rescued us from Hades and saved us from the
    hand of death,
    And delivered us from the burning fiery furnace;
    From the midst of the fire he has delivered us.
66 Give thanks to the Lord, for he is kind,
    For his mercy endures forever.
67 Bless him, all you who worship the Lord, the God of gods,
    Sing praise to him and give thanks to him,
    For his mercy endures forever."

        54–67

THE STORY OF BEL AND THE DRAGON

As the story of the youthful Daniel's vindication of Susanna fits best at the beginning of the book, so the story of his efforts to convince the king of Babylon of the falseness of his gods fits best at the end. First by setting a typical folk-lore trap Daniel proves to the king that not Bel but his priests eat the food given him. Next, by feeding an explosive cake to a serpent he is bidden to worship, Daniel causes the creature to burst apart. Then, when Daniel is cast into a den with seven starved lions, he is not only untouched but miraculously fed by the prophet Habakkuk. The miracle convinces the king of the truth of Daniel's God, and his traducers are thrown to the lions. The story was written to ridicule idolatry, probably in Greek, about 100 B.C. There is similar ridicule of idols and sacred serpents in Greek, but no dependence either way need be posited; "rationalism" of this type was in the air.

THE STORY OF BEL AND
THE DRAGON

1 WHEN KING ASTYAGES WAS GATHERED
to his fathers, Cyrus the Persian succeeded to his
2 kingdom. And Daniel was a companion of the
3 king, and was distinguished above all his other friends. Now
the Babylonians had an idol called Bel, and every day they
bestowed on it twelve bushels of fine flour and forty sheep
4 and fifty gallons of wine. And the king revered it and went
every day to worship it, but Daniel worshiped his own
God. And the king said to him,
"Why do you not worship Bel?"
5 And he said,
"Because I do not revere artificial idols, but the living
God, who created heaven and earth and is sovereign over
all mankind."
6 And the king said to him,
"Do you not think that Bel is a living God? Do you not
see how much he eats and drinks every day?"
7 And Daniel laughed and said,
"Do not be deceived, O king, for it is only clay inside and
bronze outside, and never ate or drank anything."
8 Then the king was angry and called Bel's priests, and said
to them,
"If you cannot tell me who it is that eats up these pro-
9 visions, you shall die, but if you can show me that Bel eats
them, Daniel shall die, because he has uttered blasphemy
against Bel."
And Daniel said to the king,
"It shall be as you say."
10 Now the priests of Bel were seventy in number, beside

their wives and children. So the king went with Daniel to the temple of Bel. And the priests of Bel said, 11

"See, we will go outside, and you, O king, must put the food on the table, and mix the wine and put it on, and shut the door and seal it with your signet. And when you come 12 back in the morning, if you do not find that it is all eaten up by Bel, we will die; or Daniel will who is making these false charges against us." For they scorned him, because they 13 had made a secret entrance under the table, and through it they used to go in regularly and devour the offerings.

So it happened that when they had gone, the king put 14 the food for Bel on the table. Then Daniel ordered his servants to bring ashes, and they scattered them over the whole temple, in the presence of the king alone. Then they went out, and shut the door, and sealed it with the king's signet, and went away. And the priests came in the night 15 as usual, with their wives and children, and ate and drank it all up.

And the king rose early the next morning, and Daniel 16 came with him. And the king said, 17

"Are the seals unbroken, Daniel?"

And he said,

"They are unbroken, O king."

And as soon as he opened the doors, the king looked at 18 the table, and shouted loudly,

"You are great, O Bel, and there is no deception at all about you."

But Daniel laughed and held the king back from going in, 19 and said to him,

"Look at the floor and observe whose footprints these are."

And the king said, 20

"I see the footprints of men, women, and children!"

11–20

21 Then the king was enraged, and he seized the priests and their wives and children, and they showed him the secret doors by which they got in and devoured what was on the
22 table. So the king killed them, and he turned Bel over to Daniel, and he destroyed it and its temple.

23 Now there was a great serpent in that place, and the
24 Babylonians worshiped it. And the king said to Daniel, "You cannot deny that it is a living god, so worship it."
25 And Daniel said, "I will worship the Lord my God, for he is a living God.
26 But with your permission, O king, I will kill this serpent without sword or stick."

And the king said,

"You have my permission."

27 And Daniel took pitch, fat, and hair and boiled them together, and made lumps of them, and he put them into the serpent's mouth, and it ate them and burst open. And he said,

"See the objects of your worship!"

28 When the Babylonians heard it, they were very indignant and made a conspiracy against the king, saying,

"The king has become a Jew! He has overturned Bel, and killed the serpent, and slaughtered the priests."

29 So they went to the king and said,

"Give Daniel up to us, or else we will kill you and your household."

30 And the king saw that they were pressing him hard, and
31 he was forced to give Daniel up to them. And they threw him into the lion's den and he remained there six days.
32 There were seven lions in the den; and they had been given two human bodies and two sheep every day; but now these were not given them, so that they might devour Daniel.

33 Now the prophet Habakkuk was in Judea, and he had

cooked a stew and crumbled bread into a bowl, and was
going into the field to carry it to the reapers, when the 34
angel of the Lord said to Habakkuk,

"Carry the dinner that you have to Babylon, to Daniel,
in the lions' den."

And Habakkuk said, 35

"Sir, I have never seen Babylon, and I do not know the
den."

Then the angel of the Lord took hold of the crown of 36
his head, and lifted him up by his hair and with the speed
of the wind set him down in Babylon, right over the den.
And Habakkuk shouted, 37

"Daniel! Daniel! Take the dinner which God has sent
you."

And Daniel said, 38

"You have remembered me, O God, and have not forsaken those who love you."

Then Daniel arose and ate. And the angel of God im- 39
mediately put Habakkuk back in his own place again.

On the seventh day, the king came to mourn for Daniel; 40
and he came to the den and looked in, and there sat Daniel.
Then the king shouted loudly, 41

"You are great, Lord God of Daniel, and there is no other
beside you!"

And he lifted him out, and the men who had tried to bring 42
about his destruction he threw into the den; and they were
instantly devoured before his eyes.

THE PRAYER OF MANASSEH

Just as the Letter of Jeremiah and the Prayer of Azariah supply documents hinted at in canonical books, so the present document purports to be the prayer which II Chronicles 33.18 asserts was recorded "in the books of the kings of Israel." The prayer is well constructed and well proportioned, and it expresses a deep personal religious feeling. It was written, possibly in Greek, about 100 B.C.

THE PRAYER OF MANASSEH

ALMIGHTY LORD,
  God of our forefathers,
  Abraham, Isaac, and Jacob,
And of their upright descendants;
You who have made the heaven and the earth with all their
    system;
Who have fettered the sea with your word of command;
Who have shut up the great deep, and sealed it with your
    terrible, glorious name;
Before whom all things shudder, and tremble before your
    power,
For the majesty of your glory is unbearable,
And the anger of your threatening against sinners is unen-
    durable,
Immeasurable and unsearchable is the mercy you promise,
For you are the Lord Most High,
Tender-hearted, long-suffering, and most merciful,
And regretful of the wickedness of men.
You therefore, Lord God of the upright,
Have not ordained repentance for the upright,
For Abraham, Isaac, and Jacob, who did not sin against
    you;
You have ordained repentance for a sinner like me,
For my sins are more numerous than the sands of the sea,
My transgressions are multiplied, Lord, they are multiplied!
I am unworthy to look up and see the height of heaven,
For the multitude of my iniquities.
I am weighed down with many an iron fetter,
So that I bend beneath my sins,
And I have no relief,
Because I have provoked your anger,
And done what is wrong in your sight,

Setting up abominations and multiplying offenses.
Now therefore I bend the knee of my heart, begging you
    for kindness.
I have sinned, Lord, I have sinned,
And I know my transgressions.
I earnestly beseech you,
Forgive me, Lord, forgive me!
Do not destroy me in the midst of my transgressions!
Do not be angry with me forever and lay up evil for me,
Or condemn me to the lowest parts of the earth.
For you, Lord, are the God of those who repent,
And you will manifest your goodness toward me,
For unworthy as I am, you will save me in the abundance
    of your mercy,
And I will praise you continually as long as I live,
For all the host of heaven sings your praise,
And yours is the glory forever. Amen.

THE FIRST BOOK OF MACCABEES

This book is the prime account of the Jewish war of independence fought against Antiochus Epiphanes; it covers the years 167–134 B.C. Its author was apparently an eyewitness of the events and a devoted partisan of the Maccabees. But he is careful and competent as well as patriotic and devout. Although written in Hebrew the book exhibits the characteristics of Hellenistic historiography in its emotionalism, partisanship, and use of documents; but it is nevertheless a mature and reliable work, and of high excellence both as history and as literature.

The dates in I and II Maccabees are usually given according to the Seleucid era, and can be converted to our reckoning by equating year 1 of that era to 312/311 B.C.

1] IT CAME TO PASS AFTER ALEXANDER OF
Macedon, the son of Philip, who came from the land
of Chittim, had utterly defeated Darius, the king of the
Medes and Persians, that he reigned in his stead, as he had
2 before reigned over Greece. And he waged many wars and
captured fortresses and slaughtered the kings of the earth;
3 and he made his way to the ends of the earth and despoiled
a multitude of nations. The whole earth was silent before
him, and he became exalted, and his heart was uplifted.
4 He mustered a very mighty army and ruled over the lands
5 and rulers of the heathen, and they paid him tribute. After-
6 ward he fell sick, and knew that he was going to die. So he
called in his distinguished servants who had been brought
up with him, and divided his kingdom among them while he
7 was still alive. Alexander had reigned twelve years when he
died.

8 His servants succeeded him, each in his own domain.
9 After his death they all put on crowns, as did their sons after
them, for many years, and they did much evil on the earth.

10 There sprang from them a sinful shoot named Antiochus
Epiphanes, the son of King Antiochus; he had been a
hostage in Rome and he became king in the one hundred
and thirty-seventh year of the Greek kingdom.

11 In those days there arose out of Israel lawless men who
persuaded many, saying, *(gentiles)*
"Let us go and make a treaty with the heathen around
us, for ever since the time we became separated from them,
many misfortunes have overtaken us."
12,13 The plan seemed good in their eyes, and some of the
people went eagerly to the king, and he authorized them to
14 introduce the practices of the heathen. And they built a
gymnasium in Jerusalem, in the heathen fashion, and sub-

mitted to uncircumcision, and disowned the holy agree- 15
ment; they allied themselves with the heathen and became
the slaves of wrongdoing.

When his rule appeared to Antiochus to be established, 16
he conceived the idea of becoming king of the land of Egypt,
so that he might reign over the two kingdoms. So he entered 17
Egypt with a strong force, with chariots and elephants and
cavalry and a great fleet. And he made war on Ptolemy, 18
king of Egypt, and Ptolemy turned and fled before him, and
many fell wounded. And they captured the walled cities 19
in the land of Egypt, and he plundered the land of Egypt.

After subduing Egypt, in the one hundred and forty- 20
third year, Antiochus turned back and came up against
Israel and entered Jerusalem with a strong force. And in his 21
arrogance he went into the sanctuary and took the gold
altar and the lampstand for the light, and all its furniture
and the table for the Presentation Bread and the cups and 22
the bowls and the gold censers and the curtain and the
crowns and the gold ornamentation on the front of the
temple, for he stripped it all off. And he took the silver and 23
the gold, and the choice dishes, and he took the secret
treasures, which he found; he took them all and went back 24
to his own country. He massacred people and spoke with
great arrogance.

And there was great mourning everywhere throughout 25
Israel. Rulers and elders groaned, girls and young men 26
fainted away, and the beauty of the women was altered.
Every bridegroom began to lament, and she that sat in the 27
bridal chamber grieved. The very earth was shaken over 28
its inhabitants, and the whole household of Jacob was covered with shame.

After two years the king sent an officer to collect tribute, 29
to the towns of Judah, and he entered Jerusalem with a

1:15–29

30 strong force. And he spoke to them craftily in peaceful
terms, and they trusted him. Then he suddenly fell upon the
city and struck it a great blow and destroyed many of the
31 people in Israel. He plundered the city, and burned it
down, and tore down the houses in it and the walls around
32 it. And they took the women and children captive and
33 possessed themselves of the cattle. Then they fortified the
City of David with a great, strong wall, with strong towers,
34 and it became their citadel. And they put sinful heathen
there, who did not obey the law, and they entrenched them-
35 selves there. And they stored up weapons and provisions,
and they collected the spoils of Jerusalem and laid them up
36 there, and they became a great threat, and it proved a place
of ambush against the sanctuary and a wicked adversary to
Israel constantly.

37   And they shed innocent blood all around the sanctuary,
       And polluted the sanctuary itself.

38   The inhabitants of Jerusalem fled away because of them,
       And she became a place where strangers lived,
    And she became strange to her own offspring,
       And her children forsook her.

39   Her sanctuary became desolate like a wilderness,
       Her feasts were turned into grief,
    Her sabbaths became a reproach,
       And her honor became contempt.

40   Her dishonor was as great as her glory had been,
       And her exaltation was turned into grief.

41   Then the king wrote to his whole kingdom that they
42 should all become one people, and everyone should give up
his particular practices. And all the heathen assented to
43 the command of the king. And many from Israel agreed
to his kind of worship and offered sacrifice to idols and

broke the sabbath. And the king sent word by messengers 44
to Jerusalem and the towns of Judah to follow practices
foreign to the country and put a stop to whole burnt offer- 45
ings and sacrifices and drink offerings at the sanctuary, and
to break the sabbaths and profane the feasts and pollute 46
sanctuary and sanctified; to build altars and sacred pre- 47
cincts and idol temples and sacrifice hogs and unclean
cattle; and to leave their sons uncircumcised and defile them- 48
selves with every unclean and profane practice, so that they 49
might forget the Law and change all their religious ordinances; and anyone who did not obey the command of the 50
king should die. He wrote to his whole kingdom, to this 51
effect, and he appointed inspectors over all the people, and
he ordered the towns of Judah every one of them to offer
sacrifice. And many of the people and everyone who was 52
ready to forsake the Law joined with them and they did
wrong in the land, and forced Israel to hide in every hiding- 53
place they had.

On the fifteenth day of Chislev, in the one hundred and 54
forty-fifth year, he erected a dreadful desecration upon the
altar, and in the towns of Judah round about they built
altars, and at the doors of their houses and in the squares 55
they burned incense, and wherever they found the book of 56
the Law, they tore them up and burned them, and if anyone 57
was found to possess a book of the agreement or respected
the Law, the king's decree condemned him to death. The 58
Israelites who appeared from month to month in the
towns they treated with force. On the twenty-fifth of the 59
month they offered sacrifice upon the altar which was set
up on the altar of burnt offering. The women who had cir- 60
cumcised their children they put to death under the decree,
hanging the babies around their necks, and destroying 61
their families and the men who had circumcised them.

1:44–61

62 Yet many in Israel stood firm and resolved in their hearts
63 not to eat what was unclean; they preferred death to being
polluted with food or profaning the sacred agreement, and
64 so they died. And Israel suffered intensely.

2] In those days Mattathias, the son of John, the son of
Simeon, a priest of the descendants of Joarib, removed from
2 Jerusalem, and settled in Modin. He had five sons, John,
3,4 surnamed Gaddi, Simon, called Thassi, Judas, called
5 Maccabeus, Eleazar, called Avaran, and Jonathan, called
6 Apphus. He saw the impious things that were going on in
7 Judah and Jerusalem, and he said,

"Alas! Why was I born to witness the ruin of my people
and the ruin of the holy city, and to sit by while it is being
given up to its enemies, and the sanctuary to aliens?

8   "Her temple has come to be like a man disgraced,
9   Her glorious furniture has been captured and
             carried off,
      Her infant children have been killed in her streets,
      Her young men with the enemy's sword.
10   What nation has not appropriated,
      What kingdom has not seized, her spoils?

11   Her adornment has all been taken away.
      Instead of a free woman, she has become a slave.
12   Behold, our sanctuary and our beauty
      And our glory have been laid waste,
      And the heathen have profaned them!
13   Why should we live any longer?"

14   And Mattathias and his sons tore open their clothes and
put on sackcloth and grieved bitterly.

15   Then the king's officers who were forcing the people to
give up their religion, came to the town of Modin, to make
16 them offer sacrifice. And many Israelites went to them, and

Mattathias and his sons gathered together. Then the king's 17
messengers answered and said to Mattathias,

"You are a leading man, great and distinguished in this
town, surrounded with sons and brothers; now be the first 18
to come forward and carry out the king's command as all
the heathen and the men of Judah and those who are left in
Jerusalem have done, and you and your sons will be counted
among the Friends of the king, and you and your sons will
be distinguished with presents of silver and gold and many
royal commissions."

Then Mattathias answered and said in a loud voice,   19

"If all the heathen in the king's dominions listen to him
and forsake each of them the religion of his forefathers, and
choose to follow his commands instead, yet I and my sons 20
and my brothers will live in accordance with the agreement
of our forefathers. God forbid that we should abandon the 21
Law and the ordinances. We will not listen to the message 22
of the king, or depart from our religion to the right hand or
to the left."

As he ceased to utter these words, a Jew went up before 23
the eyes of all of them to offer sacrifice as the king commanded, on the altar in Modin. And Mattathias saw him 24
and was filled with zeal, and his heart was stirred, and he
was very properly roused to anger, and ran up and slaughtered him upon the altar. At the same time he killed the 25
king's officer who was trying to compel them to sacrifice,
and he tore down the altar. Thus he showed his zeal for the 26
Law, just as Phineas did to Zimri, the son of Salom. Then 27
Mattathias cried out in a loud voice in the town and said,

"Let everybody who is zealous for the Law and stands by
the agreement come out after me."

And he and his sons fled to the mountains and left all they 28
possessed in the town.

2:17–28

29 Then many seekers for uprightness and justice went down
30 into the wilderness to settle, with their sons and their wives
and their cattle, because their hardships had become so
31 severe. And news reached the king's agents and the forces
that were in Jerusalem, in the City of David, that men who
had disregarded the king's order had gone down to the
32 hiding-places in the wilderness. And they pursued them in
force and overtook them, and pitched their camp against
them and prepared to attack them on the sabbath day.
33 And they said to them,

"Enough! Come out and and do as the king commands,
and you will live."

34 And they said,

"We will not come out nor do as the king commands, and
break the sabbath."

.5,36 Then they hastened to attack them. And they made no
response to them; they did not throw a stone at them nor
37 block up their hiding-places, for they said,

"Let us all die guiltless. We call heaven and earth to witness that you destroy us unlawfully."

38 So they attacked them on the sabbath, and they died,
with their wives and their children and their cattle, to the
number of a thousand people.

39 And Mattathias and his friends learned of it, and they
40 grieved bitterly over them. And one said to another,

"If we all do as our brothers have done, and refuse to
fight against the heathen for our lives and what we believe
is right, they will very soon destroy us from the face of the
earth."

41 On that day they reached this decision:

"If anyone attacks us on the sabbath day, let us fight
against him and not all die, as our brothers died in the
hiding-places."

2:29–41

Then they were joined by a company of Hasideans, war- 42
like Israelites, every one a volunteer for the Law. And all 43
who had fled to escape harsh treatment joined them and re-
inforced them. And they mustered a force and struck down 44
sinners in their anger, and in their wrath those who disobeyed the Law, and the rest fled to the heathen to save
themselves. And Mattathias and his friends went about 45
and tore down the altars, and forcibly circumcised all the 46
uncircumcised children that they found within the limits of
Israel. And they drove the arrogant before them, and the 47
work prospered in their hands. So they rescued the Law 48
from the hands of the heathen and their kings, and would
not let the sinner triumph.

When the time drew near for Mattathias to die, he said 49
to his sons,

"Arrogance and reproach have now grown strong; it is a
time of disaster and hot anger. Now, my children, you must 50
be zealous for the Law, and give your lives for the agreement of our forefathers. Remember the deeds of our fore- 51
fathers which they did in their generations, and you will win
great glory and everlasting renown. Was not Abraham 52
found faithful when he was tried, and it was credited to him
as uprightness? Joseph in his time of distress observed the 53
commandment and became master of Egypt. Phineas our 54
forefather for his intense zeal obtained the promise of an
everlasting priesthood. Joshua for carrying out his orders 55
became a judge in Israel. Caleb for bearing witness before 56
the congregation obtained an inheritance in the land.
David for being merciful inherited a royal throne forever. 57
Elijah for his intense zeal for the Law was caught up into 58
heaven. Hananiah, Azariah, and Mishael had faith in God 59
and were saved from the fire. Daniel for his innocence 60
was delivered from the mouths of the lions. Observe this 61

2:42-61

from generation to generation, that none who hope in him
62 will fail in strength. Do not be afraid of the words of a sinful
63 man, for his glory will turn to dung and worms. Today he
will be exalted, and tomorrow he will be nowhere to be
found, for he has returned to dust, and what he plotted
64 will perish. My children, be manful and strong for the Law,
65 for by it you will obtain glory. Now here is Simon your
brother; I know that he is a man of discretion. You must
66 always listen to him; he will be a father to you. And Judas
Maccabeus has been warlike from his youth; he will be your
67 captain and conduct the people's warfare. And you must
gather about you all who observe the Law, and avenge the
68 wrongs of your people. Pay back the heathen for what
they have done, and give heed to what the Law commands."
69   Then he blessed them and was gathered to his forefathers.
70 He died in the one hundred and forty-sixth year and was
buried in the tombs of his forefathers in Modin, and all
Israel made loud lamentation for him.

3] Then his son Judas, who was called Maccabeus, arose in
2 his stead, and all his brothers and all who had stood by his
father helped him, and with gladness carried on Israel's
3 war. And he increased the glory of his people, and put on a
breastplate like a giant, and he belted on his weapons and
organized campaigns, protecting his camp with the sword.
4 He was like a lion in his actions, and like a cub roaring for
5 its prey. He pursued and hunted out those who disobeyed
the Law, and those who harassed his people he consumed.
6 Those who disobeyed the Law were convulsed with fear of
him and all who broke the Law were dismayed and de-
7 liverance was accomplished by his hand. He angered
many kings and gladdened Jacob by his deeds, and his
8 memory will be blessed forever. He went among the towns
of Judah and destroyed the ungodly and cast them out of

her, and averted wrath from Israel. He was renowned to 9
the ends of the earth, and rallied those who were perishing.

Then Apollonius gathered the heathen together, with a 10
large force from Samaria, to make war on Israel. And 11
Judas learned of it and went out to meet him and he struck
him down and killed him. And many fell wounded, and the
rest made their escape. And they took their spoils, and 12
Judas took the sword of Apollonius and fought with it all
his life.

Then Seron, the commander of the Syrian army, heard 13
that Judas had gathered a following and a company of the
faithful about him, and of men used to going out to war. 14
And he said,

"I will make myself a reputation and gain distinction in
the kingdom, and I will make war on Judas and those who
are with him, who set the king's command at naught."

And with him there went up again a strong body of un- 15
godly men, to help him to take vengeance on the Israelites. 16
And he approached the pass of Bethhoron. And Judas went
out with very few men to meet him. But when they saw 17
the army coming to meet them, they said to Judas,

"How can we, few as we are, fight with such a strong host?
Besides we are faint, for we have had nothing to eat today."

And Judas said, 18

"It is easy for many to be inclosed in the hands of a few,
and there is no difference in the sight of heaven between saving through many or through few, for victory in war does not 19
depend upon the size of the force, but strength comes from
heaven. They come against us full of violence and lawless- 20
ness, to destroy us and our wives and our children, and to
plunder us, but we are fighting for our lives and our laws. 21
He himself will crush them before us, and you must not be 22
afraid of them."

3:9–22

23 When he ceased to speak, he fell suddenly upon them, and
24 Seron and his army were crushed before him, and they
pursued him from the pass of Bethhoron to the plain, and
eight hundred of them fell, and the rest made their escape
25 into the country of the Philistines. So the fear of Judas and
his brothers and the dread of them began to fall upon the
26 heathen around them, and his fame reached even the king,
and the heathen talked of the tactics of Judas.

27 When King Antiochus heard these reports, he was very
angry, and he sent and gathered all the forces of his king-
28 dom, a very strong army. And he opened his treasury and
gave his forces a year's pay, and ordered them to be in readi-
29 ness for any need that might arise. And he saw that the
money in his treasuries was exhausted, and the tribute of
the country was small because of the division and distress
that he had brought upon the land in doing away with the
30 laws which had been in effect from the earliest times, and
he feared that he would not have enough, as he formerly
had, for his expenses and for the presents which he had been
used to give before with a lavish hand, beyond the kings
31 that went before him. So he was very much perplexed and
resolved to go to Persia and get the tribute of those coun-
32 tries and raise a large sum of money. And he left Lysias, a
man of distinction, of the royal blood, to have charge of the
king's affairs from the river Euphrates to the borders of
33 Egypt, and to take care of Antiochus his son until his return.
34 He turned over to him half his forces and his elephants and
gave him orders about everything he wanted done, and
35 about the inhabitants of Judea and Jerusalem, against
whom he was to send a force to crush out and destroy the
strength of Israel and what was left of Jerusalem, and to ef-
36 face their memory from the place, and settle aliens in all
their borders, and distribute their land among them.

3:23–36

Then the king took the remaining half of his forces and 37
set off from Antioch, his royal city, in the one hundred
and forty-seventh year and crossed the Euphrates River
and went through the interior.

Then Lysias chose Ptolemy, son of Dorymenes, and Nica- 38
nor and Gorgias, warlike men among the Friends of the
king, and he sent with them forty thousand men and seven 39
thousand horse to go to the land of Judah and destroy it,
as the king had commanded. And he set off with all his 40
force, and they came and encamped near Emmaus in the
level country. And the merchants of the country heard 41
about them and they took a great quantity of silver and
gold, and fetters, and came to the camp to get the Israelites
for slaves. And they were joined by forces from Syria and
the land of the Philistines.

And Judas and his brothers saw that the situation was 42
very grave and that the forces were encamped within their
borders, and they knew what the king had said, when he
ordered them to inflict utter destruction on the people, and 43
they said to one another,

"Let us repair the destruction of our people, and let us
fight for our people and for the sanctuary."

And the congregation gathered together to make ready 44
for war and to pray and ask for mercy and compassion.

Jerusalem was uninhabited like a wilderness, 45
There was not one of her children who came in or
went out,
The sanctuary was trodden down,
The sons of aliens were in the citadel, it was a
stopping-place for heathen.
Joy vanished from Jacob,
And the flute and harp ceased to play.
Then they gathered together and went to Mizpeh, oppo- 46

site Jerusalem, for Israel formerly had a praying-place in
47 Mizpeh. And they fasted that day and put on sackcloth,
and sprinkled ashes upon their heads, and tore open their
48 clothes. And they unrolled the roll of the Law, such as the
heathen used to hunt out and look through for pictures of
49 their idols. And they brought out the priestly garments
and the first fruits and the tithes and they gathered the
50 Nazirites who had fulfilled their vows, and they called aloud
to heaven,

"What are we to do to these men, and where can we take
51 them, when your sanctuary is trodden down and profaned,
52 and your priests are grieved and humiliated? Here the
heathen are gathered together against us to destroy us; you
53 know their designs against us. How can we make a stand
before them unless you help us?"

54 And they sounded the trumpets and gave a great shout.
55 Then Judas appointed officers over the people, colonels and
56 captains and lieutenants and sergeants. And he ordered
those who were building houses or planting vineyards or
betrothed to women or were afraid, every one of them to
57 return home, as the Law provided. And the army moved
58 and encamped to the south of Emmaus. And Judas said,

"Prepare yourselves and be brave men and be ready in
the morning to fight these heathen who are gathered to-
59 gether against us, to destroy us and our sanctuary, for it is
better for us to die in battle than to witness the ruin of our
60 nation and our sanctuary. But he will do just as shall be the
will of heaven."

4] Then Gorgias took five thousand men and a thousand
2 picked horse, and his army moved under cover of night so
as to fall upon the camp of the Jews and attack them sud-
3 denly; and the men of the citadel were his guides. And
Judas heard of it and he and his gallant men moved to

3:47–4:3

attack the king's force in Emmaus, while the forces were 4
still scattered from the camp. And Gorgias came into the 5
camp of Judas in the night, and found no one there, and he
hunted for them in the mountains, for he said,

"They are fleeing from us!"

And at daybreak Judas appeared in the plain with three 6
thousand men, though they did not have such armor and
swords as they wished. And they saw the camp of the 7
heathen strongly fortified, with horsemen patrolling it, and
these, expert in war. And Judas said to the men who were 8
with him,

"Do not be afraid of their numbers, and do not fear their
charge. Remember how our forefathers were saved at the 9
Red Sea, when Pharaoh pursued them with an armed force.
So now let us cry to heaven, if perhaps he will accept us 10
and remember his agreement with our forefathers, and crush
this camp before us today. Then all the heathen will know 11
that there is one who ransoms and preserves Israel."

Then the aliens lifted up their eyes and saw them coming 12
against them, and they came out of the camp to battle. And 13
Judas' men sounded the trumpets and attacked, and the 14
heathen broke and fled to the plain, and all the hindmost 15
fell by the sword. And they pursued them as far as Gazara
and the plains of Idumea and Azotus and Jamnia, and there
fell of them fully three thousand men.

And Judas and his force returned from the pursuit of 16
them, and he said to the people, 17

"Do not set your hearts on plunder, for there is a battle
before us, for Gorgias and his army are near us, in the 18
mountain. Now stand your ground against our enemies,
and fight them, and afterward you can take their spoils
boldly."

Before Judas had finished saying this, a detachment of 19

4:4-19

20 them appeared reconnoitering from the mountain, and they saw that they had been routed and that they were burning the camp, for the sight of the smoke showed them what had
21 happened. And when they perceived this, they were very much alarmed, and seeing Judas' army in the plain ready
22,23 to attack, they all fled to the land of the Philistines. And Judas turned back to plunder the camp, and they took a great deal of gold and silver, and sapphire and sea-purple
24 stuffs, and great wealth. And they returned singing and blessing heaven, for he is good, for his mercy endures for-
25 ever. So Israel had a great deliverance that day.
26 Those of the aliens who escaped went and reported to
27 Lysias all that had happened. And when he heard it, he was dismayed and discouraged, because it was not at all what he wished that had happened to Israel, and it had not
28 turned out as the king had ordered. So in the following year he gathered together sixty thousand picked men, to
29 conquer them. And they came into Idumea and encamped at Bethsura, and Judas met them with ten thousand men.
30 And he saw that their camp was strong, and he prayed and said,

"Blessed are you, Savior of Israel, who stopped the rush of the champion by the hand of your slave David, and delivered the camp of the Philistines into the hands of Jona-
31 than, the son of Saul, and of his armor-bearer. In like manner shut up this camp in the hand of your people Israel, and let them be ashamed of their army and their horsemen.
32 Make them cowardly and melt the boldness of their strength,
33 and let them tremble at their destruction. Strike them down with the sword of those that love you, and let all who know your name praise you with hymns."
34 Then they joined battle, and there fell of the army of Lysias fully five thousand men; they fell right before them.

4:20–34

But when Lysias saw that his army had been routed, and 35
that Judas had grown bold, and that they were ready either
to live or to die nobly, he withdrew to Antioch and hired
soldiers in the greatest numbers, to come again to Judea.

And Judas and his brothers said,   36
"Now that our enemies are crushed, let us go up to purify
the sanctuary and rededicate it."

And the whole army gathered together, and they went up 37
to Mount Zion. And they found the sanctuary desolated 38
and the altar polluted and the doors burned up, and weeds
growing in the courts as they do in a wood or on some
mountain, and the priests' quarters torn down. And they 39
tore open their clothes and uttered great lamentation and
covered themselves with ashes, and fell on their faces on the 40
ground, and sounded the ceremonial trumpets, and cried
out to heaven. Then Judas appointed men to fight the garri- 41
son in the citadel, until he should purify the sanctuary. And 42
he appointed priests that were without blemish and ad-
herents of the Law, and they purified the sanctuary and 43
carried out the stones that had defiled it to an unclean
place. And they deliberated as to what they should do 44
about the altar of burnt offering, which had been polluted.
And a good idea occurred to them—to take it down, so that 45
it might never be thrown up to them that the heathen had
polluted it; so they took down the altar, and deposited the 46
stones in the temple mountain, in a suitable place, until a
prophet should come and declare what should be done with
them. And they took whole stones, as the Law required, 47
and built a new altar like the former one. And they built 48
the sanctuary and the interior of the temple and consecrated
the courts. And they made new holy dishes and they 49
brought the lampstand and the altar of incense and the
table into the temple. And they burned incense on the altar, 50

4:35-50

and lighted the lamps on the lampstand, and they lighted
51 the temple. And they put the loaves of bread on the table
and hung up the curtains, and completed all the work they
had undertaken.
52   And they arose early on the twenty-fifth day of the ninth
month, that is, the month of Chislev, in the one hundred and
53 forty-eighth year, and offered sacrifice according to the Law
upon the new altar of burnt offering which they had made.
54 At the time and on the day the heathen had polluted it, it
was rededicated with songs and harps and lutes and cym-
55 bals. And all the people fell on their faces and blessed
56 heaven which had prospered them. And they celebrated
the rededication of the altar for eight days and offered burnt
offerings with joy, and offered a sacrifice of deliverance and
57 praise. And they decorated the front of the temple with gold
crowns and small shields and rededicated the gates and the
58 priests' quarters, and fitted them with doors. And there
was very great joy among the people, and the reproach the
59 heathen had cast upon them was wiped out. And Judas
and his brothers and all the congregation of Israel decreed
that the days of the rededication of the altar should be observed at their season, every year, for eight days, beginning
with the twenty-fifth of the month of Chislev, with gladness
60 and joy. At that time they built high walls and strong
towers around Mount Zion, so that the heathen might not
61 come and tread them down as they had done before. And
he established a force there to hold it, and he fortified
Bethsura to hold it, so that the people might have a stronghold facing Idumea.
5]   It happened when the heathen round about heard that
the altar had been rebuilt and the sanctuary rededicated as
2 before, that it made them very angry, and they resolved to
destroy the descendants of Jacob that were among them,

and they began to kill and ravage among the people. And ₃
Judas fought against the sons of Esau in Idumea, and
against Akrabattene, because they beset Israel, and he dealt
them a severe blow and crushed them, and plundered them.
And he remembered the wickedness of the sons of Baean, ₄
who became a snare and stumbling block to the people,
lying in wait for them upon the roads. And he shut them ₅
up in their towers, and he encamped against them and
utterly destroyed them, and burned her towers with fire,
and all who were in them. He passed on to the Ammon- ₆
ites, and there he found a strong arm, and a large body
of people, with Timotheus in command of them. And he ₇
fought many battles with them, and they were crushed before him, and he struck them down. And he occupied Jazer ₈
and its villages, and returned to Judea.

Then the heathen in Gilead gathered together against ₉
Israel, to destroy those who were in their borders, and
they fled to the stronghold of Dathema, and sent a letter ₁₀
to Judas and his brothers, saying,

"The heathen around us have gathered together against
us to destroy us, and they are preparing to come and seize ₁₁
this stronghold in which we have taken refuge, and Timotheus is the leader of their force. So come and rescue us ₁₂
from his hand, for a great many of us have fallen, and all ₁₃
our brothers who were in the district of Tob have been put
to death, and they have carried off their wives and children
as captives, with their property, and they have destroyed a
regiment of men there."

They were still reading the letter when other mes- ₁₄
sengers arrived from Galilee, with their clothes torn open,
with a report to the same effect, saying that people from ₁₅
Ptolemais and Tyre and Sidon, and all Galilee of the aliens
had gathered against them, they said, "to destroy us."

5:3–15

16 When Judas and the people heard this message, a great meeting was held to decide what they should do for their brothers who were in such distress and were being attacked
17 by them. And Judas said to his brother Simon, "Choose men for yourself and go and save our brothers who are in Galilee, and I and my brother Jonathan will go into Gilead."
18 And he left Joseph, the son of Zechariah, and Azariah, a leader of the people, with the remainder of the force, in
19 Judea, to guard it. And he gave them their orders, saying, "Take command of these people, and do not join battle with the heathen until we return."
20 Simon was allotted three thousand men, to go into Galilee, and Judas eight thousand men, to go into Gilead.
21 And Simon went into Galilee, and engaged in many battles with the heathen, and the heathen were beaten before him,
22 and he pursued them to the very gate of Ptolemais. There fell of the heathen fully three thousand men, and he
23 plundered them. And he took with him those who were in Galilee and in Arbatta with their wives and children and all that they had, and brought them back to Judea with great rejoicing.
24 And Judas Maccabeus and his brother Jonathan crossed the Jordan, and marched three days' journey into the
25 wilderness. And they encountered the Nabateans and met them peacably, and told them all that had happened to their
26 brothers in Gilead, and that many of them were shut up in Bosorra and Bosor, in Alema, Chaspho, Maked, and
27 Karnaim—all large, fortified towns—and that they were shut up in the other towns of Gilead, and that they planned on the next day to attack the strongholds and take them, and
28 destroy all these men in one day. And Judas and his army turned suddenly by the wilderness road to Bosorra, and he

took the town and killed every male in it with the sword, and
he took all their spoils, and burned it with fire. And he left 29
there by night, and they arrived at the stronghold. And at 30
daybreak they looked up, and there was a crowd of people
without number, bringing ladders and engines to take the
stronghold, and they were attacking them. And Judas saw 31
that the battle had begun, and the cry from the city went
up to heaven, with trumpets and loud shouting, and he 32
said to the men of his force,

"Fight for our brothers today!"

And he went out after them in three companies, and they 33
sounded the trumpets and cried aloud in prayer. And the 34
army of Timotheus saw that it was Maccabeus, and they
fled before him, and he struck them a severe blow, and
there fell of them that day fully eight thousand men. Then 35
he turned aside to Alema and fought against it and took it,
and he killed every male in it, and plundered it and burned
it with fire. Then he moved on and seized Chaspho, Maked, 36
and Bosor and the other towns of Gilead.

After that, Timotheus gathered another army, and he 37
pitched his camp opposite Raphon, on the other side of
the torrent. And Judas sent men to reconnoiter the camp, 38
and they reported to him,

"All the heathen around us have gathered and joined
him, an immensely great force, and they have hired Arabs 39
to help them, and they are encamped across the torrent, in
readiness to attack you."

And Judas went to meet them. Then Timotheus said 40
to the officers of his army, when Judas and his army approached the stream,

"If he crosses over to us first, we will not be able to stand
against him, for he will easily defeat us. But if he is afraid 41

5:29–41

and pitches his camp on the other side of the river, we will cross over to him and defeat him."

42 When Judas came near the stream, he stationed the officers of the people by the stream, and gave them their orders, saying,

"Do not permit anyone to encamp, but let them all advance to battle."

43 And he crossed over against them first, with all the people after him, and all the heathen were beaten before them, and they threw away their arms and fled to the

44 temple inclosure of Karnaim. Then they took the town, and burned the temple inclosure with all who were in it. So Karnaim was conquered, and they could not make a stand before Judas any longer.

45 And Judas gathered all the Israelites that were in Gilead, from the least to the greatest, with their wives and children and their belongings, a very great body of people, to go to

46 the land of Judah. And they reached Ephron; it was a large town, strongly fortified, on their way; they could not turn aside from it to the right or left, but had to go through the

47 center of it. And the people of the town shut them out and

48 blocked up the gates with stones. And Judas sent them a peaceful message, saying,

"We are going through your country to reach our country, and no one will do you any harm, we will simply pass by on foot."

49 But they would not open to him. Then Judas ordered proclamation to be made throughout the body that every-

50 one should encamp where he was. So the men of the army encamped, and he fought against the city all that day and all that night, and the town was delivered into his hands.

51 And he destroyed every male with the sword, and he destroyed it and plundered it, and he passed through the

city over the slain. And they crossed the Jordan to the great 52
plain opposite Bethshean. And Judas kept gathering up 53
those who fell behind and encouraging the people, all the
way until he reached the land of Judah. And they went up 54
to Mount Zion with gladness and joy, and offered whole
burnt offerings because not one of them had fallen before
they returned in peace.

In the days when Judas and Jonathan were in the land of 55
Gilead and Simon his brother was in Galilee, opposite
Ptolemais, Joseph, the son of Zechariah, and Azariah, the 56
leaders of the forces, heard of the warlike exploits they had
performed, and they said, 57

"Let us also make a name for ourselves, and let us go and
fight the heathen around us."

And he gave orders to the part of the army that was with 58
them, and they marched to Jamnia. And Gorgias came out 59
of the town with his men to meet them in battle. And 60
Joseph and Azariah were routed, and they were pursued
to the borders of Judea. And there fell that day of the people of Israel fully two thousand men. And there was a great 61
rout among the people, because they had not listened to
Judas and his brothers, but thought they would perform
some exploit. They did not belong to the family of those 62
who were permitted to save Israel with their hands.

This man Judas and his brothers were greatly renowned 63
in all Israel and among all the heathen, wherever their
name was heard of; and men gathered about them com- 64
mending them.

And Judas and his brothers went forth and made war on 65
the sons of Esau in the country to the south, and he struck
down Hebron and its villages, and he tore down its fortifications and burned its towers around it. And he set off to go 66
to the land of the Philistines, and reached Mareshah. Some 67

5:52-67

priests fell in battle that day, when they went out to war without due consideration, because they wished to dis-
68 tinguish themselves. And Judas turned aside to Azotus, to the land of the Philistines, and he tore down their altars and burned up the carved images of their gods and plundered the towns, and returned to the land of Judah.

6] As King Antiochus was making his way through the interior, he heard that there was in Persia a town called
2 Elymais, renowned for its wealth, its silver and gold. The temple in it was very rich, and there were there gold shields and breastplates and arms left there by Alexander, the son of Philip, king of Macedon, who was the first to reign over
3 the Greeks. And he went and tried to take the town, and plunder it, but he could not do it, because his design became
4 known to the men of the town, and they opposed him in battle, and he fled and set out from there in great distress to
5 return to Babylon. And someone came to him in Persia to bring him word that the forces that had marched into the
6 land of Judah had been routed, and that Lysias had gone at first with a strong force, and had been put to flight before them, and that they had grown strong by reason of the quantity of arms and spoils they had taken from the armies
7 they had destroyed, and that they had taken down the horror which he had built on the altar in Jerusalem, and had surrounded the sanctuary with high walls, as it had
8 been before, and also his town of Bethsura. And it happened when the king heard these accounts, that he was astounded and dreadfully shaken, and he took to his bed, and fell sick with grief, for matters had not gone as he in-
9 tended. He was sick for a long time, for his grief was in-
10 tensified, and he concluded that he was going to die. So he called in all his Friends and said to them,
11   "Sleep departs from my eyes, and my heart fails with

anxiety. I have said to myself, 'What distress I have reached, and what a great flood I am now in.' For I was gracious and beloved in my exercise of power. But now I 12 remember the wrongs which I did in Jerusalem, when I took away all the gold and silver dishes that were in it, and sent to destroy the inhabitants of Judah without any cause. I know that it is because of this that these misfortunes have 13 overtaken me. Here I am dying of grief in a strange land."

And he summoned Philip, one of his Friends, and put him 14 in charge of his whole kingdom. He gave him his diadem 15 and his robe and his signet ring, so that he might educate his son Antiochus and bring him up to be king. And 16 King Antiochus died there in the one hundred and forty-ninth year. And when Lysias learned that the king was 17 dead, he set up Antiochus his son to reign, whom he had taken care of as a boy, and he named him Eupator.

The men in the citadel kept hemming Israel in about the 18 sanctuary, harassing them continually and giving support to the heathen. So Judas planned to destroy them, and he 19 called all the people together to lay siege to them. And they 20 assembled and laid siege to it in the one hundred and fiftieth year, and he built siege towers and engines. And some of 21 them escaped from the blockade, and some ungodly Israelites joined them, and they made their way to the king and 22 said,

"How long will you delay doing justice and avenging our brothers? We agreed to serve your father and to con- 23 duct ourselves in accordance with his orders and to follow his commands. On account of this the sons of our people 24 have besieged it and become hostile to us. Such of us as they found, they put to death, and they have plundered our property. They have stretched out their hands not only 25 against us but against all the lands on their borders. Here 26

6:12–26

today they have encamped against the citadel in Jerusalem to capture it, and they have fortified the sanctuary and
27 Bethsura. And unless you act against them quickly, they will do greater things than these, and you will not be able to check them."
28 When the king heard this, he was angry, and he gathered all his Friends, the officers of his army, and those in charge
29 of the cavalry. And mercenary forces came to him from
30 other kingdoms and from the islands in the sea. And his forces numbered a hundred thousand infantry and twenty thousand cavalry, and thirty-two elephants trained for war.
31 And they passed through Idumea and pitched their camp against Bethsura and fought against it for a long time, and built engines of war. And they sallied out and burned them down, and fought bravely.
32 Then Judas left the citadel and pitched his camp at Beth-
33 zechariah, opposite the king's camp. And the king got up early in the morning and moved his army precipitately along the road to Beth-zechariah, and his forces armed
34 themselves for battle, and sounded the trumpets. And they showed the elephants the juice of grapes and mulberries to
35 incite them to battle. They distributed the animals among the phalanxes and stationed with each elephant a thousand men in chain armor with brass helmets on their heads, and five hundred picked horsemen were assigned to each animal.
36 These were posted in advance wherever the animal was to be, and wherever it went they accompanied it; they did not
37 leave it. There were wooden towers upon them, strong and covered over, on each animal, ingeniously fastened on, and on each one were four powerful men who fought on them,
38 beside the Indian driver. The rest of the cavalry he stationed on this side and on that, on the two wings of the army, threatening the enemy and again finding shelter among

6:27-38

the phalanxes. And when the sun fell on the gold and brass 39
shields, the mountains flashed back and shone like blazing
torches. One wing of the king's army spread over the high 40
mountains, while some were on low ground, but they advanced steadily, in good order. And all who heard the noise 41
of their multitude and of the marching of the multitude and
the rattle of their arms trembled, for the army was very
great and strong.

Then Judas and his army advanced to battle, and six hundred men from the king's army fell. And Eleazar Avaran 43
saw that one of the animals was armed with royal armor,
and stood higher than all the other animals, and he thought
that the king was on it; and he gave his life to save his people 44
and win everlasting renown for himself. For he ran boldly 45
up to it in the midst of the phalanx slaying to right and left,
and they opened before him on this side and on that, and 46
he slipped under the elephant and stabbed it underneath
and killed it, and it fell to the earth upon him, and he died
there. And when they saw the strength of the kingdom and 47
the impetuosity of its forces, they gave way before them.

But the men of the king's army went up to Jerusalem to 48
meet them, and the king pitched his camp in Judea, and
opposite Mount Zion. And he made peace with the men of 49
Bethsura, and they evacuated the town, because they had
no food there to support a siege, for it was a sabbatical year.
So the king occupied Bethsura and stationed a garrison 50
there to hold it. And he encamped against the sanctuary 51
for a long time, and set up siege towers there and war
engines and machines to throw fire and stones, and ballistas
to shoot arrows, and slings. And they also built war engines 52
against their war engines and fought for a long time. But 53
there were no provisions in the storerooms, because it was a
sabbatical year, and those who had taken refuge in Judea

6:39-53

from the heathen had consumed what was left of the stores.

54 And there were few men left in the sanctuary, for the famine had been too much for them, and they had scattered, each man to his home.

55 Then Lysias heard that Philip, whom King Antiochus before his death had appointed to bring up his son to be

56 king, had returned from Persia and Media, with the forces that had gone with the king, and that he was seeking to get control of the government. So he hastily agreed to with-

57 draw, and he said to the king and the officers of the army and the men,

"We are growing weaker every day, and our provisions are getting short and the place we are besieging is strong,

58 and the affairs of the kingdom depend upon us, so let us now come to terms with these men, and make peace with them

59 and with all their nation, and make an agreement with them that they shall follow their own laws, as they used to do, for it was on account of their laws which we abolished that they became angry and did all this."

60 And the proposal pleased the king and his officers, and he

61 sent to them, to make peace, and they agreed. And the king and the officers made oath to them; then they evacuated the

62 stronghold. But when the king went into Mount Zion and saw the strength of the place, he broke the oath that he had sworn, and gave orders to tear down the wall that encircled

63 it. Then he departed in haste and returned to Antioch and found Philip in possession of the city, and he fought against him and took the city by force.

7} In the one hundred and fifty-first year Demetrius, the son of Seleucus, came out from Rome and went with a few men

2 to a seaside town and became king there. And it happened when he sought to enter the royal city of his forefathers, that

the troops seized Antiochus and Lysias, to bring them before him. When the matter was made known to him, he said, 3 "Do not let me see their faces."

So the soldiers killed them, and Demetrius took his seat 4 upon his royal throne. And all the lawless and ungodly men 5 of Israel came to him, and Alcimus who wished to be high priest was their leader. And they accused the people to the 6 king, and said,

"Judas and his brothers have destroyed all your Friends, and have scattered us out of our land. So now send a man in 7 whom you have confidence, and let him go and see all the damage he has done to us and to the king's country, and let him punish them and all their helpers."

And the king chose Bacchides, one of the king's Friends, 8 who was governor of the country beyond the river, and was a great man in the kingdom, and faithful to the king. And he sent him and the ungodly Alcimus, and assured him 9 of the high priesthood, and ordered him to take vengeance on the Israelites. And they set forth and came with a 10 strong force to the land of Judah, and he sent messengers to Judas and his brothers, with a peaceful message, but in guile. But they paid no attention to their message, for they 11 saw that they had come with a strong force. And a body of 12 scribes gathered before Alcimus and Bacchides, to ask for justice. The foremost among the Israelites that asked for 13 peace from them were the Hasideans, for they said, 14

"A priest of the blood of Aaron has come with the forces, and he will not do us any wrong."

And he talked peaceably with them, and made oath to 15 them, saying,

"We will not attempt to injure you or your friends."

And they trusted him. And he arrested sixty of them and 16 killed them in a single day, just as he said who wrote,

7:3-16

17   "The flesh and blood of your saints they scattered
         Around Jerusalem, and they had no one to bury them."
18   Then the fear and dread of them fell upon all the people,
     for they said,
         "There is no truth or justice in them, for they broke the
     agreement and the oath that they swore."
19   And Bacchides left Jerusalem and pitched his camp in
     Bethzaith and he set and seized many of the deserters that
     had been with him, and some of the people, and he slaugh-
20   tered them and threw them into the great pit. And he estab-
     lished Alcimus over the country, and left a force with him
     to help him. Then Bacchides went back to the king.
21,22   Alcimus strove to maintain his high priesthood. And all
     those who harassed their people gathered about him, and
     they took possession of the land of Judah and did great harm
23   in Israel. And Judas saw all the damage that Alcimus and
     his men had done to the Israelites, more even than the
24   heathen had, and he went out into all the outer borders of
     Judea and took vengeance on the men who had deserted
25   him, and kept them from going out into the country. But
     when Alcimus saw that Judas and his men were growing
     strong, and realized that he could not withstand them, he
     returned to the king and and made wicked charges against
     them.
26   Then the king sent Nicanor, one of his distinguished of-
     ficers, who hated Israel bitterly, and ordered him to de-
27   stroy the people. And Nicanor went to Jerusalem with a
     strong force, and he deceitfully sent a peaceful message to
     Judas and his brothers, saying,
28   "Let us have no battle between me and you. I will come
     with a few men to have a peaceable personal meeting."
29   So he came to Judas, and they greeted one another peace-
30   ably. But the enemy were ready to kidnap Judas. And the

7:17–30

fact that he had come to him in deceit became known to Judas, and he was very much afraid of him and would not meet him again. And Nicanor knew that his plan had been 31 discovered, and he went out to meet Judas in battle at Caphar-salama, and about five hundred of Nicanor's men 32 fell, and they fled to the City of David.

After this, Nicanor went up to Mount Zion, and some 33 of the priests came out of the sanctuary with some of the elders of the people to greet him peaceably, and show him the whole burnt offering that was being offered for the king. And he jeered at them and laughed at them and polluted 34 them, and spoke arrogantly and swore angrily, 35

"If Judas and his army are not immediately delivered into my hands, it will happen that if I return safely, I will burn this house up!"

And he went away in great anger. And the priests went 36 in and stood before the altar and the sanctuary and they wailed and said,

"You chose this house to bear your name, to be a house 37 for prayer and petition for your people. Take vengeance 38 on this man and on his army, and let them fall by the sword. Remember their sacrilegious words and let them not continue."

And Nicanor set out from Jerusalem and pitched his 39 camp in Bethhoron, and the Syrian army met him there. And Judas encamped in Adasa with three thousand men, 40 and Judas prayed and said,

"When the king's men uttered blasphemy, your angel 41 went forth and struck down a hundred and eighty-five thousand of them. Crush this army before us today, in the same 42 way, and let the rest know that he spoke wickedly against your sanctuary, and judge him as his wickedness deserves."

And the armies met in battle on the thirteenth of the 43

7:31–43

month of Adar, and Nicanor's army was beaten, and he
44 himself was the first to fall in the battle. But when his army
saw that Nicanor had fallen, they threw down their arms
45 and fled. And they pursued them a day's journey, from
Adasa until you come to Gazara, and they sounded the
46 ceremonial trumpets behind them. And people came forth
out of all the villages of Judea around, and hemmed them
in, and turned them back toward the pursuers, and they
47 all fell by the sword; not one of them was left. And they
took the spoils and the plunder, and they cut off Nicanor's
head and his right hand, which he had stretched out so arrogantly, and brought them and displayed them at Jeru-
48 salem. And the people rejoiced greatly, and they observed
49 that day as a day of great gladness. And they decreed
that that day should be annually observed, on the thirteenth
50 of Adar. Then the land of Judah was quiet for a short time.
8] And Judas heard of the reputation of the Romans, that
they were powerful, and favored all who joined them, and
established friendly relations with those who approached
2 them, and were powerful. And they told him about their
wars and the exploits they had performed among the Gauls,
and how they had subdued them and made them pay trib-
3 ute, and what they had done in the land of Spain, in getting
4 possession of the silver and gold mines there, and how by
their planning and patience they had become masters of
that whole region, though it was very far away from them,
and about the kings who had come against them from the
ends of the earth, until they had crushed them and inflicted
great losses upon them, and how the rest paid them tribute
5 every year; and how they had crushed Philip and Perseus,
the king of Chittim, and those who had opposed them they
6 had beaten in battle and subdued; and how Antiochus, the
great king of Asia, had marched against them with a

7:44-8:6

hundred and twenty elephants and horses and chariots and
a very great force, and had been beaten by them, and they 7
had captured him alive and had required him and those
who succeeded him to pay a great tribute and give hostages,
and a section of country, in India, Media, and Lydia, of the 8
best lands, and they had taken them from him and given
them to King Eumenes; and how the men of Greece had 9
planned to come and destroy them, and they had learned 10
of the matter, and they sent one general against them, and
they fought with them and many of them fell wounded, and
they took their wives and children captive and they plundered them and conquered the land and tore down their
strongholds and enslaved them unto this day; and how they 11
had destroyed and enslaved all the other kingdoms and
islands that had ever opposed them, but had maintained 12
friendly relations with their friends and those who relied
upon them; and how they had conquered kings far and
near, and all who heard their name were afraid of them.
Those whom they wished to help and make kings, became 13
kings, and those whom they wished, they deposed; and
they were greatly exalted. Yet with all this they never any 14
of them put on a diadem, or wore purple, as a mark of
magnificence. And they had built themselves a senate 15
house, and every day three hundred and twenty men deliberated, constantly planning for the people, that they
might conduct themselves properly, and they intrusted the 16
government to one man every year, and the authority over
all their country, and they all obeyed that one man, and
there was no envy or jealousy among them.

And Judas chose Eupolemus, the son of John, the son of 17
Hakkoz, and Jason, the son of Eleazar, and sent them to
Rome, to establish friendly relations and an alliance with

8:7-17

18 them, so that they might relieve them of their yoke, for they
saw that the rule of the Greeks was reducing Israel to
19 slavery. And they went to Rome, though the journey was
very long, and they went into the senate house and answered
and said,

20   "Judas, who is called Maccabeus, and his brothers and
the Jewish people have sent us to you, to make an alliance
and firm peace with you, and that we may be enrolled as
allies and friends of yours."

21,22 They were pleased with the proposal, and this is a copy
of the letter which they wrote in answer, on brass tablets,
and sent to Jerusalem, to remain there among them, as a
memorial of peace and alliance.

23   "Good fortune to the Romans and to the Jewish nation
by sea and land, forever! May sword and foe be far from
24 them! But if war is made on Rome first, or on any of their
25 allies, in all her dominion, the Jewish nation will act as their
allies, as the occasion shall demand of them, with all their
26 hearts. And to those who make the war they shall not give
or supply wheat, arms, money, or ships, as Rome decides,
and they shall observe their obligations, accepting nothing
27 from the other side. In like manner, if war is made on the
Jewish nation first, the Romans will heartily act as their al-
28 lies as occasion demands, and no wheat, arms, money, or
ships will be supplied to the allies, as Rome decides, and
29 they shall observe these obligations in good faith. On these
terms the Romans have made a treaty with the Jewish peo-
30 ple. But if hereafter one party or the other decides to add
or subtract anything, they shall do as they choose, and
whatever they add or subtract shall be valid. And about
31 the wrongs that King Demetrius is doing you, we have
written to him, saying, 'Why have you made your yoke
32 heavy upon our friends and allies the Jews? So if they appeal

8:18–32

to us against you again, we will do them justice and make war upon you by land and sea.' "

When Demetrius heard that Nicanor and his troops had [9 fallen in battle, he sent Bacchides and Alcimus into the land of Judah again a second time, with the right wing of his army. And they marched by the Gilgal road, and pitched 2 their camp against Mesaloth, in Arbela, and took it, and destroyed many people. And in the first month of the one 3 hundred and fifty-second year they encamped against Jerusalem. Then they set out and marched to Berea with 4 twenty thousand men and two thousand horse. And Judas 5 was encamped at Elasa, and had three thousand picked men with him. And they saw that the number of the troops 6 was great and they were greatly terrified, and many slipped out of the camp; not more than eight hundred men were left. And Judas saw that his army had slipped away, and 7 and that the battle was imminent, and he was troubled in mind, for he had no time to rally them. And in desperation 8 he said to those who were left,

"Let us get up and go against our opponents; perhaps we can fight against them."

And they tried to dissuade him, saying, 9

"We certainly cannot; but let us save our lives now, and come back with our brothers and fight against them; we are so few."

And Judas said, 10

"I will never do this thing, and flee from them; and if our time has come, let us die bravely for our brothers, and not leave a stain upon our honor."

So the army set out from the camp and formed its lines to 11 join battle, and the cavalry was divided into two parts, and the slingers and archers marched before the army, and all the powerful men who formed the front line. But Bacchides 12

9:1-12

was on the right wing. And the phalanx advanced on the
13 two sides, and they sounded their trumpets, and Judas' men
also sounded their trumpets, and the earth shook with the
shout of the armies, and the battle raged from morning till
14 evening. And when Judas saw that Bacchides and the
strength of his army were on the right wing, all the stout-
15 hearted went with him, and the right wing was beaten back
by them, and he pursued them as far as Mount Azotus.
16 And the men on the left wing saw that the right wing was
beaten back, and they turned and followed the track of
17 Judas and his men from behind. And the fight became
18 desperate, and many on both sides fell wounded. And Judas
19 fell and the rest fled. And Jonathan and Simon took their
brother Judas and buried him in the tombs of his forefathers
20 in Modin. And they wept over him, and all Israel lamented
him greatly and mourned for a long time, saying,
21   "What a hero is fallen, the Savior of Israel!"
22   The rest of the deeds of Judas, and his wars, and the
exploits that he performed, and his greatness are un-
recorded, for they were very many.
23   It happened after the death of Judas that those who had
no regard for the Law raised their heads all over Israel, and
24 all the wrongdoers reappeared. In those days there was a
very great famine, and the country went over to their side.
25 And Bacchides chose the ungodly men and appointed them
26 masters of the country. And they searched and sought out
the friends of Judas and brought them to Bacchides, and he
27 punished them and mocked them. And there was great
distress in Israel, such as there had not been since the time
28 when the prophets ceased to appear to them. And all the
friends of Judas gathered together and said to Jonathan,
29   "Since the death of your brother Judas, there has been no
one like him to go in and out against our enemies and

Bacchides and among those of our nation who are hostile.
So now we have chosen you today to be our ruler and 30
leader in his place, to carry on our war."

And Jonathan accepted the command at that time, and 31
took the place of his brother Judas.

And Bacchides learned of this, and tried to kill him. 32
And Jonathan and his brother Simon and all his men 33
learned of it, and they fled into the wild country about
Tekoa, and they pitched their camp by the waters of the
pool of Asphar. And Bacchides learned of it on the sab- 34
bath, and he and all his army came across the Jordan.

Now Jonathan had sent his brother, a leader of the 35
multitude, and entreated the Nabateans, as his friends, to
let them leave with them their baggage, of which there
was a great deal. But the sons of Jambri, from Medaba, 36
came out and seized John and all that he had, and went off
with it. Afterward, news came to Jonathan and his brother 37
Simon that the sons of Jambri were making a great wedding,
and were conducting the bride, the daughter of one of the
great nobles of Canaan, with a great retinue, from Nada-
bath. And they remembered the blood of their brother
John, and they went up and hid under the shelter of the 38
mountain. And they looked up and saw, and there was 39
confusion, and a great deal of baggage, for the bridegroom
had come out with his friends and his kinsmen to meet
them, with drums and musicians and many weapons. Then 40
they fell upon them from their ambush and killed them, and
many fell wounded, and the survivors fled into the mountain, and they took all their spoils. So the wedding was 41
turned into grief and the voice of their musicians into lamentation. And when they had fully avenged their brother's 42
blood, they turned back to the marshes of the Jordan.

And Bacchides heard of it, and he came on the sabbath 43

44 to the banks of the Jordan, with a strong force. And Jonathan said to his men,

"Let us get up now and fight for our lives, for today is not
45 like yesterday or the day before, for here is the battle in front of us and behind us, and on one side the water of the Jordan, and on the other marsh and thicket, and there is no
46 room to retreat. So now, cry out to heaven that you may be delivered from the hands of our enemies."

47 And the battle was joined, and Jonathan stretched out his hand to strike Bacchides down, and he gave ground be-
48 fore him. Then Jonathan and his men jumped into the Jordan and swam over to the other side; and they did not cross
49 the Jordan in pursuit of them. And fully a thousand of Bacchides' men fell that day.

50 And he returned to Jersualem, and they built fortified towns in Judea; the stronghold in Jericho, and Emmaus, and Bethhoron, and Bethel, and Timnath Pharathon, and
51 Tephon, with high walls and barred gates; and he put garri-
52 sons in them to harass Israel. And he fortified the town of Bethsura, and Gazara, and the citadel, and he put troops
53 in them, and stores of provisions. And he took the sons of the principal men of the country as hostages, and put them in custody in the citadel at Jerusalem.

54 In the one hundred and fifty-third year, in the second month, Alcimus gave orders to tear down the wall of the inner court of the sanctuary; he thus destroyed the work of the
55 prophets, but he began to tear it down. At that very time, Alcimus was stricken, and his work hindered and his mouth stopped, and he was paralyzed and could no longer utter a
56 word, or give orders about his household. So Alcimus died
57 at that time, in great agony. And when Bacchides saw that Alcimus was dead, he went back to the king, and the land of Judah was quiet for two years.

9:44–57

Then all those who disregarded the Law plotted, saying, 58
"Here Jonathan and his men are living undisturbed and
secure, so now we will bring Bacchides back, and he will
arrest them all in a single night."

And they went and consulted him. And he set out and 59
came with a strong force and he sent letters secretly to all 60
his allies in Judea to arrest Jonathan and his men, but they
could not because their plan became known to them. And 61
they seized fully fifty of the men of the country who were
ring-leaders in this wickedness, and killed them. And 62
Jonathan and Simon and their men withdrew to Bethbasi,
in the wild country, and he rebuilt the parts that had been
torn down, and they strengthened it. And Bacchides learned 63
of it, and he gathered all his host and sent word to the men
of Judea, and he came and pitched his camp against Beth- 64
basi, and fought against it for a long time and set up siege
engines.

Then Jonathan left his brother Simon in the town and 65
went out into the country, and he went with a small force.
And he struck down Odomera and his brothers, and the 66
sons of Phasiron in their tent, and they began to strike and 67
attacked with their forces. And Simon and his men went
out of the town and set fire to the siege engines, and they 68
fought with Bacchides, and he was beaten by them, and they
pressed him very hard, for his plan and his attack were in
vain. And he was very angry with the men who disre- 69
garded the Law who had advised him to come into the country, and he killed many of them, and resolved to go back
to his country. And Jonathan learned of it, and he sent 70
envoys to him to make peace with him, and obtain the release of his prisoners. And he agreed and did as he promised
and made oath to him that he would not seek to injure him 71
so long as he lived. And he released to him the prisoners 72

9:58-72

that he had taken before from the land of Judea, and he went away and returned to his own country, and did not
73 come into their borders again. So the sword ceased in Israel. And Jonathan lived in Michmash. And Jonathan began to judge the people, and he destroyed the ungodly out of Israel.

10] In the one hundred and sixtieth year, Alexander Epiphanes, the son of Antiochus, went up and took possession of Ptolemais, and they welcomed him, and he became king
2 there. When King Demetrius heard of it, he mustered very strong forces and went out to meet him in battle.

3 And Demetrius sent letters to Jonathan in peaceful terms
4 to flatter him, for he said to himself,
"Let us be the first to make peace with them, before he
5 makes peace with Alexander against us, for he will remember all the wrongs we have done him and his brothers and his nation."

6 And he gave him authority to muster troops, and to procure arms and to be his ally, and he gave orders that they should turn over to him the hostages that were in the citadel.
7 So Jonathan went up to Jerusalem, and read the letters in the hearing of all the people, and of the men who were in
8 possession of the citadel; and they were dreadfully frightened when they heard that the king had given him author-
9 ity to muster troops. And the men in the citadel turned over the hostages to Jonathan, and he gave them back to
10 their parents. And Jonathan lived in Jerusalem, and he
11 began to build and renovate the city. And he ordered those who did the work to build the walls and encircle Mount Zion with four-foot stones for its fortification, and they did
12 so. And the foreigners who were in the strongholds that
13 Bacchides had built fled; each one left his post and went
14 back to his own country, except that in Bethsura there were

9:73–10:14

left some of those who had forsaken the Law and the commandments, for it served as a refuge for them.

And King Alexander heard of all the promises that 15
Demetrius had sent to Jonathan, and they related to him
the battles and exploits that he and his brothers had performed, and the troubles they had endured, and he said to 16
himself,

"Can we find another man like him? Now we must make
him our friend and ally."

So he wrote letters and sent them to him, in the following 17
terms:

"King Alexander sends greetings to his brother Jonathan. 18
We have heard that you are a valiant warrior, and fit to be 19
our friend. Now we have today appointed you to be high 20
priest of your nation and to be called a Friend of the king"
(and he sent him a purple robe and a gold crown) "and to
side with us and maintain friendly relations with us."

So Jonathan put on the holy vestments in the seventh 21
month of the one hundred and sixtieth year, at the Camping
Out festival, and he mustered troops and provided arms in
abundance.

And Demetrius heard of these things, and he was an- 22
noyed, and said,

"Why have we brought it about that Alexander has got- 23
ten ahead of us in establishing friendly relations with the
Jews, to strengthen his position? I too will write them a 24
message of encouragement and distinction, with promises
of gifts, so that they may become a support for me."

So he sent one to them in these terms: 25

"King Demetrius sends greetings to the Jewish nation.
Since you have kept your agreement with us, and remained 26
true to our friendship, and have not gone over to our enemies, we have rejoiced to hear of it. So now continue to 27

10:15-27

keep faith with us, and we will deal favorably with you in
28 return for your dealings with us, and we will grant you many
29 exemptions and make you presents. So I do now free you
and I release all the Jews from paying tribute and from the
30 salt tax and the crown tax. And instead of one-third of the
grain and instead of half of the fruit of the trees, which it
falls to me to receive, I surrender from this day forward the
right to take them from the land of Judea and from the three
districts which are attached to it from Samaria and Galilee,
31 from this day forth and for all time. Let Jerusalem and her
32 territory, her tithes and her taxes, be holy and free. I re-
linquish also my authority over the citadel in Jerusalem, and
I give it to the high priest, in order that he may put men
33 whom he shall choose in possession of it, to garrison it. And
every Jewish person who has been carried into captivity
from the land of Judea into any part of my kingdom, I set
at liberty without payment, and let all officials cancel the
34 taxes upon their cattle also. And let all the festivals and
sabbaths and new moons and appointed days, and three
days before each festival, and three days after each festival,
be days of exemption and immunity for all the Jews in my
35 kingdom, and no one shall have authority to exact anything
36 from any of them or to trouble any of them about any matter.
And among the king's forces at least thirty thousand Jews
shall be enrolled, and they shall receive pay, as all the king's
37 forces have a right to do. And some of them shall be stationed in the king's great strongholds, and some shall be put
in positions of trust in the kingdom. And those who are set
over them and those who govern them shall be of their own
number, and they shall follow their own laws, as the king
38 has commanded in the land of Judea. And the three districts that have been added to Judea from the country of
Samaria shall be added to Judea so that they may be con-

sidered as under one man, and not obey any other authority than the high priest. Ptolemais and the land pertaining 39
to it I have presented to the sanctuary in Jerusalem, for the
expenses incident to the sanctuary. And I will give fifteen 40
thousand silver shekels every year, from the king's revenues,
from such places as are convenient. And the additional 41
grant, which the administration has not paid over as it formerly did, they shall henceforth pay in full toward the service
of the temple. In addition, the five thousand silver shekels 42
which they used to take out of the dues of the temple, from
the revenue every year, is also canceled, for it rightfully belongs to the priests who conduct the worship. And whoever 43
takes refuge in the temple at Jerusalem, and in any of its
precincts, who owes money to the king or any other obligation shall be released from it, with all his property in my
realm. The cost of rebuilding and renovating the fabric of 44
the sanctuary shall be provided out of the king's revenue.
The cost of rebuilding the walls of Jerusalem and of fortify- 45
ing it all around, and of building the walls in Judea, shall
also be provided out of the king's revenue."

But when Jonathan and the people heard these terms, 46
they did not believe them or accept them, for they remembered the great injury he had done to Israel, and that
he had distressed them intensely. And they took Alexander's 47
side, for he had been first in addressing them in peaceful
terms, and they always remained his allies.

Then King Alexander gathered large forces and pitched 48
his camp against Demetrius. And the two kings joined bat- 49
tle, and the army of Demetrius fled, and Alexander pursued
him and defeated them, and he pressed the fighting hard, 50
until sunset, and Demetrius fell that day.

Then Alexander sent envoys to Ptolemy, king of Egypt, 51
with this message:

10:39–51

52 "Since I have returned to my kingdom, and have taken my seat on the throne of my forefathers, and have taken over the government, and have defeated Demetrius and
53 taken possession of our country—for I have met him in battle, and he and his army were defeated by us, and we
54 have taken our seat on the throne of his kingdom—let us now establish friendly relations with one another, so give me your daughter to be my wife, and I will be your son-in-law, and give you and her gifts worthy of you."

55 And King Ptolemy answered,
"It was a happy day when you returned to the country of your forefathers and took your seat on the throne of their
56 kingdom. I will now do for you what you wrote, but meet me in Ptolemais, so that we may see each other, and I will be your father-in-law, as you have said."

57 So Ptolemy came up from Egypt, with his daughter Cleopatra, and reached Ptolemais in the one hundred and sixty-
58 second year. And King Alexander met him, and he gave him his daughter Cleopatra in marriage, and he celebrated her wedding at Ptolemais with great pomp, as kings do.

59 Then King Alexander wrote to Jonathan to come to meet
60 him. And he went in splendor to Ptolemais and met the two kings, and gave them and their Friends silver and gold and
61 many gifts, and was well received by them. Some malcontents from Israel, who disregarded the Law, gathered against him, to lay charges against him, but the king paid
62 no attention to them. And the king gave orders, and they took Jonathan's clothes off and clothed him in purple; they
63 did as he ordered. And the king made him sit beside him, and said to his officers,
"Go out with him into the middle of the city, and make a proclamation that no one is to appeal against him on any

10:52-63

ground, and no one must interfere with him on any account."

So it happened that when those who were complaining of 64 him saw the distinction with which he was treated, as the herald proclaimed, and saw him clothed in purple, they all fled. And the king treated him with distinction, and enrolled him among his Best Friends, and made him general and governor. So Jonathan returned to Jerusalem in peace 66 and gladness.

In the one hundred and sixty-fifth year, Demetrius' son 67 Demetrius came from Crete to the country of his forefathers. When King Alexander heard of it, he was greatly disturbed 68 and returned to Antioch. And Demetrius appointed 69 Apollonius who was in command of Coelesyria, and he gathered a strong force and pitched his camp at Jamnia, and sent to Jonathan the high priest saying,

"You are all alone in resisting us, but I am laughed at 70 and reproached because of you. Why do you claim your authority against us up in the mountains? If you really 71 trust in your troops, come down into the plain to us and let us measure our strength together there, for I have control of the towns. So inquire and find out who I am, and who the 72 others are who help us, and they will tell you that you will have no foothold before us, for your forefathers have been routed twice in their land. So now you will not be able to 73 stand against the cavalry and such a force as this on the plain, where there is no stone or pebble, or place to escape to."

When Jonathan heard the message of Apollonius, his 74 heart was stirred, and he chose ten thousand men, and set out from Jerusalem, and his brother Simon joined him to help him. And he pitched his camp against Joppa, and the 75 men of the town shut him out, for Apollonius had a garrison

76 in Joppa; and they fought against it. Then the men of the town were frightened and they opened the gates, and Jona-
77 than took possession of Joppa. And Apollonius heard of it, and he mustered three thousand horsemen and a strong force and he marched to Azotus as though he meant to travel on, but at the same time he advanced into the plain, because he had a large force of cavalry and relied upon it.
78 And he pursued him to Azotus, and the armies joined battle.
79 And Apollonius had left a thousand horse in hiding in their
80 rear, and Jonathan learned that there was an ambuscade in his rear. And they surrounded his army and showered their
81 arrows upon the people from morning till evening, but the people stood fast, as Jonathan had ordered, while the
82 enemy's horses were tired out. Then Simon advanced his force and joined battle with the phalanx, for the cavalry were exhausted, and they were defeated by him, and fled,
83 and the cavalry were scattered over the plain. And they fled to Azotus and took refuge in Beth-dagon, their idol's
84 temple. And Jonathan burned Azotus and the towns around it, and plundered them, and he burned up the temple of
85 Dagon and those who had taken refuge in it. And those who had fallen by the sword, together with those who were
86 burned up came to fully eight thousand men. And Jonathan set forth and pitched his camp against Askalon, and the men of the town came out to meet him with great
87 pomp. Then Jonathan returned to Jerusalem with his men,
88 with a great quantity of plunder. And it happened that, when King Alexander heard of these things, he treated
89 Jonathan with still more distinction, and he sent him a gold buckle, such as are usually given to the members of the royal family; and he gave him Ekron and all that district for settlement.

11] And the king of Egypt gathered strong forces, like the

sand on the seashore, and many ships, and undertook to possess himself of Alexander's kingdom by deceit, and to add it to his own kingdom. And he set out for Syria with peace- 2 ful professions, and the people of the towns opened their gates to him, and met him, for King Alexander had ordered them to meet him, as he was his father-in-law. But when 3 Ptolemy entered the towns, he placed a garrison of his troops in each town. And when they reached Azotus, they showed 4 him the temple of Dagon burned, and Azotus and its suburbs torn down and corpses lying about, and those who had been burned, whom he had burned in the war, for they had piled them in heaps in his way. And they told the king 5 what Jonathan had done, in order to throw blame on him, and the king was silent. And Jonathan met the king with 6 pomp at Joppa, and they greeted one another and spent the night there. And Jonathan traveled with the king as far as 7 the river called the Eleutherus, and then returned to Jerusalem. But Ptolemy made himself master of the coast towns 8 all the way to Seleucia which is by the sea, and formed wicked designs about Alexander. And he sent envoys to 9 King Demetrius, saying,

"Come, let us make an agreement with each other, and I will give you my daughter, whom Alexander had, and you shall reign over your father's kingdom. For I regret having 10 given him my daughter, for he has undertaken to kill me."

But he threw blame on him because he coveted his king- 11 dom. So he took his daughter away from him, and gave her 12 to Demetrius, and was estranged from Alexander, and their enmity became manifest. And Ptolemy entered Antioch, 13 and assumed the diadem of Asia, so he put two diadems upon his head, that of Egypt and that of Asia.

But King Alexander was in Cilicia, at that time, for the 14 people of those regions were in revolt. When Alexander 15

11:2-15

heard of it, he marched against him. And Ptolemy led out
his army and met him with a strong force, and routed him.
16 And Alexander fled to Arabia to find shelter, but King
17 Ptolemy was triumphant. And Zabdiel the Arab cut off
18 Alexander's head and sent it to Ptolemy. Three days later
King Ptolemy died, and his men in the strongholds were
19 destroyed by the men of the strongholds. And in the one
hundred and sixty-seventh year, Demetrius became king.
20   In those days Jonathan mustered the men of Judea to
attack the citadel, and he set up many siege engines against
21 it. And some breakers of the Law, who hated their own nation, went to the king and reported to him that Jonathan
22 was besieging the citadel. When he heard of it, he was
angry, but upon hearing it he immediately set out and came
to Ptolemais, and wrote Jonathan not to continue the siege
but to meet him as soon as possible at Ptolemais, for a con-
23 ference. When Jonathan heard this, he gave orders to continue the siege, and he selected some of the elders of Israel
24 and of the priests and put himself in danger, for he took
silver and gold and clothing and a great many other presents, and went to the king, at Ptolemais, and he pleased the
25 king. And when some of the men of his nation who disre-
26 garded the Law complained of him, the king treated him
just as his predecessors had done, and showed him great
27 honor in the presence of all his Friends. He confirmed him
in the high priesthood, and all the other honors he had received before, and made him chief of his Best Friends.
28 Jonathan asked the king to free Judea and the three provinces and Samaria from tribute, and promised him three
29 hundred talents. The king agreed, and wrote a letter to
Jonathan on all these matters as follows:
30   "King Demetrius sends greetings to his brother Jonathan
31 and to the Jewish nation. This copy of the letter which we

11:16–31

have written to Lasthenes our kinsman, we have written to you also, so that you may be acquainted with it. 'King De- 32 metrius sends greeting to his father Lasthenes. We have 33 determined to favor the Jewish nation, who are friends of ours, and observe their obligations to us, because of the good will they have shown us. So we have recognized as 34 theirs the territory of Judea and the three districts of Aphaerema, Lydda, and Ramathaim (they were transferred from Samaria to Judea) and everything pertaining to them, for all those who offer sacrifice in Jerusalem, instead of the royal dues which the king formerly took from them annually from the produce of the land and the fruit of the trees. And 35 the other things that fall to us, of the tithes and dues that fall to us, and the salt pits and the crown tax that fall to us, all these we will from henceforth make over to them. And 36 not one of these things shall be annulled from this time forth forever. So now take care to make a copy of this, and have 37 it given to Jonathan and set up in a prominent place on the holy mount.' "

And King Demetrius saw that the country was quiet be- 38 fore him, and that there was no opposition to him, and he dismissed all his troops, every man to his home, except the foreign forces that he had hired from the islands of the heathen, so the old soldiers of his fathers had a grudge against him. Now Trypho was one of Alexander's old party, 39 and when he saw that all the troops were grumbling at Demetrius, he went to Imalkue the Arab who was bringing up Antiochus, the little son of Alexander, and he insisted 40 that he should turn him over to him, to become king in his father's place. And he reported to him all that Demetrius had done, and told him of the animosity his troops felt for him; and he stayed with him a long time.

Then Jonathan sent to King Demetrius asking him to 41

11:32-41

expel the garrison of the citadel from Jerusalem, and the
garrisons from the strongholds, for they kept fighting against
42 Israel. And Demetrius sent to Jonathan and said,
"I will not only do this for you and your nation, but I will
greatly honor you and your nation if I find an opportunity.
43 So now please send me men who will fight for me, for all my
troops are in revolt."

44 So Jonathan sent three thousand able-bodied men to
Antioch, and they came to the king, and he was glad they
45 had come. And the people of the city, fully a hundred and
twenty thousand of them, gathered in the midst of the city,
46 and wanted to kill the king. And the king fled to the palace,
and the people of the city seized the thoroughfares of the
47 city, and began to fight. Then the king summoned the Jews
to his aid, and they all together rallied about him, and
scattered over the city and killed that day fully a hundred
48 thousand people. And they set the city on fire, and took a
49 great quantity of spoil that day, and saved the king. When
the people of the city saw that the Jews controlled the city as
they pleased, their hearts failed them, and they cried out to
the king in entreaty, saying,
50 "Give us your pledge and make the Jews stop fighting
against us and the city."
51 And they threw down their arms and made peace. And
the Jews were in high honor with the king, and with all his
subjects, and they returned to Jerusalem with a great quan-
52 tity of spoil. And King Demetrius sat on his royal throne,
53 and the land was quiet before him. But he lied in all that he
had said, and became estranged from Jonathan and did not
return the favors he had done him, but treated him very
harshly.
54 Now after this Trypho returned, bringing with him the
little child Antiochus. And he became king and assumed

11:42–54

the diadem. And all the troops that Demetrius had cast off 55
rallied about him, and they fought against Demetrius and
he was routed, and fled. And Trypho took the animals 56
and took possession of Antioch. And the youthful Antiochus 57
wrote to Jonathan, saying,

"I confirm you in the high priesthood and appoint you
over the four districts, and to be one of the king's Friends."

And he sent him gold plate and table service, and gave 58
him the right to drink from gold goblets, and dress in purple
and wear a gold buckle. And he made his brother Simon 59
governor from the Ladder of Tyre to the frontier of Egypt. 60
And Jonathan set out and traveled across the river and
among the towns, and the whole army of Syria rallied
about him, to ally themselves with him. And he went to 61
Askalon, and the people of the town received him with
honor. And he went from there to Gaza, but the people of
Gaza shut their gates against him, so he laid siege to it, and
fired its suburbs and plundered them. Then the people of 62
Gaza asked for terms, and he gave them his pledge and took
the sons of their leaders as hostages, and sent them to
Jerusalem; and he went through the country as far as
Damascus.

And Jonathan heard that the officers of Demetrius were 63
at Kadesh in Galilee, with a strong force, wishing to remove him from his office, so he went to meet them, but he 64
left his brother Simon in the country. And Simon pitched 65
his camp against Bethsura, and fought against it a long time,
and shut it in. And they asked him to give them pledges 66
and he did so; and he put them out of it and took possession of the town and put a garrison in it.

And Jonathan and his army pitched their camp by the 67
water of Gennesaret, and early in the morning they went
to the Plain of Hazor. And, behold, the army of the

11:55-67

68 foreigners met him in the plain; they had set an ambush
for him in the mountains, but they themselves met him face
69 to face. But the ambush rose out of their places and joined
70 battle, and all who were on Jonathan's side fled; not one was
left of them except Mattathias, the son of Absalom, and
Judas, the son of Chalphi, who were captains of the forces.
71 And Jonathan tore open his clothes and threw dust on his
72 head and prayed. And he turned against them again in bat-
73 tle and routed them, and they fled. Those who were fleeing
on his side saw it and returned to him and pursued them
with him as far as Kadesh all the way to their camp, and they
74 pitched their camp there. And there fell of the foreigners
that day fully three thousand men. And Jonathan returned
to Jerusalem.

12] And Jonathan saw that the time was favorable, and he
selected men and sent them to Rome to confirm and renew
2 friendly relations with them. And he sent letters to the
3 Spartans and to other places to the same effect. And they
went to Rome and went into the senate house and said,

"Jonathan the high priest and the Jewish people have sent
us to renew friendly relations and alliance on their behalf,
as they have been heretofore."

4 And they delivered to them in each place letters addressed to them, asking them to see them off for the land of
Judah in peace.

5 This is the copy of the letter that Jonathan wrote to the
Spartans:

6 "Jonathan, the high priest, and the council of the nation
and the priests and the rest of the Jewish people send greet-
7 ing to their brothers the Spartans. In former times a letter
was sent to the high priest Onias from Arius who was then
king among you, to say that you are our kinsmen, as the
8 copy of it that is appended to this shows. And Onias showed

11:68–12:8

honor to the man who was sent to him, and accepted the letter, which contained a declaration of alliance and friendliness. So, though we are in no need of these, since we 9 find our encouragement in the sacred books that are in our keeping, we have undertaken to send to renew relations of 10 brotherhood and friendliness with you, so that we may not become entirely estranged from you, for it is a long time since you sent to us. So we on every occasion unremittingly 11 at our festivals and on other appropriate days remember you at the sacrifices that we offer and in our prayers, as it is right and proper to remember kinsmen. We rejoice in your 12 renown. But many hardships and wars have beset us, and 13 the kings around us have made war on us. We have not 14 wished to trouble you or our other allies and friends about these wars, for we have the help that comes from heaven to 15 aid us, and we have been saved from our enemies, and our enemies have been humbled. So we have chosen Numenius, 16 the son of Antiochus, and Antipater, the son of Jason, and have sent them to the Romans to renew our former relations of friendliness and alliance with them. So we have in- 17 structed them to go to you also and greet you, and to deliver to you our letter about the renewal of our fraternal relations. Now please reply to us about this." 18

And this is the copy of the letter which they had sent to 19 Onias:

"Arius, king of the Spartans, sends greetings to Onias, the 20 chief priest. It has been found in a writing concerning the 21 Spartans and Jews, that they are kinsmen, and that they are descended from Abraham. Now since we have learned this, 22 please write us about your welfare. We for our part write 23 you that your cattle and property are ours and ours are yours. So we command them to report to you to this effect."

12:9-23

24 And Jonathan heard that Demetrius' officers had returned
25 with a stronger force than before to make war on him And
he set out from Jerusalem and met them in the country
of Hamath, for he did not give them time to make their
26 way into his own country. And he sent spies into their
camp and they came back and reported to him that they
were forming in a certain way so as to fall upon him that
27 night. But when the sun set, Jonathan ordered his men to
be on the watch and to remain under arms so as to be ready
for battle all night long, and he stationed outposts around
28 the camp. And his adversaries heard that Jonathan and his
men were ready for battle, and they were frightened and
were terrified at heart, and they lighted fires in their camp.
29 But Jonathan and his men did not know of it until morning,
30 for they saw the fires burning. Then Jonathan pursued
them, but he could not overtake them, for they had crossed
31 the river Eleutherus. So Jonathan turned aside against the
Arabs who are called Zabadeans, and he defeated them and
32 plundered them. And he set forth and went to Damascus,
and traveled all through the country.

33 And Simon set out and made his way to Askalon, and the
strongholds near it, and he turned aside to Joppa and took
34 it by surprise, for he had heard that they wanted to turn over
the stronghold to Demetrius' men, and he stationed a garrison there to hold it.

35 When Jonathan returned, he called together the elders
of the people, and planned with them to build strongholds
36 in Judea, and to increase the height of the walls of Jerusalem, and to build a great mound between the citadel and
the city, to separate it from the city, so that it might be by it-
37 self, so that they could not buy or sell in it. So they gathered
together to build up the city, and part of the east wall by the
ravine collapsed, and he replaced it with the so-called Cha-

12:24–37

phenatha. And Simon built Adida in the lowlands and he 38
fortified it and fitted it with barred gates.

And Trypho undertook to become king of Asia and as- 39
sume the diadem, and to raise his hand against King
Antiochus. But he was afraid that Jonathan would not 40
permit him to, but would fight against him, so he undertook
to seize him, in order to destroy him. And he set out and
came to Bethshean. And Jonathan went out to meet him 41
with forty thousand picked fighting men, and came to
Bethshean. And Trypho saw that he had come with a strong 42
force, and he was afraid to raise his hand against him, so he 43
received him with honor, and he introduced him to all his
Friends, and gave him presents, and instructed his Friends
and his forces to obey him as they would himself. And he 44
said to Jonathan,

"Why have you burdened all these people, when there
is no war between us? Come, send them home, and choose 45
yourself a few men to remain with you, and come with me
to Ptolemais and I will turn it over to you, together with the
rest of the strongholds and the rest of the forces and all
the officials, and I will go back again, for it was for this
that I came."

And he trusted him and did as he said and dismissed 46
his forces, and they returned to the land of Judah. He left 47
himself three thousand men, two thousand of whom he left
in Galilee, and one thousand went with him. But when 48
Jonathan entered Ptolemais, the people of Ptolemais closed
the gates and seized him, and all who had come in with
him they put to the sword. And Trypho sent forces and cav- 49
alry to Galilee and the great plain to destroy all Jonathan's
men. And they found out that he had been taken and had 50
perished with his men, but they encouraged one another
and marched away in close order, ready to fight. And when 51

12:38-51

their pursuers saw that they were ready to fight for their
52 lives, they turned back. And they all reached the land of
Judah unmolested, but they mourned over Jonathan and
his men, and they were greatly frightened; and all Israel
53 mourned for him bitterly. And all the heathen around
them tried to destroy them utterly, for they said,

"They have no leader or helper, so now let us make war
on them and destroy their memory from among men."

13] And Simon heard that Trypho had gathered a strong
2 force to invade the land of Judah and destroy it utterly. And
he saw that the people were trembling and alarmed, and he
3 went up to Jerusalem and gathered the people together
and encouraged them and said to them,

"You know yourselves all that I and my brothers and my
father's house have done for the laws and the sanctuary, and
4 the wars and hardships we have been through. As a result,
my brothers have all perished for Israel's sake, and I
5 alone am left. Now I never want to spare my own life in
6 any emergency, for I am no better than my brothers. But I
will avenge my nation and the sanctuary and your wives
and children, because all the heathen have gathered out of
hatred, to destroy us utterly."

7 And when they heard these words, the spirit of the people
8 revived, and they answered with a great shout,

"You are our leader, in the place of Judas and Jonathan
9 your brothers. Carry on our war, and we will do all that you
tell us."

10 So he called together all the fighting men, and made
haste to finish the walls of Jerusalem and put fortifications
11 around it. And he sent Jonathan, the son of Absalom, with a
considerable force to Joppa, and he drove out the men who
were in it and remained there in possession.

12 Then Trypho set out from Ptolemais with a strong force

to invade Judah, taking Jonathan with him in custody. But Simon pitched his camp in Adida facing the plain. And 13,14 Trypho learned that Simon had risen to take the place of his brother Jonathan and that he was going to make war on him, and he sent envoys to him, saying,

"It is for money that your brother Jonathan owed the 15 royal treasury in connection with the offices that he held, that we are holding him. So now send a hundred talents 16 of silver and two of his sons as hostages, so that when he is released he will not revolt against us, and we will let him go."

And Simon knew that they were speaking to him treach- 17 erously, but he sent to get the money and the children, so that he should not incur deep animosity on the part of the people, and they should say, "Because I did not send him 18 the money and the children, he perished." So he sent the 19 children and the hundred talents. But Trypho played him false and would not let Jonathan go. After this he came to 20 invade the country, and destroy it, and they went around by the road to Adora, and Simon and his army kept abreast of him everywhere he went. And the men in the citadel sent 21 envoys to Trypho urging him to come to them by way of the wild country and send them provisions. And Trypho got all 22 his cavalry ready to go, but that night there was a very heavy snow, and he could not go because of the snow, so he set forth and went into Gilead. And when he approached 23 Bascama, he killed Jonathan, and he was buried there. And 24 Trypho went back to his own country again.

And Simon sent and got the bones of his brother Jona- 25 than, and buried him in Modin, the town of his forefathers. And all Israel lamented him greatly and mourned over 26 him for a long time. And Simon built a monument over 27 the grave of his father and his brothers, and made it high

13:13-27

THE FIRST BOOK OF MACCABEES   431

so that it could be seen, with polished stone on back and
28 front. And he erected seven pyramids in a row, for his
29 father and his mother and his four brothers. And he made
devices for these, setting up great columns and putting on
the columns trophies of armor for an everlasting memorial,
and beside the armor carved prows of ships, so that they
30 could be seen by all who sailed the sea. Such was the monument that he built at Modin, and that still stands today.

31 Now Trypho dealt treacherously with King Antiochus
32 the younger and killed him and became king in his place
and assumed the diadem of Asia, and brought great calam-
33 ity upon the country. But Simon built the strongholds of
Judea and surrounded them with high towers and thick
walls and barred gates, and he stored up provisions in the
34 strongholds. And Simon chose men and sent them to King
Demetrius so that he should give the country relief, because
35 all that Trypho did was to plunder. And King Demetrius
sent him a message in these terms, and answered him and
wrote a letter, as follows:

36 "King Demetrius sends greeting to Simon, the high priest
and the Friend of kings, and to the Jewish elders and nation.
37 The gold crown and the palm branch which you sent we
have received, and we are ready to make a lasting peace
with you, and to write to our officials to grant you the im-
38 munities you ask. The things we have guaranteed to you
stand assured, and the strongholds which you have built
39 shall be yours. Any oversights and deficiencies up to this
time we forgive, as well as the crown tax that you owe, and
if any other tax was collected in Jerusalem, it shall no longer
40 be collected. And if any of you are suitable persons to be
enrolled at our court, they shall be so enrolled, and there
shall be peace between us."

41 It was in the one hundred and seventieth year that the

yoke of the heathen was lifted from Israel. And the people 42
began to write in their contracts and agreements, "In the
first year of Simon, the great high priest and governor and
commander of the Jews."

In those days he pitched his camp against Gazara, and 43
surrounded it with troops; and he built a siege engine and
brought it up to the town and attacked a tower and took it.
And the men who were on the engine sprang out into the 44
town. And there was a great stir in the town, and the 45
people of the town with their wives and children went up on
the wall with their clothes torn open and cried with a great
shout asking Simon to treat with them, and they said, 46

"Do not treat us as our wickedness deserves, but have
mercy on us."

So Simon came to terms with them and did not fight 47
them, but he put them out of the city and purified the houses
in which the idols were, and then he entered it with songs
and praise. And he expelled all impurity from it, and 48
settled men in it who observed the Law, and he fortified it
more strongly and built himself a dwelling there.

But the men in the citadel in Jerusalem were being kept 49
from going in and out of the country to buy and sell, and
they were famished and a good many of them died of starva-
tion. And they cried out to Simon to make terms with 50
them, and he did so. And he expelled them from it and
purified the citadel from its defilements. And they took 51
possession of it on the twenty-third day of the second
month in the one hundred and seventy-first year, with
praise and palm branches and with lyres and cymbals and
harps, and with hymns and songs, because a great enemy
had been destroyed out of Israel. And he decreed that they 52
should observe that day with gladness every year. And the
temple mount facing the citadel he fortified more strongly,

13:42-52

53 and he and his men lived there. And Simon saw that his son John was now a man and he made him commander of all his forces; and he lived in Gazara.

14] In the one hundred and seventy-second year King Demetrius gathered his forces and marched into Media
2 to obtain help so that he could fight against Trypho. And Arsaces, king of Persia and Media, heard that Demetrius had entered his territory and he sent one of his officers to
3 take him alive. And he went and defeated Demetrius' army and captured him and brought him to Arsaces, and he put him under guard.

4 And the land of Judah was at peace as long as Simon lived; he sought the good of his nation; his rule and his re-
5 nown pleased them all his life. With all his other glories, he took Joppa for a port and made it a way of access to
6 the islands of the sea. He enlarged the territory of his na-
7 tion, and became master of the land. He gathered many captives and made himself master of Gazara and Bethsura and the citadel, and he removed from it what defiled it, and
8 there was no one who could resist him. And they cultivated their land in peace, and the land yielded its produce, and
9 the trees in the plains bore their fruit. The old men sat in the streets; they all talked together of their well-being; and
10 the young men put on splendid warlike attire. He supplied the towns with provisions, and he furnished them with forti-fications, until his renown was spoken of to the ends of the
11 earth. He made peace in the land, and Israel rejoiced with
12 great joy. Each man sat under his vine and his fig tree, and
13 there was no one that could make them afraid. There was no one left in the land to fight them, and the kings were de-
14 stroyed in those days. He re-established all those of his people who had been humbled; he sought out the Law, and
15 removed everyone who was lawless and wicked. He made

the sanctuary glorious and increased the equipment of the
sanctuary.

It was reported in Rome and as far as Sparta that Jona- 16
than was dead, and they grieved bitterly. But when they 17
heard that his brother Simon had been made high priest
in his place, and that he was in control of the country and
the towns in it, they wrote to him on brass tablets to renew 18
with him the friendly relations and alliance they had
established with his brothers Judas and Jonathan; and they 19
were read before the assembly in Jerusalem. And this is the 20
copy of the letter which the Spartans sent:

"The chief magistrates and the city of the Spartans send
greeting to Simon, the chief priest, and to the elders and the
priests and the rest of the Jewish people, our kinsmen. The 21
envoys that were sent to our people told us of your splendor
and wealth, and we were glad of their coming. We have re- 22
corded what they said in the decrees of the people, as follows:

" 'Numenius, the son of Antiochus, and Antipater, the
son of Jason, envoys of the Jews, came to us to renew their
friendly relations with us. And the people were pleased to 23
receive the men with honor and to deposit the copy of what
they said among the public records, so that the Spartan people may have a record of it. And they sent a copy of this to
Simon the high priest.' "

After this Simon sent Numenius to Rome with a great 24
gold shield weighing a thousand pounds, to confirm their
alliance with them.

But when the people heard these things, they said, 25
"How shall we thank Simon and his sons? For he and his 26
brothers and his father's house have stood fast, and have
fought and driven from them the enemies of Israel, and
secured his freedom."

14:16–26

27 So they engraved it on brass tablets and set it on pillars on Mount Zion. And this is the copy of what they wrote: "On the eighteenth day of Elul, in the one hundred and seventy-second year—that is, the third year of the high 28 priesthood of Simon, the prince of God's people—in a great congregation of priests and people and leaders of the nation and elders of the country, this has been reported to us: 29 On the frequent occasions when wars have arisen in the country, Simon, the son of Mattathias the priest, of the descendants of Joarib, and his brothers have exposed themselves to danger and resisted the adversaries of their nation so that their sanctuary and their law might be upheld, and 30 they have reflected great glory upon their nation. Jonathan rallied their nation and became their high priest, and was 31 gathered to his people. And when their enemies resolved to 32 invade their country, and attack their sanctuary, Simon resisted them, and fought for his nation, and spent a great deal of money of his own, and armed the warlike men of his na-33 tion, and gave them wages. And he fortified the towns of Judea and Bethsura on the borders of Judea, where their enemies formerly kept their arms, and he stationed a garri-34 son of Jews there. And he fortified Joppa, on the seacoast, and Gazara, on the borders of Azotus, where their enemies formerly lived, and he settled Jews there, and all that was 35 necessary for the restoration of them he put in them. And when the people saw Simon's faithfulness and the glory that he designed to bring to his nation, they made him their leader and high priest, because he had done all these things and because of the uprightness and fidelity he had shown to his nation, and because he had sought in every way to exalt 36 his people. In his days matters prospered in his hands so that the heathen were driven out of their country, as well as those in the City of David, in Jerusalem, who had built

14:27–36

themselves a citadel, from which they would go out and pollute the surroundings of the sanctuary, and did great damage to its purity. He settled Jews in it and fortified it to 37 make the land and the city safe, and he made the walls of Jerusalem high. In view of these things, King Demetrius 38 confirmed him in the high priesthood, and made him one 39 of his Friends, and treated him with great honor. For he 40 had heard that the Jews had been addressed by the Romans as friends and allies and kinsmen, and that they had received Simon's envoys with great honor. And the Jews and 41 their priests resolved that Simon should be their leader and high priest forever until a true prophet should appear, and 42 that he should be their general, to appoint them to their duties, and to set them over the country and over the arms and over the fortifications; and that he should take care of the sanctuary, and that all should obey him, and that all 43 contracts in the country should be dated in his reign and that he should be clothed in purple and wear gold. And no 44 one of the people or of the priests shall be allowed to set aside any of these things, or to contradict what he shall say or to gather an assembly in the country without him, or to be clothed in purple or pin on a gold buckle. Whoever dis- 45 obeys these actions or disregards any of them shall be liable to punishment."

And all the people agreed to decree that they should do 46 these things to Simon, and Simon accepted them and agreed 47 to be high priest and general and governor of the Jews and the priests, and to preside over them all. And they ordered 48 that this decree should be inscribed on brass tablets and that they should be set up in a conspicuous place in the sanctuary enclosure, and that copies of it be deposited in the treasury, so that Simon and his sons might have it. 49

And Antiochus, the son of King Demetrius, sent a letter [15

14:37–15:1

from the islands of the sea to Simon, the priest and governor
2 of the Jews, and to the whole nation, and it ran as follows:
"King Antiochus sends greeting to Simon, the chief priest
3 and governor, and to the Jewish nation. As some ruffians
have made themselves masters of the kingdom of our forefathers, and I wish to claim the kingdom, so that I may restore it to its former state, and have raised a large force of
4 mercenaries and prepared ships of war, and propose to land
in the country to go in search of the men who have ruined
our country and have laid waste many towns in my king-
5 dom, I now guarantee to you all the immunities which the
kings before me have granted you, and whatever other gifts
6 they have released you from. And I give you authority to coin
7 money for your country with your own stamp, and Jerusalem and the sanctuary shall be free, and all the arms you
have prepared and the strongholds you have built and now
8 hold, shall remain yours. And any royal obligation and all
future royal obligations shall be remitted for you from this
9 time forth forever. And when we get possession of our kingdom, we will greatly glorify you and your nation and the
temple so that your glory will be visible to the whole earth."
10 In the one hundred and seventy-fourth year Antiochus
went forth into the country of his forefathers, and all the
troops joined him, so there were very few left with Trypho.
11 And Antiochus pursued him, and he came in his flight to
12 Dor by the sea, for he knew that misfortune had overtaken
13 him and his troops had deserted him. And Antiochus
pitched his camp against Dor with a hundred and twenty
14 thousand soldiers and eight thousand horse. And he surrounded the town, and ships joined in the attack from the
sea, and he pressed the town hard by land and sea, and did
not allow anyone to go out or in.
15 And Numenius and his companions came back from

Rome with letters to the kings and the countries, in which this was written:

"Lucius, consul of the Romans, sends greeting to King 16 Ptolemy. The envoys of the Jews have come to us as our 17 friends and allies, to renew the old friendly relations and alliance, having been sent by Simon, the high priest, and the Jewish people, and they have brought a gold shield 18 weighing a thousand pounds. It is our pleasure therefore 19 to write to the kings and the countries not to injure them or fight them or their towns or their country, and not to ally themselves with those who fight against them. And we have 20 determined to accept the shield from them. So if any mis- 21 creants flee from their country to you, hand them over to Simon, the high priest, so that he may punish them in accordance with their law."

He wrote the same message to King Demetrius and to At- 22 talus, and to Ariarathes, and to Arsaces, and to all the 23 countries, and to Sampsames and the Spartans, and to Delos, and to Myndos, and to Sicyon, and to Caria, and to Samos, and to Pamphylia, and to Lycia, and to Halicarnassus, and to Rhodes, and to Phaselis, and to Cos, and to Side, and to Aradus and Gortyna and Cnidus and Cyprus and Cyrene. And they wrote a copy for Simon, the high 24 priest.

And King Antiochus attacked Dor on the second day, 25 continually throwing his forces against it, and erecting war engines, and he prevented Trypho from going in or out. And Simon sent him two thousand picked men to fight for 26 him, and silver and gold and a quantity of war material. But he would not accept them but disregarded all the 27 agreements he had made with him before, and he was estranged from him. And he sent one of his Friends named 28 Athenobius to him, to confer with him, saying,

"You are holding Joppa and Gazara, and the citadel in

29 Jerusalem, cities of my kingdom. You have laid waste their territories and done great injury to the country, and you
30 have taken possession of many places in my kingdom. So now give up the towns that you have seized, and the tribute of the places you have taken possession of outside the bor-
31 ders of Judea, or else give me five hundred talents of silver for them, and five hundred talents of silver more, for the damage you have done and for the tribute of the towns; or else we will come and make war on you."

32 So Athenobius the king's Friend came to Jerusalem, and saw Simon's splendor, and the sideboard with gold and silver plate and his great pomp, and he was amazed; and he
33 gave him the king's message. And Simon said to him in reply,

"We have neither taken other men's land, nor are we in
34 possession of other men's property, but of the inheritance of our forefathers; it was wrongfully held by our enemies at one time, but we, grasping our opportunity, hold firmly
35 the inheritance of our forefathers. But as for Joppa and Gazara, which you demand, while they have done great damage to our people and in our country, we will give a hundred talents for them."

36 He made him no answer, but went back to the king in anger, and reported these words to him, and Simon's splendor and all that he had seen, and the king was extremely angry.

37 But Trypho embarked on a ship and fled to Orthosia.
38 And the king appointed Cendebaeus commander-in-chief
39 of the seacoast, and gave him infantry and cavalry, and ordered him to pitch his camp before Judea, and he ordered him to wall Kedron and fortify its gates and fight against
40 the people, but the king pursued Trypho. And Cendebaeus arrived at Jamnia, and began to provoke the people and to invade Judea, and to take the people captive and to kill

them. And he built the walls of Kedron, and he stationed 41
cavalry and other forces there, so that they might go out
and make raids on the highways of Judea, as the king had
ordered him to do.

And John went up from Gazara and told his father [16
Simon what Cendebaeus had done. And Simon called in 2
his two eldest sons, Judas and John, and said to them,

"I and my brothers and my father's house have fought the
battles of Israel from our youth until today, and we have
succeeded in delivering Israel many times. But now I am 3
old, and you by his mercy are old enough; you must take
my place and my brother's, and go out and fight for our
nation, and the help that comes from heaven be with
you!"

And he chose twenty thousand soldiers and cavalry from 4
the country, and they marched against Cendebaeus and
spent the night at Modin. And they got up in the morning 5
and marched into the plain, and here a great force came
to meet them, horse and foot, and there was a stream between them. And he encamped opposite them, with his 6
people. And he saw that his people were afraid to cross the
stream, so he crossed first; and his men saw him and
they crossed after him. And he divided the people, putting 7
the cavalry in the midst of the infantry, for the enemy's
cavalry were very numerous. And they sounded the 8
trumpets, and Cendebaeus and his army were routed, and
many of them fell wounded, and those who were left fled to
the stronghold. At that time Judas, John's brother, was 9
wounded, but John pursued them until he came to Kedron,
which had been walled. And they fled to the towers in the 10
fields of Azotus, and he burned it up, and fully two thousand of them fell. And he returned to Judea in peace.

Now Ptolemy, the son of Abubus, had been appointed 11

governor over the plain of Jericho, and he had a great deal
12 of silver and gold, for he was the son-in-law of the high
13 priest. And his heart was elated and he plotted deceitfully
14 against Simon and his sons, to remove them. Simon was making visits to the towns in the country, and providing for their care. And he went down to Jericho with his sons Mattathias and Judas, in the one hundred and seventy-seventh year, in
15 the eleventh month, the month of Shebat. And Abubus' son deceitfully entertained them in the fortress called Dok, which he had built, and he had a great banquet for them,
16 and he had men hidden there. And when Simon and his sons were drunk, Ptolemy and his men got up and got their weapons and went to the banquet hall to attack Simon and
17 killed him and his two sons and some of his servants. So he committed an act of great treachery and returned evil
18 for good. And Ptolemy wrote of this and sent it to the king, so that he might send troops to his aid, and that he might
19 turn over to him their country and towns. And he sent others to Gazara to make away with John, and he sent letters to the colonels, telling them to come to him, so that
20 he might give them silver and gold and presents; and he sent others to take possession of Jerusalem, and the temple
21 mount. And a man ran ahead to Gazara and informed John that his father and his brothers had perished, and said, "He has sent to kill you also!"
22 He was greatly amazed when he heard it, and he seized the men who came to destroy him and killed them, for he knew that they meant to destroy him.
23 The rest of the acts of John, and his wars and the exploits that he performed, and the building of the walls that he ef-
24 fected, and his deeds—behold, they are written in the chronicles of his high priesthood, from the time that he became high priest after his father.

16:12–24

THE SECOND BOOK OF MACCABEES

II Maccabees is not a continuation of I Maccabees but a parallel account, covering the years 175–160 B.C. *Its author describes it as an abridgment of a five-book work by Jason of Cyrene which he condensed with the aim of making the material more attractive and useful (2.24). It is neither. Though it too rests ultimately on eyewitness accounts it is more emotional, more rhetorical, more stilted, and more obviously propagandistic. The story of the martyrdom of Eleazar and of the seven youths with their mother (chapters 6 and 7), which is probably the best-known section of the book, is more effectively told in IV Maccabees (not in the Apocrypha), where it is the central subject.*

THE SECOND BOOK
OF MACCABEES

1] **T**O THE JEWISH BROTHERS IN EGYPT, THE
Jewish brothers in Jerusalem and the land of Judea
2 send greetings and wish you perfect peace. May God
bless you, and remember his agreement with Abraham,
3 Isaac, and Jacob, his faithful slaves, and give you all a mind
to worship him and do his will with a stout heart and a
4 willing spirit. May he open your mind with his Law and his
5 statutes, and make peace and listen to your prayers and be
6 reconciled to you, and not forsake you in adversity. This is
7 our prayer for you here. In the reign of Demetrius, in the
one hundred and sixty-ninth year, we Jews wrote you in the
extreme distress that overtook us in those years, from the
time that Jason and his men revolted from the holy land
8 and the kingdom, and set fire to the gateway and shed innocent blood. And we besought the Lord, and were heard,
and we offered sacrifice and the meal offering, and we
9 lighted the lamps, and set out the Presentation Loaves. And
10 you must keep the Camping Out festival in the month
of Chislev. The one hundred and eighty-eighth year.

Those who are in Jerusalem and those in Judea and the
senate and Judas send greetings and good wishes to Aristo-
bulus, the teacher of King Ptolemy, who is of the stock of
11 the anointed priests, and to the Jews in Egypt. As we have
been saved by God from great dangers, we offer devout
thanks to him as men who array themselves against a king;
12 for he drove out those who arrayed themselves against him
13 in the holy city. For when their leader reached Persia, with
an army about him that seemed irresistible, they were cut
down in the temple of Nanaea, through treachery on the
14 part of the priests of Nanaea. For Antiochus with his

Friends came to the place on the pretext of marrying her, in order to get a large sum of money by way of dowry. And 15 when the priests of the temple of Nanaea had brought out the money, and he had come with a few followers inside the wall of the temple inclosure, they shut the temple when Antiochus had gone in, and opened the secret door in the 16 ceiling, and threw stones and struck down the leader, and dismembered him and threw their heads to the people who were outside. (Blessed in every way be our God who 17 brought the impious to justice!)

As we are about to celebrate the purification of the 18 temple, on the twenty-fifth day of the month of Chislev, we think it necessary to inform you, so that you too may observe the Camping Out festival and the kindling of the fire, when Nehemiah, who built the temple and the altar, offered sacrifices. For when our forefathers were being taken to 19 Persia, the pious priests of that day took some of the fire on the altar and hid it secretly in the hollow of an empty cistern, where they made it secure, so that the place was unknown to anyone. Many years after, when it pleased 20 God, Nehemiah was commissioned by the king of Persia, and sent the descendants of the priests who had hidden the fire to get it. But when they reported to us that they could not find any fire but only muddy water, he ordered them 21 to dip some out and bring it to him. And when the things to be sacrificed had been put in place, Nehemiah ordered the priests to sprinkle the water on the wood and the things that were laid on it. And when this was done and some time 22 had passed, and the sun, which had been clouded over, shone out, a great blaze was kindled, so that they all wondered. And the priests uttered a prayer while the 23 sacrifice was being consumed--the priests and all present,

1:15-23

Jonathan leading and the rest responding, as Nehemiah
24 did. And this was the prayer:

"O Lord, Lord God, creator of all things, who are terrible
and strong and upright and merciful, who alone are king
25 and good, the only patron, who alone are upright and almighty and eternal, who save Israel from every evil, who
26 chose our forefathers and sanctified them, accept this
sacrifice on behalf of all your people Israel, and watch over
27 your allotment, and make it holy. Gather together our
scattered people, set at liberty those who are in slavery
among the heathen, look upon those who are despised and
abhorred, and let the heathen know that you are our God.
28 Afflict our oppressors and those who are violent in their
29 arrogance. Plant your people in your holy place, as Moses
said."

30,31 Then the priests struck up the hymns. And when the
things that were sacrificed were consumed, Nehemiah
ordered them to pour the water that was left on large stones.
32 And when this was done, a flame was kindled, but when the
33 light shone back from the altar, it went out. And when the
thing became known, and the king of Persia was told that in
the place where the priests that were deported had hidden
the fire, water had appeared, and with it Nehemiah's people
34 had burned up the things they sacrificed, the king, after in-
vestigating the matter, made the place a sacred inclosure,
35 and the king exchanged many different gifts with his favor-
36 ites. Nehemiah's people called this Nephthar, which is
translated "Purification," but most people call it Nephthai.

2} It is also found in the records that the prophet Jeremiah
ordered those who were carried away to take some of the
2 fire, as has been described, and that after giving them the
Law, the prophet charged those who were carried away not
to forget the Lord's commands, and not to be led astray in

1:24–2:2

their minds when they saw gold and silver idols and their ornamentation. And with other similar exhortations he 3 told them that the Law should not pass from their hearts. It was also in the writing that the prophet, in obedience 4 to a revelation, gave orders that the tent and the ark should accompany him, and that he went away to the mountain where Moses went up and beheld God's inheritance. And 5 Jeremiah came and found a cave-dwelling, and he took the tent and the ark and the incense altar into it, and he blocked up the door. And some of those who followed him came up 6 to mark the road, and they could not find it. But when 7 Jeremiah found it out, he blamed them and said,

"The place shall be unknown until God gathers the congregation of his people together and shows his mercy. Then 8 the Lord will show where they are, and the glory of the Lord will appear, as they were shown in the days of Moses, and when Solomon asked that the place might be made very sacred." It was also stated that he, in his wisdom, offered a 9 dedicatory sacrifice at the completion of the temple, and 10 just as Moses prayed to the Lord, and fire came down from heaven and consumed the offerings, so Solomon also prayed, and the fire came down and burned up the whole burnt offerings. And Moses said, 11

"Because the sin offering had not been eaten, it was consumed."

In like manner Solomon also kept the eight days. 12

The same thing was related also in the records and 13 memoirs about Nehemiah, and that he founded a library and collected the books about the kings and the prophets, and the works of David, and royal letters about sacred gifts. In like manner Judas also collected for us all the books that 14 had been scattered because of the outbreak of war, and they are in our hands. So, if you want them, send men to get 15 them for you.

2:3-15

16 So as we are about to celebrate the Purification, we write
17 to you. Please observe these days. It is God that has saved
all his people and given them back their heritage and king-
18 dom and priesthood and consecration, as he promised
through the Law; for in God we have hope that he will
speedily have mercy on us, and gather us together from
under heaven to the holy place, for he has delivered us from
great misfortunes and has purified the place.

19 Now the story of Judas Maccabeus and his brothers, and
the purification of the great temple, and the rededication
20 of the altar, and also of the wars with Antiochus Epiphanes
21 and his son Eupator, and the heavenly manifestations
shown to those who zealously championed the Jewish
religion, so that few as they were, they plundered the whole
22 country and drove out the barbarian hordes and recovered
the world-renowned temple, and freed the city, and restored
the laws which were on the point of being destroyed, since
the Lord, with great forbearance had shown mercy to them
23 —all this, as related by Jason of Cyrene in five books, we
24 will try to condense into one volume. For in view of the
flood of statistics and the difficulty created by the abundance of the material, for those who wish to plunge into the
25 historical narratives, we have aimed at attracting those who
like to read, and at making it easy for those who are disposed to memorize, and at being of use to all our readers.
26 For us, who have taken upon ourselves the painful task of
abridgment, the thing is not easy, and takes sweat and mid-
27 night oil, just as it is no easy matter for a man who prepares
a banquet and strives to benefit others. Still, to win the
gratitude of so many, we will gladly endure the painful task,
28 leaving to the historian the investigation of details, but tak-
29 ing pains to follow the lines of an epitome. For as the
builder of a new house must have the whole structure in
mind, while the man who undertakes to decorate and paint

2:16–29

it has only to seek out what is suitable for its adornment, so I
think it is with us. To enter upon the subject and discuss 30
matters fully and elaborate the details is the task of the original historian, but one who re-writes it must be permitted 31
to seek brevity of expression, and to forego the labored treatment of the matter. Here then let us begin the story, with- 32
out adding more to what has already been said; for it is
foolish to write a long preface to the history and then ab-
breviate the history itself.

When the holy city was inhabited in perfect peace, and [3
the laws were strictly observed, because of the piety of
Onias, the high priest, and his hatred of wickedness, it came 2
to pass that even the kings themselves did honor to the place,
and glorified the temple with most noble gifts, so that even 3
Seleucus, king of Asia, from his own revenues provided all
the expense of the sacrificial service. But a man named 4
Simon, of the tribe of Benjamin, who had been appointed
governor of the temple, had a difference with the high priest
about the conduct of the city market. When he failed to 5
carry his point against Onias, he went to Apollonius of
Tarsus, who was at that time governor of Coelesyria and
Phoenicia, and reported to him that the treasury in Jerusa- 6
lem was full of such untold quantities of money that the
amount of the funds was beyond computation; and that
they did not belong to the account of the sacrifices and they
might fall under the control of the king. When Apollonius 7
met the king, he informed him of the money that had been
pointed out to him. And he appointed Heliodorus, who was
his chancellor, and sent him with instructions to effect the
removal of this money. Heliodorus immediately set out on 8
his journey, under the guise of visiting the towns of Coelesyria and Phoenicia, but in reality to carry out the king's
design.

2:30–3:8

9 When he reached Jerusalem, and had been cordially welcomed by the high priest and the city, he laid before them the disclosure that had been made to him, and explained why he had come, and inquired whether this was really true. 10 The high priest pointed out that some deposits belonged to 11 widows and orphans, and one belonged to Hyrcanus, son of Tobias, a man of very high position—so falsely had the impious Simon spoken; that it all amounted to four hundred 12 talents of silver and two hundred of gold, and that it was absolutely impossible that those who were relying on the sacredness of the place and on the sanctity and inviolability of the temple, which was respected all over the world, should be wronged. 13 But Heliodorus, because of the royal orders he had received, said that anyway this must be confiscated for the 14 royal treasury. So he set a day, and went in to conduct an inspection of these funds; and there was no little distress 15 all over the city. The priests in their priestly robes threw themselves down before the altar, and called to heaven on him who had given the law about deposits to keep these 16 safe for those who had deposited them. One could not observe the appearance of the high priest without being pierced to the heart, for his expression and his change of 17 color revealed the anguish of his soul. For terror and bodily shuddering had come over the man, which plainly showed to those who looked at him the pain that was in his heart. 18 Moreover the people in the houses came flocking out to make a general supplication because the place was on the 19 point of being treated with contempt. The women, with sackcloth girt under their breasts, thronged the streets, while maidens who were kept indoors ran together, some to the gateways, some to the walls, and some looked out from the 20 windows; and all raised their hands to heaven and uttered

3:9–20

their supplication. One could not help pitying the multi- **21**
tude, all prostrating themselves in a body, and the anxiety
of the high priest in his great anguish.

While they therefore called upon the Almighty Lord to **22**
keep the things that had been intrusted to him in perfect
security for those who had intrusted them to him, Heliodo- **23**
rus was carrying out what had been decided upon. But no **24**
sooner had he and his guards arrived before the treasury
than the Sovereign of spirits and of all authority caused a
great manifestation so that all who had been daring enough
to come with him were appalled at the power of God and
fainted with terror. For there appeared to them a horse **25**
with a dreadful rider, adorned with magnificent trappings,
and rushing swiftly at Heliodorus it struck at him with its
forefeet. His rider seemed clad in golden armor. Two **26**
young men also appeared to him, remarkably strong and
gloriously beautiful and splendidly dressed, who stood on
each side of him and flogged him continually, inflicting
many stripes on him. He fell suddenly to the ground and **27**
was enveloped in deep darkness, and men picked him up
and put him on a stretcher and carried him off—the man **28**
that had just entered that treasury with a great retinue and
his whole guard but was now rendered helpless—and they
clearly recognized the sovereign power of God. So through **29**
the divine intervention he lay prostrate, bereft of all hope
of deliverance, while they blessed the Lord who had **30**
marvellously honored his own place; and the temple, which
a little while before had been full of fear and commotion,
now that the Almighty Lord had manifested himself was
filled with joy and gladness.

Some of the intimate friends of Heliodorus soon asked **31**
Onias to call upon the Most High and grant him his life, as
he lay at his very last gasp. The high priest suspected that **32**

:21–32

the king might form the opinion that some villainy had been practiced upon Heliodorus by the Jews, and offered a
33 sacrifice for the man's recovery. But as the high priest was offering the sacrifice of propitiation, the same young men again appeared to Heliodorus, clad in the same clothes, and they stood beside him and said,

"Be very grateful to Onias the high priest, for the Lord
34 has spared your life for his sake; and since you have been flogged from heaven, proclaim to all men the sovereign power of God."

35 When they had said this, they vanished. So Heliodorus offered a sacrifice to the Lord and made very great vows to him who had saved his life, and after a friendly meeting with
36 Onias marched back to the king. And he bore witness before all men to the deeds of the supreme God which he had seen.

37 When the king asked Heliodorus what kind of man was suitable to be sent once more to Jerusalem, he said,

38 "If you have an enemy or a conspirator against the government, send him there, and you will get him back soundly flogged, if he escapes with his life, for there is cer-
39 tainly some divine power about the place. For he whose dwelling is in heaven watches over that place and helps it, and strikes down and destroys those who come to injure it."

40 This was the way the matter of Heliodorus and the protection of the treasury turned out.

4] But this Simon who had informed about the money and against his country, made accusations against Onias, saying that he had incited Heliodorus and had been the actual au-
2 thor of these troubles. He dared to charge with conspiracy against the government the benefactor of the city, the pro-
3 tector of his countrymen, and the champion of the laws! But when his enmity reached such a point that murders were

committed by one of Simon's trusted men, Onias, becoming 4
aware of the danger of their contention, and that Apollonius, the son of Menestheus, the governor of Coelesyria
and Phoenicia, was increasing Simon's malice, resorted 5
to the king, not to be an accuser of his fellow-citizens, but as
looking after the welfare, public and private, of all the people; for he saw that without the king's interest it was im- 6
possible for the government to secure peace again, and that
Simon would not abandon his folly.

But when Seleucus departed this life and Antiochus, who 7
was called Epiphanes, succeeded to the kingdom, Onias'
brother Jason obtained the high priesthood by corruption,
promising the king in his petition three hundred and sixty 8
talents of silver, and eighty talents from other revenues.
Besides this he promised to pay a hundred and fifty more, 9
if he was given authority to set up a gymnasium and a training place for youth there and to enrol the people of Jerusalem as citizens of Antioch. When the king had consented, 10
and he had taken office, he immediately brought his countrymen over to the Greek way of living. He set aside the royal 11
ordinances especially favoring the Jews, secured through
John, the father of Eupolemus, who went on the mission to
the Romans to establish friendly relations and an alliance
with them, and abrogating the lawful ways of living he
introduced new customs contrary to the Law. For he 12
willingly established a gymnasium right under the citadel,
and he made the finest of the young men wear the Greek
hat. And to such a pitch did the cultivation of Greek 13
fashions and the coming-in of foreign customs rise, because
of the excessive wickedness of this godless Jason, who was no
high priest at all, that the priests were no longer earnest 14
about the services of the altar, but disdaining the sanctuary
and neglecting the sacrifices, they hurried to take part in the

4:4–14

unlawful exercises in the wrestling school, after the summons
15 to the discus-throwing, regarding as worthless the things
their forefathers valued, and thinking Greek standards the
16 finest. As a result, they found themselves in a trying situation, for those whose mode of life they cultivated, and whom
they wished to imitate exactly, became their enemies and
17 punished them. For it is no small matter to sin against the
laws of God, as the period that followed will show.

18 Now when the quinquennial games were being held at
19 Tyre, and the king was present, the vile Jason sent envoys
who were citizens of Antioch to represent Jerusalem, to
carry three hundred silver drachmas for the sacrifice to
Hercules. But even those who carried it thought it should
not be used for a sacrifice, as that was not fitting, but should
20 be spent in some other way. So this money intended by its
sender for the sacrifice to Hercules, was applied because of
those who carried it to the fitting out of triremes.

21 When Apollonius, the son of Menestheus, was sent into
Egypt to attend the coronation of King Philometor, Antiochus, learning that the latter was disaffected toward his government, took measures for his own security, so he came to
22 Joppa and visited Jerusalem. He was magnificently welcomed by Jason and received with torches and acclamations.
Then he marched into Phoenicia.

23 After the lapse of three years, Jason sent Menelaus, the
brother of this Simon, to take the money to the king and to
24 present papers relating to necessary business. But he, on
being presented to the king, extolled him with such apparent
authority that he obtained the high priesthood for himself,
25 outbidding Jason by three hundred talents of silver. Upon
receiving the royal commission, he came back, possessing
nothing that qualified him for the high priesthood, but with
the passions of a savage tyrant and the rage of a wild beast.

So Jason, who had supplanted his own brother, was sup- 26
planted by another, and driven as a fugitive into the country
of the Ammonites. So Menelaus held the office, but he 27
did not pay any of the money he had promised to the king,
and when Sostratus, the governor of the citadel, demanded
it, for it was his duty to collect the revenues, the two men 28
were summoned by the king to appear before him on account of it. Menelaus left his brother Lysimachus to act 29
in his place in the high priesthood, and Sostratus left
Crates, the viceroy of Cyprus, to act in his.

In this state of things, the people of Tarsus and Mallus 30
made an insurrection because they had been given as a
present to Antiochis, the king's mistress. So the king went in 31
haste to Cilicia to adjust matters there, leaving a man of
high rank named Andronicus to act in his place. Then 32
Menelaus, thinking he had found a favorable opening, presented Andronicus with some gold dishes from the temple,
which he had appropriated; he had already sold others at
Tyre and the neighboring towns. When Onias was certain 33
of this, he sternly rebuked him, after retiring to a place of
sanctuary at Daphne, near Antioch. So Menelaus took 34
Andronicus aside and urged him to arrest Onias. And he
went to Onias, and having been persuaded to use treachery,
offered him sworn pledges and gave him his right hand,
and persuaded him, notwithstanding his suspicions, to
leave his sanctuary, and immediately without regard to
justice put him in prison. This made not only Jews but 35
many people of other nationalities indignant and angry over
the wicked murder of the man. And when the king came 36
back from Cilicia, the Jews in the city, with the support of
the Greeks who abhorred the crime, appealed to him about
the unjustifiable killing of Onias. So Antiochus, as he was 37
sincerely sorry, and moved to pity, and shed tears over the

4:26–37

38 sober and well-ordered life of the departed, in a fiery passion
stripped the purple robe from Andronicus and tore off his
underclothes and led him about through the whole city to
the very place where he had sinned against Onias, and there
he dispatched the murderer, and the Lord rendered him the
punishment he deserved.

39   When many thefts from the temple had been committed
in the city by Lysimachus with the connivance of Menelaus,
and the report of them spread abroad, the people gathered
against Lysimachus, as a great deal of gold plate had al-
40 ready been scattered. But when the people made an uprising and were inflamed with anger, Lysimachus armed about
three thousand men, and commenced hostilities with a man
named Avaranus, who was as foolish as he was aged, in
41 command. And when they were aware of Lysimachus'
attack, some picked up stones and others sticks of wood and
others caught up handfuls of the ashes that were lying about,
42 and flung them pell-mell at Lysimachus and his men. As a
result, they wounded many of them, and felled many, and
put them all to flight, and the temple-robber himself they
killed beside the treasury.

43   Charges were made against Menelaus about this affair,
44 and when the king visited Tyre, the three men sent by the
45 senate presented the case before him. Menelaus was now
facing defeat, but he promised a large sum of money to
46 Ptolemy, son of Dorymenes, to prevail upon the king. So
Ptolemy took the king aside into a colonnade, as if to take
47 the air, and persuaded him to change his mind, and he
acquitted Menelaus, who was to blame for all the trouble,
of the charges against him, and condemned to death the
wretched men who would have been dismissed as innocent
48 if they had pleaded even before Scythians. So the advocates
of the city and the people and the sacred plate promptly

4:38–48

suffered this unjust punishment. This caused some Tyrians, 49
in their detestation of the crime, to provide magnificently for
their burial. But Menelaus, because of the covetousness of 50
the authorities, remained in power, increasing in wickedness and persistently plotting against his fellow-citizens.

About that time Antiochus made his second attack upon [5
Egypt. And it happened that all over the city for about 2
forty days, there appeared horsemen charging in mid-air, in
robes inwrought with gold, fully armed, in companies, with
spears and drawn swords; squadrons of cavalry drawn up, 3
charges and countercharges taking place on this side and on
that, with brandishing of shields, forests of spears, showers
of missiles, the flash of gold trappings, and armor of every
kind. Therefore all men prayed that the manifestation be- 4
tokened good.

There arose a false rumor that Antiochus had departed 5
this life, and Jason took fully a thousand men and made a
sudden attack upon the city. As the troops upon the walls
gave way, and the city was already virtually captured,
Menelaus took refuge in the citadel. Then Jason unspar- 6
ingly slaughtered his fellow-citizens, regardless of the fact
that success gained over one's kindred is the greatest failure,
and fancying that he was winning trophies from his
enemies, not from his countrymen. He did not get control 7
of the government, however, and in the end got only shame
from his conspiracy, and had to take refuge again as a fugitive in the country of the Ammonites. So finally he met a 8
miserable end; accused before Aretas, the sovereign of
Arabians, fleeing from city to city, pursued by all men,
hated as an apostate from the laws, and abhorred as the
butcher of his country and his fellow-citizens, he was driven
into Egypt, and he who had sent many from their own coun- 9
try into exile died in a strange land, crossing the sea to the

4:49–5:9

Lacedaemonians hoping to find protection there because
10 of his relationship to them. So he who had thrown many out
to lie unburied had none to mourn for him, and had no
funeral at all and no place in the tomb of his forefathers.
11 When news of what had happened reached the king, he
thought that Judea was in revolt; so he set out from Egypt
12 like a wild beast and took the city by storm. And he
ordered his soldiers to cut down without distinction anyone
13 they met and to slay those who took refuge in their houses.
Then there was a massacre of young and old, an annihilation of boys, women and children, a slaughter of girls and
14 babies. In no more than three days eighty thousand people
were destroyed, forty thousand of them in hand-to-hand encounter, and as many were sold into slavery as were slain.
15 Not content with this, he dared to go into the most holy
temple in all the world, guided by Menelaus who had be-
16 trayed both the laws and his country; and took the sacred
plate in his polluted hands, and with his profane hands he
swept away what had been dedicated by other kings to en-
17 hance the glory and honor of the place. In the elation of
his spirit, Antiochus did not realize that it was because of
the sins of the inhabitants of the city that the Lord was
angered for a little, so that he had not had regard for the
18 place. But if they had not happened to be entangled in so
many sins this man, like Heliodorus, who was sent by King
Seleucus to inspect the treasury, would have been flogged
and turned back from his presumptuous purpose as soon as
19 he approached. But the Lord did not select the nation for
the sake of the place, but the place for the sake of the nation.
20 Therefore the place itself, after sharing in the misfortunes
that overtook the nation, participated afterward in its benefits; and what was forsaken by the Almighty in his wrath

5:10–20

was restored in all its glory when its great Master became reconciled to it.

So Antiochus carried away eighteen hundred talents from 21 the temple, and hurried off to Antioch, thinking in his arrogance that he would make the land navigable and the sea traversable on foot, he was so intoxicated in mind. And 22 to harass the people he left governors—in Jerusalem, Philip, a Phrygian by nationality, but in character more barbarous than the man who appointed him; in Gerizim, Andronicus, 23 and besides these, Menelaus, who was worse than the others in his overbearing treatment of his townsmen. In his hostile attitude to the Jewish citizens, he sent Apollonius, the 24 Mysian captain, with a force of twenty-two thousand, with orders to slay all the grown men, and to sell the women and younger men as slaves. When this man arrived at Jeru- 25 salem, he pretended to be peacefully disposed, and waited till the holy sabbath day; then finding the Jews refraining from work, he ordered his men to parade under arms and 26 put to the sword all those who came out to see them, and rushing into the city with his armed men he destroyed them in great multitudes. But Judas Maccabeus with some nine 27 others got away to the wild country and kept himself alive with his comrades in the mountains as wild animals do, and they lived on what grew wild rather than suffer pollution with the rest.

Not long after, the king sent an old Athenian to force the [6 Jews to forsake the laws of their forefathers and cease to live according to the laws of God, but to pollute the temple in 2 Jerusalem and to call it that of the Olympian Zeus, and to call the one in Gerizim that of Zeus the Hospitable, in keeping with the character of those who lived there. This harsh- 3 ly and most grievously intensified the evil. For the heathen 4 filled the temple with profligacy and revelry, amusing them-

selves with prostitutes and lying with women within the sacred precincts, and bringing into it things that were for-
5 bidden. The altar was covered with abominable offerings,
6 which the laws forbade. A man could not keep the sabbath or celebrate the festivals of his forefathers, or admit he
7 was a Jew at all. On the monthly celebration of the king's birthday, they were taken by bitter necessity to taste the sacrifices, and when the festival of Dionysus was celebrated, they were compelled to wear wreaths of ivy and march in
8 procession in his honor. At Ptolemy's suggestion a decree was issued to the neighboring Greek towns, that they should adopt the same policy toward the Jews and make them
9 taste the sacrifices, and that they should slay any who would not agree to adopt Greek customs. So anyone could see how
10 their misery was intensified. For two women were brought in for circumcising their children, and they led them publicly about the city with their babies hanging at their breasts,
11 and then threw them down from the top of the wall. Others who had gathered in caves near by, to keep the seventh day in secret, were betrayed to Philip and all burned together, because they had scruples about defending themselves, in their respect for the dignity of that most holy day.
12 So I beseech those who read this book not to be cast down by such misfortunes but to consider that these punishments were meant not for the destruction of our people but for
13 their correction. For it is a mark of great benevolence not to let the impious alone for a long time but to punish them
14 promptly. For in the case of other nations, the Master is long-suffering and waits before he punishes them until they
15 have reached the full measure of their sins; but in our case he has decided differently, so that he may not take vengeance on us afterward when our sins have reached their
16 height. So he never withdraws his mercy from us, and al-

though he disciplines us with misfortune, he does not abandon his own people. This much let us say by way of reminder; after these few words we must resume our story. 17

Eleazar, one of the leading scribes, a man of advanced 18 age and fine appearance, was being forced to open his mouth and eat pork. But he, welcoming a glorious death in 19 preference to a life of pollution went up of his own accord to the torture wheel, setting an example of how those 20 should come forward who are steadfast enough to refuse food which it is wrong to taste even for the natural love of life. Those who were in charge of that unlawful sacrificial 21 meal, because of their long-standing acquaintance with the man, took him aside, and privately urged him to bring meat provided by himself, which he could properly make use of, and pretend that he was eating the meat of the sacrifice, as the king had ordered, so that by doing this he might escape 22 the death penalty, and on account of his lifelong friendship with them be kindly treated. But he, making a high resolve, 23 worthy of his years and the dignity of his age and the hoary hair which he reached with such distinction, and his admirable life even from his childhood, and still more of the holy and divine legislation, declared himself in accord with these, telling them to send him down to Hades at once.

"For," said he, "it does not become our time of life to 24 pretend, and so lead many young people to suppose that Eleazar when ninety years old has gone over to heathenism, and to be led astray through me, because of my pretense for 25 the sake of this short and insignificant life, while I defile and disgrace my old age. For even if for the present I escape the 26 punishment of men, yet whether I live or die I shall not escape the hands of the Almighty. Therefore by manfully 27 giving up my life now, I will prove myself worthy of my

6:17–27

28 great age, and leave to the young a noble example of how to die willingly and nobly for the sacred and holy laws."

29 With these words he went straight to the torture wheel, while those who so shortly before had felt kindly toward him became hostile to him, because the words he had uttered

30 were in their opinion mere madness. As he was about to die under the strokes, he said with a groan,

"The Lord, in his holy knowledge, knows that, though I might have escaped death, I endure dreadful pains in my body from being flogged; but in my heart I am glad to suffer this, because I fear him."

31 And so he died, leaving in his death a pattern of nobility and a memorial of virtue not only to the young but to the mass of his nation.

7] It happened that seven brothers were also arrested with their mother, and were tortured with whips and thongs by the king, to force them to taste of the unlawful swine's meat.

2 One of them made himself their advocate and said,

"What do you expect to ask and learn from us? For we are ready to die, rather than transgress the laws of our fore-fathers."

3 The king was infuriated and gave orders that pans and

4 caldrons should be heated. And when they were immediate-ly heated, he commanded that the tongue of the one who had been their advocate should be cut out, and that they should scalp him and cut off his extremities, while his

5 brothers and his mother looked on. And when he was utterly crippled, he ordered them to bring him to the fire and fry him. And as the vapor from the pan spread thickly, they with their mother encouraged one another to die nobly, saying,

6 "The Lord God is looking on, and he truly relents toward us, as Moses declared in his Song, which bore witness against

6:28–7:6

them face to face, when he said, 'And he will relent toward his slaves.' "

When the first one had departed in this manner, they 7 brought the second one to be mocked, and they tore off the skin of his head with the hair, and asked him,

"Will you eat, or have your body punished limb by limb?"

But he replied in the language of his forefathers and 8 answered,

"No."

So he also underwent the same series of tortures as the first suffered. But when he was at his last gasp, he said, 9

"You wretch, you release us from this present life, but the king of the world will raise us up, because we have died for his laws, to an everlasting renewal of life."

After him, the third was mocked, and when he was told 10 to put out his tongue, he did so quickly, and courageously stretched out his hands, and said nobly, 11

"I got these from heaven, and for the sake of its laws I disregard them, and from it I hope to receive them back again," so that the king himself and those who were with him 12 were amazed at the young man's spirit, because he made light of his sufferings.

And when he had departed, they tortured and maltreated 13 the fourth in the same way. And when he was near his end, 14 he spoke thus:

"It is better to die by men's hands and look for the hopes God gives of being raised again by him; for you will have no resurrection to life."

Next they brought up the fifth and maltreated him. 15 But he looked at him and said, 16

"Since you have authority among men, though you are mortal, you do what you please; but do not suppose that

7:7–16

17 our race has been abandoned by God. But follow your course and see how his mighty power will torment you and your posterity."

18 After him they brought the sixth. And when he was at the point of death, he said,
"Do not be falsely deceived; for we suffer these things because of ourselves, for we sin against our own God, so
19 these amazing things have happened. But you must not suppose that you will go unpunished for having attempted to fight against God."

20 But their mother was surpassingly wonderful, and deserves a blessed memory, for though she saw her seven sons perish within a single day, she bore it with good courage,
21 because of her hope in the Lord. And she encouraged each of them in the language of their forefathers, for she was filled with a noble spirit and stirred her woman's heart with manly courage, and said to them,
22 "I do not know how you appeared in my womb, for it was not I that gave you life and breath, and it was not I that
23 brought into harmony the elements of each. Therefore the creator of the world, who formed the human race and arranged the generation of all things, will give you back again life and breath in his mercy, as you now are regardless of yourselves for the sake of his laws."

24 Now Antiochus, thinking that he was being treated with contempt, and suspecting her reproachful cry, as the youngest still survived, not only appealed to him in words but also promised him with oaths that he would make him rich and envied, if he would give up the ways of his forefathers, and
25 would make him his Friend and intrust him with office. But when the young man paid no attention to him, the king called the mother to him and urged her to advise the boy
26 to save himself. After he had labored with her a long time,

7:17–26

she undertook to persuade her son. She bent over him, and 27 mocking the cruel tyrant, she spoke thus, in the language of her forefathers:

"My son, have pity on me, who carried you nine months in the womb, and nursed you for three years, and brought you up and brought you to your present age, and supported you. I beseech you, my child, to look up at the heaven and 28 the earth, and see all that is in them, and perceive that God did not make them out of the things that existed, and in that way the human race came into existence. Do not be afraid 29 of this butcher, but show yourself worthy of your brothers, and accept death, so that by God's mercy I may get you back again with your brothers."

Before she could finish, the young man said, 30

"What are you waiting for? I will not obey the command of the king, but I obey the command of the Law that was given to our forefathers through Moses. But you, who have 31 designed every kind of evil against the Hebrews, will not escape the hands of God. For we are suffering because of 32 our own sins. And though our living Lord is angry for a 33 little while, to rebuke and discipline us, he will be reconciled with his own slaves again. But you, impious man, 34 the vilest of all men, do not foolishly buoy yourself up in your insolence with uncertain hopes, when you raise your hand against the children of heaven; for you have not yet 35 escaped the judgment of the Almighty all-seeing God. For our brothers after enduring a brief suffering have drunk 36 everlasing life, under the agreement of God. But you, by the judgment of God, will receive the rightful penalty of your arrogance. I, like my brothers, give up body and soul for 37 the laws of my forefathers, calling upon God speedily to show mercy to our nation, and to lead you to confess, in trials and plagues, that he alone is God; and to stay through 38

7:27-38

me and my brothers the wrath of the Almighty, which has justly fallen on our whole nation."

39 But the king was infuriated and treated him worse than
40 the others, being embittered at his mockery. So he passed
41 away unpolluted, trusting firmly in the Lord. Last of all, the mother met her end, after her sons.

42 So much then for the eating of sacrifices and excessive barbarities.

8] But Judas, who was called Maccabeus, and his followers secretly entered the villages and called on their kinsmen to join them, and by enlisting those who had clung to the Jew-
2 ish religion, they mustered as many as six thousand. And they called upon the Lord to look upon the people who were oppressed by all men and to have pity on the sanctuary
3 which had been profaned by the godless, and to have mercy on the city which was being ruined and would soon be leveled with the ground, and to hearken to the blood that
4 cried to them, and to remember the lawless destruction of the innocent babies and the blasphemies uttered against his
5 name, and to hate their wickedness. And as soon as Macca-beus got them organized, the heathen found him irresistible,
6 for the wrath of the Lord now turned to mercy. He would go unexpectedly to towns and villages and set fire to them, and in recovering advantageous positions and putting to
7 flight not a few of the enemy, he found the nights especially favorable for such attacks. And the country rang with talk of his valor.

8 When Philip saw that the man was gaining ground little by little, and that his successful advances were becoming more frequent, he wrote to Ptolemy, the governor of Coele-
9 syria and Phoenicia, to support the king's side. And he promptly selected Nicanor, the son of Patroclus, one of the king's chief Friends and sent him, putting him in command

of not less than twenty thousand heathen of various nationalities, to wipe out the whole race of Judea. And he associated with him Gorgias, a general and a man of experience in military service. But Nicanor resolved by taking the 10 Jews captive to make up for the king the tribute which he owed to the Romans, which amounted to two thousand talents. And he immediately sent to the coast towns, inviting 11 them to buy Jewish slaves, and promising to deliver them at ninety for a talent, little expecting the judgment from the Almighty that was to overtake him.

When news of Nicanor's advance reached Judas, and 12 when he informed his followers of the arrival of the army, those who were cowardly and doubtful about the judgment 13 of God ran away and took themselves off. And others sold 14 everything they had left and besought the Lord together to deliver those who had been sold in advance by the impious Nicanor; if not for their own sakes, for the sake of the agree- 15 ments made with their forefathers, and because they had been called by his revered and glorious name. And Macca- 16 beus gathered his men together, to the number of six thousand, and exhorted them not to be panic-stricken at the enemy, or to fear the vast multitude of the heathen who were coming against them wrongfully, but to fight nobly, keeping before their eyes the lawless outrage they had com- 17 mitted against the holy place, and the tormenting of the derided city, and besides, the destruction of their ancestral mode of life. "For they," he said, "trust in arms and daring, 18 but we trust in the Almighty God, for he is able with a mere nod to strike down not only our enemies but the whole world."

And he told them besides of the times when help had been 19 given them in the days of their forefathers, and how in the time of Sennacherib a hundred and eighty-five thousand

8:10-19

20 had perished, and the help that came in Babylonia, in the
battle with the Galatians, when they went into the affair
eight thousand in all, with four thousand Macedonians, and
when the Macedonians were hard pressed, the eight thousand destroyed the hundred and twenty thousand, because
of the help that came to them from heaven, and took a great
21 quantity of booty. When he had revived their courage with
these words, and made them ready to die for their laws and
22 their country, he divided his army into four parts. He put
his brothers Simon and Joseph and Jonathan each in command of a division, putting fifteen hundred men under each,
23 besides Eleazar also, and he read aloud from the holy book,
and gave "the Help of God" as the watchword, and taking
command of the first division himself, he joined battle with
Nicanor.

24 And the Almighty was their ally, and they slaughtered
more than nine thousand of the enemy, and wounded and
disabled most of Nicanor's army, and forced them all to
25 flee. And they captured the money of those who had come
to buy them. And after pursuing them for a considerable
distance, they were obliged to turn back because of the time
26 of day; for it was the day before the sabbath, and for that
27 reason they could not prolong their pursuit of them. But
after collecting the enemy's arms and stripping them of their
spoils, they busied themselves about the sabbath, fervently
blessing and thanking the Lord who had preserved them
to see that day, because he had begun to show them mercy.
28 After the sabbath, they gave some of the spoils to the
wounded and to the widows and orphans and divided the
29 rest with their children. When they had accomplished
this, they made a common supplication, and besought the
merciful Lord to be wholly reconciled to his slaves.

30 When they encountered the forces of Timotheus and

8:20–30

Bacchides, they killed more than twenty thousand of them,
and obtained possession of some exceedingly high strongholds, and they divided a great amount of plunder, giving
shares equal to their own to the wounded and orphans and
widows, and also to the older people as well. And they 31
carefully collected all their own arms and deposited them
in the advantageous places, and the rest of the spoils they
carried to Jerusalem. And they killed the cavalry com- 32
mander of Timotheus' forces, a most impious man, who
had greatly injured the Jews. And in celebrating their 33
victory in the city of their forefathers, they burned those
who had set fire to the sacred gates, and Callisthenes, who
had taken refuge in a cottage; so he received the proper reward for his impious conduct. But the thrice-accursed Nica- 34
nor, who had brought the thousand slave-dealers to buy
the Jews, after being humbled through the Lord's help by 35
those whom he had thought of no account, took off his fine
clothes and going alone like a runaway across country
reached Antioch, having been supremely successful—in destroying his army! So the man who had undertaken to 36
secure tribute for the Romans by the capture of the people
of Jerusalem proclaimed that the Jews had a champion,
and that the Jews were invulnerable because of their way of
life, because they followed the laws laid down by him.

Now about that time it happened that Antiochus returned [9
in disorder from the region of Persia. For he had entered 2
the city called Persepolis, and tried to rob the temples and
get control of the city. At this the people naturally had swift
recourse to arms, and they were routed, and the result was
that Antiochus was put to flight by the people of the country
and left in disgrace. And while he was at Ecbatana, news 3
came to him of what had happened to Nicanor and the
forces of Timotheus. And excited by anger, he thought 4

he would fasten upon the Jews the injury done him by those who had put him to flight, so he ordered his charioteer to drive without stopping until he finished the journey, although the judgment of heaven accompanied him. For in his arrogance he said,

"I will make Jerusalem the common graveyard of the Jews, when I get there."

5 But the All-seeing Lord, the God of Israel, struck him down with an incurable but unseen blow, for he had hardly uttered the words when he was seized with an incurable pain

6 in his bowels and sharp internal pains—very justly, for he had tormented the bowels of others with many unusual

7 miseries. He did not desist at all from his insolence, but was more and more filled with arrogance, breathing fire in his fury against the Jews, and giving orders to hasten the journey. But it happened that he fell out of his chariot as it was rushing along, and was racked in every part of his body

8 from the fall. And the man who just now presumed to command the waves of the sea, in his superhuman boastfulness, and thought he could weigh the mountain heights in his scales, was flat on the ground and had to be carried in a

9 litter—making the power of God manifest to all men; so that worms swarmed from the impious creature's body, and while he was still alive in anguish and pain, his flesh fell off, and because of the stench the whole army turned from

10 his corruption in disgust. The man who shortly before thought he could touch the stars of heaven, no one could

11 now bear to carry, because of his intolerable stench. So it was then that, broken in spirit, he began for the most part to give up his arrogance, and under the scourge of God to attain some knowledge, for he was tortured with pain every

12 instant. And when he could not even endure his own stench, he said this:

9:5–12

"It is right to submit to God and, since man is mortal, not to think he is God's equal."

And the vile fellow made a vow to the Lord who would 13 no longer have mercy on him, stating that he declared the 14 holy city, which he was hastening to level with the ground and to make a common graveyard, free; and as for the 15 Jews, who he had decided were unworthy of burial, but should be thrown out with their children to the wild animals, for the birds to pick, that he would make them all equal to citizens of Athens; and the holy sanctuary, which 16 before he had plundered, he would adorn with the finest offerings, and he would give back all the sacred dishes many times over, and the expenses incident to the sacrifices he would supply from his own revenues; and in addition to 17 this, he would become a Jew and visit every inhabited place to proclaim the power of God. But when his suffering by no 18 means ceased, for God's judgment had come justly upon him, in despair about himself he wrote the Jews the following letter, assuming the attitude of a suppliant. It ran thus:

"To the esteemed Jewish citizens, Antiochus, the king 19 and general, sends hearty greetings and wishes for their health and prosperity. If you and your children are well 20 and your affairs are going as you wish, I am glad. As my 21 hope is in heaven, I remember with affection your esteem and good will. On my way back from the regions of Persia, I have been taken seriously ill, so I have thought it necessary to plan for the general welfare of all. Not that I despair of 22 myself, for I have strong hopes of recovering from my sickness. But observing that my father, on the occasions when 23 he campaigned in the upper country, appointed his successor, so that, if anything unexpected happened, or any dis- 24 turbing news came, the people at home, knowing to whom the government was left, should not be disturbed; and in 25

9:13–25

addition to this, perceiving that the adjacent princes, who
are neighbors to the kingdom, watch for opportunities and
are expectant of what may turn up, I have appointed my son
Antiochus king, whom I have often committed and commended to most of you, when I hurried off to the upper
provinces; and I have written him what is written below.

26 So I beg and beseech you to remember the public and private services rendered you and to continue your good will

27 to me and my son. For I am convinced that he will follow
my policy with mildness and kindness, in his relations with
you."

28   So the murderer and blasphemer, after the most intense
sufferings, such as he had inflicted on other people, ended
his life most pitiably, among the mountains, in a foreign

29 land. And his foster-brother Philip took his body home,
and then, as he feared the son of Antiochus, he went over to
Ptolemy Philometor in Egypt.

10]   Now Maccabeus and his followers under the Lord's
2 leadership regained the temple and the city, and tore down
the altars that had been built by the aliens in the public

3 square, and also the sacred inclosures. And when they had
purified the sanctuary, they built another altar of sacrifice,
and striking flints and getting fire from them, they offered
sacrifices, after an interval of two years, and they burned
incense and lighted lamps and set out the Presentation

4 Loaves. And when they had done this, they fell on their
faces and besought the Lord that they might never again encounter such misfortune, but that, if they should ever sin, he
would discipline them with forbearance, and not hand them

5 over to blasphemous and barbarous heathen. And it came
about that on the very same day on which the sanctuary
had been profaned by aliens, the purification of the sanctuary took place, that is, on the twenty-fifth day of the same

month, which was Chislev. And they celebrated it for eight 6
days with gladness, like the Camping Out festival, and re-
called how, a little while before, during the Camping Out
festival they had been wandering in the mountains and
caverns like wild animals. So carrying wands wreathed with 7
leaves and beautiful branches and palm leaves too they offered hymns of praise to him who had brought to pass the
purifying of his own place. And they passed a public ordinance and decree that the whole Jewish nation should ob- 8
serve these days every year. Such was the end of Antiochus, 9
who was called Epiphanes.

We will now set forth what took place under Antiochus 10
Eupator, who was the son of that godless man, summarizing
the principal disasters of the wars. For this man, upon suc- 11
ceeding to the kingdom, appointed one Lysias to have
charge of the government, and to be governor-in-chief of
Coelesyria and Phoenicia. For Ptolemy who was called 12
Macron instituted the practice of showing justice to the
Jews because of the wrong that had been done them, and attempted to carry on his dealings with them amicably. As a 13
result, he was accused before Eupator by the king's Friends,
and on all sides heard himself called a traitor, because he
had abandoned Cyprus which Philometor had intrusted to
him, and gone over to Antiochus Epiphanes, and, as he
could not maintain the dignity of his office, he took poison
and ended his life.

But Gorgias, when he became governor of the region, 14
maintained mercenaries and kept on warring against the
Jews at every turn. In addition to that, the Idumeans, who 15
held important forts, were harassing the Jews, and enlisting
those from Jerusalem who took refuge there, they sought to
continue the war. But Maccabeus and his men made a supplication and besought God to be their ally, and then threw 16

10:6–16

17 themselves upon the forts of the Idumeans, and attacking
them vigorously they made themselves masters of the positions, and fought off those who manned the wall, and
slaughtered those whom they encountered, killing not less
18 than twenty thousand. As fully nine thousand had taken
refuge in two very strong towers well supplied for a siege,
19 Maccabeus left Simon and Joseph and in addition Zaccheus
and his men, making a force strong enough to besiege them,
20 and set off for places that were more urgent. But the men
with Simon were covetous and were bribed by some of the
men in the towers, and on receiving seventy thousand
21 drachmas let some of them escape. But when news of what
had happened reached Maccabeus, he gathered the leaders
of the people together, and charged them with having sold
their brothers for money, by freeing their enemies to fight
22 them. So he killed those men for having proved traitors,
23 and immediately captured the towers. And as he was successful in arms in everything he undertook, he destroyed
more than twenty thousand men in the two forts.

24 But Timotheus, who had been defeated by the Jews before, gathered enormous mercenary forces, and mustering
no small number of Asiatic cavalry, came as though he
25 would take Judea by storm. But when he approached,
Maccabeus and his men sprinkled earth on their heads and
26 put sacksloth on their loins, and falling down upon the step
before the altar begged him to favor them and be the enemy
of their enemies, and oppose their adversaries, as the Law
27 declares. And when they had ended their prayer, they took
their arms, and advanced a considerable distance from the
28 city, and when they got near the enemy, they halted. And
just as the dawn was breaking, the two armies joined battle,
those on one side having besides their valor their assurance
of success and victory in having taken refuge with the Lord,

10:17–28

while those on the other followed their passions as leader in the contest. And when the fighting had become fierce, there 29 appeared to the enemy from heaven five splendid figures on horses with gold bridles, leading the Jews, and they sur- 30 rounded Maccabeus and protected him with their armor and kept him unhurt, while they shot arrows and hurled thunderbolts at the enemy, so that, confused and blinded, they were thrown into disorder and cut to pieces. Twenty 31 thousand five hundred were slaughtered, and six hundred horsemen. Timotheus himself took refuge in a strong- 32 hold called Gazara, which was strongly garrisoned and under the command of Chaereas. Then Maccabeus and 33 his men were glad, and they besieged the fort for four days. And those who were inside, relying on the strength of the 34 place, blasphemed dreadfully and uttered impious speeches. But at dawn the fifth day, twenty young men in the army 35 of Maccabeus, fired with anger by these blasphemies, man- fully assaulted the wall and in savage fury cut down every- one they met. Others who had climbed up in the same 36 way, in the confusion over those who had gotten in, set the towers on fire and starting fires burned the blasphemers alive. Still others broke open the gates, and let in the rest of the force, capturing the city. They killed Timotheus, who 37 was hidden in a cistern, and his brother Chaereas and Apol- lophanes. When they had accomplished this, with hymns 38 and thanksgivings they blessed the Lord who does great services to Israel, and gives them victory.

A very short time after, Lysias, the guardian and relative [11 of the king, who was in charge of the government, being greatly annoyed at what had happened, mustered about 2 eighty thousand men and all his cavalry, and came against the Jews, with the intention of making the city a place for

10:29–11:2

3 Greeks to live in, and of imposing tribute on the temple, as
they did on the other sacred places of the heathen, and of
4 offering the high priesthood for sale every year, taking no
account at all of the power of God, but uplifted by his tens
of thousands of infantry, and his thousands of cavalry, and
5 his eighty elephants. And he entered Judea, and approached Bethsura, a fortified place about five-eighths of
a mile from Jerusalem, and pressed it hard.
6 But when Maccabeus and his men got news that he was
besieging the strongholds, with lamentations and tears they
and the people besought the Lord to send some valiant angel
7 to save Israel. Maccabeus himself was the first to take up
arms and called on the others to risk their lives with him and
go to the aid of their brothers. So they hurried off eagerly
8 together. But there, while they were still near Jerusalem, a
rider, clothed in white, appeared at their head, brandishing
9 gold weapons. And they all blessed the merciful God together, and their hearts were strengthened, and they felt
equal to overcoming not only men but the fiercest animals
10 and iron walls. So they advanced in good order with their
11 heavenly ally, for the Lord had had mercy on them. And
flying at the enemy like lions, they killed eleven thousand of
them and sixteen hundred horsemen, and forced all the rest
12 to flee. The most of them got away stripped and wounded,
and Lysias himself escaped only by a disgraceful flight.
13 But as he was not without understanding, he thought over
the defeat he had met with, and perceived that the Hebrews
were invincible, because the mighty God was their ally, so
14 he sent to them and persuaded them to come to a general
settlement on just terms, because he would persuade the
15 king and prevail upon him to become their friend. And
Maccabeus agreed to all that Lysias proposed, thus looking
out for the common good, for the king granted all the de-

11:3–15

mands that Maccabeus made in writing to Lysias for the Jews.

For the letter written to the Jews by Lysias was as fol- 16 lows:

"Lysias sends greeting to the Jewish people. Your emis- 17 saries John and Absalom have presented the accompanying petition and asked about the matters set forth in it. So I in- 18 formed the king of the matters that needed to be laid before him, and he has agreed to all that was possible. If then you 19 will continue your loyalty to the government, I will en- deavor to further your interests in the future. But about the 20 details of these matters, I have ordered these men and my representatives to confer with you. Goodbye. The hundred 21 and forty-eighth year, Dioscorinthius twenty-fourth."

The king's letter ran thus: 22

"King Antiochus sends greeting to his brother Lysias. Now that our father has departed to the gods, we desire 23 the subjects of the kingdom to be unmolested and to busy themselves with the care of their own affairs, and as we have 24 heard that the Jews will not agree to our father's policy of making them adopt Greek practices, but prefer their own way of living, and ask to be allowed to follow their own cus- toms, we wish this nation also to be undisturbed, and our 25 decision is that their temple be returned to them, and that they follow their ancestral customs. Please send messengers 26 to them therefore, and give them assurances, so that they may know our purpose and be of good cheer, and contented- ly go about the conduct of their affairs."

The king's letter to the nation ran as follows: 27

"King Antiochus sends greeting to the Jewish senate and to the rest of the Jews. If you are well, it is what we desire; 28 we too are well. Menelaus has informed us that you want 29 to go home and look after your own affairs. Therefore 30

11:16–30

those who go home by the thirtieth of Xanthicus will have
31 our assurance that the Jews can fearlessly enjoy their own
food and laws, as before; and none of them shall be molested
32 in any way for what he may have ignorantly done. I have
33 sent Menelaus also to cheer you. Goodbye. The hundred
and forty-eighth year, Xanthicus fifteenth."

34   The Romans also sent them a letter to this effect:
"Quintus Memmius and Titus Manius, envoys of the
35 Romans, send greeting to the Jewish people. With regard
to what Lysias, the king's relative, has granted you, we also
36 give our approval. But as to the matters which he decided
should be referred to the king, as soon as you have considered the matter, send us word, so that we may take
37 proper action. For we are going to Antioch; so make haste
and send men to us, so that we also may know what your
38 intentions are. Goodbye. The hundred and forty-eighth
year, Xanthicus fifteenth."

12]   After this agreement was reached, Lysias went back to
2 the king, and the Jews went about their farming. But some
of the local governors, Timotheus and Apollonius, the son
of Gennaeus, besides Hieronymus and Demophon, as well
as Nicanor, the governor of Cyprus, would not leave them
3 alone and let them live in peace. Some people of Joppa also
perpetrated the following outrage. They invited the Jews
who lived among them to embark with their wives and children on boats they had provided, with no hint of any ill will
4 toward them, but in accordance with the public regulations
of the town. And when they accepted, as they wished to live
peaceably and had no suspicion, they took them out to
sea and drowned fully two hundred of them.
5   When Judas got news of the cruelty that had been prac-
6 ticed on his countrymen, he called his men together, and
calling on God, the righteous judge, he attacked the murder-

11:31–12:6

ers of his brothers, and one night set the harbor on fire and
burned the boats, and put those who had taken refuge there
to the sword. But as the town shut its gates against him, he 7
retired, meaning to come back and exterminate the whole
community of Joppa. But learning that the people of 8
Jamnia meant to treat the Jews there in the same way, he 9
attacked the people of Jamnia in the night, and set fire to
the harbor as well as the fleet, so that the glow of the fire
was visible in Jerusalem, thirty miles away.

When they had gone more than a mile from there, on 10
their march against Timotheus, fully five thousand Arabs
with five hundred horsemen attacked them. After a hard 11
fight, by the help of God Judas and his men were victorious,
and the nomads, being worsted, besought Judas to make
friends with them, promising to give him cattle and to help
them in other ways. Judas thought they would really be use- 12
ful in many ways, and agreed to make peace with them, so
after receiving his assurances, they left for their camp.

He also attacked a town strengthened with earthworks 13
and encircled with walls, inhabited by heathen of all sorts,
and named Caspin. Its occupants, relying on the strength 14
of their walls and their stores of provisions, scoffed madly
at Judas and his men, and went so far as to blaspheme and
makes impious speeches. But Judas and his men called 15
upon the great Sovereign of the world, who without rams
or war engines threw down the walls of Jericho in the days
of Joshua, and rushed furiously upon the walls. And by the 16
will of God they took the city, and slaughtered untold numbers, so that the neighboring lake, a quarter of a mile wide,
seemed to be filled with running blood.

When they had gone ninety-five miles from there, they 17
reached Charax, and the Jews who are called Tybiani.
They could not find Timotheus in those regions, for he had 18

12:7-18

gone away unsuccessful, but leaving behind him in one
19 place a very strong garrison. But Dositheus and Sosipater,
who were captains under Maccabeus, marched out and destroyed the force Timotheus had left in the stronghold,
20 more than ten thousand men. Maccabeus however arranged his army in divisions and put them in command of
the divisions and hurried after Timotheus, who had with
him a hundred and twenty thousand infantry and two
21 thousand, five hundred cavalry. But when Timotheus
learned of the advance of Judas, he sent the women and
children and the rest of the baggage train ahead to a place
called Carnaim, for that stronghold was hard to besiege or
22 to reach, because of the difficulty of all that region. But
when Judas' first division appeared and terror came over
the enemy and fear came upon them at the manifestation of
him who beholds all things, they hastily fled in all directions,
so that in many cases they were hurt by their own men and
23 wounded by the points of their swords. But Judas pressed
the pursuit increasingly, putting the wretches to the sword,
and destroyed fully thirty thousand men.
24 But Timotheus himself, falling into the hands of Dositheus and Sosipater and their men, besought them with
much guile to spare his life and let him go, because he had
the parents of many of them and the brothers of some in his
25 power, and it would go hard with these. So when he had
most fully guaranteed to restore them unharmed, to save
their brothers they let him go.
26 Then Judas marched against Carnaim and the temple of
Atargatis, and slaughtered twenty-five thousand people.
27 After the rout and destruction of these, he marched against
Ephron, a fortified town, where Lysias lived and multitudes
of all nationalities. Hardy young men posted before the
walls vigorously defended it, and large quantities of war

12:19-27

engines and missiles were kept there. But they called upon 28
the Sovereign who forcibly shatters the might of his enemies,
and took the town, and slew fully twenty-five thousand of
those who were in it.

Then they set out from there and marched rapidly to 29
Scythopolis, which is seventy-five miles from Jerusalem.
But when the Jews there bore witness to the good will shown 30
them by the people of Scythopolis, and their kind treatment
of them in times of misfortune, they thanked them and ex- 31
horted them to be well disposed to their race in the future
also. Then, as the festival of Weeks was close at hand, they
went up to Jerusalem.

After the festival called Pentecost they marched hurriedly 32
against Gorgias, the governor of Idumea. And he came out 33
with three thousand infantry and four hundred cavalry.
And when they joined battle, it happened that a few of the 34
Jews fell. But a man named Dositheus, one of Bacenor's 35
men, a mounted man of great strength, caught hold of
Gorgias and grasping his cloak was dragging him off by
main strength, meaning to take the accursed rascal alive,
when one of the Thracian horsemen bore down upon him
and disabled his shoulder, so that Gorgias escaped and
reached Mareshah.

But as Esdris and his men had been fighting a long time 36
and were tired out, Judas called upon the Lord to show
himself their ally and leader in the fight; then raising the 37
war cry and war songs in their ancestral language, he
charged Gorgias' men unexpectedly and put them to flight.

Then Judas assembled his army and went to the town 38
of Adullam. And as the next day was the seventh day, they
purified themselves as they were accustomed to do, and
kept the sabbath. On the following day, as by that time it 39
had become necessary, Judas' men went to gather up the

bodies of the fallen, and bring them back to lie with their
40 relatives in the graves of their forefathers. But on every
one of the dead, under the shirt, they found amulets of the
idols of Jamnia, which the Law forbids the Jews to wear;
and it became clear to all that this was why they had fallen.
41 So they all blessed the ways of the Lord, the righteous
Judge, who reveals the things that are hidden, and fell to
42 supplication, begging that the sin that had been committed should be wholly blotted out. And the noble Judas
exhorted the people to keep themselves free from sin, after
having seen with their own eyes what had happened because
43 of the sin of those who had fallen. He also took a collection,
amounting to two thousand silver drachmas, each man
contributing, and sent it to Jerusalem, to provide a sin offering, acting very finely and properly in taking account of the
44 resurrection. For if he had not expected that those who had
fallen would rise again, it would have been superfluous and
45 foolish to pray for the dead; or if it was through regard for
the splendid reward destined for those who fall asleep in
godliness, it was a holy and pious thought. Therefore he
made atonement for the dead, so that they might be set
free from their sin.

13] In the hundred and forty-ninth year, news reached Judas
and his men that Antiochus Eupator had come with great
2 hosts against Judea, bringing with him Lysias, his guardian,
who had charge of the government, each with a Greek force
of a hundred and ten thousand infantry, and five thousand
three hundred cavalry, and twenty-two elephants and three
3 hundred chariots armed with scythes. Menelaus also joined
them, and with loud pretenses encouraged Antiochus, not
to save his country, but because he thought he would be
4 put in charge of the government. But the King of kings
aroused the anger of Antiochus against the rascal, and when

Lysias informed him that this man was to blame for all the trouble, he ordered them to take him to Berea and to put him to death in the way that is customary there. For there 5 is a tower there seventy-five feet high, filled with ashes, and it had an arrangement running all around it dropping straight into the ashes. There they all push a man guilty 6 of sacrilege or notorious for other crimes to destruction. By 7 such a fate it came to pass that Menelaus the transgressor died, not even getting burial in the ground. And very just- 8 ly, for as he had committed many sins against the altar, the fire and ashes of which were holy, through ashes he came by his death.

But the king, enraged in mind, was coming to inflict on 9 the Jews the worst of the things they had suffered in his father's time. And when Judas got news of it, he ordered the 10 people to call on the Lord all day and all night now if ever to help those who were on the point of losing their Law and their country and the holy temple, and not to let the 11 people who had just begun to revive fall into the hands of profane heathen. And when they had all done this together 12 and besought the merciful Lord for three days without ceasing, with weeping and fasting and prostrations, Judas encouraged them and ordered them to rally to him. After a 13 private meeting with the elders, he decided that they should march out and decide the matter by the help of God before the king could get his army into Judea and get possession of of the city. So committing the decision to the creator of 14 the world and encouraging his men to fight nobly to the death for laws, temple, city, country, and government, he pitched his camp at Modin. And giving his men "God's 15 Victory," for the watchword, he threw himself upon the camp in the night and reached the royal tent, and killed fully two thousand men, and stabbed the leading elephant

13:5-15

16 and his driver, and finally filled the camp with terror and
17 confusion, and got away successfully. This happened by
the Lord's help and protection, just as day was dawning.
18   After this taste of the Jews' hardihood, the king resorted
19 to strategem in attempting their positions. He advanced
against Bethsura, a strong Jewish fort; he was turned back,
20 stumbled, failed. Judas sent what was necessary in to the
21 garrison. But Rhodocus, a man of the Jewish force, gave
secret information to the enemy; he was found out, ar-
22 rested, and put in prison. The king again approached the
people in Bethsura, gave assurances, received them, with-
23 drew, attacked Judas and his men, was worsted, got news
that Philip, who had been left in charge of the government
at Antioch, had gotten desperate, was dismayed, conciliated
the Jews, yielded, and swore to do all that was just, settled
with them and offered sacrifice, honored the sanctuary and
24 respected the holy place, received Maccabeus, left Hege-
25 monides as governor in control from Ptolemais to Gerar. He
went to Ptolemais; the people of Ptolemais were angry about
the treaty, for they were so indignant that they wanted to
26 annul the agreements. Lysias appeared to speak publicly,
made as good a defense as was possible, convinced them,
appeased them, won them over, and set out for Antioch.
This was the course of the king's attack and withdrawal.
14]   Three years later, news reached Judas and his men that
Demetrius, the son of Seleucus, had sailed into the harbor
of Tripolis with a strong force and a fleet, and had made
2 away with Antiochus and his guardian Lysias and taken
3 possession of the country. But Alcimus, who had formerly
been high priest, but had polluted himself of his own accord
in the days when there was no communication with the
heathen, considering that there was no way for him to save
4 himself or to obtain access to the holy altar, went to King

Demetrius in the hundred and fifty-first year, and presented him with a gold crown and palm, and in addition to them some of the customary olive branches from the temple; and he kept silence that day. But when he found an opportunity favorable to his mad purpose, being invited by Demetrius to a council, and asked about the temper and intentions of the Jews, he answered, 5

"It is the Jews who are called Hasidaeans, under the leadership of Judas Maccabeus, that keep the war alive, and stir up sedition, and will not let the kingdom enjoy tranquillity. That is why, renouncing my ancestral glory (I mean the high priesthood), I have now come here, first, because I am genuinely concerned for the king's interests, and secondly out of regard for my fellow-citizens; for through the inconsiderate behavior of those whom I have mentioned, our whole nation is in no small misfortune. Inform yourself, O king, about these things in detail, and act in the interests of our country and our hard-pressed nation, with the courteous consideration that you show to all. For as long as Judas lives, it is impossible for the government to find peace." 6 7 8 9 10

When he said this, the rest of the Friends, who were hostile to Judas, immediately inflamed Demetrius further against him. He immediately chose Nicanor, who had been master of the elephants, and appointed him governor of Judea, and sent him out with orders to make away with Judas himself, and scatter his men, and instal Alcimus as high priest of the sublime temple. And all the heathen in Judea who had driven Judas into exile flocked to join Nicanor, thinking that the reverses and disasters of the Jews would be to their advantage. 11 12 13 14

But when they heard of Nicanor's expedition and the attack of the heathen, they sprinkled themselves with earth 15

14:5-15

and intreated him who had established his own people
forever, and always upholds his own portion by manifesting
16 himself. Then, when the leader gave the order, he set forth
at once from there and joined battle with them at the village
17 of Adasa. Simon, Judas' brother, had encountered Nicanor, and had recently been checked because of the conster-
18 nation his antagonists inspired. Still Nicanor, hearing of the
valor of Judas and his men, and their courage in their
battles for their country, hesitated to decide the matter by
19 the sword. So he sent Posidonius and Theodotus and
20 Mattathias to propose terms. After full consideration of
these, when each leader had communicated them to his
people, and their judgment proved favorable, they agreed
21 to the treaty. So they fixed a day on which to meet by themselves, a chariot advanced from each side, couches were
22 placed in position; Judas posted armed men in readiness at
suitable points, through fear that some treachery might suddenly develop on the part of the enemy; they held the ap-
23 propriate conference. Nicanor stayed in Jerusalem, and
did nothing improper, but sent home the thronging crowds
24 that had gathered. He kept Judas constantly in his com-
25 pany; he had become warmly attached to the man; he urged
him to marry and have children. He did marry, settled
down, took his part in life.

26   But when Alcimus realized their good understanding
with each other, and got hold of the treaty they had made,
he went to Demetrius and told him that Nicanor was dis-
loyal to the government, for he had appointed Judas, the
27 conspirator against the kingdom, as his successor. The king
was excited and incensed by the rascal's accusations, and
wrote to Nicanor stating that he was dissatisfied with the
treaty, and ordering him to send Maccabeus as a prisoner to
28 Antioch without delay. When Nicanor received the mes-

14:16–28

sage, he was troubled and annoyed at having to cancel the
agreement when the man had done no wrong. But as it was 29
not possible to oppose the king, he watched for an opportunity to accomplish this by strategy. But Maccabeus ob- 30
served that Nicanor began to treat him more stiffly and was
acting more rudely than usual, and concluding that this
stiffness was not a very good sign, he mustered no small
number of his men and went into hiding from Nicanor.

When the latter realized that he had been splendidly out- 31
maneuvered by the man, he went to the great and holy
temple as the priests were offering the customary sacrifices,
and ordered them to deliver the man up. And when they 32
protested with oaths that they did not know where the man
he sought was, he stretched out his right hand toward the 33
sanctuary and uttered this oath:

"If you do not hand Judas over to me as a prisoner, I will
level this sacred precinct of God with the ground and tear
down the altar, and build here a splendid temple to
Dionysus."

With these words he left. But the priests stretched out 34
their hands to heaven and called upon him who always
fights for our nation, and said,

"Lord of all, who are self-sufficient, you consented to have 35
a temple for your habitation among us; now therefore, holy 36
Lord of all consecration, keep undefiled forever this house
that has been so lately purified."

Now one of the elders of Jerusalem named Razis was re- 37
ported to Nicanor as a man who loved his countrymen and
was very well thought of, and was called father of the Jews
for his benevolence. For in former times, when there was 38
no communication with the Gentiles, he had been accused
of Judaism, and had most zealously risked soul and body
for it. And Nicanor, wishing to manifest the enmity he felt 39

14:29-39

for the Jews, sent more than five hundred soldiers to arrest
40 him; for he thought that in arresting him he would be doing
41 them an injury. But when this force was on the point of
capturing the tower and was forcing the courtyard door and
demanding that fire be brought and the doors set on fire, as
42 he was surrounded he fell upon his sword, preferring to die
nobly rather than to fall into the wretches' hands and
43 suffer outrages unworthy of his rank. But he missed his
stroke in the haste of the struggle, and with the crowd
streaming in through the doors, he ran gallantly up on the
44 wall and bravely threw himself down into the crowd. But
as they quickly drew back, and a space opened, he fell in
45 the middle of the open space. But being still alive and fired
with anger he got up and with his blood gushing out,
though severely wounded, he ran through the crowd and
46 standing on a steep rock, as he was losing the last of his
blood, he pulled out his bowels with both hands and hurled
them at the crowd, and so expired, calling upon him who
is lord of life and spirit, to give these back to him again.

15] But Nicanor, getting word that Judas and his men were
in the region of Samaria, resolved to attack them in perfect
2 safety, on the day of rest. And when the Jews who were
forced to follow him said,

"Do not destroy them savagely and barbarously like this,
but show respect for the day which has been pre-eminently
3 honored with holiness by him who beholds all things," the
thrice-accursed wretch asked if there was a sovereign in
heaven who had commanded them to keep the sabbath
4 day; and when they declared,

"It is the living Lord himself, the Sovereign in heaven,
5 who bade us observe the seventh day," he said,

"I am a sovereign too, on earth, and I command you to
take up arms and finish the king's business."

14:40–15:5

Nevertheless, he did not succeed in carrying out his cruel purpose.

And Nicanor in his utter haughtiness and pretense had 6 determined to erect a public monument of victory over Judas and his men. But Maccabeus did not cease to trust 7 with perfect confidence that he would get help from the Lord, and he exhorted his men not to fear the attack of the 8 heathen but to keep in mind all the help that had come to them before from heaven, and to look now for the victory which would come to them from the Almighty. And en- 9 couraging them from the Law and the prophets and reminding them of the battles they had fought, he made them more eager. And when he had aroused their courage, he 10 gave his orders, and at the same time pointed out the perfidy of the heathen and their breaking of their oaths. Then 11 he armed each one, not so much with the security of shields and spears as with the encouragement of brave words, and cheered them all by telling a dream that was worthy of belief, a kind of vision.

The sight he saw was this: Onias, the former high priest, 12 a fine, good man, of dignified appearance, but mild in manner and one who spoke fittingly, and trained from childhood in all that belongs to character, with outstretched hands praying for the whole Jewish community; then in the 13 same fashion another man appeared, distinguished by his gray hair and dignity, and wrapped in marvelous, most majestic sublimity; and Onias answered and said,   14

"This is Jeremiah, the prophet of God, who loves the brothers, and prays fervently for the people and the holy city."

And Jeremiah stretched out his right hand and delivered 15 to Judas a gold sword, and as he gave it to him, he addressed him thus:

15:6–15

16 "Take this holy sword as a gift from God, with which you will strike down your adversaries."

17 Encouraged by Judas' words, which were so fine, and so fitted to rouse men to valor and to stir the souls of the young to manliness, they determined not to carry on a campaign but to charge gallantly and engaging them hand to hand with the utmost manfulness to decide the matter, because the city and the sanctuary and the temple were in peril.

18 For they were not so much alarmed about wives and children, or about brothers and relatives, but first and foremost

19 about the consecrated sanctuary. And those who were left in the city felt no slight distress, for they were anxious about the encounter in the open.

20 When they were all now awaiting the decisive moment, and the enemy had already joined battle, and the army was drawn up and the animals had been posted in a convenient

21 position, and the cavalry stationed on the wings, Maccabeus, realizing the hosts before him, and the elaborate supply of arms, and the fierceness of the animals, stretched out his hands to heaven and called upon the Lord who works wonders, for he knew that it is not won by arms but that as he decides he gains the victory for those who deserve it.

22 And he called upon him in these words:

"It was you, Lord, who sent your angel in the time of Hezekiah, king of Judah, and he destroyed fully a hundred

23 and eighty-five thousand in the camp of Sennacherib. So now also, Sovereign of the heavens, send forth a brave angel

24 to carry fear and terror before us. By the might of your arm may those who blasphemously come against your holy people be struck down."

25 With these words he ended. But Nicanor and his men

26 advanced with trumpets and battle songs. And Judas and

27 his men met the enemy with entreaties and prayers. So

fighting with their hands and praying to God with their hearts, they laid low no less than thirty-five thousand, being greatly cheered by God's manifest aid.

When the business was over, and they were joyfully re- 28 turning, they recognized Nicanor, lying dead, in his armor. And there was shouting and tumult, and they blessed the 29 Sovereign in the language of their forefathers. Then the 30 man who was in body and soul the perfect champion of his fellow-citizens, who maintained the good will of his youth toward his fellow-citizens, ordered them to cut off Nicanor's head and arm and carry them to Jerusalem. And when he 31 arrived there, and had called his countrymen together, and stationed the priests before the altar, he sent for those who were in the citadel. And he showed them the vile Nicanor's 32 head and the wretch's hand, which he had boastfully stretched forth against the holy house of the Almighty, and 33 he cut out the impious Nicanor's tongue, and said he would give it piecemeal to the birds, and hang up the reward of his folly in front of the sanctuary. And they all looked up to 34 heaven and blessed the Lord who had so manifested himself, and said,

"Blessed be he who has kept his own place from being defiled."

And he hung Nicanor's head from the citadel, a clear and 35 conspicuous proof to all of the Lord's help. And they all 36 decreed by popular vote of the people never to let this day go by without observing it, but to celebrate the thirteenth day of the twelfth month—which is called Adar in Aramaic—the day before Mordecai's day.

So this was the way Nicanor's efforts turned out; and as 37 the city was held by the Hebrews from that time, I too will here conclude my account. If it has been well and pointed- 38

15:28-38

ly written, that is what I wanted; but if it is poor, mediocre
39 work, that was all I could do. For just as it is harmful to
drink wine by itself, or again to drink water by itself, while
wine mixed with water is delicious and enhances one's enjoyment, so the style in which an account is composed delights the ears of those who read the work.

So this will be the end.

ABOUT THE AUTHOR

Edgar J. Goodspeed, Biblical scholar and translator, was born in Quincy, Illinois, in 1871, attended Denison University, received the degree of Doctor of Philosophy from the University of Chicago in 1898, and taught at the University of Chicago from 1899 to 1937. He brought out *The New Testament: An American Translation* in 1923, and continued to work on a translation of the entire Bible, completing his work with the publication of this translation of *The Apocrypha* in 1938. His other works include *An Introduction to the New Testament* (1937), *A Life of Jesus* (1950), and *As I Remember* (1953), his autobiography. He died in 1962.